HIGHER EDUCATION
IN CANADA

GARLAND STUDIES IN HIGHER EDUCATION
VOLUME 11
GARLAND REFERENCE LIBRARY OF SOCIAL SCIENCE
VOLUME 1099

GARLAND STUDIES IN HIGHER EDUCATION

This series is published in cooperation with the Program in Higher Education, School of Education, Boston College, Chestnut Hill, Massachusetts.

PHILIP G. ALTBACH, *Series Editor*

THE FUNDING OF HIGHER EDUCATION
International Perspectives
edited by Philip G. Altbach
and D. Bruce Johnstone

REFORM AND CHANGE
IN HIGHER EDUCATION
International Perspectives
edited by James E. Mauch
and Paula L.W. Sabloff

HIGHER EDUCATION IN CRISIS
New York in National Perspective
edited by William C. Barba

CHINA'S UNIVERSITIES, 1895–1995
A Century of Cultural Conflict
by Ruth Hayhoe

JESUIT EDUCATION AND SOCIAL
CHANGE IN EL SALVADOR
by Charles J. Beirne

DIMENSIONS OF THE
COMMUNITY COLLEGE
*International, Intercultural,
and Multicultural Perspectives*
edited by Rosalind Latiner Raby
and Norma Tarrow

THE SOCIAL ROLE
OF HIGHER EDUCATION
Comparative Perspectives
edited by Ken Kempner
and William Tierney

SCIENCE AND TECHNOLOGY IN
CENTRAL AND EASTERN EUROPE
The Reform of Higher Education
edited by A.D. Tillett
and Barry Lesser

THE LIBERAL ARTS COLLEGE
ADAPTING TO CHANGE
The Survival of Small Schools
by Gary Bonvillian
and Robert Murphy

HIGHER EDUCATION RESEARCH
AT THE TURN OF THE NEW CENTURY
Structures, Issues, and Trends
edited by Jan Sadlak
and Philip G. Altbach

HIGHER EDUCATION IN CANADA
*Different Systems,
Different Perspectives*
edited by Glen A. Jones

HIGHER EDUCATION IN CANADA
DIFFERENT SYSTEMS, DIFFERENT PERSPECTIVES

EDITED BY
GLEN A. JONES

GARLAND PUBLISHING, INC.
NEW YORK AND LONDON
1997

Library of Congress Cataloging-in-Publication Data

Higher education in Canada : different systems, different perspectives / edited
by Glen A. Jones.
       p.   cm. — (Garland studies in higher education ; v. 11. Garland
reference library of social science ; v. 1099)
    Includes bibliographical references and index.
    ISBN 0-8153-2299-2 (alk. paper)
    1. Education, Higher—Canada—Provinces.   2. Higher education and
state—Canada—Provinces—Planning.   3. Universities and colleges—
Canada—Provinces—Administration—Planning.   I. Jones, Glen A.
II. Series: Garland reference library of social science ; v. 1099.
III. Series: Garland reference library of social science. Garland studies in
higher education ; vol. 11.
LA417.5.H54   1997
378.71—dc21   96-46286
                                                                CIP

Printed on acid-free, 250-year-life paper
Manufactured in the United States of America

SERIES EDITOR'S PREFACE

Higher education is a multifaceted phenomenon in modern society, combining a variety of institutions and an increasing diversity of students, a range of purposes and functions, and different orientations. The series combines research-based monographs, analyses, and discussions of broader issues and reference books related to all aspects of higher education. It is concerned with policy as well as practice from a global perspective. The series is dedicated to illuminating the reality of higher and postsecondary education in contemporary society.

Philip G. Altbach
Boston College

Contents

Acknowledgments

The publication of this volume is a tribute to the contributions made by each individual member of the project team, and to their ongoing support of the ideas which underscored this project. I am grateful to each member of the project team for agreeing to participate in this initiative and for sharing ideas and interpretations on the evolution of Canadian higher education. The team was composed of Michael Andrews, Ron Baker, Kathryn Bindon, Sheila Brown, David Cameron, Brian Christie, John Dennison, Janet Donald, Sandy Gregor, Gail Hilyer, Ted Holdaway, Gordon Mowat, Bill Muir, Aron Senkpiel, Michael Skolnik, and Paul Wilson.

Janice Clark, a doctoral student in the Higher Education Group at the Ontario Institute for Studies in Education, worked as a editorial assistant on this volume and was responsible for copy-editing almost all of the draft chapters. Her dedication to this project while so many other things were occurring in her life was above and beyond the call of a traditional graduate assistantship. Paul Stortz, another doctoral student, used all of the skills he obtained from his work as editor of the *Ontario Journal of Higher Education* to prepare the camera-ready version of the manuscript. His tremendous professionalism, as well as his attention to detail, always make Paul a pleasure to work with.

I am particularly grateful to Philip Altbach for his interest in publishing this volume as part of the higher education series he supervises for Garland Publishing. Thanks to his work and support, this manuscript represents one of only a handful of books on Canadian higher education published outside Canada and available to a broader international audience.

Much of the early work in coordinating this project took place while I was a post-doctoral fellow supported by the Social Sciences and Humanities Research Council of Canada. I am also grateful for the support provided by Brock University and the Ontario Institute for Studies in Education which assisted in various components of this project.

The number of individuals who have both influenced and challenged my understanding of Canadian higher education is large and growing, but I would like to especially acknowledge Michael L. Skolnik, George L. Geis, Cicely Watson, Ian Winchester, Ruth Hayhoe, Saeed Quazi, John D. Dennison, Alexander Gregor, and David Cameron. I am also grateful for all that I have learned through my ongoing conversations with Jamie-Lynn Magnusson, Ellen Herbeson, and Stephen Bell. Every day my students teach me that there are questions I have never asked and perspectives that I have never considered, while Renée Martens provides a constant reminder that there are many things more important than the study of higher education. Hilliard Lawrence Jones taught me that you can build a very good life on a foundation of honesty and hard work, and, in the last few years, Doris Jones has taught me that there is a vital, inner strength inside all of us.

Glen A. Jones
May, 1996

Preface

Glen A. Jones

What we see in higher education depends on where we look. Given the diversity associated with the various higher education systems in Canada, the decentralized nature of the Canadian federation, and the limited number of scholars who explore issues related to Canadian higher education, relatively few scholars have tried to look at Canadian higher education from a broad perspective, preferring to use the classroom, the institution, or a particular policy initiative as the unit of analysis. Scholars who have analyzed higher education research in Canada have noted a shortage of studies adopting a federal or national perspective (Dennison, 1992; Sheffield, 1982).

Broad analyses of Canadian higher education do exist, though most contributors to this body of work have tended to focus either on Canadian universities (Cameron, 1991; Gregor, 1995; Jones, 1996) or Canadian community colleges (Dennison and Gallagher, 1986; Dennison, 1995). By focusing on one of the two broadly defined institutional types in Canadian higher education, these studies represent major contributions to our understanding of how these sectors evolved and the common challenges they face. The major limitation of this approach is that component parts of higher education are discussed in relative isolation, providing a comprehensive view of a cross-section of the whole. The national and international literature also includes several broad essays on Canadian higher education, though given the space limitations associated with encyclopaedia entries and journal articles, contributors have tended to provide an overview of Canadian higher education structures while acknowledging the major differences which exist between jurisdictions (Skolnik, 1991; Watson, 1992).

This book represents an attempt to describe and analyze higher education in Canada using the provincial/territorial jurisdiction as the central unit of analysis. This approach is based on the assumption that there is no such thing as a national system of higher education in Canada. While there are some national structures and the Government of Canada continues to play a limited role in this policy arena, it is clear that the provinces and territories now play the major role in terms of Canadian higher education policy. Higher education in Canada, therefore, is viewed as a collection of different provincial/territorial systems operating in parallel. Even the term system in this context must be used in the broad sense of referring to the totality of structures and institutions associated with postsecondary education in a particular jurisdiction; few provinces are characterized by a comprehensive, system-wide policy approach to higher education.

The genesis of this project can be traced back to an international conference that I attended in Finland in 1990 (Jones, 1991). I was invited to present a paper on higher education policy in Ontario in parallel with other researchers who were describing policy change in national systems of higher education, and several of my international colleagues asked me to describe the degree to which the Ontario experience was the same or different from the experience of other Canadian jurisdictions.

Attempting to answer that simple question led to the notion of a research project involving the description and critical analysis of higher education in each Canadian jurisdiction. Like almost all of my ideas, it turned out to be far from original. Shortly after Robin Harris had been appointed Canada's first Professor of Higher Education in 1964, he organized a series of seminars focusing on how higher education was evolving in different ways in different regions of the country (Harris, 1966). Less than a decade later, Edward Sheffield organized a similar project (Sheffield, Campbell, Holmes, Kymlicka and Whitelaw, 1978). Even in these early volumes, the concept of a regional approach to describing Canadian higher education was viewed as an organizational tool of convenience. Differences in provincial approaches to higher education policy within regions had become as great as those between regions.

By the early 1990s it had become clear that different provinces were moving in different directions in terms of higher education policy (Jones, 1996), but, with a few important exceptions, these different approaches received little attention in the higher education literature. Those working within a specific provincial system might be extremely familiar with what was taking place in that jurisdiction in terms of policy developments but unaware of what was taking place in a neighboring jurisdiction. Even worse, they might assume that trends and changes in one jurisdiction reflected what was taking place across the country.

In 1991 I wrote a project proposal based on the notion of a collection of papers describing and analyzing the evolution of Canadian higher education since 1945 and began the process of developing a team of collaborators with the expertise necessary to prepare the critical essays on each Canadian jurisdiction. I began with a list of acknowledged experts in certain jurisdictions, almost all of whom agreed to participate, and then used the advice of these early collaborators to complete the team. In 1992 the project team was complete, and early drafts of chapters were prepared. These drafts were then circulated to two or more other members of the team as part of an "internal" process of peer review. Eleven of the thirteen core essays were presented at a special session of the 1993 meeting of the Canadian Society for the Study of Higher Education in Ottawa, providing team members with additional feedback on their work. Each essay was further revised and updated in 1995 or early 1996 in final preparation for this publication.

The volume begins with an introductory chapter designed to acquaint the reader with a number of basic historical and structural features of Canadian higher education. This is followed by David Cameron's essay on the evolving role of the federal government. The next ten essays focus on provincial systems and are organized geographically, moving from west to east. The last two jurisdictional essays focus on Canada's territories, jurisdictions which tend to be ignored in the Canadian literature on higher education. In the concluding essay, Michael Skolnik attempts to pull the various pieces together in order to illuminate common themes and clarify important differences between jurisdictions.

This book represents an attempt to discuss different systems of higher education in Canada from different perspectives. It is our hope that the volume will assist both Canadian and international readers in obtaining a clearer understanding of Canadian higher education.

References

Cameron, D.M. (1991). *More than an academic question: Universities, government, and public policy in Canada*. Halifax, NS: Institute for Research on Public Policy.

Dennison, J.D. (1992). Higher education as a field of inquiry in Canada. In A.D. Gregor and G. Jasmin (Eds.), *Higher education in Canada* (pp. 83-91). Ottawa, ON: Department of the Secretary of State of Canada.

Dennison, J.D. (Ed.). (1995). *Challenge and opportunity: Canada's community colleges at the crossroads*. Vancouver, BC: UBC Press.

Dennison, J.D., and Gallagher, P. (1986). *Canada's community colleges: A critical analysis*. Vancouver, BC: UBC Press.

Gregor, A.D. (1995). The universities of Canada. In *Commonwealth universities yearbook 1995-96* (pp. 257-283). London, UK: Association of Commonwealth Universities.

Harris, R. (Ed.). (1966). *Changing patterns of higher education in Canada.* Toronto, ON: University of Toronto Press.

Jones, G.A. (1991). Modest modifications and structural stability: Higher education in Ontario. *Higher Education, 21,* 573-387.

Jones, G.A. (1996). Governments, governance, and Canadian universities. In J.C. Smart (Ed.), *Higher education: Handbook of theory and research* (Vol. XI, pp. 337-371). New York, NY: Agathon Press.

Sheffield, E., Campbell, D.D., Holmes, J., Kymlicka, B.B., and Whitelaw, J.H. (Eds.). (1978). *Systems of higher education: Canada.* New York, NY: International Council for Educational Development.

Sheffield, E.F. (1982). *Research on postsecondary education in Canada. A review for the Canadian Society for the Study of Higher Education and the Social Sciences and Humanities Research Council of Canada.* Ottawa, ON: Canadian Society for the Study of Higher Education.

Skolnik, M.L. (1991). Canada. In P.G. Altbach (Ed.), *International higher education: An encyclopaedia* (Vol. 2, pp. 1067-1080). New York, NY: Garland.

Watson, C. (1992). Canada. In B.R. Clark and G. Neave (Eds.), *The encyclopaedia of higher education* (Vol. 1, pp. 109-125). Oxford, UK: Pergamon.

A Brief Introduction to Higher Education in Canada

Glen A. Jones

Canada is a challenging country, both to understand and to describe. It is as varied in geography and climate as it is immense. The second largest nation on earth has a population of just under 30 million, less than Colombia or Iran, and a population density of three inhabitants per square kilometer, only slightly higher than Australia. Its ethnically and culturally diverse population is spread unevenly, with the vast majority living within only a few hundred kilometers of its border with the United States. It is a nation of intense regionalism and subtle nationalism, of bilingualism and multiculturalism. It is a country where constitutional reform, like keeping warm, appears to be an annual pastime. As J.M.S. Careless has noted, the history of Canada is very much "a story of challenge" (Careless, 1963, p. iii).

Attempting to understand and describe higher education in Canada is equally challenging. All of the factors that have made the Canadian nation unique, especially matters of geography, federalism, regionalism, language, and culture, have played a direct role in the evolution of higher education structures and programs. The challenge of describing and analyzing Canadian higher education is made even more difficult by the fact that there is no such thing as a Canadian "system" of higher education; instead one can argue that each Canadian province and territory has created a unique network of postsecondary structures and policies.

This book tells the story of higher education in Canada from the perspective of each of the thirteen political jurisdictions which play a central role in this enterprise: the Government of Canada (the federal perspective), ten provinces, and two territories. These thirteen essays describe and analyze the evolution of higher education in Canada from 1945 to 1995.

While each of the thirteen jurisdictional chapters stands on its own, the purpose of this chapter is to provide a broad overview of higher education in Canada in order to provide a clearer sense of the national context. I will begin by describing the Canadian federation, followed by brief sections on provincial coordination, institutions, institutional governance, faculty and students.

The Canadian Federation

Postsecondary education in Canada can be traced back to the early permanent settlements of New France (Harris, 1976), but universities did not emerge until after Canada became a British colony, and the American Revolution forced many of those loyal to the Crown to move north of the 49th Parallel. The first universities were created in the colonies of Nova Scotia, Upper Canada (Ontario), Lower Canada (Quebec), and New Brunswick.

The Dominion of Canada was created by the British North America Act of 1867, a piece of British legislation which created a federal government and four provinces (Ontario, Quebec, Nova Scotia, and New Brunswick). Over time, additional colonies joined the federation and new provinces were carved out of the vast western territories. Manitoba became a province in 1870. British Columbia joined the federation in 1871, followed by Prince Edward Island in 1873. Alberta and Saskatchewan became provinces in 1905. Newfoundland became the tenth Canadian province in 1949.

Canada has a federal system of government with some responsibilities assigned to the Government of Canada and others to the provinces. Under the British North America Act, the provinces have the sole responsibility for education, though as the following chapter by David Cameron clearly argues, the Government of Canada has played a major role in the development of higher education. There is no federal government department of education or higher education.

The British North America Act also established a parliamentary system of government, following the British tradition, at both the federal and provincial levels of authority. Members of the federal House of Commons, like their counterparts in the provincial legislatures, are elected by citizens in, and represent, geographically defined constituencies. Most elected representatives are associated with a political party, and the leader of the party that wins the most seats in a federal or provincial election is asked to form a government by the Governor General, at the federal level, or the Lieutenant Governor, at the provincial level. The Prime Minister or Premier forms a cabinet which constitutes the executive level of authority under the parliamentary system.

The Canadian constitution was repatriated in 1982. While the structure and division of powers within the Canadian federation has been controversial almost since the creation of the Dominion, constitutional issues, especially the future of Quebec, have been a major preoccupation of Canadian politics for more than a decade.

Provincial Coordination

The provincial and territorial governments now play the central role in terms of the coordination of Canadian higher education. Each provincial or territorial government has assigned the responsibility for higher education to a member of the cabinet, though in some cases the responsibility for specific sectors or component parts of higher education has been delegated to different government departments. In many provinces the Minister responsible for postsecondary education is also responsible for elementary and secondary education.

Provincial coordinating or advisory structures for higher education are recent phenomena in Canadian higher education; in fact no structures or mechanisms of this sort existed before 1950. While the structures and mechanisms that currently exist differ by province, it is important to note that every Canadian province except Newfoundland (with only one university) has experimented with intermediary bodies. Generally speaking, these bodies provide the relevant department with advice concerning the coordination and regulation of provincial universities. Other than sharing a broadly similar role as an intermediary between institutions and government, the actual structures and powers of these intermediary bodies have varied considerably (Skolnik and Jones, 1992). These bodies were abandoned in British Columbia, Alberta, and Saskatchewan. The creation of the Maritime Provinces Higher Education Commission, a regional coordinating agency, led to the dissolution of provincial intermediary bodies in Nova Scotia, New Brunswick, and Prince Edward Island, though as Brian Christie notes in his chapter, Nova Scotia has recently returned to the notion of a provincial coordinating agency. In addition, Manitoba, Ontario, and Quebec continue to have provincial intermediary bodies for the university sector.

While Canadian universities are generally treated as autonomous institutions, the relationship between non-degree institutions and the state varies dramatically by jurisdiction. In some provinces community colleges are essentially component parts of government departments, while in others they operate independently within the framework of government regulation.

Institutions

According to Statistics Canada, there were 281 institutions of postsecondary education in Canada in 1992-93 (Statistics Canada, 1994), not including private training schools. This figure includes 75 universities, approximately 30% of which have full-time enrollments of over 10,000. Of the 75 universities, 54 offer both undergraduate and graduate degree programs. Almost all Canadian universities are public institutions in the sense that provincial operating grants represent their single largest source of revenue. The remaining 206 institutions are broadly categorized as community colleges, though it is important to note that there is considerable variation in the role and level of programming associated with different institutional types in different provinces and territories. Of the 206 colleges, 61 have enrollments of over 3,000 full-time students. National data on the number of institutions and postsecondary enrollment by province are presented in Table 1.

Institutional Governance

One of the unique aspects of Canadian higher education has been the development of a common model of university governance. Since universities are regarded as autonomous institutions, the structures for institutional decision making have been the subject of considerable discussion within Canadian higher education. Almost all Canadian universities have a bicameral governance structure involving a corporate board of governors with responsibility for administrative and financial matters and a senate with responsibility for academic matters. The composition and authority of each body are specified in the institutional charter. In the 1960s, almost every Canadian university revised its governance structure in order to allow for increased participation of faculty and students (see Cameron, 1991; Jones, 1996).

It is far more difficult to generalize about institutional governance in the community college sectors. In some jurisdictions, community colleges operate under the direct authority of the provincial government and institutional governing boards do not exist. In other jurisdictions there has

Table 1

Postsecondary Institutions and Full-Time Enrollment in Canada, Provinces, and Territories

Jurisdiction	Number of Institutions		Full-Time Enrollment	
	CCs*	Us**	CCs	Us
British Columbia	10	7	29,304	45,091
Alberta	18	9	25,323	50,344
Saskatchewan	1	4	3,541	22,920
Manitoba	9	6	3,850	20,576
Ontario	32	21	117,113	230,570
Quebec	94	8	169,583	135,024
New Brunswick	8	5	3,194	19,110
Nova Scotia	9	13	3,375	29,427
Prince Edward Island	2	1	926	2,724
Newfoundland	12	1	4,758	13,213
Yukon	1	0	262	0
Northwest Territories	1	0	282	0
CANADA	206	75	361,511	568,999

* Community Colleges; ** Universities

All data from Statistics Canada for 1992-93 (1994, pp. 20-21). Note that there are differences in the way institutions are defined, and therefore the numbers and categories of institutions in this table are different from the numbers and categories employed by some chapter authors.

been a strong tradition of community-based decision making through governing boards composed of local citizens. The notion of faculty and student participation within community college governance structures is a relatively new phenomenon in many jurisdictions (Dennison, 1994).

Faculty

There are approximately 37,200 full-time faculty employed by Canadian universities. Since almost all Canadian universities are established as independent, not-for-profit corporations under provincial legislation, labor relations are an institutional matter within the context of provincial laws concerning employment. The majority of full-time university faculty are members of institution-based faculty unions which negotiate collective agreements covering salaries and other matters with the university. Even at those institutions where a recognized union does not exist, there are often agreements in place which guide the negotiation or discussion of salaries and other terms and conditions of employment.

While both the number and percentage of female university teachers are increasing, it is important to note that only 8% of full professors and 20% of associate professors are female (Education Support Branch, 1994), and there are tremendous differences in the gender mix by program of study. Approximately 10% of Canadian university presidents are women.

Statistics Canada estimates that there are 25,200 full-time faculty employed by Canadian community colleges (Statistics Canada, 1994). In some provinces, community college faculty are members of provincial, rather than institutional, labor unions.

Students

Accessibility to postsecondary education has been a major public policy issue in every Canadian jurisdiction. Total enrollment and participation rates have tended to increase at a faster rate in Canada than in most other western nations, and Canada and the United States are now virtually tied in terms of having the highest participation rates in the world. Data on university enrollment suggest that Canadian participation rates may actually be higher than in the United States (Lynd, 1994), and since the private sector plays a major role in American higher education, it seems clear that Canada leads the world in terms of participation in publicly supported higher education.

There were approximately 930,000 full-time students enrolled in postsecondary education programs in 1992-93, an increase in full-time enrollment of almost 30% since 1982-83 (Statistics Canada, 1994). There were almost 570,000 full-time university students (52% female) and 321,000 part-time students (62% female). There were an estimated 360,000 full-time community college students (54% female) and 210,000 part-time students (62% female) (Education Support Branch, 1994).

Summary

In this chapter I have provided a brief overview of higher education in Canada as background for the jurisdiction-based chapters that follow. It seems clear that higher education has evolved in a unique way as political and institutional leaders have sought to meet the challenge of providing access to higher education in the context of this country's unique characteristics. Rather than a single national system of higher education, the Canadian approach has involved a combination of federal government involvement and provincial/territorial initiatives. The story of the development and evolution of higher education in Canada is a tale involving different systems and quite different perspectives.

References

Cameron, D.M. (1991). *More than an academic question: Universities, government, and public policy in Canada*. Halifax, NS: Institute for Research on Public Policy.

Careless, J.M.S. (1963). *Canada: A story of challenge*. Toronto, ON: Macmillan.

Dennison, J.D. (1994). The case for democratic governance in Canada's community colleges. *Interchange*, 20(1), 25-38.

Education Support Branch, Human Resources Development Canada. (1994). *Profile of post-secondary education in Canada: 1993 edition*. Ottawa, ON: Ministry of Supply and Services Canada.

Harris, R.S. (1976). *A history of higher education in Canada 1663-1960*. Toronto, ON: University of Toronto Press.

Lynd, D.J. (1994). Increases in university enrolment: Increased access or increased retention? *Education Quarterly Review*, 1(1), 12-21.

Jones, G.A. (1996). Governments, governance, and Canadian universities. In J.C. Smart (Ed.), *Higher education: Handbook of theory and research* (Vol. XI, pp. 337-371). New York, NY: Agathon Press.

Skolnik, M.L., and Jones, G.A. (1992). A comparative analysis of arrangements for state coordination of higher education in Canada and the United States. *Journal of Higher Education*, 63(2), 121-142.

Statistics Canada. (1994). *Education in Canada: A statistical review for 1992-93.* Ottawa, ON: Ministry of Science and Technology, Canada.

The Federal Perspective

David M. Cameron

The federal perspective on higher education in Canada has been formed under conditions akin to chronic schizophrenia. The upshot is a dual perspective, the product of a split federal personality in matters of higher education. Dressed in the garb of constitutional propriety, the federal government confronts a world that excludes it from all but minor roles, with responsibility for higher education assigned to provincial governments. But under the guise of political expediency, the federal government contends with both opportunities and pressures to assume a more prominent presence, even to the point of challenging provincial primacy in some aspects of higher education.

The Schizophrenic Pattern of Federal Policy

The federal government's schizophrenic condition has been evident virtually from Confederation in 1867. The original *Constitution Act* leaves little doubt about provincial responsibility. Section 95 states that "In and for each Province the Legislature may exclusively make Laws in relation to Education. . . ."

Seven years after Confederation, the federal government introduced legislation to establish the Royal Military College in Kingston. It was justified as falling within federal responsibility for defence, yet it was anticipated from the outset that it would graduate students for civilian as well as military careers (Cameron, 1991). Much later, when the RMC obtained degree-granting powers in 1959, the constitutional circle was squared: RMC, a wholly federal institution, now offers degrees under provincial statutory authority.

Section 95 of *The Constitution Act, 1867* does not stop with the categorical allocation of legislative responsibility to the provinces. It also confirms parental rights concerning denominational schools and grants the federal government reserve power to rectify provincial transgressions of those rights. But the federal government effectively abandoned that power when it refused to intervene in the infamous Manitoba School Question after the 1896 federal election.

True to its schizophrenic character, the federal government was by no means signalling its intention to refrain from future initiatives related to education. For the most part, federal interests in education through the first half of the twentieth century came to center on technical and vocational training either at the secondary school level or outside the formal school system altogether (Manzer, 1994). In 1910, the provinces agreed to the establishment of a federal royal commission, which subsequently recommended a comprehensive scheme of federal grants in support of provincial technical and vocational programs. That recommendation was actually anticipated by legislation passed in 1912 and 1913 authorizing federal grants to the provinces for the support of agricultural training. It is interesting that in this instance the federal government did not rely upon its concurrent jurisdiction with respect to agriculture but chose instead to act under the broader scope of its implicit spending power. The upshot was Canada's first-ever conditional grant or shared-cost program. And with that came the initiation of a half century of so-called cooperative federalism.

The First World War resulted in the postponement of plans to implement the major recommendations of the Royal Commission on Industrial Training and Technical Education. The war also led directly to a new federal initiative that would have enormous implications for higher education. It persuaded leaders of both government and business that investment in research was a necessary condition for success in the internationally competitive environment associated with the war effort and anticipated in the post-war economic recovery. The National Research Council was established in 1916, and it immediately turned to the major universities as the principal source of research facilities and personnel, offering both grants and scholarships. This initiative effectively secured the federal government's preeminence in the field of university research.

The Great Depression of the 1930s called forth a number of federal initiatives designed to create jobs or otherwise reduce the number of unemployed. Not surprisingly, training took on a new urgency under the circumstances, and the federal government increased the scope and generosity of its shared-cost programs with the provinces. Also added was the first federal program to assist students through loans, embodied in the 1939 Dominion-Provincial Student Loan Program, the precursor of the present Canada Student Loan Program.

The Depression also spawned the famous Rowell-Sirois Commission, whose 1940 report so nicely captured the essence of the schizophrenic federal perspective on higher education. Having denounced conditional grants and shared-cost programs as injurious to both sound public finance and efficient administration and proposed instead a new constitutional division of taxing and spending responsibilities, the commission nonetheless allowed that:

> Even the provinces might welcome a small Dominion grant to their universities made contingent on the maintenance over a period of some years of provincial grants to the same institutions and on the preservation of high academic standards. (Canada, Book II, 1940, p. 52)

It was the Second World War and its aftermath which opened the floodgates to the federal invasion of provincial jurisdiction over higher education. University leaders, at least in English-speaking Canada, were active in lobbying for federal participation. Having enjoyed a close and cooperative working relationship during the war, university representatives joined senior federal officials and politicians in pressing for a more activist federal role in the process of post-war reconstruction. And after the hugely successful program of support for veterans entering or returning to university, lobbying efforts shifted to the search for a more permanent arrangement.

These efforts came to focus on the Massey Commission when it was established in 1949. Four of the five commissioners had close university connections, with UBC's "Larry" MacKenzie apparently the most aggressive in pressing for a recommendation in favor of federal operating grants to universities (Waite, 1987). In pursuit of this objective, the commissioners and their university supporters were prepared to turn blind eyes to the constitutional sensitivities of Quebec. The commission's 1951 report tried to finesse the constitutional issue by asserting boldly that:

> ... universities are provincial institutions; but they are much more than that. They also serve the national cause in so many ways, direct and indirect, that theirs must be regarded as the finest of contributions to national strength and unity. (Canada, 1951, p. 132)

The St. Laurent government immediately accepted the proposal, paying grants directly to all universities and colleges for 1951-52 at the rate of fifty cents per capita, allocated by province in proportion to population and distributed among the institutions in each province in proportion to enrollment. In taking this step the federal government not only provided a much needed infusion of cash for hard-pressed universities but initiated an intergovernmental tug-of-war that may only now be reaching its denouement.

The government of Quebec was the first to object to federal grants to universities, and it did so by directing the universities of that province to refuse the grants after the first year. The universities obeyed and, despite some relief from increased provincial funding, suffered the fiscal consequences.

In due course, the federal government added a considerable number of programs designed to support university expansion in specific areas. Grants for capital construction in the humanities and social sciences were introduced via the Canada Council in 1957. Subsidized mortgage financing for student residences was added in 1960. The Canada Student Loans Program was introduced in 1964. Grants for the massive expansion of facilities in medicine, dentistry, and related health professions were initiated in 1966 through the health Resources Fund following release and acceptance of the Hall Royal Commission report and in anticipation of a national medical insurance scheme (Medicare).

Research support grew apace. From the end of the Second World War to 1959, grants to university researchers climbed from about $1 million to just over $10 million. They would quadruple over the next seven years, reaching almost $42 million by 1966 (Macdonald et al., 1969). The contemporary structure of granting councils was also taking shape. In 1960 the Medical Research Council was effectively separated from the National Research Council. Confirming its preeminence in the area of scientific research, the federal government moved in 1964 to establish a science secretariat within the Privy Council Office. This was followed two years later by the establishment of the Science Council of Canada.

The skirmish with Quebec over direct federal grants to universities was finally resolved in 1959, after the death of Premier Duplessis. The resolution was attended by the addition of yet another weapon to the arsenal of federal-provincial fiscal diplomacy: contracting out (Dupré, 1965). Instead of making payments directly to universities in Quebec, the federal government would henceforth transfer an equivalent amount to the provincial government. This device was destined to gain in provincial popularity. Not only was it extended to other programs in Quebec through the 1960s, including the Canada Student Loans Program, but it also laid the groundwork for the major overhaul of federal-provincial fiscal arrangements in higher education in 1967, by which point the term higher education had generally given way to the more inclusive postsecondary education.

The contracting out arrangement set an important precedent in the way it made use of the tax system. The transfer to Quebec was initially given effect by reducing the federal corporate income tax rate applicable in Quebec by 1%, thereby allowing the provincial government to obtain the equivalent revenue through a comparable increase in provincial taxes without imposing a heavier burden on Quebec-based corporations. The revenue obtained by Quebec through this tax "abatement" was then adjusted annually, through the mechanism of the equalization formula, so that it exactly matched the amount that would have been paid to universities in Quebec under the per-capita formula. Meanwhile, the value of federal grants under that formula had been increased to $1.00 in 1956-57 and to $1.50 in 1958-59. It would subsequently be increased to $2.00 in 1962-63 and hard on the heels of the Bladen Commission on university finance (Bladen et al., 1965), to $5.00 for 1966-67.

As the year 1966 unfolded, federal education policy shifted direction significantly, but in the course of this shift its schizophrenic character was both confirmed and magnified. Partly, this reflected the growing dissonance between the Department of the Secretary of State pushing for a stronger federal presence in education generally and postsecondary education particularly and the Department of Finance concerned about the cost of open-ended fiscal commitments. Partly also, it grew out of a new priority in federal economic policy, based on the conviction that future growth and stability would require the capacity to manage a national labor market in order to reduce bottlenecks resulting from inadequate or inappropriate skills, information, or mobility.

Thus did 1966 witness the furthest advance of the federal government in its assault on provincial constitutional responsibilities for education. One event that both signalled the extent of the federal advance and pushed the provinces to take defensive action was the appointment of Robin Ross, registrar of the University of Toronto, to advise on the appropriateness of establishing an education support branch in the Department of the Secretary of State. Faced with the prospect of a federal office of education, the provinces responded by creating the wholly provincial Council of Ministers of Education, Canada (CMEC).

An event of considerably greater substance occurred in October of 1966 when Prime Minister Lester Pearson unveiled the federal government's proposals in relation to postsecondary and technical education at a federal-provincial conference. Pearson staked out a vast new jurisdictional terrain and claimed it solely for the federal government (Dupré et al., 1973). He proposed to abandon a host of shared-cost programs in respect of technical and vocational education, along with their associated opting out arrangements, that had evolved and multiplied since the original grants for agricultural education in 1912-13. In their place, the federal government would assume unilateral responsibility for the training, retraining, counselling, placement, and financial support (including training allowances and assistance in relocation) of unemployed or underemployed adults (defined arbitrarily as persons out of school and in the labor force for at least three years). Where training was judged to be necessary, the type and duration would be defined by federal counsellors, to be located in newly established Canada Manpower Centres, and with the actual training to be purchased from industry, provincial institutions, or private schools.

In defence of this bold initiative, the prime minister drew a highly dubious constitutional distinction that would remain an intergovernmental irritant for at least the next quarter century. Programs directed to ". . . the training and re-training of adults for participation in the labor force . . . are not 'education' in the constitutional sense . . .," he argued, but fall within the federal government's constitutional responsibility ". . . for economic growth and full employment" (Dupré et al., 1973, p. 26).

In sharp contrast, and announced at the same October conference, the federal government beat a substantive retreat on the question of support to universities. Most significantly, it abandoned its program of direct, per-capita grants. In addition, the categorical grants that had not already run their course were allowed to atrophy. The only significant survivors were grants to university researchers administered through the granting councils and the intergovernmental Canada Student Loans Program.

The substitute was a general fiscal transfer to the provinces based on principles established in Quebec's contracting out scheme and incorporated into the quinquennial fiscal arrangements applicable from 1967 to 1972. The transfers once again made use of tax abatements with a subsequent cash adjustment. This time, the taxing capacity shifted to the provinces amounted to 4.357 points of personal income tax plus the single percentage point on corporate income that had been ceded to Quebec in 1960 and now extended to all provinces. Provincial revenues derived from the occupancy of this transferred tax room would also be eligible for equalization, assuring all provinces of at least the national per-capita average revenue.

These revenues were then further adjusted, if necessary, under one of two floor provisions. For most provinces, the applicable floor was 50% of the total operating expenditures of all universities and colleges in the province. For three provinces with both weak fiscal capacities and relatively low levels of expenditure on postsecondary education (Newfoundland, Prince Edward Island, and New Brunswick), a higher floor of $15 per capita was available.

Despite the expectations of some provincial officials that the tax transfers would yield annual provincial revenues well above the floor (Cameron, 1991), this did not turn out to be the case. The upshot was that the arrangement became, in effect, an open-ended federal commitment to cover half of whatever was spent for operating purposes in universities and colleges. And what was spent increased dramatically. Federal cash payments to the provinces exceeded the estimates of federal officials by over 40% in the first year alone and increased by approximately 30% per year thereafter. It was not an arrangement that could last indefinitely and, of course, it did not. When intergovernmental discussions failed to produce an alternative, the federal government simply capped the annual rate of growth after 1972 at 15%.

Research continued as a mostly federal responsibility. In 1977, the federal government reorganized its granting councils, in part to extend coverage to all academic disciplines. Based on the advice of both the Macdonald study group (Macdonald et al., 1969) and the Lamontagne committee (Canada, 1972), the role of the Canada Council was restricted to the fine and performing arts, while the National Research Council was stripped of its granting function altogether. Two new councils were established which, with the Medical Research Council, comprised the tri-council structure that has survived to the present. The two new councils were the Natural Sciences and Engineering Research Council and the Social Sciences and Humanities Research Council.

In this restructuring, the federal government rejected a fundamental principle and an explicit recommendation contained in both reports. The principle was that the federal government should move to accept full responsibility for funding research, leaving the support of teaching wholly to the provinces, recognizing all the while that the two activities would mostly continue to be undertaken in tandem in the same institutions. As Lamontagne put it in his second volume:

> The Committee suggests that teaching . . . and basic research . . .
> be conceived as two separate and distinct functions, to be
> supported according to different criteria. . . . [T]he Canadian
> government would assume the financial responsibility for basic

research in universities and other centres of excellence . . .
(Canada, 1972, Vol. 2, p. 435)

The specific recommendation that followed from this principle was
that the federal research councils should meet the full costs, direct and
indirect, associated with council-supported research in universities. Past
failure to do this, argued Macdonald,

> . . . has meant that federal research grants distort the university
> budget process: Accordingly, the availability of federal research
> funds restricted to direct-cost coverage impoverishes universities
> through a budgetary substitution effect similar to that which can
> be induced by conditional grants. (Macdonald et al., 1969, pp.
> 136-7)

This recommendation to cover the full costs of sponsored research has
been made repeatedly by virtually every investigation into the funding of
research. So far, the arguments have fallen on deaf ears. Considerable
irony, therefore, attaches to the fact that the federal government did move,
virtually at the same time as it reorganized its research granting councils,
to address the priority-distorting effects inherent in the conditional grant
arrangements applicable to postsecondary education generally. In doing so
it created a whole new set of problems that once again bore witness to the
federal government's schizophrenic approach to matters of education.

Reconciling the Irreconcilable: The Rise and Demise of EPF

The Established Programs Financing (EPF) arrangement put in place
for 1977 represented the apotheosis of schizophrenia. In seeking to regain
control of its own expenditures, the federal government was prepared to
sacrifice all elements of conditionality in its transfers to the provinces in
support of postsecondary education. Yet at precisely the same time, it not
only treated the ensuing transfers as though they were earmarked for
specific programs but it also argued that they constituted a de facto
invitation to participate with the provinces in the formulation of
postsecondary policy.

The original design of EPF was complicated by a number of
encumbrances that were for the most part intended to smooth out the
transition to the new order. The principles underlying the design, however,
were quite simple. First, the program was intended to replace three shared-

cost or conditional grant programs: Medicare, hospital insurance, and postsecondary education. Second, the base amount upon which continuing federal support for these programs was calculated was the average per-capita level actually paid to all provinces combined in 1975-76. This amount was then to be indexed annually in proportion to GNP and multiplied by each province's population. Finally, half of the resulting amount was paid in cash and the remainder raised by the provinces through an additional transfer of income tax room.

An additional element of EPF had nothing to do with any of the established programs directly. It arose from the federal withdrawal from an earlier guarantee to protect provincial treasuries against revenue losses resulting from the income tax reforms of 1972. As compensation, provincial entitlements under EPF were increased by the equivalent of another two points of personal income tax, half to be added to the cash entitlement and half to the tax transfer. The cash entitlement turned out to be $113.95 per capita, before annual indexing, and the transferred personal income tax room came to 13.5% (the 4.357% transferred in 1967 plus an additional 9.143%) along with the 1% of taxable corporate income originating in the Ottawa-Quebec deal of 1959. Revenues from the transferred tax room continued to be subject to equalization.

Federal schizophrenia went to the very heart of EPF and, most particularly, to the postsecondary education component. Three examples warrant additional comment here. First, the arrangement was legally unconditional, leaving the federal government no leverage whatsoever over the way provincial governments used the attendant revenues. Yet from the very beginning, federal politicians and officials refused to accept that this was so. Prime Minister Trudeau underscored his government's Janus-like perspective when he introduced the proposals in June 1976. On the one hand, he conceded, the transfers were unconditional, and provincial governments ". . . would not have to make matching expenditures of any kind from their own resources." But on the other hand, he asserted, ". . . when funds are made available by Parliament under the spending power . . . the federal government . . . does nevertheless have to concern itself with what is done with the funds . . ."(Canada, 1976, pp. 216-17). Conditional or unconditional, that was the unanswered question. Federal officials thought they might even have it both ways. The key to this would be an invitation to the federal Secretary of State to participate in the deliberations of the inter-provincial Council of Ministers of Education. For more than a decade, the provincial ministers refused to issue such an invitation, sometimes treating their federal counterpart quite rudely.

The second example laid the groundwork for subsequently giving substance to the myth of conditionality. In the actual administration of EPF, the cash grants were divided into health and postsecondary components and paid to the provinces through separate departments: Health and Welfare on the one hand and Secretary of State on the other. The funds were divided in proportion to the average payments prior to EPF, with 67.9% allocated to health and 32.1% to postsecondary education. Federal and university officials found it both easy and convenient to argue that 32.1% of the transfer was intended to be earmarked for postsecondary education.

The third example made it possible to extend this argument even to the transferred tax points, which was no mean accomplishment. Here we have to appreciate how the transfer of tax points actually worked. After 1972, when the system of tax abatements gave way to separate provincial income taxes in all provinces (which the federal government agreed to collect if the tax bases were essentially the same), a tax transfer was accomplished by the federal government reducing its tax rate and the provinces increasing theirs, with the result that individual taxpayers paid the same total amount but paid it in different proportions to the two orders of government (more to the province and less to the federal government). Once done, this transfer was final; it could not be reversed by one party alone. Yet federal officials have always calculated provincial revenues from tax points transferred in 1960, 1967, and 1977 as though these were annual grants from the federal treasury. It might seem to be a neat trick to be able to turn provincial tax revenues into federal grants, but it is still a trick. Stefan Dupré went to the heart of the issue when he described the federal practice as coming ". . . at the top of my list of the Big Lies of Canadian public finance" (Dupré, 1994, p. 250). In truth, only the cash portion of EPF qualifies as a federal grant to the provinces.

Hardly had the ink dried on the EPF legislation when federal representatives began hinting at impending changes. Initially, the objective seemed to be to pressure the provinces into including federal officials in discussions on postsecondary policy, but by the early 1980s it seemed to be more a matter of reducing the rate of growth in transfer payments. The first clear signal of the federal government's intentions came in October 1980, when the minister of finance announced that he expected savings to accrue from reductions in transfers to the provinces. The details were to be worked out by a parliamentary task force chaired by Hon. Herb Breau. Reporting almost a year later, the task force rejected the minister's condition and instead recommended that the health and postsecondary education components of EPF be split formally and ". . . be considered earmarked for each program area and not meant for other purposes" (Canada, 1981, p. 78).

The government responded in its 1981 budget by threatening to freeze EPF payments if the provinces were not prepared to consult with federal officials with a view to shifting their spending priorities in favour of labour market training. It also proposed to eliminate the portion of the transfer associated with the 1972-77 revenue guarantee.

The latter meant that a portion of the 1977 transfer of tax room would have to be returned. But this was beyond the reach of the federal government to obtain unilaterally. In order to achieve the same effect, and at the same time to implement one of the recommendations of the Breau task force, that total EPF transfers (cash and tax room) have the same per-capita value in all provinces, the federal government proposed a change in the EPF formula. The change, legislated in 1982, simplified the formula considerably. It eliminated the transition and levelling features of the original approach and at the same time made it easy for the federal government to cap its cash transfers to the provinces. Under the new formula, the calculation of provincial entitlements remained the same (the average per-capita payment in 1975-76 escalated annually according to GNP). The cash grants were now simply the difference between the entitlement and the amount attributed to each province as revenue from the transferred tax room, along with any associated equalization.

Within the year, the federal government used the revised formula to put the first of a series of escalating caps on postsecondary cash grants under EPF. This was done as part of the so-called "6&5" anti-inflation program and limited increases in provincial entitlements to 6% and 5% for 1983-84 and 1984-85, respectively. But these limits applied to postsecondary education and not health, and that required a further change in the legislation. And when that legislation was before the House of Commons, the government accepted an all-party compromise by which the lurking conditionality of the EPF scheme was more formally recognized. The key clause required that the Secretary of State submit annually to Parliament a report setting out:

(a) cash contributions and total equalized tax transfers in respect of the post-secondary education financing program applicable to each province; [and]
(b) expenditures by each province on post-secondary education. (Canada, 1984, p. 2729)

The intention was clear: Even if EPF was an unconditional fiscal transfer, the federal government would report to Parliament as though the postsecondary education component were conditional. The "Big Lie" was now embodied in legislation and annual reports.

A year later Al Johnson tendered a report to the Secretary of State in which further quantitative substance was added to the Big Lie. He started with the now-fashionable notion that 32.1% of the total annual cash grants under EPF, plus the same proportion of the imputed revenues from the transferred tax room (including equalization) could be considered a federal grant earmarked for the support of provincial expenditures on postsecondary education. Johnson argued that the provinces were generally substituting these "grants" for their own expenditures, with the result that larger and larger shares of provincial expenditures were coming from federal grants. He calculated that the federal share of postsecondary expenditures had increased from 69% in 1977-78 to 80% in 1984-85 and actually exceeded 100% in five of the provinces (Johnson, 1985). His recommended solution, after proposing to reallocate a portion of the funds to cover the indirect costs of sponsored research and establish centres of research excellence, was to "re-conditionalize" the EPF arrangement. Annual increases in total federal transfers, he argued, should be limited to increases in provincial expenditures on postsecondary education.

By the time Johnson submitted his report, a new party was at the helm in Ottawa, and any prospect that his advice on EPF would be followed was dashed with the Conservative's first budget, tabled in May 1985. Finance Minister Michael Wilson announced that a new and permanent cap would be placed on cash transfers. By this device, he ensured that the whole EPF structure would eventually wither away.

Wilson changed the formula so that per-capita provincial entitlements would no longer grow at the rate of increases in GNP but at the rate of GNP—2%. This meant that over time, and commensurate with economic growth, provincial revenues from the transferred tax room would grow faster than their EPF entitlements. Cash transfers would thereby decline and eventually disappear. This process was speeded up in 1989 when the EPF escalator was reduced to GNP—3%, and accelerated again in 1990 when the escalator was suspended altogether.

Given all this, it is possible to see at least poetic justice in the fact that in 1988 the CMEC finally agreed to establish a "Ministerial Postsecondary Committee" that would consult with the federal Secretary of State and other federal ministers on matters related to certain aspects of postsecondary education policy. This was one of the few tangible outcomes of the

National Forum on Postsecondary Education co-sponsored by the federal Secretary of State and the CMEC in the autumn of 1987. The federal government, meanwhile, found other avenues to explore.

New Initiatives, New Frustrations

Research has been the one aspect of higher education in which the federal government has historically had clear and accepted responsibilities. This, too, is changing as provincial governments have begun to see a connection between research and economic growth. The federal government remains the preeminent patron of basic research in Canadian universities, but its objectives and administrative arrangements have changed significantly since the reorganization of the granting councils in 1977.

The first significant signal of a changing agenda came with the 1986 budget and the announcement that, henceforth, additional funding for the granting councils would be tied to matching contributions from the private sector, to a maximum increase of $369 million (subsequently increased to $380 million) over four years (6% per year) beginning in 1987. The rules governing the program turned out to be so loose that the increase in funds deemed to be "matching" far exceeded the annual limits. Not only were crown corporations considered to be in the private sector, but income from university endowments was included. As the Senate committee on national finance concluded in its 1988 evaluation of the program: ". . . there is nothing to indicate one way or another whether the program has been instrumental in generating any **additional** support from the private sector" (Canada, 1988a, p. 47:16).

In its next initiative, the federal government copied the experience of Ontario in launching a program of support for explicitly designated "centres of excellence." The preliminary step, paralleling a similar move in Ontario shortly after David Peterson's election as premier, was the establishment in 1987 of the National Advisory Board on Science and Technology, nominally chaired by the prime minister and made up of cabinet ministers, officials, the heads of the granting councils, and representatives of universities and the private sector. On the recommendation of this board, the government quickly launched a $1.3 billion research initiative. The initiative had three major components: $200 million in additional funding through the granting councils, $80 million for a program of scholarships in math, science and engineering, and $240 million for a national version of Ontario's centres of excellence program.

In choosing research projects under the centres program, the highest priority was assigned to scientific merit. In this, the government earned considerable respect from the research community, respect that was augmented considerably when the task of screening proposals was assigned to an international panel of scholars. Projects recommended by the international panel were then further assessed by a Canadian advisory committee, which mostly confirmed the recommendations of their international peers. The government made the official announcement in October 1989, indicating that fourteen projects would be supported, all of them recommended by the two panels. A fifteenth project was added six months later, the only one in the social sciences, and focusing on problems associated with an aging society. Most of the approved projects have now been approved for a second round of funding, although the overall magnitude of the program has been scaled back somewhat.

One of the more significant features of the successful projects was the extent to which they involved researchers from several universities, public agencies, and private firms. Indeed, the official title of the program was "networks" of centres of excellence. Over 30 universities were represented in the fifteen projects, many of them in several projects, and a few in virtually all of them. One assessment of the program noted the essentially Canadian character of this approach:

> Networking was an ingenious device for satisfying political needs and parochial interests without totally sacrificing scientific standards. The most eminent universities viewed "networking" as a way to ensure their continued prominence in research and the less eminent institutions saw it as enhancing their opportunities for gaining financial support. (Friedman and Friedman, 1990, p. 289)

An important component of the government's initiatives related to scientific research was the reorganization of the federal bureaucracy. In particular, it was announced in 1987 that the Ministry of State for Science and Technology would be merged with the industry branch of the former Department of Regional Industrial Expansion to create a new Department of Industry, Science, and Technology, subsequently shortened to just Industry. In many ways this was the culmination of a new federal emphasis on research, designed to harness it to the agenda of enhanced economic competitiveness. The government made no bones about its expectations of the new super department: "It will be a flagship economic policy department emphasizing the development and application of strategic technologies to promote a more internationally competitive industrial economy" (Canada, 1988b, p. 5). And with that, it was not entirely surprising that the Science Council was included in the list of public agencies to be scrapped as a consequence of the 1992 budget.

One dimension of federal policy with respect to postsecondary education that had always been driven by an economic agenda was labour market training. And here we witness the resurgence of federal schizophrenia. The Adult Occupational Training program, announced with such fanfare back in 1966, turned out to be a good deal less than promised. For one thing, the federal Department of Manpower and Immigration was simply not up to the challenge of its own grand design, which called upon it to predict future job opportunities and then select, council, train, and relocate workers whose skills and experience would precisely match future jobs. For another thing, provincial governments, and especially Ontario, moved quickly to protect their new community colleges from federally dictated priorities. The upshot was that the Canada Manpower Training Program, the institutional component of federal support for labour market training, turned rapidly into a typical shared-cost program with the provinces (Dupré et al., 1973).

There followed a number of federal initiatives which marked the abandonment of a centrally designed national training strategy. Two objectives seemed paramount: to break free of the monopoly of the provinces over institutional training and to direct federally sponsored training more specifically to the labour market needs of individual trainees and employers. In 1976 the Department of Manpower and Immigration became the Employment and Immigration Commission, a change designed to facilitate closer relations with the private sector. Then, in 1982 the Adult Occupational Training Act was replaced by the National Training Act, the latter providing considerably more flexibility in the design and delivery of training programs.

The Conservatives moved quickly after their election in 1984 to take advantage of this flexibility, unveiling the Canadian Jobs Strategy in 1985. This new approach, still operating under the National Training Act, emphasized training in combination with work experience, under projects tailored to the needs of individual employers. This was followed in 1989 by the announcement of a much more active labour market training policy, styled the Labour Force Development Strategy and supported by a new agency and a new approach to unemployment insurance.

The strategy got off to a promising start. In November 1989 all of the provincial premiers accepted the prime minister's invitation to consider a national task force on human resource development. The premiers turned the issue over to the CMEC for further consideration. There appeared to be some prospect of success, until the Meech Lake constitutional debâcle put an end to federal-provincial cooperation in such matters as education.

The federal government, meanwhile, amended the Unemployment Insurance Act in 1990 so as to free up a substantial pool of money which would be available for the training of insurance claimants. Then, the final element of the new strategy was added in 1991 with the creation of the Canadian Labour Force Development Board (CLFDB), comprising representatives of business, labour, and equity groups and intended to operate at arm's length from government in formulating a strategy for labour market training. The CLFDB was intended to work closely with parallel provincial agencies and, through them, with local boards, but provincial governments have been less than enthusiastic about the prospect of having their training priorities coordinated by a federal agency. The board has so far survived the election of a Liberal government in 1993, but it has been stripped of most of its advisory and coordinating functions.

We see here the federal government's attempt to confront one of the stark realities of Canada: the fact that economic circumstances vary considerably across the federation and that labour market training must therefore be designed to respond to these variations. But it is precisely at this point that federal policy returns to its schizophrenic origins. For if labour market training must be adapted to local and regional circumstances, is there any longer an appropriate role for the federal government in program design and delivery? The strategy underlying the creation of the CFLDB was to answer yes and no simultaneously. The Liberals, after 1993, set out to define a different approach. Lloyd Axworthy was put in charge of the recently created Department of Human Resources Development, formed in part from the merger of the Employment and Immigration Commission with the education branch of the Secretary of State's Department, and charged with reconstructing the entire array of federal social security programs—including labour market training and postsecondary education.

The Social Security Review

Axworthy's marching orders were issued as part of the 1994 federal budget. Committed to reducing the deficit to 3% of GDP in the short run, the Minister of Finance indicated that the Axworthy review would be expected to hold total federal spending on postsecondary education via EPF and social assistance via the Canada Assistance Plan (CAP) in 1996-97 to not more than the amount spent in 1993-94. Expenditures would be allowed to increase in the interim, however, with the result that some $1.5 billion would have to be cut in 1996-97 (Canada, 1994a).

Axworthy's plan was set forth in a discussion paper issued in October 1994. It proposed a radical new approach for federal support of postsecondary education (Canada, 1994b). The paper accepted that EPF cash transfers were destined to run out and suggested that this might happen within as few as ten years. Rather than letting that happen, Axworthy proposed to cancel what was now referred to as EPF/PSE and to substitute an expanded scheme of federal loans to students. It was a very clever proposal.

Cash payments to the provinces under EPF/PSE would stand at approximately $2 billion by 1996-97. Axworthy proposed to eliminate these transfers altogether. It was then assumed that the provinces would respond by allowing their universities and colleges to raise tuition fees by an equivalent amount, roughly doubling existing fees. Then, to relieve the burden of higher fees, the federal government would offer students an "income contingent repayment loan plan" (ICRLP), available without a means test and repayable after graduation in proportion to students' future incomes. What was so clever about the scheme was the calculation that the proposed ICRLP could sustain total loans of $2 billion with annual costs of about $500 million. This meant that the whole of the $2 billion withdrawn from transfers to the provinces could be put back into the postsecondary system via higher tuition and student loans, while saving the federal treasury the required $1.5 billion annually. Dealing only with the cash side of EPF forced Axworthy to confront the Big Lie of counting provincial revenues from transferred tax room as annual federal transfers. This he proposed to do in a diplomatic finesse which conceded the substance but not the principle of the traditional federal position:

> The tax room transferred to the provinces under the EPF arrangements . . . is there in perpetuity. The federal tax points amount to a permanent, growing federal endowment to help support provincial post-secondary education costs. (Canada, 1994b, p. 61)

That was the essence of the conceptual plan. The details, however, belied the cleverness of the concept.

For one thing, ICLR plans require a host of detailed decisions before their actual impact can be discerned, and few of these were specified in the discussion paper. One detail that was included was that no means test would be applied, as is the case for the Canada Student Loans Program. The absence of a means test meant, in turn, that interest rates would have to approximate commercial rates, or else students and their parents would be induced to borrow excessively in order to capture the subsidy. But commercial rates would mean that students could face enormous debts after graduation, as interest compounded on their original loans. One study in New Brunswick came to the discomforting conclusion that some students (mainly women) might never repay their student loans (New Brunswick, 1994).

The Axworthy proposal elicited opposition from almost every quarter. Student groups were most vocal, demonizing the ICRLP as a thinly disguised device to lever up tuition fees. Universities were concerned not only about the potentially uneven impact of the proposal on different institutions but also about its failure to address the lingering problem of indirect research costs and the possibility that it might put these out of the reach of many provinces and universities. The provinces were fearful of the magnitude of the cuts proposed and the fact that their allocation among provinces could vary enormously (Cameron, 1995). The prospects for Axworthy's proposals were not good, given the nature and strength of the opposition. But what finally doomed them was the relentless pressure on federal finances and the higher priority assigned by the government to deficit reduction over social policy reform.

The 1995 Budget

The Liberals' second budget, delivered at the end of February 1995, killed Axworthy's proposed reforms. Instead of scrapping EPF and substituting an expanded loan scheme, the Minister of Finance announced the expansion of EPF to incorporate the Canada Assistance Plan as well as health and postsecondary education and to be designated the Canada Health and Social Transfer (CHST). But the budget went much further than this. It also proposed to cut provincial entitlements under the new CHST by some \$4.3 billion by 1997-98 (Canada, 1995). And because the CHST would initially work much as had EPF (with cash grants equal to the difference between entitlements and provincial tax revenues attributed to transferred tax points and associated equalization) comparing entitlement levels greatly understated the proposed cuts in actual cash transfers. Rather than the 4.4% cut claimed by the federal Minister of Finance, the real cut amounted to some 37% (Cameron, 1995). Moreover, the CHST will continue to wither away, just like EPF.

Two questions remain as a consequence of these cuts. The first concerns their distribution among the provinces after 1996-97, which remain to be negotiated. The second concerns the disposition of these cuts within individual provinces, which will reflect the relative priorities provincial governments assign to postsecondary education as opposed to other expenditure items, including deficit reduction. And federal withdrawal from the support of postsecondary education does not stop here. The granting councils were also hit, by 10% in the case of the Medical Research Council, and by 14% in the case of the Natural Sciences and Engineering Research Council and the Social Sciences and Humanities Research Council. Coupled with the cuts in transfers to the provinces, and the eventual demise of the CHST, this has to raise serious concerns about the future funding of university research. Then, the Department of Human Resources Development is slated to reduce its overall spending by some 35% as a result of the program review exercise. Can this be accomplished without touching the Canada Student Loans Program administered by that department? Finally, the whole question of federal involvement in labour market training remains in limbo. Axworthy's plans for reform of unemployment insurance, included in his October 1994 discussion paper, have gone nowhere, while the prospect of turning responsibility for training over to the provinces remains a much-discussed option.

And so the federal perspective on higher or postsecondary education remains as it began, profoundly schizophrenic. Bold proposals bequeath budgetary backtracking. Federal and provincial priorities conflict, yielding outcomes that differ from intentions. Constitutional morality succumbs to political advantage. Despite this pathological disposition, federal policy on postsecondary education has scored some remarkable achievements, in building a national research enterprise, in support of provincial universities and colleges, and in a student loan program that is a testament to creative and cooperative policy formulation in a federal context (Cameron, 1991). It is a mixed record to be sure, but that in itself is consistent with the very nature of the federal perspective on higher education in Canada.

References

Bladen, V.W., Dugal, L. P., McCutcheon, M., Wallace, R., and Howard, I. (1965). *Financing higher education in Canada: Report of a Commission to the Association of Universities and Colleges of Canada*. Toronto: University of Toronto Press.

Cameron, D.M. (1991). *More than an academic question: Universities, government, and public policy in Canada*. Halifax: IRPP.

Cameron, D.M. (1995). Shifting the burden: Liberal policy for post-secondary education. In S. Phillips (ed.), *How Ottawa spends 1995-96: Mid-life crisis*. (pp. 159-184). Ottawa: Carleton University Press, 1995.

Canada. (1940). Royal Commission on Dominion-Provincial Relations. *Report*. Ottawa: King's Printer.

Canada. (1951). Royal Commission on National Development in the Arts, Letters, and Sciences. *Report*. Ottawa: King's Printer.

Canada. (1972). Senate, Special Committee on Science Policy. In Maurice Lamontagne (Chair), *Targets and strategies for the seventies*. *(Vol. 2)*, Ottawa: Information Canada.

Canada. (1976, June 14-15). *Federal-provincial conference of First Ministers*.

Canada. (1977, Amended in 1984). *Federal-provincial fiscal arrangements and Federal Post-Secondary Education and Health Contributions Act*.

Canada. (1981). Parliamentary Task Force on Federal-Provincial Fiscal Arrangements, *Fiscal federalism in Canada*. Ottawa: Minister of Supply and Services.

Canada. (1988a, July 27). Senate, Standing Committee on National Finance. *Twenty-sixth report*.

Canada. (1988b). Department of Industry, Science and Technology. *Science and technology: The federal government record*.

Canada. Department of Finance. (1994a, February 22). *Budget speech*.

Canada. Department of Finance. (1995). *Budget plan*.

Canada. Department of Human Resources Development. (1994b). *Improving social security in Canada: A discussion paper*. Ottawa: Supply and Services Canada.

Dupré, J.S. (1965). Contracting out: A funny thing happened on the way to the Centennial. In *Report, 1964 Conference*. Toronto: Canadian Tax Foundation.

Dupré, J.S. (1994). Comment: The promise of procurement federalism. In K. Banting, D.M. Brown, and T. Courchene (Eds.), *The future of fiscal federalism*. (pp. 249-254). Kingston: School of Policy Studies, Queen's University.

Dupré, J.S., Cameron, D.M., McKechnie, G.H., and Rotenberg, T.B. (1973). *Federalism and policy development: The case of adult occupational training in Ontario*. Toronto: University of Toronto Press.

Friedman, R.S., and Friedman, R.C. (1990). The Canadian universities and the promotion of economic development. *Minerva, xxviii* (3), 272-293.

Johnson, A.W. (1985). *Giving greater point and purpose to the federal financing of post-secondary education and research in Canada*. Ottawa: Report prepared for the Secretary of State of Canada.

Macdonald, J.B., Dugal, L.P., Dupré, J.S., Marshall, J.B., Parr, J.G., Sirluck, E., and Vogt, E. (1969). *The role of the federal government in support of research in Canadian universities*. Ottawa: Queen's Printer.

Manzer, R. (1994). *Public schools and political ideas: Canadian educational policy in historical perspective*. Toronto: University of Toronto Press.

New Brunswick. (1994). Department of Advanced Education and Labour. *Income based rebates (IBR): An alternative for dealing with student debt load*. Fredericton.

Waite, P.B. (1987). *Lord of Point Gray: Larry MacKenzie of U.B.C.* Vancouver: UBC Press.

Higher Education in British Columbia, 1945-1995: Opportunity and Diversity

John D. Dennison

Introduction

To many Canadians, British Columbia is conceived of as a remote, and in some respects, a frontier province. Certainly, the symbolic barrier of the Rocky Mountain Range has tended to isolate the extreme western region of the country, even from the prairie provinces. From well before the time of its entry into confederation, much of the economy of British Columbia has relied upon resource extraction industries, agriculture, and more recently, tourism. Covering a vast area of 950,000 square kilometres, the province has a highly populated coastal region in the southwest, the Lower Mainland, in which more than half the population resides. Another 20% of its people are located in the capital city, Victoria, and a number of smaller communities on Vancouver Island. The remainder reside in numerous widely scattered towns and villages in the interior of the province. Of the latter, only four regions, centred by Nanaimo, Kelowna, Kamloops and Prince George, contain more than 50,000 people (Barman, 1991).

This combination of geographic and population disparities, coupled with the pattern of the economy, has had an important bearing upon the development and design of higher education in British Columbia. As described vividly by Barman (1991) British Columbia developed for most of its first century in an atmosphere of rugged entrepreneurial activity in which its rich natural resources were exploited with heavy injections of outside capital to feed the engines of manufacture and processing in other regions of Canada and the United States. Political leadership was largely confined to finding better and more efficient ways of resource extraction as a way to cultivate the "good life" which became so deliberately descriptive of the province.

In an economy based upon forestry, fishing, mining, and the harnessing of hydroelectric power, which characterized the first half of the twentieth century, there was little need to invest in those sophisticated training and educational programs which would have provided the basis for a more diversified economy. Eventually, it was public pressure which translated into government policy during the sixties and seventies, culminating in the creation of a galaxy of postsecondary educational and training institutions which offered a much wider range of learning opportunities than had previously been the case. Ultimately, it was a long-established and uncertain dependence upon the economic health of other constituencies to maintain the British Columbia economy, coupled with the impact of increasingly competitive global markets, which contributed to the realization that economic survival in British Columbia must rest upon better and more sophisticated utilization of human resources.

While there has been a continuing overall increase in the population of the province since 1945, from 1.6 million in 1961 to 3.25 million in 1991, the proportion of college-age students, age 16–24, has actually declined in recent years (from 18.5% in 1978 to 15% in 1986). And whereas the participation rate of these students in postsecondary studies grew rapidly in the sixties and earlier seventies, this increase was largely the result of greater participation by women. [1] Although the overall participation rate has levelled off to some extent in recent years, the actual numbers of applicants continue to grow and enrollment pressures upon universities and colleges remain high.

In a province with an economic base described above, it is perhaps not surprising that higher education has only recently become a major "industry." While there had been spasmodic attempts to establish private postsecondary colleges, the provincial university was the only institution of higher education in the province until well into the second half of the twentieth century. The University of British Columbia (UBC) began first in a high school, later as a university college affiliated with McGill University in Montreal, and achieved independent status as a degree-granting institution in 1915 (Logan, 1958). Enrollment grew slowly in the years before World War II, drawing students primarily from a small and selective segment of the population. Often regarded by those living in the interior of the province as a "lower mainland" institution, the university remained geographically, socio-culturally, and financially inaccessible to most young people. It is fair to say that, for many years, continuation to advanced education has not been an activity characteristic of the culture of most young British Columbians. Apart from socio-cultural obstacles, the attraction of quick and relatively substantial incomes from employment in the forests, fishing boats, and mines spread throughout the province has always been difficult for young people to resist.

It is against this background that the remainder of this essay has been prepared. The primary purpose is to describe and analyze the development of higher education in British Columbia since the end of the Second World War.

1945-1975: Autonomy, Diversity, and Expansion

As noted earlier, to the end of World War II the history of higher education in British Columbia was virtually synonymous with the development of the province's only public university. By 1995 the university and its affiliate, Victoria College, together with two Normal Schools, comprised the entire spectrum of higher education in the province. One adult vocational school in Nanaimo provided a limited range of job training and apprenticeship programs.

The years from 1944 to 1948 were among the most dramatic in the university's history. A policy decision taken by the federal government to support financially those war veterans wishing to pursue further education, coupled with the university administration's determination to provide places for all, translated into an enrollment spurt from 3000 in 1944 to almost 9500 in 1948. The problems created by this unprecedented surge of students were massive. For example, large numbers of huts had to be procured from military authorities to provide classroom, laboratory, and residence space for a student body of which over half were veterans with young families (Logan, 1958).

After the enrollment peak in 1948, numbers declined but by 1951 began to climb again with "almost alarming acceleration" (Logan, 1958, p. 177). Growing financial difficulties, due in part to the loss of federal funds which accompanied the decline in veteran enrollees, became a major concern during the deliberations of the Massey Commission (Royal Commission on National Development in the Arts, Letters, and Sciences, 1951). The influential and energetic president of the University of British Columbia, Norman MacKenzie, a member of the commission, pressed the case for substantial and immediate fiscal intervention by the federal government if Canadian universities were to be in a position to accommodate an already escalating demand for places by a post-war generation of students.

Although the university's enrollment continued to grow, and while new faculties—Law 1945, Graduate Studies 1948, Pharmacy 1949,

Forestry 1950, Medicine 1950, Education 1956—were added together with numerous newly formed schools and departments, other public postsecondary institutions were not established in the province. Part of the explanation for this deficiency lay with the attitude of President MacKenzie. Fearful that the already precarious fiscal support for higher education from the provincial government would be diluted further by the creation of alternative institutions, MacKenzie took the view that any expansion should be confined to new affiliates with the university (Waite, 1987).

Although no material changes occurred in British Columbia's higher education system until the aftermath of the Macdonald Report in 1963, referred to later in this essay, there were a number of spasmodic proposals and also a significant amendment to the Public Schools Act in 1958. In that year the legislature, "responding to the social and economic forces of our times" (Soles, 1968, p. 58), passed permissive legislation which granted school boards the authority to establish postsecondary district colleges "in affiliation with the University of British Columbia." This last caveat reflected a concern over the need to ensure academic quality and, at the same time, to accord with the wishes of President MacKenzie. While no college was actually established under this legislative authority, one school district, Kelowna, hired a consultant to conduct a feasibility study which concluded that the time was right, economically and socially, to establish a college in its region under the conditions outlined in the legislation (Dawe, 1959). Further proposals were contained in the Report of the Royal Commission on Education in 1960. While concerned primarily with elementary and secondary school studies, the Commission did recommend the expansion of Grade 13 programs, then available in a limited number of high schools throughout the province, and their incorporation within a new type of institution, to be called collegiate academies, which were to encompass all post-compulsory school students enrolled in Grades 11, 12, and 13. No such action eventuated.

There was also some activity in the province to establish non-public institutions of postsecondary education. Notre Dame University in Nelson had opened under the authority of the Roman Catholic archbishop in 1950 with an enrollment of twelve Grade 13 level students. By 1961 considerable growth in both students (now 231) and facilities led to the addition of third- and fourth-year courses and the accrediting of a B.A. degree in affiliation with St. Francis Xavier University in Nova Scotia. Another college in Prince George, also under the auspices of the local bishop, opened in 1962 with an enrollment of sixteen Grade 13 students.

In Langley, Trinity Junior College, an institution affiliated with the Evangelical Free Church of America, began operation in 1962 with a two-year liberal studies program and an initial enrollment of seventeen students.

All of this activity was of modest significance compared to what proved to be a crucial decision taken in 1962 by the governing board of the University of British Columbia to appoint John Barfoot Macdonald to succeed Norman MacKenzie as President. But before discussing the consequences of this event it is necessary to digress. While academic institutions tended to dominate the postsecondary educational scene in the province, there is another component of this sector which deserves attention.

Adult Vocational Training in British Columbia

Vocational training for adults had begun as early as 1901 as simply a course located within a public school, although the first "institutionalized" training actually dated from 1915, as a program offered in Vancouver's King George High School (Meredith, 1983). However, the only self-contained vocational school established before World War II opened in Nanaimo in 1936 as the Dominion-Provincial Youth Training School. Subsequently, with fiscal support from the federal government, Vancouver became the site of the Vocational Institute in 1949 under the aegis of the local school board. The need for greater opportunities for trades training during the post-war boom, coupled with federal fiscal initiatives under the Technical Vocational Training Assistance Act (1960), resulted in an unprecedented expansion of facilities for vocational training throughout the province between 1960 and 1970. New vocational schools were constructed during that period in Burnaby, Kelowna, Nelson, Dawson Creek, Prince George, Terrace, and Victoria all administered centrally by the Department of Education in Victoria. These institutions, together with provincial schools of art in Nelson and Vancouver, constituted a geographically dispersed galaxy of capital facilities which were later to become key factors in the development of the community college system.

One other notable institution was also created during the sixties. Again, with the incentive of capital funding from Ottawa, the provincial government established the B.C. Institute of Technology (BCIT) in 1964. The latter provided the first significant opportunity for students in the province to complete two-year technology diplomas in engineering, business, and a variety of specialities within the health sciences.

Whether the aforementioned vocational schools (as distinct from BCIT) constituted a legitimate component of the postsecondary educational sector in the province might well be a matter of debate. In general, their curricula comprised short-term trades training, apprenticeship courses, and academic upgrading for post-school age students. Admission requirements were usually grade 10 completion, although competitive entry to many programs called for better qualified and more mature applicants. A large percentage of these students were selected and supported financially under a variety of federal programs.

The Macdonald Report

To quote Soles (1968) :

The importance of the Macdonald Report (as it is now commonly called) to the future of higher education in British Columbia, and for that matter to all of Canada, cannot be over-emphasized. In clear, unmistakable terms, and perhaps for the first time in the history of Canadian education, a university president set out a plan for the future. (p. 59)

John Macdonald, a Canadian-born Professor of Prosthetic Dentistry at Harvard University, came from a research position to the presidency of the only university in a relatively small and isolated province in the midst of rapid economic and human expansion. One of his first acts was to assume personal responsibility for a study of the future needs in postsecondary education in the province. While the study team included a number of selected colleagues from the university, Macdonald was the prime influence behind the Report. The project which he undertook was neither encouraged nor overtly supported by the government of the time, although the results were to become very much the concern of the latter.

In the initial chapter of the final Report, Macdonald set the theme and context for the recommendations which were to follow with an explicit commitment to excellence, which, in a postsecondary educational system, the Report stated, could be promoted only through the creation of alternative institutions, which must be diversified in their mandates and autonomous in their governing structures. In the words of the Report:

Excellence cannot be legislated; it cannot be purchased; it cannot be proclaimed; and it cannot be assigned. It can be sought and

encouraged and rewarded, and this is the task in planning for
higher education in British Columbia—to seek, encourage and
reward excellence. (Macdonald, 1962, p. 19)

What followed was a carefully reasoned rationale for the establishment
of two four-year colleges and six two-year colleges in various locations
throughout the province. The latter, in response to a widely expressed
demand for university-level studies, particularly in the interior of the
province, were to offer academic, or "university-equivalent" courses, which
would be designed to carry transfer credit towards a baccalaureate degree
for those students who elected to continue their studies in a university or
four-year college. The colleges would also offer technical programs for
those seeking employment in occupations characteristic of their regions.
Apparently impressed by arguments contained in briefs presented in local
communities, Macdonald recommended that the two-year colleges should
operate under the auspices of the local school boards, "which have the
widest knowledge and experience in financing and developing educational
facilities" (p. 87).

The Report was remarkably comprehensive. Not only did it describe
the kinds of institutions needed, it also provided detailed arguments for the
locations which were proposed, estimates of their capital and operating
budgets, projected enrollments, and in the case of the colleges, proportions
of the budgets to be borne by government, students, and local taxpayers,
respectively. Furthermore, the Report contained detailed advice on
governing structures at the institutional and provincial levels. At the latter,
two bodies, an academic board and a grants commission, were
recommended. The board was to supervise academic standards in the new
institutions, while the commission was to become an advisory body
independent of government which would consider, coordinate, and
recommend on the "allocation of capital and operating funds for
universities and colleges" (p. 84).

Public and media response to the Macdonald Report was immediate
and enthusiastically supportive, a reality which the provincial government
could hardly ignore. In a rapid burst of activity, Victoria College was
authorized as the autonomous University of Victoria, and action was taken
immediately to plan the future Simon Fraser University. The latter was
completed and enrolled its first students in less than two years. With respect
to college development, however, the government took a unique and more
cautious approach. A complicated series of plebiscites and referenda at the
community level were required as a precondition to fiscal support from the

province. The college funding formula included a tax-driven local contribution which, with student tuition fees, amounted to approximately half of the operating budget. Given the degree of community leadership and time-consuming procedures required to establish a college, it was not surprising that British Columbia's new postsecondary institutions came to fruition one by one. Ten were eventually established by the mid-seventies when the procedure for creating a college was changed.

The original recommendation contained in the Macdonald Report, to establish four-year colleges, was rejected by the government, and Victoria and Simon Fraser were both given a mandate to become fully fledged universities. Enrollments in both new institutions grew rapidly. Partly to attract and satisfy the expectations of new highly qualified faculty, at the time difficult to recruit, each new university quickly established graduate and professional programs in concert with a strong research focus.

Another notable event of the early seventies was a decision taken by the government in Victoria to meld several colleges with the most proximate provincial (although constructed with federal funds) vocational schools. This policy decision was partly initiated by the unwillingness of voters in almost all college regions to pass referenda to elicit local tax support for capital construction. The alternative was to continue operation of the colleges in temporary leased facilities, a situation which was most unsatisfactory. The government recognized that a potential solution lay in the amalgamation of the college with each respective regional vocational school, an action which would result in joint sharing of the building in which the latter was located. A second explanation for the meld, as articulated by the deputy minister of the day, was to help overcome the traditional status gap between vocational and academic studies by placing them together in one institution and at the same time providing a better opportunity for introducing general education into essentially job training programs. Whatever the reason for the decision, the ultimate result was a network of comprehensive colleges offering program options ranging from adult upgrading and basic literacy to the first two years of a university degree.

The brief political tenure of the New Democratic Party from 1972 to 1975 did have some impact upon the postsecondary system, particularly with respect to the universities. The idea of coordination, at least within the university sector, had been explored by a committee chaired by a Deputy Minister of Education in the previous government (Perry, 1969). For reasons never explained, Dr. Perry's advice was not made public until the election of the NDP. Nevertheless, the new government began yet another examination of the issue by appointing a University Governance Committee, chaired by Professor Walter Young of UBC, which eventually recommended the creation of an intermediary body, a Universities Council, with powers to ensure coordinated planning. The Council became reality within a new Universities Act in 1974. It was granted legislated power "to require" the universities to submit long- and short-term plans and "to approve" the establishment of new degree programs and faculties. Another important change in the new Act was the inclusion of faculty, support staff, and student representatives on the universities' governing boards, a provision consistent with the government's policy respecting participatory democracy.

The Minister of Education also established a broadly representative commission of enquiry into the college sector, which produced a report containing recommendations for far-reaching changes (L'Estrange, 1974). The general thrust of the recommendations was to widen the base of community involvement in college operations and to encourage greater responsiveness to traditionally disadvantaged students. The government was defeated before many policies regarding the colleges could be initiated. However, in one of her last actions, the minister did respond to one recommendation in the L'Estrange Report by establishing four more colleges in regions of the province which had been excluded to that time. By taking this action the organizational steps required by the previous government were removed. Another initiative taken by the NDP government was to pass a legislative act which removed the B.C. Institute of Technology from direct control by the Department of Education and to create its own Board of Governors, which also included a number of institutional representatives. With the autonomy which ensued, BCIT began a long process of defining an identity and seeking a mandate somewhat different from either the colleges or the universities.

Thus ended the first important post-war phase, from 1945 to 1975, for higher education in British Columbia. It was an era of remarkable change in the numbers, kinds and, perhaps of greatest importance, the geographic dispersal of postsecondary institutions. This phenomenon was, of course, shared by other provinces during the same period, but there was an important difference in British Columbia. Growth and expansion of the system, particularly in the college sector, was not so much the product of direct intervention by the government. Rather, the latter provided enabling legislation which required the expenditure of considerable energy and commitment at the grass roots of the community before new colleges could be established. Nevertheless, there was remarkable growth in a period of extensive public support and comparatively strong fiscal health. Simon Fraser University was unquestionably a monument to government support for higher education. It was designed, constructed, and opened within a two-year period and became, both physically and symbolically, an example of how effectively government could respond to a popular public issue. As so often the case, it was largely public pressure which elevated postsecondary education to the top of the policy agenda.

But the era of growth was slowing. The fiscal appetites of both colleges and universities seemed to be insatiable, and with more limited financial contributions from Ottawa, the government of British Columbia had already restricted annual budget increases for the colleges to 10%. The stage was set for a very different era for postsecondary education, one which was to begin with controlled growth but would end eventually with varying degrees of consolidation and constraint.

1976-1981: Controlled Development and Consolidation

The Social Credit party was returned to power in 1975, and the driving forces in postsecondary education for the next seven years became the new minister, Dr. Patrick McGeer, and his deputy-minister, Dr. Walter Hardwick. Dr. McGeer was a member of the Faculty of Medicine at UBC, engaged largely in neurological research, but with very strong views about many aspects of postsecondary education. His themes were the preservation of high academic standards, a strong commitment to research, particularly in science and technology, and to finding new and less expensive ways of ensuring greater access to higher education than by necessarily constructing new institutions.

One of Dr. McGeer's first acts was to create committees of enquiry into ways to increase access to university programs in the interior of the province (Winegard, 1976), and to explore the status of continuing education for the post-school-age population (Faris, 1976). Each report eventually recommended somewhat expensive solutions to each respective issue, and most were not implemented. Winegard advanced the idea of a multi-campus university to serve the non-metropolitan areas of the province. Faris saw the need for greater expansion of adult learning opportunities under a variety of formats.

Two other committees began work in 1977, and their conclusions proved to be of greater significance. The first, a study of vocational training (Goard, 1977) addressed the issue of better control and coordination of trades training in the colleges, a role which Dr. McGeer viewed as a priority. Provision of vocational training had been beset by jurisdictional disputes and bureaucratic problems between the Ministries of Education and Labour and between the two major levels of government. The situation had resulted in confusion and limited access for those seeking training in a variety of trades. The Goard Report suggested several strategies to alleviate the problem, including the creation of a single provincial body to coordinate the planning and administration of vocational training. The second committee, under the direction of Patricia Carney, outlined a coordinated approach to the planning of distance education in the province (Carney 1977). In doing so, her Report addressed both the need for and the feasibility of distance learning as an alternative to conventional educational institutions in more isolated regions.

Meanwhile, a problem which was to have a number of consequences emerged in relation to the operation of Notre Dame University in Nelson. Notre Dame, the province's only private denominational degree-granting institution to that time, having been awarded that status in 1965, encountered serious financial difficulties. A Royal Commission on Postsecondary Education in that region of the province, under the direction of Ian McTaggart-Cowan, had been appointed in 1973 and eventually recommended the creation of a public multi-campus institute to include Notre Dame and Selkirk College. No action was taken as a result of this exercise. Faced with continuing financial problems, the Notre Dame board requested that the government take control of the university in 1977. Consequently, Dr. McGeer established the David Thompson University Centre on the Notre Dame site, administered by the University of Victoria. Despite its popularity and success, reinforced through a formal evaluation in 1983, David Thompson proved to be, in the view of government, too expensive with respect to per-student costs and for this reason was closed in 1984. Not surprisingly, the decision was highly unpopular in the Nelson region and further exacerbated the debate over access to university education in the non-metropolitan regions of the province.

Dr. McGeer also took the initiative in several other policy matters. He argued for the establishment of "discovery parks," in association with the universities and BCIT, which would serve as "town-gown" research centres in pursuit of new advances in science and advanced technology. Furthermore, McGeer's interest in research was exemplified by his role in the creation of the Science Council of B.C., the Biomedical Research Centre, and Discovery Foundation, all enterprises which gave new energy to those groups and individuals who had argued for an expanded role for the province in the "knowledge industry."

The new minister also supported a private member's bill which ensured that Trinity Junior College would be granted degree-granting status as Trinity Western University. He also offered incentives to the University of British Columbia to double admissions to its Faculty of Medicine. With respect to the latter, McGeer emphasized the need for expanded opportunities for British Columbians to study medicine rather than the alleviation of any short-fall in the supply of physicians, a problem which the province did not face. While a number of these decisions were taken largely outside the auspices of the Universities Council, McGeer lent his support to the continuation of the latter.

But perhaps Dr. McGeer's most significant contribution was to direct the creation of a College and Institute Act (1977). For the first time non-university institutions were awarded corporate status under their individual governing boards, granting them a legal authority previously held by school boards. Furthermore, the act provided for the creation of three intermediary councils to coordinate planning and funding of academic and vocational programs and general support of college operations. The idea of a vocational coordinating council had been recommended previously in the Goard Report.

The new legislation, however, was not free from controversy. Some observers (Dennison, 1986; Mitchell, 1986) saw it as a centralizing initiative in that it placed the control of college operations within the appropriate department of government, with a consequent reduction in the role played by local college boards. In fact, as a result of the legislation, "community" colleges might now be viewed more accurately as "provincial" colleges. One additional feature of the new legislation, which added to this assertion, was a section delineating the extensive and explicit powers of the minister in setting policy for the college sector. Another somewhat controversial aspect of the legislation was the decision to include BCIT under its authority. As noted earlier, BCIT had been operating under its own act, a provision which had allowed for the pursuit of a distinct identity and had generated a variety of expectations as to its future role in the educational spectrum. Not surprisingly, the institution argued strongly for continuation under its own legislation. These appeals were of no avail and, among other consequences, BCIT's faculty and student representatives on its governing council were removed.

The minister's energies were also directed towards the establishment of a number of provincial institutes, concerned largely with specialized programs. BCIT was joined in this category by Emily Carr College of Art and Design, Pacific Vocational Institute, The Justice Institute of B.C., and the Pacific Marine Training Institute. But perhaps the most imaginative addition to the galaxy of postsecondary educational institutions was the creation of the Open Learning Institute, a distance education enterprise offering academic degrees and a range of technical-vocational programs. The idea for O.L.I. had come from several sources, including the Carney and Winegard Reports, but also through the efforts of John Ellis, a professor at Simon Fraser University, who had long promoted the concept of a British Columbia Open University modelled on its British counterpart. Ellis was to become the first principal of the new institute (Moran, 1991). Later, McGeer was also to take a leadership role in the establishment of a public television channel, The Knowledge Network of B.C., which supplemented several programs of study offered by O.L.I. as well as providing publicly supported educational television throughout the most isolated regions of the province.

The early years of the McGeer-Hardwick influence were productive indeed. By the end of the seventies the province's postsecondary educational offerings included three universities, fifteen community colleges, five provincial institutes, and a distance learning institution which provided a full range of programs, largely by correspondence. But the era of growth and expansion had peaked, and the next few years ushered in the first policies of restraint, consolidation, and reassessment of the higher education system.

1982-1986: The Years of Restraint

In the early eighties a number of predominantly fiscal factors were to impact upon postsecondary education. The federal government imposed limits upon the growth of transfer payments; the province entered a period of relatively deep recession and public support for education seemed to wane as other policy concerns—energy, health care, social welfare, and the environment—seized priority. Government's response with respect to higher education was both subtle and direct. Universities and colleges were confronted with two consecutive years of decremental operating budgets (5% for universities, 3.5% for the colleges, although inflationary factors made the cutbacks more severe), with the result that programs suffered accordingly. As other ministers had now assumed responsibility for postsecondary education, several of the policies of their predecessor were either changed or modified.

The Universities Council, long unpopular with at least two of the universities who saw it as an expensive additional level of bureaucracy which obstructed their access to government, was abolished, partly as a cost-saving measure. Another contributing factor to the demise of the Council was that neither the government nor the universities perceived it as representing their respective interests. The universities were now free to address their concerns directly to the appropriate department of government. However, a need for voluntary cooperation was recognized when the presidents formed a tri-universities council to consider joint planning initiatives.

During the same period important amendments were made to the College and Institute Act (1977). In an era of financial restraint a variety of provincial initiatives were put in place, largely as budgetary control measures (Mitchell, 1986). For example, legislation was introduced to control salary increases of public-sector employees, including university professors and college personnel, but other initiatives were also introduced that controlled college budgets. The three intermediary councils were abolished and their residual powers assumed largely by the department of government. The composition of governing boards was changed to ensure that all members were government appointed. This change removed those representatives appointed via school board election. In addition, a funding formula increased provincial control over the development and accompanying costs of college programs.

The period of restraint between 1983 and 1986 translated into numerous reductions in programs and in restriction of student access. In an unprecedented action, the University of British Columbia had to remove $6 million from its base budget by the elimination of several programs and the termination of a number of teaching faculty, some of whom were tenured (Dennison, 1987). The theme of the period, articulated by the Minister of Education and others, was that significant "downsizing" of institutions was a reality which had to be addressed. Other policy decisions taken under this rubric were the amalgamation of the Pacific Vocational Institute with the BCIT and major changes in the fiscal management of the Justice Institute. The Knowledge Network was also melded with the Open Learning Institute to become the Open Learning Agency.

1986-1990: Concern over Access

The years between 1986 and 1990 might be described in British Columbia as *between recessions*. The government began a process of recovery in the postsecondary educational sector after the destructive years which preceded. One issue which soon emerged was the matter of access to postsecondary education, a topic which the University of British Columbia, among others, had addressed previously in its mission statement (Second to None, 1989). A report prepared by a Provincial Access Committee (Access Committee, 1988) drew attention to some disconcerting facts. British Columbia ranked ninth among the provinces in Canada with respect to degrees awarded and seventh in full-time enrollment as a percentage of the 18–24 age group. Furthermore, problems of access to postsecondary education were particularly difficult for those living in rural and remote regions, and for selected groups such as Native people. In conclusion, the report noted an immediate need to create 15,000 new places in degree programs if the province was to meet comparable national standards.

Many solutions to the access problem were proposed. A new independent public university to serve the northern regions of the province was to be planned for Prince George. The creation of a provincial Council on Admission and Transfer, a quasi-independent body, was recommended. The Council was to facilitate admission and credit transfer policies among institutions. The Access Report also recommended that the colleges be given the authority to develop Associate Degree programs similar to practice common in the United States.

But the most significant initiative of the Access Report was the recommendation that "in more densely populated regions outside the Lower Mainland and south Vancouver Island, university degree programs be expanded by means of the establishment of an upper-level 'university college' component." (Access Committee, 1988, p. 16) These expanded institutions were to be created by the granting of degree-granting status to three community colleges in Kamloops, Kelowna, and Nanaimo (Fraser Valley College was added later) although for an initial period the degrees were to be awarded by one or more of the established public universities. Although at first the Ministry assumed that the Open Learning Agency would be involved in the planning of degrees, the three colleges chose to collaborate with the more conventional universities (Dennison, 1992). After some initial concern over budgets, the latter cooperated by jointly planning degree programs with the colleges in Arts, Science, Education, Business, Social Work, and Nursing. Actually, the idea of expanding opportunities for degree completion by collaborative arrangements between universities and colleges was not entirely new. It had been tried in limited ways, primarily with degrees in Education for some time and had been further proposed by the universities themselves.

The new model of postsecondary education, as yet untried in Canada, was not devoid of problems (Dennison, 1992). Although its initial success must be acknowledged in the first graduates who received their degrees in 1991, ongoing relationships between the colleges and their parent universities generated some difficulties for both old and new college faculty. Among issues which have arisen are those which concern the role of faculty in academic governance, more specifically, whether university colleges should establish senates or equivalent bodies; the meaning and importance of scholarly activity; an expectation of faculty performance more characteristic of that found in universities; and the desire of the colleges to preserve the broad program comprehensiveness of their curricula. Moreover, as the current plan evolved to award degree granting status to the colleges in their own right, the debate has centred around what kind of institutions will emerge, i.e, should they become conventional universities, four-year degree-granting colleges emphasizing teaching rather than research, or an alternative model? It is still yet to be determined just what the mandate and values of these new and innovative institutions will be.

Meanwhile, the Open University developed as a flexible, distance-learning, degree-granting alternative to the conventional universities. The OU created a "credit bank" by which students could accumulate previously earned course credits towards a baccalaureate degree. Under its more flexible academic organization, the OU recognized courses taken from any appropriate postsecondary institution in planning a student's degree program. Furthermore, a number of colleges and institutes were able to enter into agreements with the OU to plan joint degree programs in specific areas such as Music, Fine Arts, and Health Sciences.

Planning for the new University of Northern British Columbia (UNBC) was also well underway. The process which lead to the creation of UNBC could be seen as an example of grassroots community action with strong political overtones. To a large extent, the university was promoted as an incentive to stimulate economic growth in that region of the province. Even the legislative act which established the university was pragmatic in that it included components of both the current University Act and its own unique legislation. The action plan for UNBC included ideas for cooperative delivery of academic programs with the existing community colleges in the North.

Meanwhile, in a different arena, the British Columbia Association of Colleges, a body which had been composed of board members to represent the interests of their institutions to government and the wider community, was abolished. In its place a new organization, the Advanced Education Council, was created. This body was formed through an amalgamation of the old board member group with the Council of College Presidents to be more widely representative of the non-university component of the postsecondary sector.

In yet another context the government introduced a further initiative. Under the leadership of Deputy Minister Gary Mullins and the direction of Paul Gallagher, a former college president with wide experience, the British Columbia Human Resource Development Project was set in motion. Its charge was to develop a policy framework for the future of all forms of education, training and learning for adults in the province. The project adopted a "stakeholder" approach to its organization whereby a steering committee was formed to plan and execute the process. This committee was widely representative of labour, business, public and private education at all levels, students, First Nations, and government. The exercise involved extensive discussion over an eighteen-month period with more than 3000 individuals and organizations.

Essentially, the final report (1992) covered three areas. It summarized the long and extensive history of human resource development in the province, it outlined in detail the economic, socio-cultural, and educational changes which will demand new strategies to address current deficiencies in the system, and it provided a policy framework for further action to overcome these deficiencies. The primary thrust of the proposed new policy framework was to reinforce the interdependence and interrelationship among the various sectors of education and training. Collaborative planning and offering of programmes by business, labour, and educational institutions was seen as vital if the extensive pool of human resources of the province was to access the learning opportunities so necessary in the new competitive economic environment. It was made clear that programmes could no longer stand alone, that individual learners must be given the opportunity to upgrade credentials and pursue educational mobility with appropriate transfer of credit, and that much greater liaison among government agencies, labour, business, and the educational sector was necessary to ensure program comprehensiveness and responsiveness.

The Nineties: Stability and Incentives

In 1991 the New Democratic Party was re-elected with a commitment to education at all levels. Funding for the postsecondary sector was maintained, albeit at a modest rate of growth. With respect to the universities, government influence was relatively minor. The clause in the University Act, which had denied faculty the right to organize, was removed. A temporary moratorium on tuition increases was imposed. The University of Northern British Columbia was opened on schedule in impressive capital facilities in Prince George.

After a cabinet shuffle, The Hon. Dan Miller was named Minister of Skills, Training, and Labour, with postsecondary education within his portfolio. This title was a significant reflection of the government's priority towards education as an instrument of economic growth and for the preparation of a skilled workforce. Two policy initiatives were to have major implications for the higher education system at large. The first was a legislative bill which awarded independent degree-granting authority to the four university colleges (a fifth, Kwantlen, was added later). In addition, the B.C. Institute of Technology and the Emily Carr College of Art and Design were granted similar status.

Further, a major change in the governing structure of the non-university institutions was contained in the same legislation. Faculty, support staff, and student representatives were given full membership on the boards, and an Education Council was created in each institution which, with a membership composed largely of teaching faculty, was granted statutory authority in selected areas of academic governance. In effect, this sector now operated under a form of bicameral governance, and as such, became the first in Canada to adopt such a model.

The second major initiative, entitled *Skills Now: Real Skills for the Real World* (British Columbia, 1994), was the product of advice given to government by representatives of business, labour, and education and involved a financial allocation in excess of $200 million. This program contained four major thrusts:

1. Linking high schools to the workplace by funding work experience for secondary students, offering postsecondary credits in vocational programs while still in high school, providing mandatory career planning, and creating alternative education programs.

2. Providing more seats in college and university programs and establishing ten community-based skills centres throughout the province.

3. Retraining workers close to home. The newly created B.C. Labour Force Development Board will play a major role by advising on job market and training needs.

4. Moving welfare recipients into the workforce. In this endeavour local businesses will receive funding support to provide training spaces for individuals on financial assistance.

While *Skills Now* is a formidable initiative, public postsecondary educational institutions will be challenged to plan programs which will be innovative, cost effective, and accessible. While incentives exist, funding will not flow as it has in the past. It appears that postsecondary education in British Columbia must inevitably become more responsive to government priorities if it is to maintain viability in a competitive market.

Hence, the history of higher education in British Columbia from 1945 to 1995 has been one of phases—expansion, growth, development, diversity, consolidation, restraint, retrenchment, and coordinated planning—each reflecting the contextual conditions which applied at any given time. In the last section of this essay it is now appropriate to analyze and evaluate some of the most important factors in a higher education phenomenon of almost half a century.

Government Policy

The policy of the government of British Columbia during the past half century could be described in several ways, depending upon the period under review. It might be characterized at various times as disinterest, direct intervention, benign neglect, commitment to access and expansion, or obsession with a need to control budgets. It may be argued that the attitude of the Social Credit government, which has dominated the political corridors of power during much of the post-war era, has ranged from varying degrees of support, at best, to overt antagonism, at worst. Wherever the truth lies, the facts indicate that massive expansion in the number and kind of institutions, with an accompanying increase in the number of students, occurred during this same period. It may well be that particular individuals in roles of leadership and influence should be given much of the recognition for the growth of the system. However, governments respond to their perception of popular sentiment, and education has been a priority in the public policy arena for a good part of the post-war era.

Given the foregoing, it must also be said that government policy towards postsecondary education has been erratic, unpredictable, and often unreadable, despite the fact that one party remained in control for a considerable segment of the period. While this description of public policy may not be unusual or peculiar to British Columbia, it is nevertheless disconcerting to those who seek order, predictability, and direction for the system. With respect to the university sector, the general approach from government has been non-interventional, at least in a direct sense.

Relatively minor actions have been taken, such as the introduction and later removal of an amendment to the University Act denying faculty members the right to unionize. Faculty salaries have been indirectly affected by wage control legislation, and for a brief period, it appeared that tenure might be in peril. On the other hand, university autonomy respecting budget allocation, hiring of personnel, setting student tuition fees, and establishing academic priorities has remained intact. With the exception of the brief tenure of the Universities Council, long- and short-term planning has been largely an internal matter within each university. During times of financial crises whatever solutions were necessary were planned and executed by the universities themselves, without government interference or direction.

However, government influence over the college sector has been much more real, direct, and effective. College legislation gives unambiguous authority to the minister in critical aspects of budget allocation, policy development, and program approval. Until quite recently membership on governing boards consisted entirely of ministerial appointments. But above all, policy initiatives such as formula funding and mandatory five-year planning based upon a predetermined format have been extremely influential in charting the course which colleges and provincial institutes have taken. Government has gradually become a powerful senior partner in the governance of colleges, making them, in the judgment of the courts, "agents of the crown" (B.C. Court of Appeal, 1988, p. 721).

Hence, it is extremely difficult to generalize about the intent of government policy with respect to British Columbia's institutions of postsecondary education. The latter are neither modelled nor moulded by government nor are they fully autonomous self-regulating institutions, although the university sector enjoys great autonomy. Rather they are, in a somewhat Canadian sense, quite pragmatic in their role within the public policy agenda. Nevertheless, the overall contribution of higher education to the economic and social development of the province during the post-war period has been significant.

The *Skills Now* initiative, described earlier, has the potential to influence the direction which the colleges and institutes will take in the future. In this regard British Columbia is following the path of other provinces in its overall concern for budgetary control, labour force development, and economic renewal. The inevitable conclusion, however, is that government has now entered the field of policy delineation in higher education in a more deliberate manner. Policy initiation, rather than coming through erratic and often obtuse messages, will now be cloaked in a mantle of rationality and purpose.

Coordination and Articulation of the System

It is the contention of this observer that British Columbia has developed a *system* of higher education which has been articulated and coordinated to a somewhat greater extent than is the case in other Canadian provinces, with the exception of Quebec and, perhaps, Alberta. At the beginning of the era the existence of one provincial public university and one affiliated college evoked little discussion about coordination. By the end of the era, however, the presence of over twenty independently governed public institutions might well be viewed as a largely uncoordinated *system*. But important factors deserve to be recognized.

The issue of transfer of credit among and between colleges and universities, while not exempt from short-lived crises, has been handled with reasonable sensitivity and considerable success. There are several reasons for this contention. Foremost among these are the efforts of the Academic Board in the early days of college development. The Board carefully articulated a protocol and a process by which college courses would be approved for transfer credit. The universities were thus provided with assurance that academic standards would be protected. Procedurally, questions of academic comparability among courses were addressed through a series of "articulation committees" specific to each discipline and containing representatives from both colleges and universities. Further, a number of studies (Dennison and Jones, 1970; Dennison et al., 1974; Forrester et al., 1982, B.C. Research, 1978-88) provided evidence of the success of transfer students. The universities soon recognized the advantages of a formalized transfer policy and cooperated accordingly. As a result, students are given assurance, at the beginning of their programs that, as long as they choose courses in accord with the Transfer Guide, the credits they earn will be honoured on transfer from one institution to another. No comparable situation exists with technical and vocational courses *vis-à-vis* the universities, but there is credit transfer in these areas among and between the provincial institutes and colleges.

In the last five years a good deal of accelerated activity has taken place in pursuit of greater coordination. As previously noted, one prominent recommendation of the Access Committee (1988) was to establish a provincial Council on Admissions and Transfer, a body with quasi-independent status, which would "provide a mechanism for the resolution of difficulties which may arise from time to time with respect to admissions, course and program equivalency, degree requirements, and transfer of course credits" (Access Committee, 1988, p. 22). The Council, however, was not to be given the authority to override the autonomy of university senates on credit transfer questions.

Subsequently, the Council was established, with broad representation from both the university and the college sectors, and has taken a number of initiatives. The first was to produce a single province-wide transfer guide to replace those published previously by each individual university. Another action taken by the Council was to begin discussion of the Associate Degree as a formal credential to be offered by the colleges. The forum which followed brought university and college representatives into a close relationship which allowed for better understanding of mutual concerns among the participants. The Associate Degree has been awarded for many years in the United States. Eventually, the presence of that credential in most states has rendered transfer of credit largely a matter of routine, a practice which B.C. universities would be reluctant to accept.

Conclusion

A final comment upon the development of postsecondary education in the post-war years may well address the question of just how productive and effective the system has been within a societal context. Contemporary societies anticipate, indeed they demand, a great deal from the organizations to which they provide fiscal support. Publicly funded institutions, for example, are expected to offer high quality and accessible health care, efficient and dependable transportation, or sensitive, equitable and supportive social services. In like vein, public higher education is under greater scrutiny than has previously been the case. Institutions of postsecondary education are seen to be effective if they produce graduates who can contribute to the economic and socio-cultural advancement of the state. Furthermore, institutions are required to be accountable to government and to the wider community for the proper expenditure of public funds. Accessibility is yet another criterion for earning societal approval. It translates into places available in program options consistent with student choice, availability of programs under circumstances designed to accommodate student need, while being, at the same time, financially and geographically attainable. Against these yardsticks British Columbia's institutions would earn a mixed response.

From a statistical standpoint British Columbia's record in postsecondary education is not overly impressive. In terms of enrollment as a percentage of the 18–24 age group, the province has not ranked as high in relation to other provinces as might have been expected. Hence, in spite of impressive expansion of the number and kinds of institutions, participation levels remain problematic. Many explanations have been offered for this phenomenon, for example, the attraction of high salaries in resource extraction industries, a lack of cultural tradition with respect to advanced education, the insularity of many communities, or the inability of institutions to be fully responsive to client needs. Whatever the reason, mere growth and expansion of the number and diversity of postsecondary institutions seem not to have provided a satisfactory response.

With regard to access, a similar reservation exists. While there has been a significant increase in the number of college-age students, particularly women, enrolled in advanced education, [2] many categories of the disadvantaged in the population have remained outside the system (Access Committee, 1988). In particular, Native people, the physically disabled, and the socio-culturally disadvantaged do not enrol in numbers sufficient to increase their participation in the power structures of society. Open learning opportunities at several levels do exist, but interestingly enough, in 1991 more than half the enrollees in the Open Learning Agency resided in urban centres. A recent study (B.C. Research, 1989) indicated that financial obstacles were perceived to be the primary deterrents by those high school graduates who do not continue their education. In this context, financial barriers are usually represented by the delay of opportunities to earn an income. Nevertheless, many non-participants expressed the intention of returning to education at an appropriate time in the future. For those who do continue their education, academic and cultural capital [3] is the important factor in their decision, while financial costs are of little consideration. Student profiles in the community colleges, particularly in rural areas, reveal impressive percentages of mature students, often enrolled on a part-time basis. However, the prospects for such students continuing their education at the universities are limited by distance and family responsibilities.

As noted earlier, the establishment of university colleges in selected rural regions of the province offers a potential impetus for area-bound students to complete degrees. Nevertheless, the concept of the university colleges, to this time untried in Canada, also presents a challenge both to the preservation of the comprehensive community college concept upon which they are grafted and to their future acceptance as *university-like* institutions which, as current planning prescribes, will emphasize teaching rather than research and undergraduate rather than graduate studies. To this point, British Columbia's universities have been reasonably conventional, competitive with respect to expansion of professional degree programs and research, and strongly committed to the maintenance of autonomy. If, how, and when the new university colleges will become socialized into the higher education sector in Canada will become a topic of considerable interest in the next decade.

Public attitudes to postsecondary education in British Columbia since World War II have reflected those of the government, i.e., generally fluctuating. The almost unlimited support of the sixties was followed by a period of disillusionment. However, during the restraint of the early eighties, polls indicated support for public higher education and general agreement upon the need for improved fiscal assistance. In the 1986-91 period, increased government support for the universities was expressed through a number of initiatives—expanded access, student financial aid, matching capital grants, and a Science and Technology Development Fund. At the same time, it may be argued that colleges and universities have paid insufficient attention to the need for engendering better public appreciation and support for their role in the economic and social development of the province. Very little attention has also been given to the rapidly expanding number of private institutions, including Trinity Western University, which have captured a growing market in a variety of fields. In part due to federal policy in supporting private-sector-based training, the number of independent proprietary schools has grown rapidly, over 800 existing by 1995. Immigration policies, in turn, have generated an expanded need for private language training and "visa" schools. These private colleges, now formally regulated, seem poised to play an important role in higher education. It is an issue which the public sector will be forced to accommodate in a systematic manner.

Many other issues remain not fully addressed. As in other provinces, dilemmas such as accountability versus autonomy, effective governance, particularly in the college sector, a rational and predicable policy of budget allocation to institutions, improved articulation between college-based job preparation and the realities of the workplace, technology transfer, and the dichotomy between the goals of unions and industry and the priorities of the higher education sector, all represent challenges which cannot be avoided in the future.

Postsecondary education in British Columbia is an expensive enterprise. It is also volatile, reactive, and apparently insatiable with respect to its fiscal expectations. It has played, and will continue to play, a prominent role in the social and economic growth and development of the province. Much has been accomplished in recent years towards the provision of equitable access to all who are qualified and seek further education. With imaginative and sensitive leadership, both at the government and institutional level, higher education has the capacity to exploit to the fullest the talents and potential of the province's most important resource—the people of British Columbia. This challenge, however, must be met without sacrificing those appropriate aspects of institutional autonomy which bear upon quality, nor can it be accomplished without recognition of the legitimate expectations of government respecting the role of higher education as a corporate partner in the pursuit of economic growth, productivity, and competitiveness. There is clearly a "tightrope of compromise" between these two goals which must be achieved. The realization of an effective solution will require imagination, commitment, and, of greatest importance, leadership at all levels of the enterprise.

Notes

1. In 1980, 34% of female high school graduates in B.C. continued to postsecondary education. In 1986, 45% did.

2. In 1990 the full-time equivalent enrollment in postsecondary education in British Columbia was 144,860, of which 80,231, or 55%, were women. Comparable figures in 1970 were 58,063, of which only 23,021, or 40%, were women.

3. The concept of "cultural, social, and academic capital" as a factor in the decision made by students to continue their education after high school has been developed in the work of Bourdieu (1986) and others. This topic is discussed at length in a doctoral dissertation by Lesley Bellamy (1992) at the University of British Columbia.

References

Academic Board for Higher Education in British Columbia (1965). *The role of district and regional colleges*. Victoria, BC: Academic Board.
Academic Board for Higher Education in British Columbia (1966). *College standards*. Victoria, BC: Academic Board

Academic Board for Higher Education in British Columbia (1969) *College-university articulation*. Victoria: Academic Board.

Access Committee (1988). *Access to advanced education and job training in British Columbia*. Victoria: Ministry of Advanced Education.

B.C. Court of Appeal (1988). *Douglas/Kwantlen Faculty Association vs. Douglas College*. Vancouver: Western Weekly Reports.

B.C. Research (1978-88). *College-university articulation report*. Vancouver: B.C. Research.

B.C. Research (1989). *A follow-up survey of 1987/88 grade graduates*. Vancouver: B.C. Research Corporation.

Barman, J. (1991). *The west beyond the west: A history of British Columbia*. Toronto: University of Toronto Press.

Bellamy, L.A. (1992). Paths on life's way: Destinations, determinants, and decisions in the transition from high school. Unpublished doctoral dissertation, University of British Columbia.

Bourdieu, P. (1986). Forms of capital. In J.C. Richardson (Ed.), *Handbook of theory and research for the sociology of education* (pp. 241-258). New York: Greenwood Press.

British Columbia (1994). *Skills now: Real skills for the real world*. Victoria, BC: Government Printer.

Carney, P. (1977). *Report of the Distance Education Planning Group on a delivery system for distance education in British Columbia*. Victoria: Ministry of Education.

College and Institute Act (1977). Victoria: Government Printer.

Dawe, A. (1959). *The Kelowna Junior College survey*. Kelowna: Kelowna Printing Co.

Dennison, J.D. (1978). University transfer program in the community college. *Canadian Journal of Higher Education, 8*(2), 27-38.

Dennison, J.D. (1986). Some aspects of government policy towards community colleges in British Columbia. *Journal of Educational Administration and Foundations, 1*(2), 4-16.

Dennison, J.D. (1987). Universities under financial crisis: The case of British Columbia. *Higher Education 16,* 135-143.

Dennison, J.D. (1992). The university-college idea: A critical analysis. *Canadian Journal of Higher Education,* 22 (1), 109-124.

Dennison, J.D., and Jones, G. (1970, April). How B.C. students fared in college-university hurdles. *Canadian University and College,* 5, 40-41.

Dennison, J.D., Tunner, A., Jones, G., and Forrester, G.C. (1974). *The impact of community colleges: A study of the college concept in British Columbia*. Vancouver: B.C. Research.

Faris, R. (Chair) (1976). *Report of Committee on Continuing and Community Education in British Columbia*. Victoria: Ministry of Education.

Forrester, G.C., Dennison, J.D., and Jones, G. (1982). Degree completion at British Columbia's universities, *Canadian Journal of Higher Education. 12* (2), 43-57.

Goard, D. (Chair) (1977). *Report of the Commission on Vocational Technical and Trades Training in British Columbia*. Victoria: Ministry of Education.

L'Estrange, H. (Chair) (1974). *Towards the learning community*. Victoria: Department of Education.

Logan, H. (1958). *Tuum Est: A history of the University of British Columbia*. Vancouver : Mitchell Press.

Macdonald, J.B. (1962). *Higher education in British Columbia and a plan for the future*. Vancouver: University of British Columbia.

McGeer, P. (1972). *Politics in paradise*. Toronto: Peter Martin Associates.

Meredith, J.D. (1983). *A history of vocational training in British Columbia*. Victoria: No Publisher.

Mitchell, A. (1986). Administrators' perceptions of the outcomes of implementing three provincial policies on community colleges in British Columbia. Unpublished doctoral dissertation, University of British Columbia.

Moran, L. (1991). Legitimation of distance education: A social history of the Open Learning Institute of British Columbia, 1978-1988. Unpublished doctoral dissertation, University of British Columbia.

Partners for the Future (1991). *Ministry plan*. Victoria: Ministry of Advanced Education, Training and Technology.

Perry, N. (1969). *Report of the Advisory Committee on Inter-University Relations*. Victoria.

Report of the Provincial Access Committee (1988). *Access to advanced education and job training in British Columbia*. Victoria: Ministry of Advanced Education.

Report of the Steering Committee (1992). *Human resource development project*. Vancouver: BC Human Resource Development Project.

Royal Commission on Education (1960). Sperrin Chant (Chairman). *Report*. Vancouver: Queens Printer.

Royal Commission on National Development in the Arts, Letters and Sciences (1951). Vincent Massey (Chair). *Report*. Ottawa: Government Printer.

Royal Commission on Postsecondary Education in the Kootenay Region (1974). Ian McTaggart-Cowan (Chair). *Report*. Vancouver: Queens Printer.

Second to None (1989). *The mission statement of the University of British Columbia*. Vancouver: The University of British Columbia.

Soles, A.E. (1968). *The development of the two-year college in British Columbia*. Unpublished master's of education thesis, University of British Columbia.

Universities Act (1974). Victoria: Government Printer.

Waite, P. (1987). *Lord of Point Grey: Larry MacKenzie of UBC*. Vancouver: UBC Press.

Winegard, W. (1976). *Report of the Commission on University Programs in Non-Metropolitan Areas*. Vancouver.

Postsecondary Education in Alberta Since 1945

Michael B. Andrews, Edward A. Holdaway, and Gordon L. Mowat *

The development of postsecondary education in Alberta since 1945 was heavily influenced by the system that existed prior to that time and by economic and social events which were vastly different from those which occurred prior to the end of World War II.

Setting

The Province of Alberta was founded in 1905. It is Canada's fourth largest province with a land area of 255,285 square miles. This westernmost prairie province has a population of 2.4 million. Its economy is heavily based on service industries, financial services, petroleum and natural gas, and manufacturing.

Alberta's growth during its first 40 years as a province is the story of the development of a last frontier. That part of the Northwest Territories, which became the Province of Alberta in 1905, experienced two periods of major immigration prior to World War II—from the late 1890s to 1913 and from the late 1920s to 1930.

Early governments had to deal not only with Alberta's vast size but also with its sparse population. Moreover, the decades preceding World War II were turbulent. They were marked by the social and economic

---

* Special thanks are due to David Keast who undertook an extensive literature research and assisted with preliminary planning for this chapter. Susan Bens, Lynne Duncan, Chris Elford, Asefa Gabregiorgis, Larry Henderson, Myer Horowitz, Gerry Kelly, Henry Kolesar, Brian McDonald, Terry Moore, Janice Park, Marilyn Patton, James Small, Stan Souch, Alan Vladicka, William Workman, and Walter Worth provided information and helpful suggestions for improvement to earlier versions of the chapter. Marilyn Goshko, Tracey Kremer, Georgie Kwan, and Norma Tindall assisted greatly with excellent secretarial support.

trauma associated with the adjustment of early patterns of agriculture, by the plunge from early prosperity into major economic depression, and by the shock and after-shock of a world war. The provision of postsecondary educational services was difficult.

Nevertheless, prior to 1945, Alberta had a significant number and variety of postsecondary institutions, including the University of Alberta, the Institute of Technology and Art (Calgary), the Banff School of Fine Arts, two schools of agriculture (Olds and Vermilion), the Calgary Normal School, the Edmonton Normal School, and a considerable number of private colleges (Berghofer and Vladicka, 1980, pp. 74-75). Such was the basis for post-war growth.

Factors of Post-War Growth

One of the earliest indications that education services required expansion occurred as World War II drew to a close. The federal government had provided educational benefits for ex-service personnel who swelled enrollments in existing institutions. From 1945 to 1946, for example, enrollment at the University of Alberta nearly doubled (Johns, 1981, p. 203).

These demands were minor compared with those that were created later by a rapid growth in population. First, the higher birth rates of the post-war period produced a swell of demand that worked its way through the system. Second, the economy was transformed by the discovery of major oil fields, starting in 1947. The rapid development of an industrialized economy created another wave of immigrants from Europe, the United States, and other parts of Canada. Clearly, more postsecondary education services had to be provided.

The most compelling aspect of the new demand for postsecondary education, however, went beyond serving a larger population and a new economy. The status of education seemed to have changed at the end of the war. In due course, employment opportunities were plentiful; prospective employees were scarce, and remuneration was high. Individuals saw education as the path to a good life. Access became a right, and opportunity became the mark of a desirable system. The resulting increase in the participation rate, applied to a larger population, fed the transformation of the postsecondary system.

Postsecondary Institutions in 1995

This section briefly describes the current postsecondary educational system in Alberta. While it has much in common with the other Canadian provincial systems, its emphasis upon accessibility, upgrading of qualifications, and student support are especially noteworthy.

Overview

In July 1995, the Alberta postsecondary system consisted of a number of sub-systems: (a) four universities, the Banff Centre for Continuing Education, eleven public colleges, two technical institutes, four vocational colleges, and three hospital-based schools of nursing, all of which receive substantial operating grants from the provincial government; (b) four degree-granting private colleges, four community consortia, about 90 licensed private vocational schools, 85 community adult learning councils responsible for non-credit programming, and a number of Bible colleges and seminaries; and (c) Native colleges—the Old Sun Community College established on the Blackfoot Reserve at Gleichen, the Maskwachees College in Hobbema, the Blue Quills First Nations College in St. Paul, and the Red Crow Community College at Standoff. The four private colleges receive some operating grant support from the province, as do the community adult learning councils and consortia (see Table 1).

The system full-time equivalent (FTE) student counts for 1980-81 and 1990-91 are provided in Table 2 along with the operating grants for each sector. Clearly, the postsecondary system of Alberta has responded to student demand. For example, the university sector enrollment grew by 20,369 FTEs between 1980-81 and 1990-91—an increase of 54%. Concomitantly, the effective real level of operating grants dropped 24% over the same period. This represented a definite productivity gain, but the combination of increased enrollment and decreased constant-dollar funding resulted in more enrollment quotas, higher admission requirements, and general system inelasticity in responding to demand (Alberta Advanced Education, 1991a, p. 2).

Universities

Prior to 1945, Alberta offered university education only at the University of Alberta in Edmonton. In 1945, all teacher education was transferred from normal schools to its Faculty of Education. The teacher education program was still offered in Calgary, but this resulted in the Calgary Normal School being designated as the Calgary Campus of the University of Alberta. Over the years, other faculties established programs at the Calgary Campus and pressures grew in that region to have a separate and independent university. The Universities Act of 1966 established The University of Calgary as an autonomous institution, which soon had a new campus. The Act also made provision for the formation of other universities by order-in-council. In 1967, The University of Lethbridge

Table 1

Alberta Postsecondary Educational Institutions, 1995

Type of Institution	Name of Institutions
Universities	Athabasca University, University of Alberta, The University of Calgary, The University of Lethbridge
Public Colleges	Alberta College of Art, Fairview College, Grande Prairie Regional College, Grant MacEwan Community College, Keyano College, Lakeland College, Lethbridge Community College, Medicine Hat College, Mount Royal College, Olds College, Red Deer College
Private Colleges	Alberta College, Augustana University College, Canadian Union College, Concordia College, The King's University College
Technical Institutes	Northern Alberta Institute of Technology, Southern Alberta Institute of Technology
Vocational Colleges	AVC-Calgary, AVC-Edmonton, AVC-Lac La Biche, AVC-Lesser Slave Lake
Other Institutions	Banff Centre for Continuing Education, Schools of nursing (3), Private vocational schools (90), Bible colleges/seminaries, Native colleges (4), Community learning councils (85), Community consortia (4)

Table 2

Full-Time Equivalent Enrollments (FTEs) and Operating Grants in Postsecondary Sectors in Alberta, 1980-81 and 1990-91*

Sector	FTEs		Operating Grants ($,000)	
	1980-81	1990-91	1980-81	1990-91
University	37, 495	57,864	237,021	464,900
Public College	14, 378	25,174	65,467	184,540
Technical Institute	13, 897	15,023	66,711	131,177
Vocational College	3, 967	9,355	15,985	37,257
School of Nursing	1, 172	1,543	3,700	13,380
Private College	892	2,636	2,151	7,392
Total	71, 801	111,595	391,035	838,646

* Information was provided by Alberta Advanced Education. FTEs are as reported by each institution.

was formed on its own campus from the academic division of the Lethbridge Junior College.

Other considerations of the need for a second university in the Edmonton area came to a head in 1970 when the provincial government announced that it would initiate planning of Athabasca University in St. Albert, near Edmonton. Planning was stopped briefly by the new Progressive Conservative government in 1971 but was resumed in 1972. Athabasca University was given a mandate to develop new delivery systems and to specialize in distance education. This made it the first institution of its type in Canada. In 1980, the government decided to relocate the university to Athabasca, 150 kilometres north of Edmonton. The new Athabasca University facilities were officially opened in 1985. Its enrollments have grown steadily.

The teaching, research, and service activities of Alberta's four universities are comprehensive. Some faculty members—including those in agriculture and forestry, chemistry, education, engineering, English, and physical education—have achieved international prestige. Graduate students have frequently been major contributors to this research.

The few specialized programs such as veterinary medicine, optometry, and chiropractic medicine which are not offered in Alberta are available to Albertans through interprovincial agreements. Graduate programs are extensive at both the University of Alberta and the University of Calgary. In 1991-92, the University of Lethbridge first offered an MEd program and Athabasca University received approval for a master's program in distance education.

The Banff Centre

The Banff Centre for Continuing Education, formerly the Banff School of Fine Arts, is legally constituted through the Banff Centre Act. It has "the object of providing to the public the opportunity of access to a broad range of learning experience with emphasis on the fine arts, management studies, language training and environmental training" (Banff Centre, 1980). It does not grant degrees and does not design its programs to meet requirements of other postsecondary institutions in Alberta. The Banff Centre attracts artists of international renown and representatives of business, industry, and government from many countries.

Public Colleges

The economic and industrial expansion of the 1950s and 1960s and the accompanying demand for postsecondary education stimulated interest in formation of public colleges in the province, particularly in urban areas outside Calgary and Edmonton. The Lethbridge Junior College, the first such institution in Canada, was founded in 1957 on the initiative of local school districts. After considerable debate, the University of Alberta approved an affiliation arrangement with this college, which, in its early years, mainly enrolled students in a university transfer program (Berghofer and Vladicka, 1980; Johns, 1981).

This development stimulated the province to pass the Public Junior Colleges Act (1958) which set out the policies, administrative structure, and financing of public colleges. Various reports, such as those of the Cameron Royal Commission on Education of 1959 and the Survey Committee on Higher Education of 1961, made recommendations which included increased autonomy for colleges through governance by locally elected boards, decreased influence of the University of Alberta, and created a dual role for colleges through the offering of university and non-university programming (Berghofer and Vladicka, 1980). This resulted, over time, in amendments to the Colleges Act. Although this Act and reports by committees recommended a "dual role," the government's stance on this issue in relation to its financing arrangements was inconsistent. For example, some colleges focused almost exclusively on university transfer programming, while others were concerned with more comprehensive offerings.

The number of public colleges increased substantially throughout the 1960s and 1970s. Red Deer College was established in 1964, Medicine Hat College in 1965, and Grande Prairie College in 1966. Mount Royal College, Calgary, a private institution since 1910, became a public college in 1966. Grant MacEwan Community College in Edmonton was established in 1970. In 1975, the Alberta Vocational Centre (AVC) in Fort McMurray and the agricultural school in Vermilion were renamed Keyano College and Lakeland College, with the latter becoming Canada's first interprovincial college, serving northeastern Alberta and northwestern Saskatchewan. Subsequently, in 1978, Keyano College and the three agricultural colleges/schools also became public colleges.

The last major step in development of the current public college system occurred in 1986 when the Alberta College of Art in Calgary, which offered a four-year diploma in visual arts, was separated from the Southern Alberta Institute of Technology (SAIT) and became an autonomous institution.

The 11 public colleges have a primary responsibility to respond to the educational needs of Albertans in the communities and regions served by the institutions. They offer academic upgrading ranging from career, agricultural, fine arts, and vocational programs to university transfer. In the fall of 1995, some colleges will offer applied degree programs.

Technical Institutes

The federal Technical and Vocational Training Assistance Act (TVTAA) of 1960 marked a clear and aggressive arrangement between federal and provincial governments for development of technical education in the provinces. This act, which reflected new federal-provincial cost-sharing arrangements, resulted in a massive infusion of funds into this sector. In Alberta, an expectation had developed that more students should complete grade 12 and later undertake specialized training. The need for non-university alternatives to provide this training was anticipated by the Department of Education. In particular, J.P. (Jack) Mitchell, Director of Technical and Vocational Education, understood this need, and through his efforts, the Northern Alberta Institute of Technology was created in 1960. The other technical institute—the Southern Alberta Institute of Technology (SAIT) in Calgary—was originally the Provincial Institute of Technology and Art, founded in 1916. It was renamed SAIT in 1960.

The mandate of NAIT and SAIT is to provide training that leads to employment in business, industry, and human service organizations. As specified in the Technical Institutes Act (1981), the institutes "shall provide courses or programs of instruction or training that have been determined to be required with respect to a trade designated pursuant to the Manpower Development Act by the Minister responsible for that Act" (p. 10). Over 70 different full-time programs are offered by the technical institutes, a few of which are one-year programs. In addition, both institutions have extensive offerings in continuing education courses and provide the theoretical training components of the apprenticeable trades. The involvement of technical institutes and colleges in apprenticeship training is governed through regulations outlined in the Apprenticeship and Industry Training Act 1991.

In 1979, the provincial government announced it would create another institute of technology to accommodate a perceived shortage in apprenticeship training despite the fact that about 30% of all apprentices in Canada were being trained in Alberta. Stony Plain (40 kilometers west of Edmonton) was selected as the location of the new institution. The Technical Institutes Act (1981) converted the existing institutes and the new one at Stony Plain—named Westerra—into board-governed operations from their previous status of provincially administered institutions. Westerra was a victim of the economic decline of the 1980s as it was merged with NAIT in 1991 in accordance with a government directive.

Vocational Centres/Colleges

During February 1965, the government approved in principle the establishment of three purpose-specific educational institutions to serve adult Albertans who wished to take academic upgrading and/or to acquire employment-entry skill training. In addition to technical education, Mitchell foresaw the need to provide additional facilities for vocational training of unemployed or under-educated adults. His vision and initiative resulted in the creation of the Alberta Vocational Centres (AVC's), which were funded through the TVTAA. Located in Edmonton, Calgary, and Fort McMurray, the AVCs were to become part of a network of provincially administered institutions which at that time included the technical institutes and the vocational and agricultural colleges.

AVC-Edmonton succeeded the Canadian Vocational Training Technical School which operated out of various locations including offices in NAIT. AVC-Calgary was a successor of the Canadian Vocational Training Trade school which closed in 1962. AVC-Fort McMurray was a new facility (Berghofer and Vladicka, 1980, pp. 29-30).

In 1970, the residence and vocational high school of Northland School Division at Grouard were transferred to the Department of Education to become AVC-Grouard. Shortly after, in 1972, the provincial government acquired the assets of a federal initiative called Alberta Newstart located in Lac La Biche. In 1973 the institution re-opened as the province's fifth AVC. AVC-Fort McMurray was changed to Keyano College in 1975.

Another AVC variation was the Community Vocational Centres (CVCs), which commenced operations in 1971. The CVCs provided basic education, skill-training courses, and student services for adults in 23 communities. In 1989, AVC-Grouard and the CVCs were merged to form AVC-Lesser Slave Lake.

In 1990, the name of the Alberta Vocational Centres was changed to Alberta Vocational Colleges (AVCs). These institutions continue to concentrate on academic upgrading and pre-employment skill training in business, health, and service industries. The AVCs focus primarily on meeting the educational needs of under-educated adults. Both AVC-Calgary and AVC-Edmonton have extensive programming in English as a Second Language. All AVCs operate under direct control of the Department of Advanced Education and Career Development.

Community Consortia

The community consortia of Alberta are "associations of post-secondary institutions working cooperatively and in close association with local citizens to provide postsecondary educational opportunities" (Alberta Advanced Education and Career Development, 1995c, p. 51). Originally, five were established between 1978 and 1981. Four are now operating in Alberta: the Big Country Educational Consortium (Drumheller), the Chinook Educational Consortium (Crowsnest Pass), the Pembina Educational Consortium (Drayton Valley), and the Yellowhead Region Educational Consortium (Hinton). They provide their regions with ongoing credit programs and courses through a participating postsecondary institution or recognized licensing body.

Each consortium has a board of directors comprised of regional advisory committee members and representatives of the participating institutions. An executive director facilitates delivery of the programs in the specific regions in conjunction with the responsible postsecondary institution. Since consortia do not have a legal base in a provincial statute, grants are issued to an educational institution acting as the administrative agent for each consortium. In 1993-94, credit course registrations in courses delivered through community consortia totalled 13,613.

Schools of Nursing

Until 1975, responsibility for nursing education in Alberta was divided between the Department of Advanced Education and The Department of Hospitals and Medicare. Universities and colleges provided degree and diploma programs, while major hospitals operated schools of nursing. In 1975, hospital-based schools of nursing became part of the provincial postsecondary system under the Department of Advanced Education. This shift was primarily one of funding, as the hospitals still provided the basic nursing education. Government policy changed again in 1994 with the decree that nursing education would become the sole responsibility of colleges and universities. Current plans call for the nursing schools based in the Misericordia Hospital (Edmonton) and the Royal Alexandra Hospital (Edmonton) to be phased out by 1997: those in the Foothills Hospital (Calgary) and the University of Alberta Hospitals (Edmonton) were closed in June 1995. The School of Nursing at Alberta Hospital (Ponoka) will continue to offer a diploma program in psychiatric nursing.

Private Colleges

Alberta College in Edmonton, founded in 1903 under direction of the Methodist Church, was the first institution of higher education in Alberta. Camrose Lutheran College and Concordia College in Edmonton were established by the Lutheran Church in 1910 and 1921, respectively. Mount Royal College, created in Calgary in 1910 by the Methodist Church, became a public college in 1966. Collège Saint-Jean, established by the Oblate Fathers in Edmonton in 1911, remained independent until 1970 when it became part of the University of Alberta.

In 1983, the Universities Act was amended to include the Private Colleges Accreditation Board, which consists of four academic staff members of the universities, four academic staff members of the private colleges, and four members of the public, with a chair appointed by the Minister. The board is empowered to approve a program of study leading to a baccalaureate and to recommend to the Minister that the private college be given the power to grant a degree in that approved program. From 1983 to 1991, the Minister approved three-year and/or four-year degree programs in Arts and Sciences in the four private colleges. By 1992, the following non-profit private colleges had received authority to grant baccalaureate degrees in certain program areas: Augustana University College (Camrose), Canadian Union College (Lacombe), Concordia College (Edmonton), and The King's University College (Edmonton).

Community Adult Learning Councils

Throughout Alberta, 85 community adult learning councils—formerly known as further education councils—have the responsibility to coordinate and facilitate adult learning at the community level on an inter-agency basis. The community adult learning councils, responsible for adult programming in both rural and urban communities, are unique in Canada. The Community Programs Branch of Alberta Advanced Education and Career Development is responsible for the administration of this program. In 1971, the adult education participation rate in Alberta was 10%. By 1983, this rate had risen to 25%, the highest in Canada (Devereaux, 1985). The Community Programs Branch provided over $6.3 million in grants in 1993-94 for the provision of adult further education courses approved by the councils. In that year, 22,223 courses were taken by 387,116 adults in more than 625 communities in the province. The overall impact of these councils in Alberta has been significant (Alberta Advanced Education and Career Development, 1995c).

The Management of Growth

The ultimate responsibility for provision and operation of the postsecondary system lies with the legislature acting through the Minister of Advanced Education and Career Development.

Special Boards and Councils

To further guide the Minister in overseeing the postsecondary system and to complement the functions of the Department, five special boards or committees currently exist: the Students Finance Board, the Apprenticeship and Industry Training Board, the Council on Admissions and Transfer, the Private Colleges Accreditation Board, and the Private Vocational Schools Advisory Council.

Responsibility for advice and recommendations to the Minister on supply and demand for skilled labor rests with the "Apprenticeship and Industry Training Board." In addition, the Board is responsible for regulations respecting designated trades and occupations, certification, approval, and registration of work experience programs defined under the Apprenticeship and Industry Training Act. The apprenticeship process provides for a structured combination of technical training and on-the-job experience. Alberta has 50 apprenticeable trades of which 28 are designated Interprovincial Red Seal (transferable recognition) trades. Development of the apprenticeship program has been a major part of the growth of the postsecondary system.

Functions of the other boards and councils are discussed elsewhere in this chapter.

Ministerial Powers

Various acts of the legislature, augmented by regulations issued by orders-in-council, set out the powers and duties of the bodies which govern postsecondary institutions. The powers granted to boards of governors of universities and other public institutions are both broad and specific. The acts reserve certain decisions for the Minister, require ministerial approval of certain decisions of a board, and award some discretionary powers. For example, the Universities Act stipulates that the Minister may regulate the establishment, extension, or expansion of a new school or faculty, service, facility, or program of study. Further, the Minister may approve or refuse to approve any proposal to reduce, delete, or transfer a program of study. The Minister has direct control over the function and operation of AVCs.

As in the case of universities, certain important checks and balances exist with respect to the powers of the boards of governors of public colleges and technical institutes. First, the Auditor General of the province is the auditor of each board-governed institution. Second, the Lieutenant Governor in Council has the power of dissolution of the college board. Since 1971, the Minister has twice recommended to the Lieutenant Governor in Council that a board be dissolved and an administrator appointed to run the institution.

Institutional Governance

Governance of institutions is accomplished by several means, as described below.

University sector. The universities are governed by autonomous boards of governors under authority of the Universities Act 1966. Each board is a legal corporation and has responsibility for the management and control of the university, its property, revenue, and business affairs. The chairman and eight representatives of the general public are appointed by the Lieutenant Governor in Council, while the Minister may appoint nine constituent members including alumni (2), senate (1), faculty (2), support staff (1), and students (3), who are nominated by their constituent group for consideration by the Minister. The chancellor and university president are ex-officio members of the board of governors.

The Universities Act also provides for a senate and a general faculties council. Two major duties of the senate include election of a chancellor every four years and authorization for conferring honorary degrees. Also, a senate may inquire into any matters useful to the university and make any report or recommendation that it considers advisable to the board or general faculties council. A major responsibility of a senate, which may have up to 62 members, is to provide a significant link between the university and the community. The specific composition of the senate is outlined in the Universities Act.

Another significant aspect of the Universities Act is the granting of responsibility for academic affairs to general faculties councils, subject to the authority of boards of governors. Each general faculties council is chaired by the president and has representation from administrators, faculty members, and students. The method of election to general faculties councils is described in the Universities Act.

The Universities Act also decrees that there shall be a Universities Coordinating Council (UCC) consisting of the president and senior vice-president of each university, two deans, two other members of the academic staff of each university appointed by the general faculties council of the university, and up to three other members of the academic staff of each university appointed by the UCC. This Council has authority for approving the admission standards of entry for first-year students. It also has jurisdiction over the conditions of entry to certain learned professions and callings, which is a unique responsibility in North America (L. Henderson, personal communication, March 20, 1992). Further, the UCC may take forward to the Minister any matter that it considers to be related to university issues.

A slightly different governance structure is prescribed for Athabasca University in a regulation approved by the Lieutenant Governor in Council. This established a corporation with the name "The Athabasca University Governing Council" which carries out the duties of a board of governors, general faculties council, and senate. This unicameral body is composed of a chairman appointed by the Lieutenant Governor in Council, the president and three vice-presidents of the University, one student, one non-academic staff member, five academic staff members, a tutor, and 14 additional members representative of the general public.

Non-university sector. In 1995, 11 public colleges were operating under authority of the Colleges Act, while the two technical institutes were operating under authority of the Technical Institutes Act. Governance of each public college is entrusted to a board of governors appointed by the Minister. The powers and duties of college boards, which are corporations, are specifically defined in the Colleges Act which decrees that there shall be an academic council that may make recommendations and submit reports to the college board. It normally consists of the college president, chief financial officer, three senior academic officers, up to 10 academic staff, and up to 10 elected students. The board may appoint up to five additional members. The technical institutes are also governed by autonomous boards of governors. The powers and duties of these boards are similar to those of the public colleges, as are the role and composition of the academic councils.

The form of governance for the vocational colleges differs from the public colleges and technical institutes in that the former are administered directly by the provincial government. The presidents of these institutions report to the Deputy Minister. The power and duties of the presidents are derived from the Alberta Advanced Education Act-Alberta Vocational Colleges Regulation.

The Banff Centre for Continuing Education has a board of governors whose role and responsibilities are similar to those of Athabasca University.

System Coordination and Control

During the 1960s, provision for postsecondary education in Alberta grew substantially and rapidly. Towards the end of the decade, the government considered that appraisal and assessment of the expanded postsecondary system was essential, particularly with respect to measures required for its coordination.

Some such coordinating measures did exist. For example, the Universities Act of 1966 created the Universities Coordinating Council and the Universities Commission to serve as advisory, intermediate agencies between government and the universities. Institutes of technology and other postsecondary institutions operated under the Department of Education, while schools of agriculture operated under the Department of Agriculture. These two departments exercised guidance and control within their jurisdictions, but they tended to act independently of each other. The newest members—the community colleges—were rooted in a consortium of public school districts, each of which had membership on the colleges' boards of governors which were responsible to the Department of Education.

Nevertheless, relentless demands, steady growth of services, and escalating costs prompted the government to adopt a stronger presence in the development and management of the system. Towards this end, it took two major steps in the late 1960s. First, it established the Provincial Board of Postsecondary Education in 1967, chaired by Dr. Gordon Mowat. Second, in 1969, the Minister of Education (Robert Clark) established a Commission on Educational Planning headed by Dr. Walter Worth. Table 3 provides the names of ministers, chairmen, and deputy ministers of relevant bodies.

Table 3

Ministers and Deputy Ministers of Departments, and Chairmen of Other Bodies

Educational Body	Years	Chairmen	Years	Ministers	Years	Deputy Ministers
Department of Education			1945-47 1948-52 1952-64 1964-67 1967-68 1968-71	R.E. Ansley I. Casey A.O. Aalborg R.H. McKinnon R. Reierson R.C. Clark	1946-66 1966-71	W.H. Swift T.C. Byrne
Alberta Colleges Commission	1969-73	H. Kolesar				
Alberta Universities Commission	1966-68 1968-70 1970-71 1971-73	W.H. Swift A. Stewart L.A. Thorson H.G. Thomson				

Table 3 (continued)

Ministers and Deputy Ministers of Departments, and Chairmen of Other Bodies

Educational Body	Years	Chairmen	Years	Ministers	Years	Deputy Ministers
Provincial Board of Postsecondary Education	1967-69 1969	G.L. Mowat H. Kolesar				
Department of Advanced Education,* Department of Advanced Education and Manpower,** Department of Advanced Education and Career Development***			1971-75 1975-79 1979-82 1982-86 1986-89 1989-92 1992-	J.L. Foster A.E. Hohol J.D. Horsman D. Johnson D. Russell J. Gogo J. Ady	1972 1972 1972-76 1976-87 1987-	R.E. Rees J.P. Mitchell W.H. Worth H. Kolesar G.L. Duncan

* 1971-76, ** 1976-83, ***1992-

Achieving a College System

During its brief existence from 1967-69, the Provincial Board of Postsecondary Education directed its efforts mainly to the non-university sectors. The Board noted the compartmentalized nature of the sector, the diversity of jurisdictions, and the different sources of revenues. Subsequently, in 1968 the Board presented a series of recommendations to the Minister of Education, Raymond Reierson, all of which were accepted over several years. An important outcome was the passage of the Colleges Act of 1969, which specified that all colleges were part of one system, that community colleges were to be removed from administrative contact with public school districts, and that a Colleges Commission would be established with functions similar to those of the Universities Commission. Another significant change was elimination of property taxes as one source of funds for colleges, with the Alberta Treasury assuming funding responsibility. When the Colleges Commission was formed in 1969 with Dr. Henry Kolesar as Chairman, the Provincial Board of Postsecondary Education ceased to exist.

Toward Centralism

The Commission on Educational Planning, headed by Worth, concentrated on structures and processes that would be needed for the administration and coordination of the postsecondary system and for its coordination. Among its recommendations, one of a general nature set the direction in which the government would move for the next 20 years, namely, that the provincial government should change structures in such a manner as to have more direct influence on the postsecondary system. Other recommendations accordingly urged the dissolution of the Universities Commission and the Colleges Commission, the creation of a new department to oversee all postsecondary programs, and the use of such authority as might be necessary to remove obstacles to mobility of students among postsecondary institutions.

Efforts to achieve greater coordination of postsecondary education became more authoritative, starting in 1971 when the Progressive Conservative party came to power. In the pre-election campaign, major representatives of the party had supported the Worth recommendations outlined above, challenged the desirability of coordination of commissions, and proclaimed the need for a Department of Advanced Education. Upon coming to power, the new government created such a department under the

Minister, James Foster, who, from 1971-1974, put into place a number of structures which still exist.

Formal establishment of the Department of Advanced Education in 1972 marked the beginning of a period of greater central scrutiny and control of postsecondary expansion. The costs of higher education and Alberta's dependency on non-renewable resources became important issues. In order to control and direct expenditures, while restraining the costs of system, greater central involvement seemed to be required. The government's stance thus became one of carefully considered expansion under fiscal restraint (Berghofer and Vladicka, 1980, p. 52), guided by a new policy entitled *Program Coordination: Policy, Guidelines, Procedures* (Alberta Advanced Education, 1974).

This policy stated that in order for postsecondary institutions to receive approval and funding for new programs, proposals had to be submitted to the department. Proposals were then reviewed in relationship to demand, present availability, and general impact on the system. If a proposal was approved, funds were provided to the institution through the New Course Development Fund. A major thrust of the Program Coordination/Course Development policies was the expansion of trades and technology programming to local colleges. Ironically, and partly as a result of these policies, expenditures on postsecondary education doubled in the period from 1971 to 1979.

Improving Student Mobility

No initiative of the new department incited more widespread debate than its proposals to solve problems associated with the transfer of students from one institution to another. Colleges had for some years offered university transfer programs. College personnel viewed the conditions of transfer imposed upon their students by university personnel as unnecessarily restrictive, unpredictable over the longer term, and a denial of their academic integrity. By the late 1960s, impatience had turned to anger and to determination that the transfer problems must be resolved.

In 1971, the Mowat Committee (Mowat, 1971), which was established by the Universities Coordinating Council to examine the transfer problem, proposed the establishment of a committee or council, with membership from all relevant institutions, to provide a forum to be charged with the solution of transfer problems. The Universities Coordinating Council accepted the proposal in principle and so notified the Colleges Commission. The Commission, however, had its own proposal (known as the Kolesar-Fast proposal) that "sending" institutions certify the amount of advanced standing that their students would carry to another institution and that "receiving" institutions would be obligated to honor such certification. Debate continued for another two years.

This impasse was resolved within a new structure. In 1973, the government enhanced its position as a direct presence in the system by abolishing both the Universities Commission and the Colleges Commission. In that same year, Worth became Deputy Minister of Advanced Education, and Drs. Henry Kolesar and Raymond Fast (from the now-defunct Colleges Commission) became senior officials in the Department. Conviction within the Department that it should legislate a solution to the transfer problem was strong.

Perhaps recognition of the threat of a legislated solution to years of bickering brought postsecondary institutions together. In any event, in September 1974, at the request of the Universities Coordinating Council and the presidents of postsecondary institutions, the Minister of Advanced Education announced establishment of the Alberta Council of Admissions and Transfer, with Dr. Harold Baker as its first chairman. This independent body, which reports annually to the Minister, "is responsible for developing policies, guidelines, and procedures designed to facilitate transfer arrangements among postsecondary institutions" (Alberta Council on Admissions and Transfer, 1994, p. 1).

Under the leadership of its second chairman, Dr. Terry Moore, the Council on Admissions and Transfer has become a major component of the postsecondary system. In 1993, over 9,000 students transferred within the province. The largest transfer group is from colleges to university. Notably, however, increasing numbers of university students are transferring to other sectors. For example, in the fall of 1993, 38% of the transfer students admitted to public colleges came from universities. Also the universities provided 41% of the transfer students admitted to institutes of technology.

Agreements made by institutions to recognize transfer courses for credit are published annually in the *Alberta Transfer Guide* (Alberta Council on Admissions and Transfer, 1994) which is widely distributed throughout Alberta and other provinces. The first of its kind in Canada, this transfer guide has become a useful tool for students when planning their courses as well as for institutions when assessing transfer-student transcripts. Creation of the Council on Admissions and Transfer did not indicate the provincial government's retreat from the intended use of legislation to assert its will in postsecondary education, as described below.

The "Failed Act"

Following the provincial election of 1975, and having been re-elected to power, the government announced that the Department of Advanced Education and part of the Department of Labour would be merged and renamed the Department of Advanced Education and Manpower. (This arrangement existed until 1983, when the manpower portfolio was again separated from Advanced Education.) The merger, together with concern for planning and coordination, suggested that the department would have a manpower planning role. Deputy Minister Worth further stated that a review of adult education legislation and regulations would occur. Subsequently, in July 1975, the Alberta Conservative government circulated widely a draft act entitled The Adult Education Act. This act proposed greatly increased control over all adult education institutions, including universities, and would have given the Minister sweeping power over programs, courses, and institutional operations. However, as Winchester (1984) noted,

> the response to the draft act was so negative and so violent and so articulate from so many quarters that even though the Ministry of Advanced Education and Manpower was strongly in favor of a single, system-wide act that would give enormous power to the minister, the draft was withdrawn and no similar legislation was subsequently introduced. (p. 47)

Winchester concluded that "at the present time, the universities in Alberta remain, as they do in the rest of Canada, autonomous though accountable institutions. But they were within a hairsbreadth of losing, on paper at least, that autonomy on which success depends" (p. 59).

Funding

The growth of postsecondary education in Alberta from 1945 to the present has led to substantial increases in expenditures. Institutional revenues mostly come from government grants but other sources including fees are important. The percentages of institutional revenues provided by the provincial operating grant varies substantially among types of institutions, for example, for one college and one university the percentages were 54% and 71% in 1994-95. From one period to another, the provisions under which an institution received funds have changed, as government wished either to exert influence on the system or to increase equity. The framework of the funding system can be revealed, however, by reference to a number of its longer-term features.

Federal Aid

Although education is a constitutional responsibility of the provinces, the federal government has provided substantial funds to postsecondary education. During the war, the federal government financed numerous training programs in support of the war effort and in a direct relationship with provincial institutions to provide these programs. From 1951 to 1966, federal funds were paid directly to universities, bypassing provincial authorities, who were consequently in a position of diminished control over expansion and costs. Direct federal grants to universities were discontinued in 1966 and replaced by transfer payments to provincial authorities which, in their amount, bore some relationship to previous payments to universities but which now were not earmarked for postsecondary education. The provincial authorities then had to devise a new system of paying operating grants.

Operating Grants

From 1966 until 1973, operating grants were calculated by a formula based on full-time enrollments and weighted to reflect the costs of different programs. In 1973, the use of the formula was discontinued in favor of basing grants on an approved three-year projection of operating costs. Since 1976, a system of block grants has been in force. An institution's grant is based on its grant for the previous year, adjusted for inflation. Further adjustments may be made for new programs, new space, or "special circumstances." Earmarked grants may be given for new programs until they have become established, at which time the "earmark" is removed and the grant becomes part of the block grant.

Capital Grants

When the Progressive Conservative government took office in 1971, a freeze on new capital construction was invoked including shelving plans for the St. Albert campus of Athabasca University. This freeze remained in place until 1978 when a major capital development program was announced. New buildings and expansions were provided for the universities in Alberta and Lethbridge; for Fairview, Grant MacEwan, Keyano, and Red Deer Colleges; and for the Northern Alberta Institute of Technology (NAIT). Further capital projects were announced in 1980. These included a permanent campus for AVC-Lac La Biche, residences for Grande Prairie Regional College, and new construction of a third technical institute in the Edmonton area. The government also announced that new facilities would be built for Athabasca University in Athabasca.

As the massive provision of new facilities throughout the province declined, planning turned to the renewal of furnishings and equipment, to renovations and alterations, and to site and utility maintenance. A capital renewal plan was in effect until 1993, when capital renewal funds were "rolled into" operating grants.

Special Funds

In 1970, the Three Universities Fund was established which provided $25 million in capital funds to match private contributions to universities. In 1980, the government outlined several new postsecondary initiatives. The Minister, James Horsman, announced establishment of the Medical Research Foundation, the Heritage Scholarship Fund, and the Alberta Education Endowment Fund; $480 million was withdrawn from the Alberta Heritage Trust Fund to provide long-term capital for these funds. The Endowment Fund (later the Endowment and Incentive Fund) initially allotted $80 million to match private-sector donations to postsecondary institutions. It was so successful that additional funds had to be allocated in 1986 and 1988. An extension in 1990 was to cover the period up to 1999, but in 1992 the university sector was no longer eligible for the matching grant allocation and by 1993 the fund was depleted. These programs injected approximately $412 million in government and private funds into Alberta's postsecondary education system.

The Endowment Funds had demonstrated that substantial private funding was available for postsecondary education. Even though the provision ended and government ceased its matching grants, another provision was introduced to encourage private contributions. The Advanced Education Foundations Act was proclaimed in December 1991. It permits establishment of a foundation for the Banff Centre, one for each university, and one each for the public colleges and technical institutes. The purpose was to stimulate private donations in support of educational and research activities of Alberta's advanced education institutions. Since the foundations are agents of the Crown, a person donating will be able to claim the full amount of the donation as an income tax deduction in the year in which it is made.

Alberta governments have been consistent in their policy that financial need should not be a barrier to further education for adults, so very substantial provincial funds have been allocated for the support of students. The administration and implementation of this policy rests with the Students Finance Board. In 1993-94, 65,700 needy students received direct federal and provincial assistance from programs administered by the Board, with the total level of assistance provided amounting to $329,382,395. This included 8,716 scholarship recipients who received $12,499,713 under the Alberta Heritage Scholarship program. Amendments to the Students Finance Regulation increased student assistance limits in 1993-94 to $8,300 per academic year for all eligible students (Alberta Advanced Education and Career Development, 1995c).

Recent Initiatives

The mid-1980s marked a downturn in Alberta's oil industry and in the provincial economy. This downturn was accompanied by changes in government policies. The government continued to finance some expansion, but projects were now more carefully targeted, and the government urged institutions to streamline, downsize, and strategically plan their allocation of resources.

Initiatives in 1989-92

In its *Guidelines for System Development Policy* (Alberta Advanced Education, 1989a), which succeeded the 1974 *Program Coordination: Policy, Guidelines, Procedures*, the Department outlined procedures for planning processes for institutions in the postsecondary system. Each institution was required to submit a formal development plan which included statements of purpose and aspects of program planning to the Department for approval. The policy reflected a move by government towards more centralized monitoring of the system in times of economic restraint. Institutions were encouraged to concentrate on long-range, strategic planning and to reassess their goals and missions continually.

In January 1990, John Gogo, Advanced Education Minister, circulated a discussion paper entitled *Responding to Existing and Emerging Demands for University Education: A Policy Framework* (Alberta Advanced Education, 1990). This invited stakeholder groups to provide suggestions on establishment of a framework for building the future of university-level education. Responses were received from institutions, student groups, faculty associations, and interested Albertans. Most favored building on the existing framework although there was some support for extending degree-granting status to public colleges. In fact, Red Deer College submitted a formal proposal seeking degree-granting status in October 1990. Following extensive consultations, Gogo stated that

> while I have learned a great deal in the last two years, I do not believe that I can respond with a definitive answer to degree granting status for colleges until the government has completed its consultations on *Toward 2000 Together*. Through this process, the government is encouraging public discussion of the issues and options for Alberta's future economic development. These views will have significant implications for postsecondary programs of all types, be they certificates, diplomas, or degrees. (Alberta Advanced Education, 1991e)

In April 1991, Gogo announced a revised tuition policy which established annual average fee increases for universities and colleges. The policy, which emphasized increased student contributions to higher education, set a fee revenue ceiling so that, over time, up to 20% of an institution's operating costs would be raised from student fees. The policy also raised tuition fees for international students to twice those paid by Canadian students.

Also introduced in 1991 was the *Foundations for Adult Learning and Development Policy* (Alberta Advanced Education, 1991c) which addressed the needs of adults requiring basic skills training. This policy was intended to provide clear and consistent direction for meeting the learning and development needs of adults with low-level academic skills.

In 1992, Gogo announced a number of consultative initiatives that would be undertaken to examine the challenges faced by Alberta. First, he invited all major stakeholders—boards of governors, faculty associations, and student associations—to submit their views on options for the future. In August 1992, a representative group of consultative stakeholders, named the "Strategic Options Task Force," was mandated to provide an independent report to the Minister. All information received was then synthesized as a basis for a consultative process with the people of Alberta on the future of advanced education. The whole process was put on hold in late 1992 when a change of Minister occurred.

Initiatives in 1992-95

In December 1992, Jack Ady was appointed Minister of a new department named Advanced Education and Career Development. This new department resulted from a re-merger with the Manpower portfolio which was separated from Advanced Education in 1983. Ady decided to proceed with the strategic planning process to create a vision for the future of adult learning in Alberta. From early 1993 to May 1994, Ady and his departmental officials held regional meetings throughout the province to hear from interested Albertans. The overall goal was to produce a document on new directions for adult education within a policy framework acceptable to government.

However, while the consultative process was underway, the government announced a major plan to balance the provincial budget by 1997. In order to achieve reductions of 20%-25% from its 16 ministries, the Alberta government ordered all of its departments to submit three-year "business plans" outlining their policy directions and how such directions would result in the necessary reductions in expenditures. In January 1994, Ady announced that funding for postsecondary institutions would be reduced by 21% over three years—11%, 7%, and 3%. Highlights of the 1994-95 Business Plan for Alberta Advanced Education and Career Development (AAECD) included continuation of the strategic planning process, a commitment to revise the funding formula, an emphasis on accountability, a focus on partnerships and greater adaptability and flexibility in program design, a commitment to increase access to meet the learning needs of Albertans, the creation of an Access Fund, and a statement that the tuition fee policy would be reviewed (Alberta Advanced Education and Career Development, 1994a).

In accordance with the AAECD Business Plan, the Alberta government announced a new $47 million Access Fund created through reductions in institutional grants. It was established to finance program proposals that focus on innovative cost-effective methods and partnerships that increase learning opportunities and access for Albertans. A key consideration of the approval process "will be the program's potential to provide learners with attitudes, skills and knowledge that lead to employability and personal growth" (Alberta Advanced Education and Career Development, 1994a, p. 8).

The Latest Initiative

Shortly after release of its Business Plan in 1994, AAECD produced a draft White Paper entitled *An Agenda for Change* (Alberta Advanced Education and Career Development, 1994e). Over 7,000 copies were mailed to groups or individuals who wished to participate in the planning process and to provide written submissions to the Minister. The Minister then met with stakeholder representatives for discussions on budget issues and future policy formulation. All these activities resulted in the publication in October 1994 of a policy document entitled *New Directions for Adult Learning in Alberta* (Alberta Advanced Education and Career Development, 1994c). This identifies four major goals for Alberta's public postsecondary institutions: increased accessibility, improved responsiveness, greater affordability, and more accountability. Each goal has a series of strategies. Overall, 22 strategies were identified that will shape the direction of Alberta's adult learning system, including these five major initiatives:

1. The Minister will hold an annual Minister's Forum on Adult Learning to report on the progress of the system in reaching the goals of the Department.

2. A new credential, the applied degree, will be tested at public colleges and technical institutes.

3. Tuition fees will be allowed to rise to 30% of an institution's net operating expenditures.

4. Students' ability to transfer courses between postsecondary institutions will be enhanced.

5. The Minister will request the boards of public institutions to revisit their collective agreements to meet the changing economic circumstances. Specifically, barriers to the termination of academic staff in response to fiscal restraint must be removed.

In February 1995, the Department produced a progress report entitled *Institutional Accountability in Alberta's Post-secondary System.* This describes how departmental officials worked with representatives of public colleges, technical institutes, and universities to agree on a core set of key performance indicators (KPIs) in addition to the accountability measures provided by the institutions. These KPIs focus on program/student outcomes, financial productivity, and research and knowledge development indicators. During the 1995-96 academic year, institutions will be expected to provide their data on most of the new KPIs in a pilot test. In order to interpret these data, benchmarks will be developed which allow for differences between programs offered, students served, and the contexts in which the institutions operate (Alberta Advanced Education and Career Development, 1995a). A funding mechanism proposed in June 1995 has two main parts: (a) a general operations grant tied to targets in the department's business plan, and (b) performance-driven funds to reward performance and act as incentives to meet specified objectives (Alberta Advanced Education and Career Development, 1995d).

During sessions of the Legislative Assembly in March 1995, Ady announced that, subject to the pleasure of the Assembly, colleges and technical institutes will be given authority to grant applied degrees. Subsequently, approval has been given for four applied degrees: a Bachelor of Applied Forest Resources Management, a Bachelor of Applied Petroleum Engineering Technology, a Bachelor of Applied Communications, and a Bachelor of Applied Small Business and Entrepreneurship. These degrees must combine six semesters of formal instruction and a work experience component of at least two semesters. Such programs must involve employers in program design, delivery, and the costs of the work experience element (Alberta Advanced Education and Career Development, 1995b).

Analysis and Assessment

Examination of the developments and types of institutions outlined above reveals that successive Alberta governments since 1945 have provided a comprehensive postsecondary educational system which serves the diverse needs of the population. Considerable emphasis has been placed upon giving appropriate course credit to transferring students. Substantial financial support has been made available to needy students and the public institutions.

Alberta's relatively small population is well served by a large number of postsecondary institutions, consortia, and councils which operate throughout the province. In eight aspects, Alberta has taken the initiative before any other province: (a) the first province to concentrate all teacher education in the university sector (1945); (b) the first junior college—Lethbridge (1957); (c) the first open university—Athabasca (1970); (d) the first comprehensive mechanism to facilitate transfer of students among postsecondary institutions—Alberta Council on Admissions and Transfer (1974); (e) the first interprovincial college—Lakeland (1975); (f) the first community adult learning councils

(1975); (g) the first Private Colleges Accreditation Board (1983); and (h) the first applied degrees (1995).

During Alberta's first 40 years, the postsecondary sector was clearly characterized by both pragmatism and elitism. The Provincial Institute of Technology, the agricultural schools, and the normal schools provided skills training and represented a pragmatic approach in meeting the human resource needs of Albertans. The University and the private colleges on the other hand provided broader educational opportunities. In addition the university, through legislation, had considerable control over the university courses taught by the private colleges.

The 1945-1986 period marked a reconstructionist stage in Alberta's postsecondary system (Michael and Holdaway, 1991). Emergence of the public college sector, expansion to four universities, and enlarged provision of technical and vocational training reflected the economic growth of the province in that period. This reconstructionist stage had virtually became a reductionist stage by 1990. Alberta's postsecondary system continues to be in a reductionist stage, as the government's operating grants, which increased by 3% for 1992-93, 0% for 1993-94, and then were reduced by 11% in 1994-95, are inadequate to cope with increased costs. At the University of Alberta, capital grants to cover equipment replacement and maintenance had been drastically reduced—before they were rolled into the operating grant in 1993—leading to concerns about obsolete equipment and deteriorating buildings.

Concurrent with this situation is emergence of entrepreneurialism, whereby Alberta's postsecondary institutions are energetically seeking additional revenue through fund-raising, increased linkages with business and industry, and greater emphasis on marketing inventions and discoveries. However, the combined results of these efforts are highly unlikely to meet justifiable institutional needs. Nor can increased student fees fully compensate. Probably a combination of increased government funding, higher student fees, greater emphasis on various types of entrepreneurial activities, and more serious planning and reassessment by each institution will be required in a new stage which might appropriately be labelled as pragmatic.

In light of the *New Directions* document, what can be said of the future of postsecondary education in Alberta? Government policies in the late 1980s emphasized quality programming, greater accountability, and a focus on long-range planning. The policy document of 1994 reinforced that direction with its four goals of increased accessibility, improved responsiveness, greater affordability, and more accountability. The budget speech of 1995 outlined that financial cuts will continue through 1997, yet institutions are expected to meet the four goals and maintain quality and standards within their programs!

The philosophical basis of the document, with accessibility and affordability as two of its four stated goals, clearly indicates a pragmatic approach which emphasizes availability of adult education to all Albertans. Paradoxically, tuition fees have been raised substantially over the past five years and will be further increased, thereby reducing affordability for students and consequently access. The other two goals of responsiveness and accountability focus on the relationship between the system, the learner, and the social and economic needs of the province. The document has a predominantly cost-benefit/human resources planning focus, with some gesture towards social demand.

New Directions identifies three major thrusts for Alberta's adult learning system: basic education and skills training, career and technical programs, and degree programs. Only three strategies attach any relevance to degree programs. Strategy 2.1 states that collaboration among universities, colleges, and technical institutes will be improved to create new paths for completing degrees. These new collaborative programs will build on diploma programs by offering additional university studies to complete a degree. Strategy 2.2 proposes the introduction of an applied degree to prepare Albertans for the "skill requirements of Alberta's changing economy" (p. 11). This approach is outcome-specific and directed toward training for employment. Even university degree programs are seen in the light of economic development and not as nurturers of original human thought. This would seem to neglect the perspective that we live in a rapidly changing world which requires people who can adapt, be resourceful, and advance in the face of the unexpected. Also, Strategy 2.4 states that the province must "establish a framework for university research to foster excellence in the creation and sharing of new knowledge" and that "the framework will recognize the significant relationship between the advancement of knowledge and Alberta's economy and quality of life" (p. 12).

As with other provincial systems, Alberta is attempting to cope with many issues arising from cultural needs and changes as well as from the simultaneous thrusts of increasing central coordination, maintaining local autonomy, and reducing operating grants. However, when government thrusts dating back to the 1960s are examined, these new policies mostly seem to be restatements of previously introduced policies. The major exception is the introduction of applied degrees.

Probably the most significant aspect of the document is what is not said. Alberta's health, K-12 education, and social welfare sectors are undergoing significant restructuring, downsizing, and massive changes in their organization and administration. At present in the postsecondary sector, only hospital-based schools of nursing will close and some institutions will have some changes made in their mandate. Overall, the system appears intact, but it is faced with a number of significant changes especially related to funding, accountability measures, and the provincial government's overwhelming concern with budget reduction and economic development. However, higher education must be seen as contributing more than a trained workforce to improve the economy. The societal benefits from a responsive and comprehensive postsecondary system are greater than the sum of its quantifiable parts.

The major challenge to Alberta will be to ensure that the system which emerges from the changes is indeed responsive and comprehensive. Access is clearly an issue, but what impact will the significantly higher tuition fees have? Stagnation is unacceptable and planned change must characterize new directions for the system. Whatever emerges, future developments and outcomes resulting from *New Directions* will be watched with great interest by stakeholders in postsecondary education in Alberta and other parts of Canada.

References

Advanced Education Foundations Act 1991, c, A-2.5.

Advanced Education Statutes Amendment Act 1987, c, 1.

Alberta Advanced Education. (1974). *News release,* August 1974.

Alberta Advanced Education. (1974). *Program coordination: Policy, guidelines, procedures.* Edmonton, AB: Author.

Alberta Advanced Education. (1985). *Community consortia in Alberta.* Edmonton, AB: Author.

Alberta Advanced Education. (1989a). *Guidelines for system development policy.* Edmonton, AB: Author.

Alberta Advanced Education. (1989b). *Trends and issues in postsecondary education 1989-2000.* Edmonton, AB: Author.

Alberta Advanced Education. (1990). *Responding to existing and emerging demands for university education: A policy framework.* Edmonton, AB: Author.

Alberta Advanced Education. (1991a). *Achievements of Alberta's postsecondary system.* Edmonton, AB: Author.

Alberta Advanced Education. (1991b). *Annual Report 1989-90.* Edmonton, AB: Author.

Alberta Advanced Education. (1991c). *Foundations for adult learning and development policy.* Edmonton, AB: Author.

Alberta Advanced Education. (1991d). *News release,* April 1991.

Alberta Advanced Education. (1991e). *News release,* December 1991.

Alberta Advanced Education and Career Development (1992). *For all our futures: strategies for the future of postsecondary education in Alberta.* Edmonton, AB: Author.

Alberta Advanced Education and Career Development (1994a). *Three year business plan.* Edmonton, AB: Author.

Alberta Advanced Education and Career Development. (1994b). *Keeping you informed. . . .* Edmonton, AB: Author.

Alberta Advanced Education and Career Development. (1994c). *New directions for adult learning in Alberta.* Edmonton, AB: Author.

Alberta Advanced Education and Career Development. (1994d). *Community adult learning program.* Edmonton, AB: Author.

Alberta Advanced Education and Career Development. (1994e). *An agenda for change.* Edmonton, AB: Author.

Alberta Advanced Education and Career Development. (1995a). *Institutional accountability in Alberta's post-secondary system—A progress report.* Edmonton, AB: Author.

Alberta Advanced Education and Career Development. (1995b). *News release,* March 1995.

Alberta Advanced Education and Career Development. (1995c). *1993-94 Annual report.* Edmonton, AB: Author.

Alberta Advanced Education and Career Development (1995d). *A proposed performance-based funding mechanism.* Edmonton, AB: Author.

Alberta Advanced Education and Career Development (1994e). *Adult learning: Access through innovation.* Draft White Paper: An agenda for change. Edmonton, AB: Author.

Alberta Council on Admissions and Transfer. (1976). *First annual report, 1975/76.* Edmonton, AB: Author.

Alberta Council on Admissions and Transfer. (1994). *Alberta transfer guide 1994-95.* Edmonton, AB: Author.

Alberta Council on Admissions and Transfer. (1995). *Nineteenth annual report.* Edmonton, AB: Author.

Apprenticeship and Industry Training Act 1991, c, A-42, 3.

Association of Canadian Community Colleges. (1990). *Serving the needs of a changing community.* Toronto, ON: Author.

Banff Centre Act R.S.A. 1980, c, B-1, as amended.

Berghofer, D., and Vladicka, A. (1980). *Access to opportunity 1905-80*. Edmonton, AB: Alberta Advanced Education and Manpower.

Cameron, D.M. (1991). *More than an academic question: Universities, government, and public policy in Canada.* Halifax, NS: The Institute for Research on Public Policy.

Colleges Act 1969, C-14.

Colleges Act R.S.A. 1980, c, C-18, as amended.

Dennison, J., and Gallager, P. (1986). *Canada's community colleges.* Vancouver, BC: UBC Press.

Department of Advanced Education Act 1983, c, D-11.1, as amended.

Devereaux, M.S. (1985). *One in every five: A survey of adult education in Canada.* Ottawa, ON: Statistics Canada & Education Support Sector, Department of the Secretary of State.

Dupré, J.S. (1987). *Post-secondary operating grants in Alberta: An equity study.* Edmonton, AB: Publication Services, Government of Alberta.

Institute for Research on Public Policy. (1987). *Report to the Secretary of State, Canada, and the Council of Ministers of Education, Canada: National Forum on Postsecondary Education,* Saskatoon, 1987. Halifax, NS: Author.

Johns, W.H. (1981). *A history of the University of Alberta 1908-1969.* Edmonton, AB: University of Alberta Press.

Knapp, J. (1991). Institutional planning in Alberta's public colleges. Unpublished doctoral dissertation, University of Alberta, Edmonton, AB.

Michael, S.O., and Holdaway, E.A. (1991). Entrepreneurial activities in higher education. *The Canadian Journal of Higher Education, 22*(2), 15-40.

Mowat, G.L. (1971). *A report on the concept of affiliation between colleges and universities in Alberta, with a proposal for change.* Submitted to the Universities Coordinating Council, June 30.

Public Junior Colleges Act 1958, c, 64.

Report on the Royal Commission on Education in Alberta. (1959). Edmonton, AB: Queen's Printer.

Secretary of State. (1985). *Accessibility to postsecondary education in Canada.* Ottawa, ON: Author.

Secretary of State. (1988). *Inventory of research on postsecondary education.* Ottawa, ON: Author.

Secretary of State. (1989). *Federal and provincial support to postsecondary education in Canada.* Ottawa, ON: Author.

Secretary of State. (1990). *Canadian programs and policies affecting international students.* Ottawa, ON: Author.

Survey Committee on Higher Education. (1961). *An interim report.* Edmonton,
    AB: Queen's Printer.

Technical Institutes Act 1981, c, T-3-1, as amended.

The Technical and Vocational Training Assistance Act 1960 Vol. I 1960-61 c, 6.

Universities Act 1966, C-105, as amended.

Universities Act R.S.A. 1980, c, u-5, as amended.

Winchester, I. (1984). Government power and university principles: An analysis of
    the battle for academic freedom in Alberta. *Interchange,* Informal Series 57,
    41-59.

Worth, W.H. (1972). *A choice of futures.* Report of the Commission on Educational
    Planning. Edmonton, AB: Queen's Printer.

Worth, W.H. (1974). From autonomy to system: A provincial perspective. *Library
    Association of Alberta Bulletin, 5*(2).

Higher Education in Saskatchewan

William R. Muir

Saskatchewan has a number of distinctive characteristics that have affected the development of its higher education. Its postsecondary education system has a short history, as it was the last province (along with Alberta) in Canada to experience European settlement; not much more than a century ago it was the property of a fur-trading company. Even compared to the two other prairie provinces its economic and demographic situation is unusual. Before the Depression it was the most populous of the prairie provinces; today it is the least, its population having grown by less than 10% since 1931. As recently as twenty-five years ago half its population still lived in rural areas, and half of its gross domestic product came from agriculture. These proportions have since decreased, but they are still significantly greater than the Canadian (and even the prairie) average (Friesen, 1987; Statistics Canada, 1994; Saskatchewan Bureau of Statistics, 1994).

These factors have significantly shaped Saskatchewan's system of higher education. The first architects of this system were faced with the challenge of creating educational services taken for granted at the time in the more established provinces, over widely separated settlements and under frontier conditions that often made it difficult to recruit qualified professionals. The challenge was met in part initially by relying on community resources to augment the limited professional services available, a policy that has continued to be useful to the present day. Later the same pressures would lead to the foundation of a university with innovative features. A second challenge was the Depression, which hit Saskatchewan more severely than any other part of Canada, just when it seemed that it was about to take its place among the more established provinces. As a result Saskatchewan has had to continue to innovate and to make do under unusual conditions. In particular, with educational institutions tending to develop in urban centres, it has had to find ways of serving its widely spread rural population as well.

The primary focus of this article is an examination of higher education after World War II. However, to understand developments since 1945 it will be helpful to survey what happened earlier.

Historical Synopsis

From 1670 to 1868 Saskatchewan was part of the Hudson Bay Company's colony and commercial enterprise of Rupert's Land, which was purchased in 1868 by the new Dominion of Canada. What would be Saskatchewan and Alberta were administered by Ottawa as the North-West Territories until they achieved provincial status in 1905. The Anglican Church founded a missionary school in 1840, a college in 1879, and in 1883 obtained a charter from the Dominion government licensing the future establishment of a university in the Territories. In response, residents of the Territories, objecting to a denominational university, lobbied Ottawa to endow a public institution in 1889, and upon the achievement of locally controlled responsible government, the Territorial Legislature riposted in 1903 by establishing on paper a public university with exclusive degree-granting rights in the area. Although neither institution ever came into being, the political stage was set for a clash between the ideas of sectarian and public higher education (Hayden, 1983).

An early educational concern was the training of elementary school teachers. Because of the difficulty of recruiting qualified personnel to work in primitive rural areas for the salaries paid by early school boards, many of the first teachers were local women who learned their profession largely through apprenticeship. Beginning with a provisional teaching certificate (which required only the recommendation of a local school board), a teacher could work up through four levels to a first-class certificate by acquiring approved teaching experience and passing examinations set by the Board of Education, with more experienced teachers in "normal" or model departments in the larger schools offering instruction. In 1893 a specialized Normal School was established in Regina by the territorial government to provide formal training, with a second starting in 1912 in Saskatoon and a third in Moose Jaw in 1927. (These hardly qualified as institutions of higher education, as until 1919 the only entrance requirements for this program were completion of grade six and a working knowledge of English.) The program was only for primary school teachers; the first high school teachers were recruited from Eastern Canada or abroad (Denny, 1929; Hayden, 1983).

Nursing training was also initially provided at the local level through apprenticeship for similar reasons to teaching. The first small permanent hospitals staffed by imported physicians and nurses were established at the end of the nineteenth century. St. Paul's Hospital in Saskatoon was typical; opened in 1907, it began taking in student nurses in 1909. Probationers, who had to be 18 years old and grade eight graduates, were put on ward duty immediately. They were taught bedside procedures on the job by the matron and received lectures from the doctors on fundamental medical subjects in their "leisure time" over two years. Virtually every hospital of any size had such a school at the beginning of the century for training its own nursing staff. In 1917 the Registered Nurses Act provided for certification on the basis of an examination conducted through the University of Saskatchewan, and in the 1920s some hospitals began appointing full-time nursing instructors. By 1938, when the University introduced a degree in nursing, the number of hospital schools had been reduced to 10 in larger centres (King, 1959; Robinson, 1967).

An act was passed in 1907 founding a university in Saskatoon. Realizing the pointlessness of attempting to establish a purely conventional university under frontier conditions, Walter C. Murray, its first president, set out to create a utilitarian institution that was so attractive to the voters that a sometimes reluctant provincial government would be compelled to finance it. He strove from the first to involve the university in the process and criteria of accreditation and education of every profession practised in the province, as was illustrated above in the case of nursing. He focused the university's attention on the province's principal economic activity, agriculture. Research was concentrated on areas such as plant diseases and animal breeding, and a substantial portion of the university's resources was devoted to agricultural extension activities, including many that took the university to the countryside such as "Better Farming Trains" with livestock and farm machinery demonstration cars, Homemakers' Clubs for farm women, and 4-H Clubs. Any other educational institution that showed signs of competing with the provincial university for government funding was ruthlessly suppressed or cannibalized. If institutions such as Regina College (originally founded by the Methodist Church in 1911 to provide a mix of secondary schooling, liberal arts, and vocational instruction) wanted to move into higher education, they were allowed only to teach first and second year University of Saskatchewan arts and science courses as affiliated "junior colleges" (Hayden, 1983).

In 1928 the first Bible college was established in Saskatchewan, and by 1945 there were at least 15. These institutions provided a scripture-based general education for students with a different worldview that was the equivalent of the liberal arts studies of a more affluent and urban class.

During the 1930s Saskatchewan's economy was devastated by depression and drought, followed by the disruptions of World War II. At war's end prosperity returned, not only from renewed agricultural activity but from increased diversification in resource development as well. A political change occurred with the economic one; in 1944 Saskatchewan elected the forebear of the New Democratic Party (NDP), the Co-operative Commonwealth Federation (CCF) party, as North America's first socialist government. Developments in postsecondary education in Saskatchewan have been correlated to a large extent with the political views of the provincial government of the moment. Although nominally several different parties have held power at various times, Saskatchewan basically has had a two-party system throughout its history; the province has alternated between a rightist and a leftist philosophy in its choice of administration, regardless of the title of the party elected. In prairie historian Gerald Friesen's (1987) summation,

> both Liberals and Tories [Progressive Conservatives] represented the right side of the Saskatchewan political spectrum because both were closer to business and farther from labour than their NDP opponents. Both Liberals and Tories were closer to youth and farther from the elderly than were the NDP. Both Liberals and Tories were perceived to be less sympathetic to government intervention in the economy and to social experiments. (p. 427)

At times an individualistic, business-oriented, private enterprise approach to government has seemed appropriate to the majority of voters; at other times a collective, socially conscious, interventionist orientation has appeared preferable. Educational policy has usually followed closely.

The virtually uninterrupted rightist Liberal reign from 1905-44 coincided with Walter Murray's 1907-37 presidency of the University of Saskatchewan. The government was persuaded to allow an autonomous university to dominate higher education in the province during this time because the politically astute Murray created a utilitarian institution that ministered to the province's economic needs. However, the leftist CCF government of 1944-64, faced with a deterioration of rural life and a changing provincial university whose interests were turning from extension and applied research to pure science, decided to form its own educational agenda. It did so by increasing its control over the university, integrating the remaining Teachers Colleges into it, and promoting Regina College from junior college status to a second campus of the university with an emphasis on social science and the humanities. In the area of non-university postsecondary education, it moved supervision of private vocational schools from the Department of Labour to the Department of Education. Vocational training outside the high schools had previously been offered in the province only on a short-term basis in response to such events as the Depression, World War II, and returning veterans. However, in 1958 a permanent facility was established when the Moose Jaw Normal School was converted into the Saskatchewan Technical Institute, to be followed eventually by the creation of three more permanent technical institutes in other urban centres between 1962 and 1986. Several vocational centres for training programs funded by external agencies such as Canada Manpower were also established, usually in temporary rented accommodation. In 1956 a Royal Commission on Agriculture and Rural Life recommended that the university increase its emphasis on social research that could benefit rural residents. It also advised that more opportunity be provided in adult education, using not only university resources but those of local schools and volunteer citizen organizations as well. However, almost two decades would pass before the latter recommendations were implemented.

On being returned to power in 1964 on promises to activate industry and business in the province, the Liberals embarked on a program of expansion and centralization of higher education along more conventional lines. Nursing training was moved from the Department of Health to Education, the effective supervision of private vocational schools was intensified, and another urban technical institute was initiated. However, in the late 1960s the combination of the transfer of university grants from federal to provincial control and a reduction in provincial revenues due to falling world wheat prices led to a diversion of funds formerly spent on higher education to other purposes.

In 1971 the NDP (as the CCF was now called) was re-elected, and it immediately carried out some radical changes. In 1973 a unique system of community colleges was established. Although government-funded, each college had a board of local residents who used community input to determine its program. Existing facilities such as school buildings were used whenever possible, and instruction was provided on a brokerage basis, either through instructors hired on contract or through courses provided by the university or the technical institutes. The colleges were to be agents of "community development" as well as educational institutions

(Saskatchewan, 1972, p. 59). By 1981 there were sixteen regional colleges, including one offering programs on Indian reserves. In 1974 the University of Regina became independent with its own Act, and a Universities Commission was established as an arm's-length body to coordinate the two institutions.

In 1982 the NDP was defeated by the Progressive Conservative (Tory) Party, and yet another radical restructuring of postsecondary education occurred. The contrast in educational philosophy of the two parties was starkly outlined in the departmental Annual Reports before and after the election. In 1980-81 the NDP described advances in their pre-retirement planning and counselling program, development of training programs for workers in special, home, and day care, and the establishment of an Office of Native Career Development (*Annual Report*, 1980-81). In the 1982-83 Report the Tories announced that the Department's name had been changed from Continuing Education to Advanced Education and Manpower, and that "the new Department's activities have been and will continue to be addressed toward meeting Saskatchewan's projected long-term need for skilled labour through the preparation of Saskatchewan citizens for effective entry, adaptation, and participation in the labour market" (*Annual Report*, 1982-83, p. 3). In 1983 the Universities Commission was abolished. In the same year a Task Force led to the establishment of the Advanced Technology Training Centre in 1984 as a Crown corporation to encourage Saskatchewan industries to improve productivity and competitiveness, with the expectation it would become self-funding. In 1987 in yet another reorganization the Department of Advanced Education and Manpower was reunited with the Department of Education and combined with the provincial library system. A major policy framework paper, *Preparing for the Year 2000* (Saskatchewan, 1987), was issued to describe the objectives and goals around which the government wished the province's educational institutions to coordinate their future plans. One of the new ministry's first initiatives was the amalgamation in 1987 of the Advanced Technology Training Centre, the four technical institutes, the four urban community colleges, and a northern vocational centre into a multicampus institution called the Saskatchewan Institute of Applied Science and Technology (SIAST), to be managed by a government-appointed board of directors. Another major restructuring saw the remaining rural community colleges changed to nine regional colleges, with a new mandate "to offer university and institute programs on an extension, brokerage basis, across the province. The colleges will continue to provide adult literacy training, but will be asked to transfer community interest and personal "hobby" courses to volunteer organizations or to other community groups" (pp. 9-10). Colleges were to be restricted to the conventional educational goals of brokering institute and university courses and programming career, training, and adult basic education courses; the original objective of "community development" was removed from their mandate. Recognizing the maturity of the college system, the department adopted an arm's-length policy toward the colleges and in 1989 eliminated its Regional Colleges Branch and its field staff, encouraging each college to plot its own independent course; it also relaxed the restrictions on colleges acquiring permanent facilities (Regional Colleges Committee of Review, 1993).

Distance education was advanced by the creation of a Distance Education Program Review Committee in 1987 to develop policy, coordinate programs, assess new technology, and provide advice. The Saskatchewan Tele-Learning Association (STELLA), a voluntary consortium of educational institutions and the Saskatchewan Wheat Pool, had been working for some time to deliver educational programming to sites in rural centres via satellite and SaskTel's pioneering fibre-optic network. In 1989 this service was expanded by the creation of the Saskatchewan Communications Network (SCN), a Crown corporation. The SCN Cable Network provides educational programming available to all cable television subscribers in the province through a dedicated cable channel, while the SCN Training Network delivers interactive programming for university and SIAST courses to over 80 sites throughout the province.

In 1992 the NDP were returned to power. This time, however, the changeover of administrations was stormier than usual; the predictable change in educational policy was complicated by the new government having to cope with a fiscal crisis brought on by the most recent recession and the profligate financial policies of the previous administration. To date the government has had its hands full with downsizing the provincial budget, and a climate of enforced financial restraint has allowed it to do little more than re-evaluate its educational goals. Major reviews have been conducted of the university sector, SIAST, the regional college system, and the private vocational schools. In the Department's most recent *Annual Report* (1993-94) it announced that it intended "to develop a new strategic direction for education, training and employment, and to set up a new organizational structure that reflects and implements that strategic direction" (p. 1). Among the priority areas identified were strategies for training and employment, distance education, and the education, training, and employment of Aboriginal people; the development of an integrated postsecondary sector; and the development of an effective system of accountability. To aid in the development of system-wide objectives, the clarification of institutional mandates, and the facilitation of cooperative initiatives a postsecondary strategic planning group was formed consisting of the chief executive officers of the universities, the Gabriel Dumont Institute, the Saskatchewan Indian Federated College, SIAST, representatives of the regional colleges and the private vocational schools, and six executives from the Department.

The Components of the System

Degree-Granting Institutions

The University of Saskatchewan's early constitution was unique among Canadian universities, although virtually all of its separate features were drawn from other models. It had exclusive degree-granting powers in the province; a Board of Governors managed the financial affairs of the University and appointed the President and the faculty (on the recommendation of the President); a Senate approved all academic programs, and a faculty body called the Council managed day-to-day academic matters and proposed changes in programs for the approval of the Senate. But where Saskatchewan differed was that a majority of its Senate was elected by the university graduates resident in the province, and the Senate in turn elected the majority of the Board of Governors. The government provided the major funding for the university through a statutory grant, but it did not control the institution. Ironically, a provincial government far from socialist in philosophy had created probably the closest thing in North America to a "people's university."

But in time the university moved toward a more conventional pattern. The Senate lost control over academic programs to the Faculty Council as the former became more and more unwieldy through the addition of members appointed by professional groups whose training and accreditation the university managed. The government grant changed from a statutory grant to one voted annually. After World War II the government changed the University Act to transfer the power to create new programs from the Senate to the Board. The composition of the Board was eventually changed to a majority of government-appointed members (Hayden, 1983).

Walter Murray, President of the University for most of its first three decades, had assiduously pursued a policy of discouraging the emergence of any other institution not on the university campus that might aspire to degree-granting status and thereby threaten the University of Saskatchewan's virtual monopoly of government support for higher education. Regina, for many years a larger and more important centre than the University's home of Saskatoon, had to be content with junior feeder colleges. But in 1959 both the University and the government recognized the need for a second institution to serve the southern portion of the province and sanctioned the elevation of Regina College to a second campus of the university. In 1974 Regina Campus became the independent University of Regina (Hayden, 1983; Riddell, 1974). In 1994 the two universities had a combined enrollment of 24,075 full-time equivalent students.

The universities have the sole right in the province to authorize instruction for degree credit. Fourteen colleges are connected in varying degrees of integration with the two universities in order to offer degree-credit courses. Four colleges (three at the University of Regina and one at the University of Saskatchewan) have federated status, meaning that they are financially independent but are located on the campuses of their host universities and offer academic programs that are entirely merged with them. Seven colleges have affiliated and three associated status, categories covering a range of relationships from three on-campus mainstream Protestant graduate theological colleges at the University of Saskatchewan offering degrees in divinity, to several off-campus institutions, mainly denominational, offering some courses with university transfer credit. The regional colleges and SIAST campuses in non-university cities can teach particular university courses on a proxy basis.

The original motivation for creating connected colleges was the typical Canadian answer of compromise for questions of conflicting interests. Saskatchewan had been a witness to the final stages of the nineteenth-century battle between secular and denominational higher education. It adopted the University of Toronto's solution of a secular, state-controlled, state-funded university combined with federated colleges where religious groups were allowed an adjunct function of providing an appropriate supporting environment for their students and the opportunity to teach a specialized curriculum. A variation on this theme is the sponsorship by the Federation of Saskatchewan Indian Nations of the Saskatchewan Indian Federated College (SIFC), beginning at the University of Regina in 1976 but now operating at both universities. The college provides remedial preparatory programs and a supportive learning environment for Native university students and teaches such subjects as Indian studies and languages, linguistics, and a certificate in Aboriginal business studies supported by the Bank of Nova Scotia (Lewington, 1995).

Technical/Vocational Institutes

The Saskatchewan Technical Institute was established in Moose Jaw in 1958; three more institutes were established in Saskatoon (1962), Regina (1972), and Prince Albert (1986). Each institute had a principal reporting to the deputy minister, who was responsible for the system's program development. The range of technical programs offered was broadened over time, with, for example, nursing training being transferred to the institutes from the hospitals in the late 1960s. However, as the institutes were all located in urban centres, they were not easily accessible to the large proportion of the population living in rural areas. As well, directly managed by the Department of Education and staffed by permanent instructors who were members of the government employees union, they were inhibited in responding to new or local training needs.

As part of the Tories' major reorganization in 1987, SIAST was created from the amalgamation of several existing institutions. The philosophy of the new institution was announced in the Department's 1986-87 *Annual Report*:

> SIAST will employ proven private sector techniques in managing its affairs. The institute will be expected to cover a portion of its operating costs from private sector training contracts. It will be required to operate annually on a break-even basis, and invest a percentage of annual income in new technology, applied research and development. . . . SIAST will operate independently from government, reporting to an autonomous board of directors. (p. 24)

SIAST was divided into four campuses in Moose Jaw, Prince Albert, Regina, and Saskatoon. Each campus resulted from the consolidation of the existing technical institute and urban community college in the city, with the Advanced Technology Training Centre joining the Saskatoon campus as well. In 1994 the Gabriel Dumont Technical Institute, established in 1980 for postsecondary education of Métis and Non-Status Indian students, federated with SIAST. In 1994 SIAST provided programs to 13,724 full-time and 33,175 part-time students.

Community/Regional Colleges

Much discussion preceded the passage of The Community Colleges Act in 1973. The 1956 Royal Commission on Agriculture and Rural Life referred to earlier had advocated the role of volunteer services in adult education (Hayden, 1983). At least four other studies and reports were produced prior to the establishment of an Advisory Committee on Community Colleges to the Minister of Education by the NDP, shortly after its return to office in 1971. The Committee's advice to the Minister, generally known as the Faris Report (Saskatchewan, 1972), was to create a set of community colleges. The Committee's meaning of "community college" was not the conventional one; their use of the term was based on the assumption that "the interaction of individuals who share common concerns produces a social dimension known as a community. This community, in turn, influences the people within it" (p. 8). The Committee was as much advocating the fostering of a social phenomenon as the creation of an institution. Its version of a college would coordinate but not duplicate existing educational services for providing access to lifelong learning; the heart of a community college was a representative board that determined what learning activities the community wanted and then obtained them. No degrees or credits would be granted; leased facilities would be used if possible, and permanent staff would be limited to maximize the flexibility and creativeness of the movement. As much as possible the colleges would act as brokers for other agencies such as the technical institutes and universities, which could provide courses and credits on a contract basis. It was strongly suggested that the new colleges operate independently of the rural school boards, and that all adult education and recreational activities be transferred from the latter to the new system as well. A basic principle was that "a community college shall assist in community development by offering programs of community education and service. In rural areas it will serve as a mechanism for the maintenance and development of a viable way of life" (p. 59).

The report led to The Community Colleges Act in 1973; by 1987 there were 16 colleges province-wide, each governed by a seven-member board of local residents that decided policy and appointed a principal to supervise instruction. Most colleges were funded by a base grant to cover administrative costs and a certain level of discretionary projects, grants from federal and provincial agencies for sponsored adult basic education courses (the largest source), contracts from business and government agencies, and tuition fees (Dennison and Gallagher, 1986; Minister's Advisory Committee on Community College Financing, 1987).

As part of their restructuring of postsecondary education in 1988 the Tories amalgamated the four urban community colleges with SIAST, and the rural area was divided in nine regions, each with a regional college. In 1994 approximately 30,000 individuals enrolled in regional college programs.

Private Vocational Schools

Saskatchewan's first private vocational school was established in the 1900s to offer the province's earliest training in secretarial studies. The field remained largely unregulated until 1939, when The Trade Schools Regulation Act came into force. This was replaced in 1980 by the present Private Vocational Schools Regulation Act. The principal activity at first under these Acts seems to have been mediation between schools and students on disputes over fees; however, a more active supervision policy was initiated in 1964. The popularity of the schools grew slowly until around 1980, when there were 16 with a total enrollment of 1,732, almost all in the fields of beauty culture, commercial studies, and income tax preparation. A rapid surge of interest was evidenced during the next decade, contributed to by the closing of programs in secretarial sciences and beauty culture at SIAST and the availability of several financial assistance programs for students. Total enrollments increased to 4,286 in 1987 and peaked at 5,254 in 1988; the number of schools rose from 48 in 1988 to 59 in 1989. The most popular programs in 1989 in terms of total enrollments and number of schools were business/computer (54.2%, 21 schools), Saskatchewan Safety Council (10.1%, 1 school), life skills (9.7%, 6 schools), and beauty culture (6.9%, 9 schools). However, activity in this sector has since plummeted. During 1989-91 six schools closed in mid-term, disrupting the training of several hundred students; in 1994 the number of schools registered had dropped to 41 and total enrollments to approximately 1,920 (Private Vocational Schools Review Panel, 1993).

Bible Colleges

Following World War I, a profound religious, social, and intellectual movement swept through Canada, the prairies in particular. For some time the mainstream Protestant denominations had been moving toward an increased concern for social problems and social salvation with a de-emphasis of asceticism, personal salvation, and the conversion experience. This accompanied shifts from a literal to a historical approach to biblical studies, toward a preference for ministers with university training, and toward church services that were more formal and intellectual, rather than emotional, in tone. As Mann (1955) has observed, although this movement was attractive to many educated, urban, middle-class churchgoers, it alienated numerous others, particularly less educated and less affluent people in small towns and rural areas, who left the mainstream denominations in large numbers in favour of more conservative, fundamentalist groups that stressed an emotional, charismatic, and evangelistic approach to worship.

These groups emphasized more intense involvement and fellowship in their congregations; this, combined with their disapproval of many conventional forms of entertainment such as movie-going, dancing, and cardplaying, which tended to distance them from other members of their communities, meant that their churches acquired social as well as religious significance for them. Their belief in the validity of a literal interpretation of the Bible, as well as their conviction that it was the duty of all Christians to be evangelists, led to a new form of educational institution, the Bible college.

The first of these was established in Saskatchewan in 1928, and by 1945 their number had grown to at least 15. Today there are 12, 2 of which have attached advanced theological seminaries for professional clergy. Although the colleges exist in every province except Newfoundland and Quebec, Saskatchewan has the second largest number after Ontario and the most on a per capita basis. The median enrollment in these institutions is about 100, ranging from 30 to 870 with an estimated total of around 2,600 (Anderson, 1992). Their mandate is broader than the training of professional clergy of the mainstream theological colleges. They provide vocational training for ministers and foreign and domestic missionaries; for example, one college provides training leading to a pilot's license, while another offers instruction by a former chef from a major hotel in cooking for evangelical camps. Many of the denominations sponsoring them de-emphasize professional clergy, and many young people enroll in them for shorter courses simply to acquire the knowledge of the Bible that their faith assures them is essential for making the correct decisions in everyday life. In addition there is the appeal of a social life unavailable during the dreary winter months on a farm or in a small town. In many respects the Bible college offers (in the context of a different worldview) the same attractions to a lower-income, rural population that the liberal arts college provides to a more affluent, urban group (Mann, 1955). They provide a distinctive and significant contribution to the provincial system.

Conclusion

How well is Saskatchewan served by its higher education system? This question will be addressed from two perspectives: how the various levels of the system function according to conventional standards and whether the province's needs are being met. Four reviews of the major components of the system recently commissioned by the provincial government provide invaluable assistance in answering this question. It should be borne in mind that the panels carrying out the reviews were all chosen by an NDP government and can be expected to have been operating from particular *a priori* assumptions, explicit and implicit, in performing their tasks. Two important givens for the panels were that many aspects of the system being reviewed had been introduced by the previous political administration and that a drastic economy campaign was in effect for the government.

In their examination of the university sector (which has exclusive jurisdiction over all instruction leading to degree credit), the University Program Review Panel (1993a; 1993b) had been specifically directed to look for possible cost savings. The Panel concluded that by conventional criteria the universities were doing a good job. Their principal criticism was that, ironically, perhaps the province has more of a good thing than it can afford.

> Together, Saskatchewan's universities offer a near complete range of major programs—a remarkable achievement for a province of under a million people. The question must be asked, though, given that resources are already stretched to provide the programs now offered, can the province afford the diversity of programs it now has within the universities? (1993b, p. 21)

How are such economies to be achieved? One of the questions posed by the government had been the advisability of returning to the evergreen Saskatchewan concept of a single provincial university. The Review Panel threw cold water on this idea, concluding that:

> there is a sound case to be made for two universities, and to enter
> into the "one versus two" debate deflects from addressing some
> of the more fundamental issues respecting governance and the
> delivery of high quality education. . . . It is important to drop the
> debate about one university or two. People must now turn their
> minds to what system of coordination can be developed to ensure
> that each university can grow—within its own niche—and in
> harmony with the other. (1993b, pp. 5-6)

To achieve this goal the formation of an interlocutory body was recommended that could gather and analyze information relevant to university issues, audit the public responsibilities of the universities, and provide advice to the government. The Panel stressed that the proposed body was not intended as a return of the former Universities Commission, which it saw as having operated as "a kind of 'super Board' [of Governors]" (p. 36) for the two universities, thereby infringing on their autonomy. Rather, the proposed body was to have an advisory, not an intermediary, function.

Regarding the government's concern that there was unwarranted duplication of programs within the two institutions, the Panel noted that the University of Regina had developed many of its new programs to complement the curriculum at the older University of Saskatchewan. The Panel concluded that, although some duplication exists, only in one area (fine arts) was there an argument for consolidation. Amalgamation of other programs would create accessibility and logistical problems. Rather, a more productive approach would be a rationalization of programs within each institution. In particular, it was recommended that the universities scrutinize their specializations where costs were high and enrollments low and examine noncredit programs with the view to transferring them to other institutions such as SIAST. Other areas where internal reforms were advised were in the governance and administration structures of the two universities, academic program evaluation, and faculty development.

The Panel believed that some issues needed to be dealt with at the regional or national level. Professional education was one example; it would be wasteful for every province to provide a complete set of programs. At present, for instance, rather than mounting its own occupational therapy program, Saskatchewan has an agreement with neighbouring provinces to have students accepted into their programs. Similarly, the University of Saskatchewan has a veterinary medicine school serving the four western provinces. Dentistry was suggested as a good candidate for another such cooperative program. Another issue requiring attention at the national level is Aboriginal postsecondary education, which requires provincial-federal government cooperation.

Although the Panel was generally positive about the universities' efficiency and conventional performance, it presented some subtle criticisms of how well these institutions were coping with some of the province's particular access problems.

> Saskatchewan has a small population, distributed across a wide area, and a relatively large population of aboriginal peoples who historically have not received post-secondary education. Both of these conditions pose particular problems for ensuring accessibility to university of all qualified students. Special efforts need to be made to overcome the barriers of distance, isolation, and poverty that prevent access to university level education for aboriginal people. Without these efforts, the social and economic well-being of the population and the long-term provincial growth will suffer. (1993a, p. 3)

The Panel proposed that distance education be integrated into university instruction as a fundamental element, an addition that would be of benefit to both the Native and general populations. It also warned that, although the SIFC's Native academic and cultural programs were a strong point and should be extended, the college's remedial function should be considered only a stopgap until better preparatory programs for Native students were in place.

The principal vehicle for the provision of technical and vocational training and adult upgrading is SIAST with its four campuses in the province's largest urban centres. Considering that SIAST's staff and management problems had seldom been out of the news since its merger in 1987, it is not surprising that the SIAST Committee of Review (1992) came up with a generally bleak picture of the institution's functioning. Although a structure had been designed for SIAST when it was created to combine the constituent institutions entering into it, "there appears to have to have been little, if any, consideration for the people involved in the merger" (p. 10). The Committee characterized SIAST's management as "overly centralized and top heavy," "excessively bureaucratic and authoritarian," and "operating without regard for community concerns" (pp. 13, 16). There was no effective communication between SIAST and the provincial and federal governments or, for that matter, between its central office and its campuses. The Committee concluded that, while there was no point in attempting to undo the merger, "in its immediate state, the institute is not ready to deal with the future. We believe that its existence depends on immediate action [on restructuring] being taken" (p. 6).

Surprisingly, given that the institution's reorganization had been intended to increase its responsiveness to community requirements, it was the Committee's opinion that, although SIAST may be providing courses and programs in career education as directed, its approach to job-training was narrow and inflexible, and it was slow in responding to changing needs. The Committee recommended a broadening of the curriculum to include communication, problem-solving, and decision-making skills, and the development of a plan to address the continuing education needs of the community.

The Regional Colleges Committee of Review (1993) found that the Tory government conversion of the institutions from community to regional colleges had not been generally well received. It reported a strong public appeal for the reintroduction of community interest and hobby courses to the colleges' curriculum, and the return of community development to their mandate. The predicted assumption by volunteer organizations of responsibility for these courses had not occurred; rather, their removal from the college sphere of interest had decimated the volunteer network that the colleges had relied on as their eyes and ears to determine demand for programming. Although some colleges welcomed the 1989 move toward greater autonomy, the Committee commented that:

> a provincial regional college system no longer existed. Rather, what existed were eight separate and distinct colleges each with differing philosophies on the future direction for adult education access and program delivery in rural Saskatchewan. (p. 19)

The Committee recommended stronger linkages between the colleges and the Minister of Education. As well, communication between levels of the postsecondary system was patchy. Good operational connections on course delivery with the universities were reported but not at more senior administrative levels, and relations with SIAST and the K-12 system at all levels left much to be desired.

The increased latitude in allowing the acquisition of permanent facilities introduced by the Tories had created a complex situation. The colleges favoured the provision of a central custom-designed building in each region, a program not likely to be viewed enthusiastically by a cost-cutting government. Many comprehensive high schools recently built in rural areas with good teaching facilities were underutilized and had school boards willing to share them with the colleges; however, some colleges resisted this solution, arguing that many adult learners needed an institution with a distinct identity, clearly separate and apart from the K-12 system.

It would be tempting to predict that an NDP-appointed commission might take a negative view of the role of private enterprise in education, but the report of the Private Vocational Schools Review Panel (1993) belies that preconception by presenting a commendatory assessment of the province's commercial schools. The Panel pointed out that private schools differ from ones in the public sector in several ways. Their curricula are more structured because of their direct connections with particular job skills. They are cost effective, in that most have short programs, can operate with few staff, generally give all students in a program the same sequence of courses, and start new classes several times a year. They are flexible, as decision making is usually done by the owner without the necessity of input from others, and so they can react more quickly to changing market conditions. Perhaps most importantly, making a profit is an important goal. The Panel concluded that the commercial schools serve the valuable function of filling the cracks in the programs designed by the state.

> No single model of delivering post-secondary education will meet all students' requirements. There is a need for a diversity of programs and delivery mechanisms. Within this framework, private vocational schools play a legitimate and valuable role. They offer programs that are unavailable elsewhere and deliver these programs in ways that reflect both students' requirements and labour market demand. Private vocational schools are an important component of the post-secondary education system of this province. (p. 7)

In summary, the reviewers concluded that the provincial institutions in the best health were those at the top and at the bottom of the pecking order, the universities and the private vocational schools. Interestingly, these are the two sectors that are subject to the least government intervention. The regulation of private schools is principally for purposes of consumer protection, while the financial assistance they receive is virtually restricted to student loan programs. The private school reviewers did not recommend changing this situation. Although the universities were created by, are largely government funded and administered through boards mainly appointed by the government, they have benefitted from the traditional arm's-length relationship with the civil power. As a result of this government inattention, in their different ways both sectors have evolved to their present forms largely through market pressures: this is the case for the private schools by definition, while for the universities the situation came about because the newer University of Regina had to expand into areas that did not compete with the more senior University of Saskatchewan. And while the university reviewers' terms of reference certainly encouraged a critical approach to their task, their report gave little support for any proposal of radical change. By contrast, SIAST and the regional colleges, the sectors most directly controlled by the government (and bearing most strongly the imprint of the previous Tory administration), received the most negative verdicts and the most drastic recommendations for change. Although SIAST's amalgamation of several institutes into a single organization directed by an appointed board seemed to have been a good move, its internal organization was poor; although it was making courses in career education available, it was deficient in its provision of adult upgrading. The regional colleges were drifting on separate courses and losing contact with their constituency. It remains to be seen what measures a cash-strapped provincial government will be able to take to change these situations.

Two major themes pervade the reports on the public sector institutions. The first is the need for more communication and coordination among the components of the system. The universities should better harmonize their basic programs with each other and should engage in cooperative ventures with other provinces to jointly mount expensive professional courses. SIAST should improve virtually all its channels of communication, both with its own campuses and with other institutions. The regional colleges should return to being part of a provincial system, rather than autonomous entities. The recent restructuring of the Department of Education, Training and Employment, and the Department's creation of a strategic planning group for postsecondary education were intended to deal with this situation. Only time will show if these moves can effectively solve the problem.

The second theme is the distance that the system still has to travel to provide accessibility to every resident of Saskatchewan. SIAST was castigated for "operating without regard for community concerns" (SIAST Committee of Review, 1992, p. 16). The universities were reminded that "special efforts need to be made to overcome the barriers of distance, isolation, and poverty that prevent access to university level education for aboriginal people" (University Program Review Panel, 1993a, p. 3) Even the regional college system, the jewel in the crown of the NDP social-educational enterprise, received a gentle nudge in this direction. Directed by the Minister of Education to "review the mandate of community colleges and recommend a vision for the future," the Regional Colleges Committee of Review (1993) stated:

> Saskatchewan people hold deep attachment to regional colleges. Rural people expect access to the same quality of post-secondary and adult education opportunities as their urban counterparts. . . .
>
> The future vision places community at the centre of the Saskatchewan Regional College system. The vision requires colleges to extend themselves into their local and regional communities. It challenges regional colleges to develop new partnerships with educational institutions, Aboriginal people, agriculture, business, industry, labour and government departments and industry. It foresees distance education and technologies as important means to extend educational access. . . .
>
> Saskatchewan Regional Colleges are strategically positioned to assist communities through a time of changing attitudes about what "community" is. Regional colleges are flexible organizations, responsive to locally and regionally identified community needs. They provide a successful, functional model of regional service delivery. Regional colleges, working in educational partnership with local and regional communities, will serve as one vehicle for social and economic renewal in rural Saskatchewan. (pp. iii-iv)

Again, time will tell what progress the sectors of the system can make in improving access for its various constituencies in a chilly financial climate and whether yet another provincial election may alter the picture by changing the parameters of the future vision by which the system is judged.

References

Note: Unless otherwise specified, the source of information for factual statements in this paper is the appropriate *Annual Report* of the variously titled government departments responsible for postsecondary education over the period covered.

Anderson, D. (1992). *Directory of theological education in Canada.* Regina: Canadian Bible College.

Annual report (1980-81). Regina: Saskatchewan Department of Continuing Education.

Annual report (1982-83). Regina: Saskatchewan Advanced Education and Manpower.

Annual report (1986-87). Regina: Saskatchewan Education.

Annual report (1993-94). Regina: Saskatchewan Education, Training and Employment.

Community Colleges Act (1973). Regina: Queen's Printer.

Dennison, J.D, and Gallagher, P. (1986). *Canada's community colleges: A critical analysis.* Vancouver: UBC Press.

Denny, J.D. (1929). *The organization of public education in Saskatchewan.* Toronto: Ontario College.

Friesen, G. (1987). *The Canadian prairies: A history.* Toronto: University of Toronto Press.

Hayden, M. (1983). *Seeking a balance: University of Saskatchewan, 1907-1982.* Vancouver: UBC Press.

King, C. (1959). *The first fifty: Teaching, research and public service at the University of Saskatchewan 1909-1959.* Toronto: McClelland and Stewart.

Lewington, J. (1995, August 21). The learning beat. *The Globe and Mail,* p. A3.

Mann, W.E. (1955). *Sect, cult, and church in Alberta.* Toronto: University of Toronto Press.

Minister's Advisory Committee on Community College Financing (1987). *Final report of the Committee to the Hon. Lorne H. Hepworth.* Regina: Saskatchewan Education.

Private Vocational Schools Regulation Act (1980). Regina: Queen's Printer.

Private Vocational Schools Review Panel (1993). *The proposed government direction for the licensing of private vocational schools in Saskatchewan.* Regina: Minister of Education.

Regional Colleges Committee of Review (1993). *Regional colleges: Partners in rural renewal.* Regina: Saskatchewan Education.

Riddell, W.A. (1974). *The first decade 1960-1970.* Regina: University of Regina.

Robinson, M. (1967). *Saskatchewan Registered Nurses' Association: The first fifty years.* Regina.

Saskatchewan (1972). *Report of the Minister's Advisory Committee on Community Colleges.* Regina: Department of Continuing Education.

Saskatchewan (1987). *Preparing for the year 2000: Adult education in Saskatchewan.* Regina: Saskatchewan Education.

Saskatchewan Bureau of Statistics (1994). *Economic Review.* (No. 48). Regina.

SIAST Committee of Review (1992). *Final Report.* Regina.

Statistics Canada (1994). *Agriculture Economic Statistics.* (Catalogue No. 21-603E, Issue 94-002). Ottawa.

Trade Schools Regulation Act (1939). Regina: King's Printer.

University Program Review Panel (1993a). *Looking at Saskatchewan universities: Programs, governance, and goals. Executive summary.* Regina.

University Program Review Panel (1993b). *Looking at Saskatchewan universities: Programs, governance, and goals. Final report.* Regina.

Higher Education in Manitoba

Alexander D. Gregor

Preface

In the early decades of the new Canadian confederation, Manitoba enjoyed a position of marked prominence in Western Canada. The first of the western territories to become a province of the new nation, Manitoba was the first to establish a degree-granting institution of higher education. Although the economic and technological changes of the next century would slowly diminish Manitoba's pivotal position within western Canada, the years of preeminence were enough to foster a university of international reputation and a higher education legacy that still manages to belie the financially beleaguered circumstances of a so-called "have-not" province.

The University System

In the years following World War II, the higher education system of Manitoba consisted of a single university, albeit the oldest in western Canada (1877). This modest establishment was a reflection of public policy: the "one university" notion that was meant to offset the sectarian conflicts that were seen to have plagued the development of provincial systems to the east. To accomplish this goal, the government modelled the provincial university after the University of London: to be an examining and degree-granting superstructure to a federation of denominational colleges which would carry out the actual teaching task. By this device, the new University of Manitoba encompassed French Catholic St. Boniface College, Anglican St. John's College, and Presbyterian Manitoba College. In the years following, the federated structure took on additional partners: Methodist Wesley College (which subsequently amalgamated with Manitoba College to re-emerge as United College), Brandon College, and the province's colleges of law, medicine, and agriculture.

With the increasing demands for science and the influence of the American state university and land grant college, the University gradually took on the role of teaching. By the end of the war, the University was coming to overshadow the collectivity of denominational colleges which until then had dominated the life and governance of the federated institution. Another twenty years passed before the strains of that relationship finally brought matters to a breaking point. In 1967, United College became the University of Winnipeg and Brandon College became Brandon University. The ninety-year-old policy of *one University* had come to an end.

The Colleges

For those colleges (that is, St. John's and St. Paul's) which stayed with the University of Manitoba, the problems of the previous era were to be resolved in a different way. A report (Manitoba, 1967) of the provincial Council on Higher Learning led in 1970 to an agreement based on what became known as the "Community of Colleges" concept. Under this arrangement the arts and science teaching functions of the colleges—and the accompanying faculty—became part of the University Faculty of Arts and Science. This solved the colleges' financial difficulties leaving them responsible only for theological studies (in the case of St John's) and any private activities and property. Teaching space, however, came under University timetabling authority with the colleges surrendering any final control over who taught and who studied within the college boundaries. The colleges could and did find means to continue the functions they felt to be their *raison d'être*: in offering a college ethos to those faculty and students who sought it. In cooperation with the departments of the University Faculty of Arts, the colleges were able to provide office space and an interdisciplinary collegial community to a substantial cross-section of subject specialists. With the same cooperation, they fostered opportunities for concentration on thematic areas of interdisciplinary study within the general undergraduate arts program: Canadian Studies at St. John's College, and Catholic Studies at St. Paul's. The accommodation was not, of course, a perfect one. The colleges frequently felt their interests submerge under the monolith of the larger institution. But the *modus vivendi* was one that did allow continuation of the college tradition within the provincial university and, with the careful distinction made between *private* and *public* in the Community of Colleges arrangement, the public university was able to continue one of its distinguishing historical characteristics—the ability to respond to the cultural diversity of its province.

In furthering this traditional goal, other forms of accommodation were found for those institutions for which the Community of Colleges approach did not quite fit. Because of its unique cultural and language mission, le Collège Universitaire de Saint-Boniface could not consider the degree of assimilation undertaken by St. John's and St. Paul's. In its case, an arrangement of separate provincial funding permitted administrative autonomy, including appointing faculty. On academic matters, the college was responsible to the University Senate; and, at the level of specific program regulations, was responsible to the respective University Faculties: Arts, Education, and Graduate Studies. After almost two decades of unresolved discussion, another arrangement was worked out for Ukrainian Orthodox St. Andrew's College. In 1981, the University Senate and Board of Governors endorsed special affiliation status for the college. Under this agreement, the two institutions would jointly participate in a Centre for Ukrainian Canadian Studies, which, in addition to a range of other educational activities, would coordinate, under the jurisdiction of the Faculty of Arts, a major and minor program in Canadian Ukrainian Studies. By this arrangement, the college itself, although situated on the University campus, was not formally linked as an institution; its relationship was limited to partnership in the jointly-sponsored Centre. Its constituency could be offered access to University credit without the college having to surrender the autonomy it felt it needed for the other aspects of its mission.

A number of Bible colleges which wanted to maintain a discrete distance from the secular provincial universities, but yet felt the need to offer some university credit courses to attract students, required yet a different agreement. Again the University responded, this time with an arrangement that became known as Approved Teaching Centres. By this device, the University could approve the offering of specific courses at the colleges. This approval was granted on an annual basis and involved endorsing the proposed instructors. A perennial concern in such relationships was that of academic freedom and scholarly ambience, and consideration of that matter was a central part of the initial review of any institution requesting Approval Teaching Centre status. Under this policy the University of Manitoba entered relationships with the Canadian Mennonite Bible College and the Canadian Nazarene College, both of which are located in Winnipeg. The University of Winnipeg in its turn entered a similar arrangement with the College of the Nazarene, Menno Simons College, and Concord College.

Although a good deal of the motivation behind these various arrangements had to do with honouring historical relationships, the college idea as an approach to institutional organization has more than once been considered by the University. By the early 1960s, the unprecedented increases in enrollment were causing many within the University to fear that incoming students would feel themselves lost on the undergraduate sea of a commuter campus. One response came in 1963 with establishment of a nondenominational University College as a constituent element of the Faculty of Arts. Developed under the guidance of its first Provost, the eminent Canadian historian Professor William L. Morton, University College was inspired by the Oxford model, but the forces of the later 1960s made short shrift of that vision. As in the case of the affiliated denominational colleges, membership in the new institution was voluntary for staff and students. After a period of experimentation, University College did evolve its own academic and social identity, but it was to be the last such experiment. Later discussions about organizing subsequent University undergraduate growth into relatively small college groupings met the fiscal wall of the 1970s. Needless to say, however, the two new universities—Brandon and Winnipeg—were quick to point to the college-like ambience their own smaller size permitted.

A Provincial System

With the two new universities came the first accoutrements of a "provincial system," to the extent that the term can be applied to higher education in Canada. As did all but one of the other provinces, Manitoba introduced its own variation of the United Kingdom's University Grants Committee—the Universities Grants Commission, incorporated by an act of the provincial legislature in 1967. Like its counterparts in other provinces, the UGC (as it came to be called) was assigned two basic tasks: to provide the government with an objective assessment of the universities' needs, and to apportion the annual provincial grant among the four public institutions (that is, the three autonomous universities—Brandon, Manitoba, and Winnipeg—and the separately funded St. Boniface College). Unlike so many of the other provinces, Manitoba has retained its commission to the present day, although not without some changes in character and tone. The most significant change has been in the gradual *de facto* movement away from the theoretical arm's-length relationship to government (which is, of course, the primary rationale for such so-called buffer agencies). The appointment in the mid-1980s of the Deputy Minister of Education as Chairman of the Commission flagged its evolving character as a semi-autonomous arm of government. Its membership—all of which is at the discretion of Cabinet—has also been a matter of concern to the universities. During most of its existence, the Commission has had a small number of university members. These have, however, been selected by government and not by the institutions, even by nomination or recommendation. The assurance of a consistent university *voice* on the body has thus been problematic. Most recently, moreover, the replenished composition of the Commission has made no provision for university members. Because of this and the fact that the fiscal responsibilities of the UGC make it necessary for most of its work to be conducted *in camera*, the university community is understandably uncertain of the degree to which its perspective is appreciated or championed. While there is a general acceptance in principle of the desirability of having some neutral referee between the universities and the political process, there are serious reservations about a perceived ineffectiveness of the present arrangement as a device for conveying university needs to government or of providing a public forum for broader discussion of higher education in the province. Of concern as well is the fact that the UGC is limited in its mandate to consideration of the university sector alone. No agency inside or outside of government is charged with responsibility for considering the development of higher education in its full scope—community colleges, technical institutes and universities. As a consequence, the two sectors have effectively operated in isolation and in parallel streams of development, operationally, and in the realm of public policy.

Ironically, even in the university sector, the enacting legislation for the UGC provided powers considerably in excess of what the Commission has ever chosen to exercise. Although permitted by that legislation to intrude into the existing programs of the provincial universities, the UGC has limited its scrutiny to new program proposals for which it must give final approval. In an interesting fulfilment of the use it or lose it admonition, a recent attempt on the part of the UGC to define the respective roles of the four higher education institutions in the provincial system was sternly rebuffed by the University of Manitoba as an unacceptable infringement on its traditional autonomy. Although the other institutions implicitly accepted the initiative, the subsequent inaction on the part of the UGC would suggest that it accepted the University of Manitoba's definition of the Commission's jurisdictional boundaries, at least for the time being.

Because government funding for the universities of Manitoba is in the form of block grants allocated by the UGC, it is not normal for any existing or new programs to be targeted for specific or supplementary funding. The usual message, upon approval of a new program, is that the university concerned may make the necessary adjustments in its general operating budget if it wishes to implement the new venture. This approach has meant that the Commission will be generally willing to endorse new initiatives, provided that the other institutions—which are invited to comment on new program proposals, regardless of their nature—do not have compelling arguments to make about overlap or redundancy. On occasion, special overtures have persuaded the UGC to allocate supplementary targeted funds for a new undertaking, but this has not been something with which the universities have been particularly comfortable. Because of the nature of government granting procedures, it is difficult to be convinced that such money is really "new," rather than a portion of the total funds that had been allocated for the university system. Moreover, there has been an inevitable uneasiness about the gradual growth of external intervention, and the concomitant diminishing in institutional autonomy, that such targeted allocations imply. The universities have for the most part favoured the freedom that block funding gives; although in a system in which the grants are annual and not driven by a formula (be it student numbers, program type, or other), planning is problematic and inter-institutional antagonisms over the outcomes of the yearly allocations inevitable.

For a period in the 1970s, the province experimented with the establishment of a separate ministry dedicated to postsecondary education (albeit sharing the same minister as the Department of Education). This new Department of Colleges and Universities Affairs was seen by many as an indication that the government was ready to give a higher priority, or at least more attention, to that element of the educational system. Despite its name, however, the new department concentrated its attention on the non-university sector, leaving the universities to the UGC. A subsequent policy decision to reunite the offices of government concerned with the various elements of the educational system—under the somewhat ironic rationale of ensuring better coordination of educational planning for the system as a whole—affected the universities hardly at all. The community colleges, however, lost their position of prominence in the government agenda with their management now relegated to a division (Postsecondary, Adult, Continuing Education and Training Division) within a ministry quite naturally consumed by the demands of the province's public school system. In the course of the 1980s, financial "restraint" gradually whittled away the staff resources even of that division, with the result that the institutions under its jurisdiction—which by provincial policy and practice could not make their own decisions about policy, staffing, or curriculum—now really had almost no one to make those decisions for them at the ministry level.

Inter-Institutional Cooperation

The creation of two new universities in 1967 did not mark a complete break with the thinking that had stood behind the *one University* policy for almost a century. In recognition of the province's relatively small population, a revised policy was adopted, declaring that the University of Manitoba—because of its size, scope, and resources—would remain the centre for professional and graduate studies within the province. Proposals from the other institutions for programs beyond those of undergraduate arts and science would not normally be entertained unless compelling reasons could be offered. Given the ambitions that characterize new universities, however, compelling reasons were quickly discovered. Gradual adjustments to the policy occurred as time went on. The first of these arose at the University of Winnipeg, which, in its earlier manifestation as United College, had attained widespread recognition for a number of its undergraduate honours programs, particularly in such fields as Economics, History, English, and Psychology. Not surprisingly, there was a strong impulse to continue to develop this strength in the realm of graduate studies; equally unsurprising was the argument that the recruitment and nurturing of first-class faculty would be made easier by the opportunity to teach and advise at the graduate level. On the nudging of the Universities Grants Commission, a cooperative arrangement reasonably consistent with the overriding provincial policy was struck. This took the form of the Joint Master's Program, which in four fields of study—History, English, Religion, and Public Administration—would have master's-level work administered under the aegis of a joint committee appointed by the Senates of the two universities. In its turn, the Joint Senate Committee would oversee the work of similar joint discipline committees in the four areas. Students would be able to take coursework at both institutions and to receive the final degree from the university of their choice.

The approach worked with variable success. In some cases—Religion and Public Administration—a successful working relationship has been maintained. The two English departments parted company at an early date, and History, although favouring a joint venture, has felt that the existing administrative and financial arrangements do not encourage continuation of the *status quo*. At the undergraduate level, a rather more successful experiment—"encouraged" by the province in response to the University of Winnipeg's desire to involve itself in teacher training—is an arrangement surrounding the Bachelor of Education program. By this agreement, the University of Winnipeg is able to admit to the program, to a number half of that entering the University of Manitoba's B.Ed. For those former students, the first three years of the B. Ed. program are completed at the University of Winnipeg (these are the years heavily comprised of arts and science courses); the final or "certificate" year—which is normally comprised exclusively of Education courses—is done at the University of Manitoba. The degree awarded for that group is from the University of Winnipeg. The general question of relationships among the various institutional members of the provincial system was one of the matters addressed by the 1993 Roblin Commission (considered below), and the question is an open one as to whether the almost thirty-year policy about centralization of professional and graduate programs will hold.

A number of political currents infuse the discussion, not the least of which is a concern that concentrating graduate and professional studies at the University of Manitoba—while perhaps defensible on academic and resource grounds—nonetheless militates against ready access to such programs on the part of people living at any distance from Winnipeg. This was an argument developed with some force by Brandon University, which has always seen itself as serving the broad catchment area of western Manitoba. In concert with vocal professional groups, Brandon has been able to persuade the Universities Grants Commission to approve master's-level programs in Music and in Education. In its turn, St. Boniface College was able to make the case that the regional francophone constituency that it serves (a community largely but by no means exclusively situated in the former city of St. Boniface, now a constituent part of Greater Winnipeg) required the opportunity for advanced study in its mother tongue. This initiative translated into a French-language Master of Education degree substantially different in approach from that offered through the Faculty of Education at the Ft. Garry campus.

Notwithstanding these initiatives, access has remained a long-standing concern in the province, particularly for inner-city, northern, and Aboriginal communities. In the absence of any institution dedicated to distance education, this concern has had to be met by a number of individual initiatives. Brandon University, for example, has been particularly prominent in this area. That institution, along with the University of Manitoba, has worked in cooperation with the province—with some measure of federal cost-sharing—in a number of access programs that have brought opportunities to those communities for study in engineering, education, social work, and the health professions. Brandon University's innovative community-based teacher education programs and the University of Manitoba's Winnipeg Centre Project are examples of these initiatives. The latter project, originally inherited from Brandon University, provides access to undergraduate professional programs—Education and Social Work—for inner-city (primarily Aboriginal) and immigrant groups which would not normally avail themselves of conventional university offerings. The University of Winnipeg, in its turn, has taken seriously its proclaimed mission as an urban university and introduced a range of opportunities for part-time and off-campus study. The University of Manitoba made its unique contribution through technology, in the development of various opportunities for distance education. Another notable initiative has been that university's special armed forces program, in which defence personnel are able to aggregate credits taken from a range of institutions attended in the course of career postings.

One enterprise does, in fact, come close to being a provincial distance education agency. In a long-standing government-supported venture, the three universities act jointly to manage what is known as "Inter-Universities North." Managed on a rotating basis by an officer of one of the three universities, the project involves the offering of credit courses to northern communities, usually in the form of a series of "fly-in" classes conducted by university faculty. The courses are those of the respective institutions but are easily transferred to the university in which the student ultimately decides to complete the degree. More recently, the province, concerned that communities to the south were similarly disadvantaged by the remoteness of the principal provincial university, persuaded a somewhat cautious University of Manitoba to assist in an arrangement by which first-year offerings would be made available in four provincial centres using, where feasible, local resources (material and human). In this way, students are able to undertake the first portion of their university studies without the expense or personal dislocation of moving to Winnipeg or Brandon.

The Community College System

If Manitoba has a postsecondary system that is not in fact a system (in the sense that no formal or informal provision has been made for coordination of the two sectors, university and community college), it has a community college sector composed of institutions which, by Canadian norms as discerned by Dennison and Gallagher (1986), are not really community colleges. The reason for this is easily enough discerned: the three institutions now carrying that label were previously vocational institutes whose basic character remained essentially unchanged when the spirit of the 1960s prompted a change in nomenclature and rhetoric. The origins of those institutions stretched back to the early 1940s and their history was in large part a response to federal funding initiatives: the Vocational Training Co-ordination Act of 1942 and the Adult Occupational Training Act of 1967. The strong dependence on these federal sources resulted in institutes whose basic mandate was occupational training and whose principal stakeholder was industry.

By the 1960s, the original Winnipeg-based Manitoba Technical Institute (established in 1948) had become the Manitoba Institute of Technology/Manitoba Institute of Applied Arts (1966), with the latter division expanding its mandate to include industrial and vocational teacher training as well as business and commercial programs. The Brandon Vocational Training Centre, which had been set up in 1961 to serve the western region of the province, became the Manitoba Vocational Centre in 1966. A northern regional institute, the Northern Manitoba Vocational Centre, was established at The Pas in the same year. Then, in 1969, as part of the new national wave toward broader community-oriented postsecondary opportunity, the three institutions suddenly became Red River Community College, Assiniboine Community College, and Keewatin Community College, respectively. Although the curriculum of the colleges expanded modestly, it and the institutional ambience remained decidedly vocational, emphasizing two-year technological programs as well as apprenticeship training in the designated trades, adult basic education, health and personal services, applied arts, business and administrative studies, and tailored programs for specific businesses, industries, and non-profit organizations. Although extensive efforts have been made to provide for part-time study throughout the province and to facilitate access to groups not yet properly represented in the province's postsecondary programs, the overall size of the college enterprise has tended to be modest in comparison to other provinces.

In addition to charges of limitations in scope and narrowness of focus, the community colleges of Manitoba were criticized for not assuming the organizational features that define an institution of higher education. Of particular concern was the colleges' bureaucratic subservience to the provincial government. Under this arrangement, detailed budget scrutiny, staffing decisions, curriculum planning and modification were all beyond the final authority of the college presidents, who were directly responsible to the Assistant Deputy Minister in charge of the Postsecondary, Adult and Continuing Education and Training Division (PACET) of the Department of Education and Training. This Division, moreover, was responsible for a range of other activities, not all directly bearing on postsecondary education *per se*. These included not just various adult education programs, the Manitoba Technical Training Centre, the ACCESS Initiative programs, the Manitoba Student Financial Assistance Program, joint training programs with other provinces but also the development, coordination, and monitoring of provincial job creation activities, coordination of immigrant language services, and provision of direct employment-related training. It is possible to see the community colleges, then, as having been as much a part of the province's economic and social policy as they were of its educational policy. This explains in part the tendency to maintain a close central control over the colleges and the reluctance to accord them the normal autonomy of educational institutions. It also underlines a major reason for the absence of any coordinated postsecondary strategy or system in the province and the absence of significant working relationships between the college and university sectors.

A major by-product of tight government control was the absence of autonomous governing boards for the colleges. With the change of rubric to community colleges in 1969, the three institutions received revamped versions of the advisory boards that had been put in place for the erstwhile technical institutes. The principal of these, the Technical and Vocational Advisory Board, which had as its mandate to counsel the minister on the system as a whole as well as to act as the specific advisory body for Red River Community College, is by a significant factor the largest participant in the system. This board was to be comprised of staff and student representatives as well as those from government, community, and local school divisions. The other two boards were similarly constituted, with the emphasis again on the qualifier "advisory," effectively ensuring that there was very little local control of college programs. Contrary to the presumed *raison d'être* of community colleges, these institutions belonged to their local communities in little more than a geographic sense.

Within the institutions themselves, 1972 saw the introduction of internal general boards which included staff and students. Unlike university senates, their role was not a legislative one but was limited once again to advice. After considerable discussion of this general issue, the provincial government finally determined in 1990 that the community college system would move to governing boards. (This was effected in 1993 through the Colleges and Consequential Amendments Act.) The ultimate role these boards will play and their impact on the character of the colleges remain yet to be seen although it is hoped that they will spur efficiency, community links, and entrepreneurship. Clearly, however, they represent a necessary if not sufficient condition for the emergence of an integrated postsecondary system.

With the enabling legislation to establish governing boards now in place, those bodies will have to come to grips with yet another perennial concern: that of the employment status of college staff. Prior to the 1993 legislation, there had been no collective bargaining unit unique to the colleges; staff are members of the broadly-based Manitoba Government Employees Association and thus public servants. Although members might in some ways benefit from representation by a large and powerful union, concerns were raised that such a bargaining unit could not take account of the special nature of an educational institution. A case in point had been the salary structure which in its public service mould was seemingly unable to correlate academic preparation and financial remuneration, a source of abiding frustration to staff wishing to improve their teaching credentials and to administrators wanting to encourage such development. With the new legislation, however, labour relations have finally been placed in the hands of the colleges themselves.

This issue of staff development has been further exacerbated by differences of academic culture within the colleges themselves, as, for example, between the trades and the professions. Although the express mandate of any community college is teaching, few of the staff have any pedagogical preparation at the time of hiring; and many do not see themselves as teachers in any professional sense. The college system has attempted to address the situation with an in-house Certificate in Adult Education which must be completed by all staff as a condition of continuing employment. But, in the view of many within the college system, only institutional autonomy—in matters such as hiring, academic qualifications, staff development, and the like—will allow the colleges to nurture the ethos and character their mandate espouses.

Like the province's universities, the colleges continue to see themselves as having regional responsibilities. Red River Community College, for example, offers courses in a number of locations in southeastern Manitoba and operates permanent regional centres in three of the larger population concentrations in the area. Assiniboine Community College, like Brandon University, has its field of responsibility in southwestern Manitoba, with a permanent Parkland Campus in Dauphin. In the special area of agricultural training, Assiniboine's mandate extends throughout the province. Keewatin Community College, of course, attends to northern Manitoba and has its own regional centres in the communities of Flin Flon and Thompson.

Shortly after the inception of the community college sector in Manitoba's postsecondary system, the province instituted a major public review of higher education—the Task Force on Postsecondary Education (the so-called Oliver Commission, after its Chairman, Michael Oliver, then President of Carleton University). This task force, which submitted its report in 1973, organized a broad range of public hearings across the province. For better or worse, however, it elicited little discernible action on the part either of government or of institutions. Among the recommendations that would have required government action were a number encouraging closer articulation between the two sectors, university and community college—that is, the development of a real postsecondary system. Other recommendations had to do with a rather dramatic decentralization of the system, with the province to be appropriately divided into manageable regions. Implicit and explicit in these recommendations was the need to make more real the community in community colleges and the desirability of breaking the tight control exercised by Winnipeg on the educational agenda of the province as a whole. Not incidentally, Winnipeg's nature as a "southern" city—in Manitoba's terms—was seen to be as much of an issue as bureaucratic centralization itself. This theme was to be repeated in subsequent years, but the concomitant vision of a northern university has yet to be realized.

Nursing Education

An ambiguous element of the higher education complex of Manitoba has been that of nursing education. While the University of Manitoba has a Faculty of Nursing offering bachelor's and master's degrees in the field, the majority of the province's nurses have received at least the first portion of their professional training in the various diploma (Registered Nurse) schools attached to the hospitals, or, in one case—Red River—to a community college. Because of the rather different educational goals and approaches of these diploma schools, as compared to the University Faculty of Nursing, an ambivalence existed in both camps as to the desirability and feasibility of so-called *ladder* approaches to professional training, by which diploma-trained nurses would be able subsequently to transfer the two years of their R.N. training to a bachelor's program. Because of this ambivalence, an arrangement allowing for some but not full transfer evolved, to no one's particular satisfaction. Recent dramatic changes in the profession and particularly the declared goal of having a bachelor's degree as the condition for entry to practice by the year 2000 have been altering the agenda quite dramatically. The hospital schools realize that they must be more closely associated with degree programs if their involvement in nursing education is to continue and the University Faculty of Nursing recognizes that it will clearly not be in a position to supply the numbers of graduates that the new policy would imply. Arrangements have therefore been painstakingly worked out to allow the Faculty and, initially, the two major hospital schools (Health Sciences Centre and St. Boniface Hospital) to collaborate in the offering of the University degree program. Because one of the hospital schools—(St. Boniface Hospital, owned by the Grey Nuns) has its own quite distinct educational philosophy—the arrangements have had to be such that the unique purposes and approach of the hospital schools and the traditional academic expectations of the University are both reasonably satisfied.

Whether these arrangements presage other such linkages between elements of the higher education system remains to be seen. In establishing its community college system, Manitoba chose what has been labelled the binary model, by which the two sectors—universities, on the one hand, and colleges and institutes, on the other—are kept distinctly separate. No university-transfer programs are offered, nor is any regular credit allowed for work taken in a community college program. One major exception to the rule exists in the case of teacher training in the areas of vocational and industrial education. That training had originally been diploma level and accordingly had been placed at Red River Community College. As teacher certification progressed to degree level, strategies were developed to link the college program with that of the University of Manitoba Faculty of Education. (Because the expensive equipment upon which those programs were based was already situated at the college, it was deemed impractical to consider duplicating those resources at the University.) The final accommodation was the currently existing joint Bachelor of Education program, of which two years are completed at Red River and two at the University of Manitoba.

The Future

By the early 1990s, it was clear that rapidly changing needs and expectations, in concert with a less than exhilarating fiscal climate, would require a fundamental re-examination of postsecondary education in the province. As the foundation to this re-examination, the provincial government established the University Education Review Commission, which quickly became known as the Roblin Commission. Unlike its predecessor of twenty years before—the Oliver Task Force—the University Education Review Commission was quite deliberately not broadly representative; like many of its contemporary counterparts, the three-member commission did not even include academic representation from inside or outside the system. It was lay leadership looking at the university under the chairmanship of a former Progressive Conservative premier of Manitoba, Senator Duff Roblin.

The provincial postsecondary institutions had the chance to make their case to the Roblin Commission—as did any other interested group or individual. The final report of December 1993 came to a conclusion not dissimilar to that of similar public inquiries elsewhere—that much of the university's case was self-serving at worst and out of touch with contemporary reality at best. The subtitle of the report conveys that message with little subtlety: *Doing Things Differently*. Ironically, the case of the community colleges was much more sympathetically received. While the universities were in effect advised to do better with less; the colleges, in the view of the Commission, should move to a doubling of enrollment over the following five years (and should enjoy first claim on any increased funding that might become available during that period).

Implicit in the commentary of the report was an assumption that, with efficiency and focus, the universities could meet the needs of the province without significant increases in their funding. The Commission operated on the assumption that there would not be any end to the existing public financial constraints "for the medium planning horizon"; it is clear that they were foreseeing an end to growth in the university sector. At the same time, they seemed to think that in the crucible of constraint those institutions could be tempered to something finer, that internal discipline could render the prospect of limited resources a challenge rather than a handicap. By the same token, there appeared to be the suspicion that the academic community might not of its own accord leap at this enticing challenge. Faculty activity must therefore be monitored by "transparent" measures of accountability and the need to "re-assert management responsibilities" recognized. Accordingly, the Boards of Governors were to "reassert their plenary role" and take a much more proactive role in working with the academic community in identifying those "strategic priorities that will contribute most to the economic, social and cultural needs of society." Clearly this would involve substantive change: "Priorities will mean program changes." And the character of that change was just as clearly implied in other of the Commission's observations. In the matter of "internal unsponsored self-directed research including graduate studies"—which the Commission saw as in fact "sponsored" by public money—there was the concern that much of the work was "only tenuously linked to Manitoba's social, cultural and economic interests." Quickly following on the heels of this observation were the shouts of alarm within the academy at the prospect of scholarship being judged primarily in terms of its relevance to elusive provincial priorities.

The same concerns with efficiency and effectiveness presumably underlay the Commission's encouragement of measures aimed at fostering a provincial system. These proposed measures included the establishment of a Cabinet-level committee on postsecondary education, which could presumably ensure inter-departmental coordination and furnish strategic guidelines. Between the government and the institutions themselves (and replacing the Universities Grants Commission) would be a Council on Postsecondary Education. This body would take a proactive role in mediating government policy into system-wide planning and budgeting and ensuring transparent accountability. To date, the government has acted to appoint a second Deputy Minister within the Department of Education and Training, with specific responsibility for advanced education and skills training. It has, however, remained silent on the larger structural recommendations.

Other perennial policy issues were pronounced upon although, here again, the ultimate governmental disposition is yet to be seen. Running through many of these specific concerns was a clear determination that the two principal sectors—universities and community colleges—should come together into something far more resembling a partnership than has been the case to date. In the matter of distance education, the conclusion clearly was that the province's postsecondary distance opportunities should continue to be provided *via* creative adjustments on the part of the existing institutions. With a rather nice twist, though, the proposal was made that Manitoba's northern community college—Keewatin—should be the postsecondary coordinating centre for that portion of the province. The government was pleased to enact this recommendation in rapid fashion, somewhat to the unease of the universities, which were uncertain about the implications for their autonomy. Another proposal—having this time to do with the very sensitive issue of Aboriginal education and Aboriginal self-determination—is still under consideration: this was the recommended establishment of a First Nations Postsecondary Education Authority. And, as in all other jurisdictions across the country, the issue of student tuition fees begged consideration. Here the Commission saw at least two problems: one having to do with basic principles and the other having to do with the historical inequities in the existing situation. It proposed that, in lieu of any further across-the-board increases, any subsequent hikes should be aimed at gradually bringing the various Faculties to the point where tuition fees covered approximately 35% of their own respective program costs. The higher program costs of graduate studies were acknowledged in the recommendation that there the proportion be in the area of 15%. It was politically important that international students be considered, of course; and there the recommendation was that fees should be double those for Canadian citizens.

In its initial response to the Roblin Commission report, the provincial government was quite frank: "The fiscal reality before the citizens of Manitoba is that there will be very little new money added to the system" (Manitoba, 1994, p. 1). Notwithstanding this recommendation, or perhaps because of this new "reality," the charge to the postsecondary system was dramatic:

> The challenge, therefore, is for our institutions to change the way they do business: establishing program priorities, transforming the learning and research environments by emphasizing multidisciplinary approaches, redefining scholarship, using information technologies, creating active partnerships with the public and private sectors of our society, cooperating with other post-secondary institutions and providing quality education on campus, at home and in the workplace to full- and part-time students. To meet the fiscal challenge and simultaneously respond to the demands of the community will require nothing short of re-engineering and redesigning the education enterprise so that universities and community colleges can improve their contribution to the social, cultural and economic development of the province. (p. 1)

In their more specific objectives, the government showed itself in fundamental agreement with the Commission itself. The "agenda for change," as it was called, was to come in the form of a "challenge":

> . . . setting institutional priorities, creating centres of specialization, redesigning how universities conduct their internal affairs, designing an effective accountability framework,

developing mechanisms for greater cooperation, coordination and articulation between and among universities and community colleges, exploring more aggressively interprovincial cooperation, adopting communications technology as a means to greater efficiency and effectiveness in the learning process, ensuring accessibility to those who wish to pursue post-secondary education. (p. 2)

On some of these matters the boards of the postsecondary institutions were to report within a six-month period; the government agencies would explore others themselves or in consultation with the institutions. That the game was to be played by new rules is to be seen in the government's admonition that priority-setting will mean the termination of programs and that the establishment of centres of specialization will be undertaken within the province's Framework for Economic Growth "and to such other areas deemed important to the province" (p. 2). Promised from the government side are a funding formula based on the desired new accountability, a process for credit transfer, a tuition fee policy, a new access policy, and a framework for inter-provincial cooperation.

Conclusions

At the moment, Manitoba clearly faces a confluence of issues concerning the character and future of its postsecondary system. These issues have affected the system's various constituencies in different ways and were the subject of a wide range of pointed submissions to the Roblin Commission. The final determination the provincial government makes respecting action on the Commission's recommendations should, in yet unpredictable ways, refashion the face of that system.

Among the principal challenges to be grappled with is the development of clear and public provincial policy on research, development, and training, such that the shape and development of the postsecondary system itself can be planned and measured against an articulated vision of the province's economic, industrial, scientific, social, and cultural future. Connected to this argument is an injunction that policy-making in the broad plane of research and development activities within the province be more effectively coordinated with that for postsecondary education itself by strategies yet to be specified but having to do with such matters as a still largely underdeveloped Research Park. Needed as well is more effective coordination among the various provincial ministries, for example, with Education and Health.

The implementation of this new vision will have some practical implications. Among these are an urgent need for provincial support of university-based research, presumably in a structure similar to the arrangements in place at the federal level. The province is seen to be seriously trailing other provinces in that respect, to the detriment of university research itself and to the detriment of provincial economic, social, and industrial development. The Manitoba Health Research Council already performs a role analogous to that of the Medical Research Council, but a compelling need is seen for provincial counterparts of the Natural Sciences and Engineering Research Council and the Social Sciences and Humanities Research Council. Not unrelated is the urgent need for significantly increased student financial assistance, particularly at the graduate level. The province has lagged behind comparable jurisdictions in provision of fellowship support, to the presumed detriment not only of its university-bound citizenry but also of the research enterprise that is so intimately associated with a strong graduate presence. The concomitant weakening of the province's position to attract and foster public and private sector "R & D" activities is also underlined by the critics.

Another matter clearly at issue is that of access, particularly in the university sector. The institutions of the province have maintained a commitment to the proposition that they should be accessible to any Manitoba resident meeting the basic admission requirements. Austerity is straining that principle, as it is everywhere in Canada, but equally as disturbing is the message conveyed, perhaps most dramatically by the *Maclean's Magazine* comparative rankings of Canadian universities, that the institutional consequences of broad access—as, for example, relatively high rates of attrition and relatively modest entrance standards—are deemed to be incompatible with national and international *status* (a matter of more than vanity in the competition for elusive research funding and in the attracting of the best students and staff). It may be that the province will have to rethink the mechanisms and agencies through which the social policy of access is to be effected.

The increasingly strident calls for a highly skilled workforce, supported by adequate opportunities for life-long learning and career development, have been a major factor in the recent implicit public policy shift toward encouraging increased collaboration between the university and community college sectors. With little experience in this kind of cooperation and in the face of several reservations and diminishing resources, the path toward a greater degree of system in the relationship of those two sectors is not yet clearly discernible. In the university sector itself, it remains to be seen whether the province is now ready to resume the initiative abandoned a few years ago by the UGC of attempting to articulate a plan that would define the roles of the component institutions. This was implicitly done some twenty years ago through publication of the Oliver Task Force Report (without, however, any subsequent legislative action), but such a demarcation of territory and mandate has never been explicitly articulated as public policy. Now the prospect of continuing austerity, the need to bring the two sectors of the postsecondary system out of their respective solitudes, and the apparent inability to nurture a coherent and appropriately diverse system through the processes of natural selection may well force the issue, with results as yet unpredictable.

References

Bedford, A.G. (1976). *The University of Winnipeg: A history of the founding colleges*. Toronto: University of Toronto Press.

Dennison, J.D., and Gallagher, P. (Eds.) (1986). *Canada's community colleges: A critical analysis*. Vancouver: UBC Press.

Gregor, A., and Hechter, F. (1993). Public Attitudes Toward the University: The 1991 Winnipeg Area Study. *CHERD Occasional Papers in Higher Education, 3*. Winnipeg: University of Manitoba.

Gregor, A., and Wilson, K. (Eds.) (1979). *Issues in higher education*. Winnipeg: University of Manitoba.

Gregor, A., and Wilson, K. (Eds.) (1979). *Higher education in Canada: Historical perspectives*. Winnipeg: University of Manitoba.

Gregor, A., and Wilson, K. (Eds.) (1984). *The development of education in Manitoba*. Dubuque: Kendall/Hunt.

Manitoba (1967). Manitoba council on higher learning. *The community of colleges: A report of the committee on college structure*.

Manitoba (1991). *Bill 49: The Colleges and Consequential Amendments Act*.

Manitoba (1993). *The colleges act. Appendix: College governance initiative*.

Manitoba (1994). *Response of the Government of Manitoba to the report of the University Review Commission*. Winnipeg.

Manitoba Delegation, National Forum on Post-Secondary Education (1987). *Discussion paper*. Winnipeg.

Manitoba. Department of Education and Training (1993). *Final report of the Task Force on Distance Education and Technology*. Winnipeg.

Manitoba. Department of Education and Training. Skills Training Advisory Committee (1990). *Partners in skills development*. Winnipeg.

Manitoba. Task Force on Post-Secondary Education in Manitoba, Michael J. Oliver, chairman (1973). *Post-secondary education in Manitoba*. Winnipeg: Queen's Printer.

Manitoba. University Education Review Commission, Honourable Duff Roblin, chairman (1994). *Post-secondary education in Manitoba: Doing things differently*. Winnipeg.

Morton, W.L. (1957). *One university. A history of the University of Manitoba*. McClelland and Stewart.

University of Manitoba (1992). *An interim executive brief to the University Education Review Commission*.

University of Manitoba (1994). *Plan 2000: Toward a new University of Manitoba*.

Higher Education in Ontario

Glen A. Jones

Introduction

The story of higher education in Ontario begins long before the creation of the Dominion of Canada, but hindsight suggests that many of the core themes of the tale emerged as part of a flurry of activity in a single decade. In the period from 1960 to the early 1970s, the basic structures and mechanisms associated with the province's two higher education sectors emerged. For the next two decades, higher education in Ontario was characterized by system growth in terms of enrollment and institutional activity, but the basic structural arrangements associated with Ontario universities and the colleges of applied arts and technology actually changed very little. Recent events suggest that Ontario is about to go through another phase of major transformation.

In this Chapter I describe the evolution and development of higher education in Ontario in terms of provincial policies and structures. The Chapter is organized chronologically, with particular emphasis to the period from 1945 to 1995.

Before 1945

The history of higher education in Ontario can be traced back to the granting of a Royal Charter for King's College, York (Toronto), in 1827. Following the American Revolution, large numbers of individuals loyal to the British Empire sought refuge in the northern colonies where they could live under the protection of the Crown and with the comfort of British culture and traditions. The movement to create an institution of higher learning in Upper Canada was based on a desire to maintain those cultures and traditions, dispel the evils of republicanism, and provide an intellectual training ground for the next generation of colonial leaders. At the forefront in the campaign for a new institution was Bishop John Strachen, a man whose influence extended far beyond the Church of England into the oligarchical political structures of the colony. He played a central role in obtaining the Royal Charter for the new institution. It turned out to be an inauspicious beginning, since King's College was to be the subject of bitter political and denominational debates for the next two decades.

The political problem created by the charter was that King's College was clearly perceived to be closely associated with the Church of England but was supported by public resources. For those associated with other denominations, the arrangement seemed unfair and inequitable. As new denominational institutions began to emerge, such as Queen's College at Kingston (Presbyterian) and Victoria College in Cobourg (Methodist), political questions concerning denominational favouritism and the appropriate structural arrangements for public higher education in the colony became the fuel for a series of heated, public debates. After years of controversy, the King's College initiative was transformed into the University of Toronto, a publicly supported university built on a secular base. In 1868, a year after the creation of the new province of Ontario through Canadian confederation, provincial leaders attempted to extinguish the flames of denominational infighting by declaring that public support would only be provided to secular (non-denominational) institutions.

This new provincial policy did little to stifle the development of denominational colleges following confederation, and over the next seven decades only Queen's (Kingston) and the University of Western Ontario (London) would move to join the University of Toronto as secular, provincially supported institutions. In fact, the most important developments in higher education in Ontario in the period between confederation and 1945 were the growth in denominational colleges, the gradual development of technical, non-university institutions, and a formal review of institutional governance at the University of Toronto.

Denominational colleges began to emerge in most large towns in the province. For example, the College of Bytown (Catholic) was created in 1849, changed its name to the College of Ottawa in 1861, and obtained a papal charter in 1889. Assumption College (Catholic) was incorporated in 1858. McMaster University (Baptist) obtained a provincial charter in 1887.

While select secondary schools were beginning to play a major role in providing technical/vocational training in response to the needs of the slowly industrializing province, a number of specialized educational institutions were also created. The Toronto Normal School, which operated school teacher education programs, opened in 1847, and other teacher training institutes were soon in operation in Guelph, Hamilton, and

Kingston. The Government of Canada created a military college at Kingston in 1874 (which, following approval of the Queen, became the Royal Military College in 1878) in order to train future officers in military tactics, engineering, and general scientific knowledge. Originally viewed as a specialized technical institution, the College would later evolve into a degree-granting college associated with the university sector. The provincial government created a School of Agriculture in 1874, later to become the Ontario Agricultural College and Experimental Farm (Guelph). Most of the College's educational activities were associated with a two-year diploma course, though the College also affiliated with the University of Toronto in order to offer degree programs.

While the University of Toronto was now firmly entrenched as a publicly supported "provincial university," by the turn of the century questions began to arise as to the relationship between the university and the government and the structure of decision-making within the university corporation. Accusations of petty patronage and partisan interference, including the appointment of professors by political leaders without consulting the University president, eventually led to the creation of a royal commission. The Flavelle Commission report of 1906 was to become one of the most important documents in the history of Ontario, and perhaps Canadian, higher education. In reviewing the situation, the Commission concluded that

> despite the zealous efforts of statesmen and educationalists the University became on many occasions in the past the sport of acrimonious party disputes. Its interests were inextricably confused in the popular mind with party politics, although with these it had, in reality, little concern. (Alexander, 1906, pp. 275-276)

Commission members studied both British and American structural arrangements and concluded that the successful operation of the University required that the institution be separated from "the direct superintendence of political powers" (Alexander, 1906, p. 276). The structural solution recommended by the Commission involved two basic concepts. The first was the delegation of government authority over the institution to a corporate board. While government was to continue to provide annual operating support, the direct supervision of the University was to be assigned to a governing board composed largely of members appointed by government. The second concept was bicameralism. While arguing that the board should play a central role in overseeing the administrative affairs of the University, the Commission also recommended that the University of Toronto Senate, with major responsibilities for academic matters, be retained. The new Senate included representatives from each faculty, the administration, the affiliated colleges, and alumni. The notion of a bicameral university governance structure was far from original since several Canadian universities had already experimented with similar arrangements, but it was the Royal Commission on the University of Toronto which clearly articulated the rationale and framework for bicameralism (Cameron, 1991; Jones, 1992). A draft University of Toronto Act, delegating responsibilities for the institution to the two governing bodies, was prepared by the Commission and was quickly passed, with few amendments, by the Ontario Legislature (Wallace, 1927). This governance structure was quickly adopted by the new universities emerging in Western Canada and gradually became the dominant model for university governance throughout the country (Jones, 1996).

In summary, by 1945, higher education in Ontario included three publicly supported universities, a variety of denominational private colleges, and a small number of specialized institutes associated with technical, professional, or occupational training. The provincial government had clearly established a policy of providing public support only to secular institutions.

Evolutionary Expansion (1945-1960)

While it is generally argued that the post-war expansion of higher education signalled a tremendous increase of activity in the sector, it is important to recall that the initial phases of this transformation, at least in Ontario, were evolutionary and that it was not until the period beginning around 1960 that the magnitude and speed of change became dramatic. In office from 1934 to 1943, the Government of Mitchell Hepburn viewed higher education as a low priority, and the provincially supported institutions languished on the margins of a political agenda dominated first by Depression-era economics and then by the enterprise of war. Ontario universities responded quickly to the national war effort and were, for a time, transformed into public service institutions whose resources were openly accessible to the public interest. When the war was over and the huge federally supported cohort of veterans began to find their way onto university campuses, the universities moved quickly, often borrowing temporary buildings, facilities, and equipment from war surplus in an attempt to expand in parallel with the new level of demand. While universities began to play a much larger role in the political and economic arena, it was a role largely supported and funded by the Government of Canada rather than the Government of Ontario.

While higher education did not seem to be an important priority of the Ontario government, the population was gradually beginning to view universities (and even more gradually, other forms of postsecondary education) as important instruments of economic and social development. War-time propaganda had highlighted the important contribution of university research to the war effort, and, as veterans began to move from military service to university to jobs in the provincial economy, the perceived role of the university began to change. As Paul Axelrod has noted:

> The Second World War, which disrupted and transformed so many facets of Canadian life, was instrumental in altering public perceptions about the respectability and value of higher education. The *actual* changes in the post-secondary system in Ontario between 1945 and 1960, however, were not profound. . . . public spending was still restrained by a frugal government more interested in highway building than higher learning. (Axelrod, 1982, p. 14)

Since higher education was a relatively low priority, there was relatively little need for a policy development infrastructure within government. Universities were considered autonomous institutions, and formal interaction between institutions and government was often limited to annual requests for operating support from the small number of provincially supported institutions. Denominational institutions, while receiving federal government support under the veterans program, were denied access to provincial support.

At the same time, there were a number of evolutionary changes taking place. The increasing diversification of the provincial economy was creating new demands for skilled labour, impoverished denominational institutions, viewing funds from the public purse as the only source of support for expansion, began to move towards secularization, and, by the late 1950s, the government was beginning to experiment with advisory bodies designed to guide the increasingly complex public policy matters associated with the sector.

The Ontario economy was a major beneficiary of Canada's successful economic transformation and almost complete demilitarization following the war. As the industrial base continued to diversify, the labour requirements of industry began to change. Since the educational requirements of business involved the need for new types of skilled labour, needs that were quite different than the education and professional training associated with the public universities, the government began to invest in technical vocational training beyond the level of basic training available through the secondary school system. The creation of the Lakehead Technical Institute in 1946 and the Ryerson Institute of Technology in 1948 represented major steps in this new direction within postsecondary education, though within a decade the former was transformed into the Lakehead College of Arts, Science and Technology on its evolutionary path towards university status. The government also went on to provide support for a small number of technical/vocational or trade training institutes throughout the province.

The number of public universities began to grow. McMaster University in Hamilton began to distance itself from Baptist control in order to become a secular institution and therefore eligible for public support. McMaster received its first government grant in 1947. Carleton, with roots going back to the Ottawa Young Men's Christian Association, became a secular university under provincial legislation passed in 1952 (Fleming, 1971). By 1960 there were five independent, secular universities obtaining direct provincial government support, though it was already clear that this number would soon grow rapidly given the level of public support for further expansion.

Until 1951, Ontario did not have a single office or agency with responsibility for higher education, and as the number of institutions grew and the Government of Canada became increasingly interested in the higher education sector, it became clear that the Government of Ontario would have to develop some mechanism for considering policy matters. From 1951 to 1956 the role was assumed by a part-time consultant to the Minister of Education, but in 1956 the Premier appointed a committee of senior government officials to evaluate provincial needs and recommend funding policy. In 1958 this group was replaced by the University Committee, composed of senior civil servants from the Departments of Economics, Education, and Treasury. By the end of the decade, however, it was clear that no one was particularly pleased with the arrangement. The demands on the Committee were simply too heavy to be accomplished by a group of individuals who viewed higher education policy as only a small component of their work, and the lack of representation from the university community raised concerns among the leaders of the publicly supported institutions (Beard, 1983).

The Structural Revolution (1960-1970)

By 1960 there was no longer a question of whether the infrastructure for higher education in Ontario should be expanded; the issue was how to do it. Evidence of the public need and desire for university expansion was coming from all directions. Opinion poll data, provincial government predictions of enrollment demand, economic arguments for increased investment in human capital, and business demands for educated labour, all reinforced the need for action to be taken.

The first matter to be dealt with concerned the question of how to expand university enrollment. While some universities argued for the creation of junior colleges, and some government officials argued for a mammoth expansion of the existing institutions, it soon became clear that both the creation of new comprehensive universities as well as a tremendous expansion in enrollment and program offerings at existing institutions would be necessary (Axelrod, 1982). In this matter, the government played more of a facilitative, rather than proactive or leadership role, by encouraging the secularization of denominational institutions (so that they could obtain public support), funding and supporting the transformation of specialized institutes into universities, and in several cases, chartering new institutions in response to community-based initiatives. Ontario was soon to have fifteen universities: Brock, Carleton, Guelph, Lakehead, Laurentian, McMaster, Ottawa, Queen's, Toronto, Trent, Waterloo, Western Ontario, Windsor, Wilfred Laurier, and York. Each of these institutions was autonomous and had its own government charter. All were secular, and all received the bulk of their operating support through government grants. Denominational institutions still existed, but many entered into affiliation or federation arrangements with public universities in order to obtain government support for students enrolled in non-theological programs, and the others functioned as theological or bible colleges offering religious studies.

As the publicly supported university sector expanded, the government struggled to find ways to determine levels of operating support per institution as well as monitor and plan in an environment of constant change. In 1961 the University Committee was replaced by the Advisory Committee on University Affairs (which included non-government members) which survived only three years. In 1964 the government created the Department of University Affairs, with William Davis as the first Minister, and a new advisory body called the Committee on University Affairs. By 1967 the job of Chair of the Committee had become a full-time position. The new Committee included representatives nominated by the university committee and was designed to play a "buffer" role as a neutral policy advisor rather than a direct appendage of government. While only a few years before government involvement in the university sector had been largely informal, there was now a distinct government ministry and, for the first time, full-time policy development and research staff.

While the government's new policy infrastructure quickly became involved in a number of important issues, they did not develop a master plan for the Ontario university sector. The government continued to support, or at least tolerate, a high level of institutional autonomy, even among the fledgeling institutions that were only just emerging within the sector. When a commission reviewing graduate program development recommended the creation of a University of Ontario, based on the model of the University of California, as a way of rationalizing the sector, the reaction was almost universally negative. It was clear that direct government control of the university sector was not a viable policy option.

Instead of direct control, a system of checks and balances was created within the sector. A formula-financing system was developed as a way of determining system needs and allocating those funds through a verifiable, equitable funding mechanism. At the root of this new arrangement was a calculation of enrollment, weighted by program in order to recognize differences in program costs. The formula provided a means for determining the amount of support the government should provide to the institutions as well as the share that each institution would receive. In order to maintain a high level of institutional autonomy, the decisions related to how these funds were to be spent were left in the hands of the individual institutions. Over time, the formula was amended in order to increase stability and allow institutions to do longer-range planning. These amendments included the introduction of a moving-average calculation based on past enrollment and a decision that government, rather than the formula, would determine the amount of support available to the system and the formula would only be used as an allocative mechanism.

The creation of the Ontario Council on Graduate Studies (OCGS) by the universities represented another important mechanism for accountability within the sector. As part of a voluntary arrangement between the institutions, new proposals for graduate programs were subjected to a review process which included an external, expert appraisal of program quality. While the Council initially focused on new graduate programs, its role was gradually extended to include the periodic appraisal of all existing graduate programs. The government eventually tied the appraisal process to the formula-funding arrangement: A successful appraisal was required before the enrollment in a new program would be included in the formula, and a successful review from a periodic appraisal was necessary in order to continue to receive support for students in an existing program.

The Ontario Council on Graduate Studies was created by the Council of Ontario Universities (COU), essentially the committee of presidents of provincially assisted universities which had been meeting regularly since 1962. In addition to providing a forum for discussing matters of common interest, COU began to play a role in providing sector-wide data to support the policy and advocacy responsibilities of the Council and gradually developed a number of provincial services supported by fees paid by member institutions, including a centralized office for processing admission applications and a transit service to transport correspondence and goods between institutions.

Organizations representing other estates within the university sector also emerged during this period. The Ontario Council (and later Confederation) of University Faculty Associations was established in 1963. Governed by a body composed of one representative from each member organization, the Confederation quickly established itself as a strong participant in provincial discussions (Fleming, 1972). The Ontario Union of Students represented student interests, though the organization was later abandoned and replaced, in the early 1970s, by the Ontario Federation of Students.

While there were tremendous changes taking place related to the expansion of university education in Ontario, even more dramatic events were taking place in the non-university sector. As the Ontario economy continued to flourish, there were increasing demands for new forms of technical/vocational education. Ontario's trade schools and technical institutions represented a patchwork quilt of educational services, but few viewed the existing institutions as having the capacity to offer the comprehensive range of programs that would be required to fuel the Ontario economy. In 1965, William Davis announced that the Government was about to create a new level and type of institution, the College of Applied Arts and Technology (CAAT).

The CAATs were designed to be both separate and distinct from the universities. As crown corporations, they would be subject to provincial regulation, but each would have its own governing board composed of representatives of the local community, as well as program advisory committees including representation from local industry, so as to ensure that colleges were responsive to community needs. This community focus was reinforced by the notion of placing colleges in various geographic regions of the province, though the government intentionally avoided the term "community college." Each college would provide a comprehensive range of postsecondary technical/vocational training programs as well as support apprenticeship and skills training/upgrading programs.

One of the more controversial elements of the CAAT mission was that the colleges were not designed to operate university-transfer programs. There were a number of reasons for this decision. There was strong opposition to a transfer role from a number of influential university presidents, and since it now seemed clear that there would soon be a university in most urban centres in the province, the central rationale for creating junior colleges in order to facilitate geographic access no longer existed. Since the new institutional infrastructure would be heavily subsidized by a federal government program, there was some concern that directing some of this financial support to transfer programs, in an environment where the federal government was also subsidizing university expansion, might be problematic. There was also a concern that a transfer function might place the new colleges in a subservient role to the university sector, creating institutions viewed as second class when the objective of government was to create first-class institutions with a distinct mission.

The speed in which the government's proposal was implemented was simply amazing. In 1967, only two years after the formal announcement, 19 colleges opened their doors. Using a combination of new buildings, existing facilities associated with the old technical institutions and vocational centres, and rented space, the CAATs moved quickly to create a unique identity and a wide range of program offerings. Within five years the CAATs enrolled more than 35,000 full-time students in postsecondary programs, and even more part-time students (Vision 2000, 1990).

The basic structure of the CAAT sector paralleled the university sector in many respects. A Council of Regents was created in order to provide the government with policy advice on the development of the sector, though the Council soon assumed a role as an agency of government rather than an intermediary or buffer body.

The pace and magnitude of change in Ontario higher education structures during the 1960s were nothing short of revolutionary. By the end of the decade, the province had a greatly expanded university sector, an entirely new network of technical/vocational colleges, and a new government department and related advisory structures.

Structural Stability (1970-1990)

The systemic and structural expansion of higher education in Ontario ended in the early 1970s as many of the influential factors which had facilitated growth began to diminish in importance. The notion that there was a direct relationship between economic growth and educational investment quickly came into question as a major recession forced the provincial economy into neutral gear, and the provincial government, concerned with the rapid speed with which higher education appeared to be able to consume public resources, began to apply the brakes. At the same time, demographic studies began to raise questions concerning the need for further expansion of higher education as the post-war baby-boom passed through the educational system leaving behind a smaller traditional cohort of secondary school students. While both the universities and government continued to predict increased demand, at least in the short term, the actual increase in applications fell well below system estimates for several years at the beginning of the decade. Within a few short years, debates over how best to expand higher education in Ontario were replaced with discussions of how to reduce or stabilize institutional expenditures within the context of the new economic climate (Axelrod, 1982).

The structures and mechanisms introduced in the 1960s in order to coordinate and facilitate growth were now employed to constrain or control system expansion. While there continued to be an expansion of programs and activities at the institutional level, the higher education superstructure in Ontario entered a period of "modest modifications and structural stability" characterized, as I have previously argued, by attempts to stimulate or initiate change within the constraints and boundaries associated with the structural arrangements that had emerged by the end of the 1960s (Jones, 1991).

Central to these structural arrangements was the emergence of two distinct higher education sectors: the university sector and the CAAT sector. With the assumption that the two sectors played very different roles, distinct mechanisms and structures emerged in each sector, in fact the two sectors operated in parallel under distinct branches of the same Ministry.

Each sector had an advisory or intermediary body designed to provide advice to government and distinct funding and regulatory mechanisms. Instead of a single higher education system, Ontario possessed two sectors, and the sector, rather than the totality of provincial higher education, was the focal point for policy discussions.

For the university sector, these structural arrangements were based on a number of important notions: institutional autonomy, the regulation of degree granting, and the equal treatment of institutions within the sector. Sectoral arrangements continued to respect, or at least tolerate, a high level of institutional autonomy. The principle of only providing government support to secular institutions gradually evolved into a policy of regulating and controlling the authority to grant degrees. Using this "public monopoly" over degree granting, an operating policy that became law under the Degree Granting Act of 1983, the government limited expansion in terms of the number of universities (except for bible colleges and theological schools offering religious instruction) and directly regulated the ability of out-of-province institutions to offer degree programs in Ontario (Skolnik, 1987). To date, only one private, degree-granting institution has emerged under this framework: The Institute for Christian Studies (Toronto). While the universities were obviously quite different in terms of program mix, size, and historical development, the province created a common formula for determining the allocation of provincial grants that treated institutions equally. Subsequent policies served to reinforce this notion of institutional equality, and almost all new sectoral initiatives involved some allocative formula or competitive component designed to depoliticize and equalize the treatment of institutions by government.

These basic principles, combined with the checks and balances associated with the structural arrangements that had emerged in the 1960s, served as the basis for a form of political equilibrium within the sector, though these arrangements were not viewed as utopian by government or any of the other sectoral interests. Government became concerned with the lack of rational planning within the system, but minor attempts to promote rationalization or tamper with the power structures of the sector were less than successful. An attempt to strengthen the role of the intermediary body ran into political difficulties resulting in the creation, by order-in-council, of a new Ontario Council on University Affairs with essentially the same advisory mandate as the former Committee on University Affairs. Two major government commissions made recommendations concerning sector rationalization and institutional differentiation (Commission on the Future Development of the Universities of Ontario, 1984; Committee on the

Future Role of the Universities in Ontario, 1981), but the government failed to even formally respond to these suggestions.

Instead of making major changes to the structural arrangements in the university sector, the government approach to university policy was one of "managerialism at the margins" (Jones, 1994). The only significant change to the mechanism for allocating operating grants was the introduction of funding corridors, negotiated benchmarks which, combined with other aspects of the formula, provided stable shares of available operating support as long as institutions did not stray beyond plus or minus 3% of the formula enrollment calculation. Most government initiatives during this period, therefore, involved attempts to stimulate or modify sectoral activity without changing the basic arrangements for core operating support. A number of new programs were created to stimulate university-industry research partnerships, including a matching-grants program (Bell, 1990). Perhaps the largest initiative involved the creation of Centres of Excellence, publicly supported research corporations. Each centre involved the linkage of expertise in one or more universities for the exploration of a specified research area involving ongoing contact with industry. Other new targeted programs provided mechanisms for supporting research overhead costs, bilingual programs, and the special costs associated with operating programs in the north.

The universities were primarily concerned with funding issues. While operating grants were allocated via a mechanism that protected institutional autonomy, the institutions felt that they had little influence over the level of support. During most of this period institutional leaders as well as representatives of other sectoral interest groups lobbied for increased support with extremely limited success. Since the operating grant allocative mechanism included a calculation of tuition fees, government also controlled the second largest source of institutional revenue, and institutional leaders found themselves in a situation where they were unable to have a significant impact on the amount of income their institutions received regardless of the administrative policies they introduced. The only major exception involved private donations, and almost all institutions initiated private fund-raising campaigns.

While the various parties were clearly frustrated with these arrangements, there was some concern that major changes might actually worsen rather than improve the situation. Government officials might dream of a rationalized higher education system, but the sectoral arrangements were successful in addressing the two most important goals of government during this period: increasing accessibility and reducing or stabilizing the level of government allocations. Universities were dissatisfied with the level of government support but were pleased with the fact that the arrangements served to prevent direct government intervention and allowed for considerable institutional freedom.

Financial issues were also a major area of concern within the CAAT sector. Like the university sector, the level of operating grant support for postsecondary programs was determined by government and allocated on the basis of a formula. Unlike the university sector, the CAAT sector formula rewarded growth. Institutions which increased enrollment at a higher rate than their peers received a larger share of available support. Another important difference between the sectors was that the CAATs had other sources of income, especially related to the non-postsecondary side of activities (trades, skills development, basic education). Federal government programs directed towards employment training began to play a major role in institutional decision making. In order to reduce the influence and impact of changing federal programs, the Ontario government intervened and began to negotiate Ontario-specific arrangements with the federal government which involved routing support through a provincial Ministry of Skills Development. Direct federal initiatives continued to have an influence on the sector. However, this influence decreased in relative importance as the level of federal activity declined and the federal approach shifted in favour of decentralized decision-making structures and the use of a broader range of training providers. Finally, contract-training arrangements came to represent another important source of revenue for many CAATs, though this source of income continued to represent only a small percentage of the budget of most colleges.

These changing patterns of support had an obvious impact on the sector, especially since many of the provincial and federal programs were targeted towards specific training activities. Colleges were forced to respond promptly to new skills development initiatives. The fact that the allocative mechanism for postsecondary programs was enrollment sensitive meant that these institutions also had to respond to changes in demand for postsecondary programs and, when appropriate, create new programs in order to maintain or increase enrollment. While the structural arrangements of the sector were relatively stable during this period, these arrangements led to changes at the institutional level. As institutions responded to changes in targeted programs and the needs of their local communities, greater institutional specialization began to emerge within the sector. Far less autonomous than their university counterparts, a subtle form of institutional differentiation began to emerge within the boundaries associated with government regulation and a common mandate.

Labour relations was another important area of concern during this period. While labour matters were an institutional concern in the university sector, CAAT employees unionized on a provincial level with the Council of Regents playing the role of management in collective bargaining. The province-wide faculty union went on strike in 1984 and again in 1989, with workload and salaries as the central issues of disagreement. Province-wide bargaining has been viewed as a major problem within the sector, both because of the complexity of creating terms of employment that are appropriate for a huge range of sectoral activities and because of the limitations that centrally negotiated contracts place on institutional decision-making structures. On the other hand, college faculty representatives, unlike their university counterparts, are able to negotiate employment contracts with the same entity which is chiefly responsible for determining the level of support that will be allocated to the system. Though a government commission recommended minor modifications to these structural arrangements, no changes were made (Gandz, 1988).

The fact that there was no formal interaction between the two sectors of Ontario higher education was becoming a subject of some discussion by the end of the 1980s. Some leaders within the CAAT sector, impressed with the transfer-program arrangements in British Columbia and Alberta, began to argue that the CAATs should offer university-transfer programs or, at the very least, that universities should do more in terms of facilitating the movement of students from one sector to the other. While most of these discussions focused on student mobility from the CAAT sector to the university sector, the number of students moving from universities to CAATs was also increasing, and several CAATs introduced after-degree programs designed to provide students with employable skills to supplement their undergraduate education.

By the early 1990s, Ontario possessed a large higher education infrastructure. Changes in the university sector included the transformation of Ryerson Polytechnical University, which evolved from a technical school into a polytechnic before obtaining full university status, and Nipissing University, a former affiliate college of Laurentian University, as well as the full integration of the Ontario Institute for Studies in Education, formerly an administratively independent entity, into the University of Toronto. These changes brought the number of provincially supported universities in Ontario to 17, with the Ontario College of Art as the only non-degree institution considered part of the sector. There were now 25 colleges of applied arts and technology, the three most recent additions being colleges where French is the primary language of instruction. In addition the Ontario higher education system, broadly defined, included the federally supported Royal Military College, 4 agricultural colleges, the Michener Institute of Applied Health Sciences, the Canadian Memorial Chiropractic College, the Canadian Coast Guard College, a variety of bible schools and theological colleges, and over 200 privately operated technical schools.

From Sectoral Approach to Macro-level Policy (From 1990)

From the mid-1970s, the funding and regulation of higher education had been split between two levels of authority within government. The level of government funds available to the two sectors had always been determined by cabinet through its traditional budget exercises, but during most of the 1960s and early 1970s the sectors were usually given what the sectors said they needed. As the importance of higher education began to diminish in political terms, the relationship between what the sectors wanted and what the government thought was appropriate became far less direct. No longer the priority it once was, the locus of control for determining the level of financial support for higher education gradually moved away from the sectors and into the much more complex and politicized arenas associated with macro-level policy. Higher education became one of a wide range of policy areas competing for scarce public resources. While the institutions and relevant interest groups seemed to have limited influence over the level of government support, the sector continued to be the focal point for discussions of regulation and resource allocation.

The Vision 2000 project provided a good example of both the strengths and weaknesses of the sectoral approach. In 1988, the Minister of Colleges and Universities asked the Council of Regents to conduct a comprehensive review of the Ontario CAATs in order to develop a vision for the CAAT sector in the year 2000. Charles Pascal, then Chair of the Council, organized a major task force with representation from a wide range of groups both inside and outside the sector. The final report of the steering committee was released in 1990 (Vision 2000, 1990).

The Vision 2000 review was as comprehensive as it was consultative. The project involved a series of original research projects, the preparation of numerous background papers and discussion documents, and the participation of over 100 individuals on working study teams. The success of the review was largely a function of the fact that Pascal and others were able to bring together various interested parties to participate in a province-wide discussion of sectoral issues, and in doing so, both reaffirm the importance of the CAATs as well as, by stimulating research activity for the review, provide a much clearer sense of what was being accomplished within the sector. One major recommendation of the review was that CAAT programs should be periodically reviewed based on sector-wide standards. Government quickly provided financial support for the initiative, leading to the creation of the College Standards and Accreditation Council.

The central core of the Vision 2000 review, however, was a reaffirmation of the mandate and role of Ontario CAATs, a perspective that was hardly surprising given the sectoral mandate of the review and the broad participation of sectoral interests. Turning to the issue of university-CAAT linkages, the task force did not stray into the issue of sectoral territoriality, instead arguing that the level of cooperative activities between the two sectors should increase, calling on the government to expand the opportunities for student mobility between sectors and recommending the creation of an institute "without walls" to facilitate the coordination of arrangements between universities and colleges. These recommendations have led to an increased level of articulation arrangements between individual universities and CAATs and some minor government initiatives, including the creation of a "transfer guide" (Ontario, 1994). Hindsight, however, suggests that the review failed to resolve this issue, in large part because issues that transcend sectoral boundaries require provincial, rather than sectoral, responses and there is no mechanism or forum that transcends these boundaries within Ontario higher education.

While Vision 2000 was based on a sectoral approach to higher education policy, a new, major provincial government initiative took higher education in a very different direction. Bob Rae's New Democratic Party had been elected on the basis of a social democratic agenda and for several years the government moved to strengthen social programs. While government spending increased, the province experienced sudden and dramatic decreases in provincial tax revenues associated with the recession of the early 1990s. The government began to shift its focus and direction as the size of the provincial deficit became an immense political issue.

The Rae Government's solution was called "The Social Contract," though neither the framework nor the implementation process would have pleased Rousseau. The general principle was that the government would reduce expenditures to every component of the broader public sector but avoid a large-scale downsizing of the civil service by providing a legislative framework allowing for the temporary reduction of salaries through unpaid vacation days. Since many of the decisions made under the "Social Contract" arrangements were unilateral but conducted under the facade of consultation, the entire program became a political time bomb in wait for the next election.

Since both the university and CAAT sectors were defined as being part of the broader public service, representatives of both sectors found themselves within the framework of this arrangement. For both sectors, the "Social Contract" meant that the cabinet was not only deciding the level of operating support but mandating the ways in which the budget shortfalls would be handled. The impact was particularly dramatic in the university sector since the process of implementation served to shift the roles of various actors in the policy community. The Council of Ontario Universities found itself playing the role of management in sectoral discussions with the Ontario Confederation of University Faculty Associations. Negotiations between faculty and management were eventually delegated to the institutional level, but even here the provincial framework left little room for institutional autonomy let alone traditional forms of collective bargaining. Macro-level policy had suddenly shifted the locus of powers within the university sector.

Another shift occurred when the Ministry of Colleges and Universities became combined with a number of other education-related units to form a new Ministry of Education and Training. The new super-Ministry is responsible for all levels of education in Ontario. While the two sectors were accustomed to interacting with distinct branches of the same Ministry, under the new organizational structure they are now interacting with policy and regulatory actors who have responsibility for specific functions that transcend sectoral boundaries.

A further shift in the balance of the university sector resulted from a review of university funding arrangements by the Ontario Council on University Affairs in response to a request by the Minister of Employment and Training. In many respects the Council inverted the process that had been used by Vision 2000: drafting an extremely controversial discussion paper which included policy options that had never been discussed within the sector (Ontario Council on University Affairs, 1994), releasing a series of background documents that had been prepared by Council staff, conducting a series of public consultations in which representatives of the sector questioned the existence of a problem let alone the appropriateness of Council policy options, and ending with a series of recommendations that were generally regarded as unworkable since they favoured more government intervention in a political environment where government was trying to pull back from its responsibilities (Ontario Council on University Affairs, 1995). While the Council raised a number of important issues as part of the review, for example the degree to which the balance between university teaching and research is appropriate, the approach employed in the review may have seriously jeopardized the Council's role as an intermediary body (see Skolnik, 1995). To date there has been no government response to the Council's recommendations.

With the defeat of Rae's New Democratic Party in the election of 1995, a new Progressive Conservative government led by Mike Harris came to power and with it a political agenda called The Common Sense Revolution. At the core of this Revolution is a macro-level policy approach focusing on deficit reduction through a major decrease in the size of government and government expenditures. Brushing aside any of the traditional consultative mechanisms associated with the sectoral approach to higher education policy in Ontario, the Government's first budget, announced in November of 1995, called for a 15% reduction in total allocations to higher education, a 10% increase in tuition, with universities having the discretion to increase tuition by a further 10%, and a broad review of higher education policy based on a government-prepared discussion paper that will be released in 1996. Subsequent to the budget, the government also announced a complete deregulation of international student fees: international students will no longer be counted within the allocative formulas of the college or university sectors, and institutions are completely free to determine the fee level.

While it is far too early to speculate on the long-term impact of these major changes, the short-term impact is already being felt. Many colleges have already announced the gradual discontinuation or immediate closure of programs, especially expensive programs like technology and nursing, as well as major reductions in teaching and support staff. Many universities are also preparing for staff reductions through early-retirement programs and by laying-off part-time teachers and support staff. It is quite clear that higher education in Ontario has moved out of the era of modest modifications and structural stability.

Conclusions

As Canada's most heavily populated province, Ontario has had an advantage over some other provinces in that it has been able to support a large higher education infrastructure. The degree to which Ontario has been successful in serving all of its population in terms of higher education is clearly debateable. The province has a high rate of participation, though its university participation rate is less than Nova Scotia, but one might argue that access to higher education in the north, as well as the participation of certain minority groups, especially Ontario's Native peoples, continues to be constrained. In a related way, there continue to be concerns regarding the degree to which women and visible minority populations are equitably represented among the ranks of university and CAAT faculty. While there have been gains in the participation of non-traditional groups both as students and faculty, the new Progressive Conservative government is far less enamoured with proactive approaches in these policy areas than several prior governments.

Other contemporary issues in Ontario higher education include operating support, accountability, and cross-sector relations. The level of government allocations to higher education has been the central policy issue for more than two decades, and the dramatic cuts announced by the Harris government have further exacerbated the financial difficulties of many institutions. As the government decreases operating support and increases or deregulates tuition, market forces and competition between institutions may come to play a much larger role in the future development of higher education in Ontario. Government cuts have already led to a modest form of program rationalization among CAATs in the greater Toronto area as some colleges abandon more expensive programs, though these changes are more closely associated with crisis management than sectoral rationalization. In the university sector, the prospect of market competition has already led to changes in institutional decision making related to tuition fees, as institutions attempt to maximize revenue while maintaining enrollment and increased experimentation with non-government supported fee-for-service programs. If the current government continues to move in the direction of deregulation in order to encourage competition while reducing the government share of operating costs, many of the factors and assumptions that have underscored the sectoral approach to decision making, especially the assumption of institutional equity and sectoral consultation processes, will probably be abandoned.

While the government is taking steps to deregulate some aspects of Ontario higher education, it is also concerned with institutional accountability. From time to time, Ontario governments have asked whether unrestricted operating grants and high levels of institutional autonomy, especially in the university sector, create an environment where institutions are appropriately responsive to the needs and desires of the populations they serve. To date, the accountability debate in Ontario has involved much talk and little action, though a review in the university sector focused attention on the accountability role of institutional governing boards and the possible need for a provincial agency to ensure that boards take this role seriously (Skolnik, 1994; Task Force on University Accountability, 1993), and there is a limited form of accountability associated with the work of the College Standards and Accreditation Council. A central difficulty in this debate is the lack of a common definition of accountability, a problem which makes it difficult to determine, given the plethora of reports published by institutions and sectoral organizations, what is currently missing from the equation. Given the new government's interest in accountability, there is a concern that its policy initiatives may involve the enigmatic approach of increased competition simultaneously with increased regulation. Regardless of how these issues are balanced, there is a certain irony in the fact that government interest in accountability seems to have grown as the government's contributions to higher education decline.

Finally, the appropriate relationship between the two sectors continues to be an issue. While recent increases in articulation agreements between colleges and universities and the clarification of credit transfer arrangements for students moving from CAATs to universities represent considerable progress, many feel that there is a need to go much further and argue that the role of the CAATs should be expanded to include associate degree and/or university-transfer functions. It will be extremely difficult to address or resolve this recurring issue in the absence of some body or agency with a system-wide, rather than a sectoral, perspective.

The story of higher education in Ontario involves a dramatic period of expansion in the 1960s, followed by a long period of structural stability within the constraints associated with clear, sectoral policy networks. Ontario has never had a higher education system, in an holistic organizational sense, or a master-plan. As Ontario moves into a new phase of transition in higher education, it seems clear that the power structures associated with the sectoral approach to higher education are now shifting. Since this huge infrastructure developed with little that might be called system planning, it comes as no surprise that while recent events signal movement, there is no clear sense as to the direction that higher education in Ontario is going.

References

Alexander, W.J. (Ed.). (1906). *The University and its colleges—The University of Toronto, 1827-1906*. Toronto, ON: The Librarian (University of Toronto).

Axelrod, P. (1982). *Scholars and dollars: Politics, economics, and the universities of Ontario 1945-1980*. Toronto, ON: University of Toronto Press.

Beard, P. (1983). *The Ontario Council on University Affairs: What, why and how*. Toronto, ON: Ontario Council on University Affairs.

Bell, S. (1990). Using matching grants to facilitate corporate-university research linkages: A preliminary examination of the outcomes of one initiative. *Canadian Journal of Higher Education*, 20(1), 57-74.

Cameron, D.M. (1991). *More than an academic question: Universities, government, and public policy in Canada*. Halifax, NS: Institute for Research on Public Policy.

Commission on the Future Development of the Universities of Ontario (1984). *Ontario universities: Options and futures*. Toronto: The Commission.

Committee on the Future Role of the Universities in Ontario (1981). *The report*. Toronto: The Committee.

Fleming, W.G. (1971). *Post-secondary and adult education*. Toronto, ON: University of Toronto Press.

Fleming, W.G. (1972). *Educational contributions of associations*. Toronto, ON: University of Toronto Press.

Gandz, J. (1988). *The report of the Colleges Collective Bargaining Commission*. Toronto: Colleges Collective Bargaining Commission.

Jones, G.A. (1991). Modest modifications and structural stability: Higher education in Ontario. *Higher Education*, 21, 573-587.

Jones, G.A. (1992). *University governance in the 1990s: An issues paper*. Paper prepared for the Association of Universities and Colleges of Canada.

Jones, G.A. (1994). Higher education policy in Ontario. In L. Goedegebuure, F. Kaiser, P. Maassen, L. Meek, F. van Vught, and E. de Weert (Eds.). *Higher education policy: An international comparative perspective* (pp. 214-238). Oxford: Pergamon.

Jones, G.A. (1996). Governments, governance, and Canadian universities. In John C. Smart (Ed.) *Higher education: Handbook of theory and research Volume XI* (pp. 337-371). New York, NY: Agathon Press.

Ontario Council on University Affairs (1994). *Sustaining quality in changing times: Funding Ontario universities, a discussion paper*. Toronto, ON: Ontario Council on University Affairs.

Ontario Council on University Affairs (1995). *Advisory memorandum 95-III. Resource allocation for Ontario universities*. Toronto, ON: Ontario Council on University Affairs.

Ontario, Ministry of Education and Training (1994). *Ontario transfer guide: A guide to transfer agreements among Ontario colleges and universities*. Toronto: Ministry of Education and Training.

Skolnik, M.L. (1987). State control of degree granting: The establishment of a public monopoly in Canada. In C. Watson (ed.), *Governments and higher education—The legitimacy of intervention* (pp. 56-83). Toronto: Higher Education Group, Ontario Institute for Studies in Education.

Skolnik, M.L. (1994). University accountability in Ontario in the nineties: Is there a role for a provincial agency? *Ontario Journal of Higher Education 1994*, 108-127.

Skolnik, M.L. (1995). Upsetting the balance: The debate on proposals for radically altering the relationship between universities and government in Ontario. *Ontario Journal of Higher Education 1995*, 4-26.

Task Force on University Accountability (1993). *University accountability: A strengthened framework*. Toronto, ON: Task Force on University Accountability.

Vision 2000. (1990). *Vision 2000: Quality and opportunity*. Toronto: Ontario Ministry of Colleges and Universities.

Wallace, W.S. (1927). *A history of the University of Toronto 1827-1927*. Toronto, ON: University of Toronto Press.

Higher Education in Quebec: 1945-1995

Janet G. Donald

"Education" in French has an extended meaning: it encompasses not only learning but character development and the ensuring of a good life. Recognition of the broader meaning of education has undoubtedly contributed to the importance accorded educational issues in Quebec and to the development of an extensive system of education. The earliest influences in Quebec education were, as elsewhere in the western world, religious, but the religious influence continued longer in Quebec. Although their ecclesiastical origins may today be overlaid with the demands of a technological society, institutions of higher education in Quebec are the product of an intense interaction between religion, politics and economics. An analysis of changes and development in postsecondary education must take into account the context of the changes, the specific events which were harbingers of change, the policies which conceptualized and represented the changes, the outcomes or actual changes effected, and the values which informed them. This chapter is an attempt to bring together context, events, policies and outcomes in order to understand the higher education system in Quebec and how it has functioned during the last half century.

Massive changes in Quebec higher education have occurred over the second half of the twentieth century. Of the 890,000 students enrolled in Canadian universities in 1992-93, over 257,000 or 29% were in Quebec universities, and another 219,000 (40% of the college population of Canada) were registered in college level programs (Human Resources Development Canada, 1994). The participation rate, once the lowest in Canada, is now the highest, with 29% of the 18–24 age group in full-time postsecondary education. Contributing to the high participation rate in Quebec is the Cegep (Collège d'enseignement général et professionnel) system, in which first year is the twelfth year of schooling while in other provinces the twelfth year is part of secondary school. If first year Cegep students were excluded from the calculation, the participation rate in

Quebec would be similar to that of Ontario (24%), still higher than the national average of 23%. To what can we attribute this change?

Primarily to the Parent Commission and the seriousness with which its recommendations were taken. From 1945 to 1959, Maurice Duplessis and the Union Nationale government were in power. The Union Nationale was a coalition of local entrepreneurs, workers and farmers, allied to both big business and the clergy (Black, 1977). This was a period of rapid economic and population growth, due in large part to a high birthrate but also to immigration. Postwar industrial development led to a new middle class. Quebec society as a whole was still rural and was categorized according to religion and language. A compulsory school education law was enacted in Quebec only in 1943, and Duplessis, while in opposition, voted against it (Magnuson, 1980). The British North America Act guaranteed the right to be educated in either the Catholic or Protestant faith, and two separate educational systems had developed. In francophone Quebec, the church was the authority in education, and Duplessis warned against the creation of a post of Minister of Education, implying it would end religious schooling (Black, 1977). During this period, French Quebec had the highest elementary school dropout rate (52% from grade 2 to grade 8) in Canada, and English Quebec the lowest (10%) (Dominion Bureau of Statistics, 1960). For francophone students, academic preparation at the secondary level was the province of the classical colleges. A small French public secondary school system provided a practical, vocationally oriented training. Thus the number of students who could acquire the academic preparation to enter postsecondary education was severely limited in French Quebec compared to English Quebec and other provinces.

Entry to French university education in Quebec, through the classical college, was open only to those who could pay the cost of attending. A francophone student attending classical college would have four years of secondary school, then another four years leading to a baccalaureate upon graduation from college, followed by three years in university. In comparison, an anglophone could go directly from secondary school grade eleven into a four-year university program. The classical colleges, moreover, were organized to provide a classical and general education, rather than to meet postwar needs for science, technology and commerce. The colleges were vulnerable because they "depended upon volunteer religious teachers, and the curriculum focused almost entirely on the humanities" (Superior Council of Education, 1990, p. 85). Efforts were made to increase the number of students pursuing postsecondary education in the 1940s and 50s by revising the classical college curriculum to prepare more students in the pure and applied sciences and in the social sciences. But in francophone Quebec, broader and more fundamental change was needed if the demands of postwar society were to be met.

At the university level, francophone education had been relatively slow to develop, although Laval University in Quebec City was founded in 1852 and had existed since 1663 as the Petit Séminaire. Laval University played a particularly important role in the socio-political life of Quebec. It trained the political, legal, social and religious elite, the senior civil servants of the Quebec government, and many of the critics and reformers who were later to challenge this elite (Henchey and Burgess, 1987). McGill University, founded in 1821, was the first English language university. Bishops University in Lennoxville in the Eastern Townships received its charter in 1853, and Loyola College, serving the English Catholic population in Montreal, was founded in 1896. University education for francophones, particularly in the Montreal region, developed more slowly. The University of Montreal was a branch of Laval University from 1876, receiving its charter in 1920. The Quebec government had authorized an École des Hautes Études Commerciales (HEC) in Montreal in 1907; it was affiliated with Laval University in 1914 (Rumilly, 1966). All of the universities were founded through private initiative and were governed by private charters. The slow development of the francophone universities was further marked by their stated missions.

In postwar Quebec, while most North American universities were adding the responsibility of research to their teaching duties, the francophone universities resisted this change (Magnuson, 1980). According to Magnuson, the University of Montreal in 1954 saw the role of the university as preserving and transmitting knowledge rather than increasing it and did not consider research an essential activity. The outcome was a lag in the development of science and technology. A third francophone university, the University of Sherbrooke, received its charter in 1954. Sir George Williams College was granted a university charter in 1948, bringing the number of universities in Montreal to three, two English and one French. Thus French postsecondary education in the commercial center of Quebec and of Canada was relatively slow to develop in the postwar years.

The Quiet Revolution

The death of Duplessis in 1959 and the access to political power of the Liberal party in 1960 ushered in the Quiet Revolution. A fundamental shift in consciousness in Quebec, the Quiet Revolution symbolized a change in the sense of identity, values, and aspirations of the province (Henchey, 1973). Francophone Quebec, prior to 1960, had been attached to tradition, loyalty to the Church, and an elitist view of society and was detached from economic concerns. Now the orientation was toward the present and the future, the secular, and an egalitarian view of society committed to change and economic control. The Liberal government brought in a new labor code that granted public servants the right to organize and strike, opened up the government planning process to labor and business groups, and enfranchised younger voters by lowering the voting age from 21 to 18 (Clarkson and McCall, 1990). This change in perception required a more highly educated population and a revamped postsecondary school system. At the same time, educational institutions had lost their way; several classical colleges went into bankruptcy, and life as a member of one of the religious orders, which had provided teaching staff, was no longer attracting sufficient numbers of young people to continue that practice (Paltiel, 1992).

Given the new secular orientation, the retention of students, the rescue of faltering educational institutions, and access to postsecondary education were critical problems. The problem of access was exacerbated by the rate of population increase, nearly 30% between 1951 and 1961. But Quebec was not alone in its sense of a need for change. In Great Britain, the Robbins Commission had been appointed in 1961 to review the pattern of higher education and to make suggestions for improving it (Higher Education, 1963). The point of departure of the Robbins Commission was the belief that "a highly educated population (was) essential to meet competitive pressures in the modern world" and that therefore a much greater effort was necessary if they were to "hold their own" (p. 268). Access to education, and particularly the requirement for places in higher education, were national priorities. In the same manner, the Government of Quebec recognized the need for development of its educational resources. This led to the naming of the Parent Commission with the mandate to investigate the entire educational system in Quebec.

The Royal Commission of Inquiry on Education in the Province of Quebec (Parent Commission) (1963-1966)

The Parent Commission conducted public hearings, visited more than 50 institutions throughout the province, interviewed more than 200 experts, and visited educational institutions in other Canadian provinces, the United

States, and Europe (The Royal Commission of Inquiry on Education, 1963). Democratization and access were key words which emerged from the report (Edwards, 1990). *Democratization* of the system of education occurred in spite of pressure on the Commission to preserve some aspects of elitism; *access* referred to students not being prevented by geography or finances from going as far as possible in the system. A universal right to education was acknowledged. This premise was revolutionary, for accepted thinking at the time in Quebec, backed by legislation, was that post-compulsory education (after the age of 14) was a privilege or a luxury, not suitable for everyone.

The Parent report noted the need for an expansion of the universities and a demand for mass education, based on recognition of the relationship between general and professional education and its economic importance. But it also based its recommendations on a recognition of cultural diversity, that is, humanistic, scientific, and technical cultures, and the necessity of instilling in students different methods of perceiving reality. The report referred explicitly to C.P. Snow's (1964) comparison of the two cultures—the humanities and the sciences—and to the need to reconcile them if Quebec schools were to provide worthwhile education. One effect of this approach was the insistence that teacher training focus, above all, on a thorough knowledge of psychology, to enable teachers to understand personal development, a brave heresy in the educational milieu of the time. Another effect was the stress put on an activist pedagogy in the colleges. According to the second volume of the Parent Commission report, college teachers were to make use of seminars, group discussions, personal and joint projects in order to give their instruction an activist, dynamic spirit which would require students to participate and to express themselves.

The first recommendation of the Commission was that a cabinet minister be fully responsible for all aspects of education in order to represent the "complex and vital claims of education" (p. 13). The second recommendation was the formation of a Superior Council of Education as an advisory or consultative body to the Minister to assist in determining priorities. The Commission also recommended expanded enrollments, an improvement in the holding power of schools, and greater emphasis on scientific, technical, and practical education.

More directly affecting higher education, a new network of institutes at the college level was envisioned to provide free general and professional education, and the number of university places was increased. The Parent report advocated that college level enrollments increase from 16% of the population to 45% and that university-level places be increased to accommodate 20% from the 7% in attendance in 1961. The institutes, which were incorporated as Collèges d'enseignement général et professionnel (Cegeps), were designed to encompass the role of both the classical colleges and the existing technical schools and institutes. They were also to harmonize to some extent the Quebec system with other European and North American systems that had twelve or thirteen years of schooling before university.

The colleges were expected to be comprehensive, that is, they would offer both pre-university and advanced technical programs within the same institution, bringing together what were previously classical and technical streams. They were also to be public institutions, legally established as public corporations, although the first colleges to open were amalgams of private classical colleges, teacher training institutions, and institutes of technology. They were to be free to all full-time students, providing equality of educational opportunity in one institution (Henchey and Burgess, 1987). Quebec students would enter Cegep after eleven years of schooling, pursuing either a two-year general program leading to university entrance or a three-year professional program leading to the workplace. The rationale for the new organization was that it would encourage more Quebec students to continue their education and would put higher education on the same footing for French and English students in Quebec. The colleges were also intended to link secondary and university levels, education and work, school and community, young and adult learners.

The forecasted need for increased university places was responded to with three proffered solutions. One was the maximum use of existing universities. The second was the establishment of limited charter universities which would provide undergraduate instruction. The third solution, in regions where it was impossible to establish a limited charter university, was the opening of centers of university studies which would provide the first and second years of university instruction in a sufficient number of basic disciplines and specialties. To deal with the development of research and graduate studies, the Commission recommended that adequate scholarships be provided to attract candidates to graduate school and that laboratories, equipment, and technicians be made available to researchers. To avoid the dispersion of resources, Laval, McGill, and the University of Montreal were asked to develop graduate programs, and a provincial research council was to be set up to foster research. The universities were also to take on the responsibility of training teachers to ensure the adequate preparation of students entering university (Paltiel, 1992).

To achieve more democratic management of the universities, the Commission recommended that there be greater participation in administrative councils and that faculty participate more extensively in administrative and educational decision making. Students were also to be brought into the decision-making process. Coordination among universities was to be the responsibility of the newly formed Conférence des Recteurs et Principaux des Universités du Québec (CRÉPUQ), initiated and funded by the presidents, that is, the rectors and principals of Quebec universities. Thus an active, participative framework was envisaged within and between universities.

The Conseil Supérieur

The second major recommendation of the Parent Commission was the formation of a Superior Council of Education as an advisory or consultative body to the Minister to assist in determining priorities. The Council was designed as

> ... the keystone of a vast system of consultation through which the actions that the Department of Education has the duty to undertake in the interests of true progress in Quebec education may become deeply rooted in every level of society and in every region. ... To attain its objectives, the Department of Education has to meet an immense challenge. It would undoubtedly fail were it not to share this task with all the dynamic elements of our society. (Superior Council of Education, 1966, p. x)

For the educational policies to be effective, participation was considered a critical factor. The first annual report of the Council (1964-1965), entitled *Participation in Educational Planning*, began with a recognition of the suddenness of the changes taking place which were giving rise to a certain disorder and causing confusion, anxiety and distress. Rapid industrialization and urbanization, new ideas, processes, and tools were identified as contributing to a clash of opinions and a vast socializing movement. Educational planning thus became one of the state's foremost duties:

> The administration of the plan for educational development, including the coordination of university education, requires guidance and control by the State. One of the latter's fundamental

tasks consists in making provision for drawing up the plan, accepting it and putting it into operation according to predetermined stages. . . . Moreover, major decisions in the field of education have a political side. In modern society, education is at the Centre of everything. It engages the future of the nation as well as that of each citizen. The financial demands of education have become very significant. It costs millions of dollars to equip a nuclear physics Centre in a university . . . (p. 46).

The Superior Council envisaged participation to consist of the will to dialogue and the spirit of partnership, in order to bring down the barriers between educational sectors and to reduce the distances which were seen to often paralyze communication. Planning would take place through dialogue, a receptivity to others' ideas, and an active interest in the common good. This philosophy led to the organization of the Council with four Commissions appointed to study issues in elementary, secondary, technical and vocational, and higher education, and two confessional committees (Catholic and Protestant) that were watchdogs for all religious aspects of education. In higher education, a variety of problems were examined in the first year of the Council. Some had to do with the development of resources: the establishment of a second French-language university in Montreal; an estimate of the number of university professors needed; and a survey of professors in Canada and the United States who were qualified to teach in French-language universities. Others concerned research: its importance in relation to other university functions, the functions of the university professor (teacher, researcher, administrator), and the establishment of a provincial research council.

In its section of the Council's report, the Commission of Higher Education listed a number of problems requiring study, among them university autonomy and academic freedom, and the relations between the state and the universities. Several problems concerned standards: standards of admission to various faculties; equivalences between Canadian university faculties and those abroad; and the requirements of professional licensing bodies of international associations with regard to courses of study and standards in various faculties. The rapid increase in professional knowledge and its effect on university teaching posed problems and the new philosophy guiding the determination and elaboration of courses of study also required attention. The number of issues considered to merit study was substantial.

A special committee reporting to the Council on pre-university and vocational education recommended institutions with a dynamic social climate in which 50% to 70% of Quebec adolescents from 15 to 19 years would take different programs while being able to meet each other in the institution. The report detailed steps to the establishment of the Cegeps, starting with the formation of public corporations consisting of local groups or organizations. Thus the first set of recommendations of the Superior Council were both practical and far reaching.

Results of the Recommendations of the Parent Commission

The first twelve francophone Cegeps opened in 1967, with an additional eleven in the following year, accommodating 38,000 students. The first English-language Cegep, Dawson College, opened in 1969; the second, Vanier, in 1970. With the development of the Cegeps, the universities of Quebec were to reduce their undergraduate programs from four to three years. This was to free them to focus on the development of graduate teaching and research. The fourth and final volume of the report of the Parent Commission had recommended that research money be made available and that the business community and alumni be called upon to aid education. Soon after the release of the report, the two Catholic universities, Montreal and Laval, were secularized, in 1965 and 1970, respectively. The appointment of a scientist as rector at the University of Montreal ensured attention to the development of science and technology programs.

The democratization recommended by the Parent Commission was echoed in the sixties in student demands for representation on the governing bodies of Cegeps and universities (Edwards, 1990). At McGill University, students were elected to serve on Senate and, by the end of the decade, were providing evaluations of their professors' teaching. At Dawson College, students were members of the Board of Directors. The student unity movement was reflected in student protests in October 1968. Fifteen francophone Cegeps were occupied by students; at the University of Montreal students boycotted classes, and at McGill, students moved resolutions in support. A major concern for students was that a second French university in Montreal would not be open in time to receive the expanded cohort of students graduating from Cegeps in 1969.

To increase student access to university, the University of Quebec was established in 1969, with campuses in Trois-Rivières, Chicoutimi, Rimouski, and Montreal (Magnuson, 1980). The University of Quebec was organized as a public provincial university with a central administration located in Quebec City but with campuses in other regions of Quebec and with other constituents. These included a research institute, the Institut National de Recherche Scientifique, and a school of public administration, the École nationale d'administration publique, both founded in 1969. The mandate of the University of Quebec was to expand university services to the population, especially adults; regional leadership was deemed crucial to its success. Its novel academic organization was based on modules consisting of groups of professors and students who developed and then followed a program of studies.

Between 1962 and 1970, full-time enrollments in francophone universities tripled and those in anglophone universities doubled, from a total of 24,631 to 55,429. Government annual operating grants to the universities rose substantially, while students were aided by low fees and a program of student financial assistance. A policy of *rattrapage*, that is, a *catching up*, was instituted to provide francophone universities with extra funding in order to speed their development. This policy was officially ended in 1970, although funding disparities between francophone and anglophone universities continued well after that year.

To respond to the need for development of graduate teaching and research, the Minister of Education created a program to support the development of teams of researchers, "Formation des chercheurs et action concertée (FCAC)." The program funded research in the sciences, technologies, and humanities, including education. It encouraged cooperation among university professors within and across universities, supported the publication and presentation of research results, and provided support and training for graduate students. It thus fulfilled the recommendations of the Parent Commission but went beyond it to develop a research network.

The Seventies: A Decade of Planning and Development

During the seventies, postsecondary enrollments once again multiplied. Cegep enrollments doubled in the two-year pre-university programs and tripled in the three-year technical programs (Henchey and Burgess, 1987). The colleges undertook major programs in continuing education and in community development. English language universities had developed Cegep equivalent programs in the late sixties to accommodate the requirement for college-level education. In the seventies, as five English language Cegeps (four public and one private) came into full operation, the anglophone universities phased out their college programs. Technical institutes and most classical colleges were integrated into the Cegep system. Much time and effort were spent in establishing the curriculum for courses in Cegep programs and then evaluating them for the *Cahiers*, or course curriculum guides, which consisted of course outlines, evaluation criteria, and bibliographies for each approved course. Most college instructors were unionized, and differing visions of teachers and administrators over college policies and working conditions meant conflict and turbulence.

In the universities, the student population also increased by 87% in full-time equivalents, with an increase in part-time students from one-third to one-half of the university population (Conseil des Universités, 1979). The student population now had a more heterogeneous background, with increased numbers of women and older students. Fifty new undergraduate programs were approved in the seventies, 86 at the masters level, and 26 at the doctoral level, as well as shorter certificate and diploma programs. To meet the demands of more students and new programs, the number of professors increased from 4500 to 6500, and financing for the universities jumped from $121 million to $622 million, a 250% leap in constant dollars. As in the Cegeps, demands and resources for continuing education were increasing, and more professors were unionized. Budgeting and planning processes were hitting snags. But this was not for want of attention to the planning process in Quebec higher education. For example, a Comité de liaison de l'enseignement supérieur et de l'enseignement collégial (CLESEC) was established in 1971 to coordinate programs in the Cegeps and universities and to clarify admissions standards. Wide participation in the planning process continued.

Consultation

A prominent feature of higher education in Quebec was the number of consultative bodies, commissions, and councils that functioned during this period. Analysis of their reports provides insight into the evolution of the Quebec system of education. To usher in the seventies, an eighteen-person advisory body to the Minister of Education, the Council of Universities, was mandated to study the needs of higher education and university research and to make recommendations on the measures to be taken to respond to these needs. The Council was to consider short- and long-term objectives, the creation of new establishments, the budgets of the universities, and laws concerning university teaching and research (Loi du

Conseil des Universités, 1968). Increased government organization provoked counter organization in the universities. In its annual report for 1976-77, the Council began by stating its concern over the effect that syndicalization was having in the universities (Conseil des Universités, 1977). The year (1976) had seen a change in government from Liberal to Parti Québecois, which would continue in office until 1985. The negotiation of nine collective agreements, at Bishop's, Laval, Sherbrooke, and several of the University of Quebec campuses had taken place that year. Conflicts had paralyzed the campuses of Laval and the University of Quebec at Montreal for four months. Study days were taken at other universities. University autonomy and responsibility were central themes in the report of the Council.

One of the goals of the Council of Universities was to put into place a triennial budgeting system for the allotment of resources to the universities. Another goal was to study scientific research policies. The universities were to be accountable, with each member of the "system" providing progress reports on the steps taken to achieve accountability. The universities responded uneasily to these propositions. Some studies undertaken by the Council were, however, responded to more favorably. For example, in the study on basic sciences, greater attention to their development in the universities was recommended. This found approval. Recommendations for improved teaching and research, and programs (formation) for secondary school science teachers received a positive response overall. A report on training in medical sciences and clinical research also met with positive response. A review of the program of research funding, for the training of researchers and team research (Formation des Chercheurs et Actions Concerteé) led to recommendations for an expansion of the program to support new researchers and programs of research, and a larger budget. The report of the Council of Universities covered all aspects of university life and was both precise and prognostic in its recommendations. Although some of these plans would not be put into effect for several years, they were more than clues to the future of the universities of Quebec.

In addition to the work of the Council of Universities, there were Commissions and more specific studies on the universities done for the Minister of Education. One detailed study on student graduates from the universities established that those graduating from programs in the humanities or in education had greater difficulty in finding jobs than those graduating from programs in pure and applied sciences (Audet, 1982). Although this might be expected, given the continued tendency of greater numbers of Quebec students to pursue studies in the arts rather than the sciences, it indicated a lack of coordination between the aspirations of the state and those of Quebec adolescents.

The lack of coordination was noted and led to major studies of the directions being taken in higher education. For example, a Commission d'étude sur les universités (1978), consisting of some 32 members, was appointed to study the future of the universities. The rationale for the Commission was the tremendous growth of the universities over the previous 15 years, the difficulties experienced by some of the developing universities and by the students in them, and the problem of financial constraints. The study document called upon universities to consider their role in the development of new knowledge as a primordial objective. The second objective was the development of highly qualified personnel. The Commission noted the need for universities not to abandon the ideas of equality and of continuing education while they pursued technological excellence. Finally, the universities were exhorted to continue their role as social critics.

The objectives recommended to the universities exhibit concerted conceptualization. But it is not only in their philosophical conceptualization that the planning groups excelled. I would suggest that their attention to and belief in conceptual model building in order to understand the phenomena of higher education has rarely been matched. For example, to place the discussion of the Commission d'étude sur les universités in context, the study document presented a table of differing conceptions of the university, from Newman's concept of the university through the German and American models to more utilitarian models such as that of the USSR. In the document, the place of Quebec universities in this schema was then described, with Laval and McGill following the Newman ideal of liberal education and newer universities adopting more specialized or utilitarian goals. Philosophy stated and models developed, the Commission then proceeded to operationalize with a vengeance, recommending how the universities and colleges should proceed. The study concluded with concerns of how the universities were going to adapt to the need for qualified personnel in the "productive" sectors (industry, transport, tele-communications) and with how members of the Quebec university network, pluralistic and differentiated, would define their roles and hence their financing.

The study was comprehensive and collaborative in its approach. It did not, for example, neglect to examine the relationship of the Cegeps to the universities. Recognizing that the advent of the Cegeps had created new pressures on the universities, the Commission suggested that new patterns of liaison were needed to deal with problems of selection and orientation of Cegep graduates, with evaluating student motivation and aptitude for higher-level study, and with the fact that certain courses in the university were duplicating Cegep courses.

At the end of the decade, in its evaluation of the first ten years of its existence, the Council of Universities (1979) took up the question of the redundancy of programs between college and university levels. It was, however, more concerned with the unionization of professors over the decade, going from 0 in 1969 to 61% in 1979, with all of the francophone universities unionized. Even more troubling, because it showed the extent to which interest groups had formed and could create bottlenecks within the *collectivité*, one of the unions of sessional lecturers (chargés de cours) at the University of Quebec at Montreal had prevented the University of Quebec from negotiating a collective agreement with sessional lecturers' unions at the other campuses. The Council of Universities was no happier with the lack of progress on the budgeting front. Although many steps had been taken to move from the historical method of budgeting, which was based on salary indexation and the change in student numbers, to a more systematic approach based on the cost of education in different disciplines, little had changed. But an unpredicted budget cut to the universities and expected continuing budget cuts due to the recession had eliminated the possibility of moving to a more rational basis for the allocation of educational funds.

More to the point, after ten years of planning endeavors, the Council of Universities saw little advance in the collection of information on the universities, little change in the operations of the universities due to the Council's studies, and a feeble level of response to the Council's exhortations to the universities to create *axes* or main lines of development. In its review, the Council of Universities was pleased with the rich and extended planning efforts made over the decade but reserved in its evaluation of actual outcomes.

The Superior Council of Education in its annual report of 1979 on *The State and Needs of Education* was even less sanguine about the role and efforts of the universities in the 70s. It expressed its concern with the unsettled situation in which the universities found themselves and berated the universities for their lack of attention to student life and learning. From the perspective of the Superior Council, the expansion of the Quebec universities had posed organizational problems and had modified their operating patterns, with the result that students were not their primary concern. To illustrate, it was noted that university meetings tended to deal with the status of professors, research, faculties, and university organization to the neglect of students. Trade unionism had changed the relationship between different groups within the university community and between professors and students. The interruption of academic sessions, that is, strikes, and the participation of professors as union representatives were considered to endanger the attention paid to students and their learning. The Superior Council further noted that although students had been invited to participate in the collective decision making of the university, they were poorly informed and could therefore only play a reduced role in the consultative and decision-making process.

Accessibility was another important consideration in this report. Given the major investment in higher education in the past two decades, what had been accomplished in terms of the democratization of education? From 1971 to 1976, the rate of graduation from undergraduate programs for the Quebec population between the ages of 18 to 24 had dropped from 4.5% to 3.9%. During that same period, the rate in Ontario had risen from 5.2% to 7.4%. Program quotas in some fifty undergraduate programs had further impeded student access. In addition, 30% of the students consulted in a study of Quebec student life considered that their professors gave the impression of not having time to spend on them (Dandurand, Fournier, and Hétu, 1979).

At the same time, the development of the universities had led to the need for a much larger complement of administrative personnel. The need for support services and for coordination in the university led to centralization, which had, in turn, deprived professors and faculties of a significant share of their traditional responsibilities, for example, guaranteeing the quality of teaching provided. In response to these trends, there had been a movement toward the consumer university, in which programs had proliferated and students chose job-oriented programs, often maintaining full- or part-time jobs while pursuing their studies. As had the 1978 Commission report, that of the Superior Council called upon universities to devote more attention to their mission as critics of society. Universities were to examine factors which affect university life, to innovate, and to make student participation more worthwhile.

The decade of planning, with its many commissions, councils, and studies, appeared at this point to have produced relatively little activity let alone change in the way universities planned but a great deal of frustration among those called to consult as members of the social planning process. Evidently, great strides had been made in the actual numbers of students served by the system, but the quality of their educational experience was somewhat suspect. Increases in size brought their own problems of organization and coordination. The paucity of effects of the planning bodies in this decade did not, however, lead to decrements in planning. The Council of Universities ended its 1979 report with a set of objectives for the 1980s. The first objective for the universities was to move from a conception of accessibility as quantitative to one of qualitative accessibility, in which the university mission would be examined. The second objective was to maintain the quality of education in a period of financial restriction, and the third was for each university to use its resources better to meet its priorities. The Council saw its role in the 1980s to be one of providing better planning and coordinating mechanisms and called upon the government to supply it with the information and resources to do so.

Years of Reflection and Retrenchment: The Eighties

During the eighties, the number of students enrolled in postsecondary studies once again surpassed the forecasts of the demographers in the Ministry of Education, then levelled off (Superior Council of Education, 1990). The forecast for 1986, the expected zenith of the postsecondary age population, was 100,000 in the colleges; that year there were actually 160,000 (p. 27). In 1987 the number of Cegep registrants in the Montreal area dropped slightly, but the report predicted that applications would soon begin to increase again due to demographics. In the universities, with a predicted enrollment of 90,000, actual enrollment was 115,000.

Economically, demands were outpacing resources, and the decade began with talk of budget cuts, accountability, and the need for a reallocation of the available resources in higher education. A major recession in 1981-82 led to increased levels of unemployment and reductions in salaries. A series of budget cuts to the universities left them to deal with increasing numbers of students with reduced resources. The Parti Québecois lost its referendum for political independence in 1980 and the repatriation of the Canadian constitution in 1982 changed the political context further. Quebec now moved economically from a welfare state to greater privatization and deregulation. How would this affect higher education?

An opinion poll of the role of the universities in Quebec at the beginning of the decade showed that 55% of Quebecers were very satisfied or sufficiently satisfied with the contribution the universities were making to Quebec society; 69% considered that the universities were fulfilling their role well (Sorécom, 1982). Fifty-one percent felt that everyone who wanted to could go to university. A majority felt that it was very important for the universities to do basic and applied research. Eighty percent of the respondents with 16 or more years of education felt that the financial situation of the universities was bad, and 85% thought that government funding should be augmented (37%) or maintained (48%). Thus, public sentiment was favorable toward the universities, in spite of continuing labor problems and confrontations.

Meanwhile, the policy studies of the Councils in the eighties became more detailed and reflective. The 1981-82 annual report of the Superior Council (1983) on *Educational Activity: Present Practices and Ways of Renewal* was a discussion of teaching methods, particularly the relationship of teachers and students in the colleges in light of the recent power struggles in the Cegeps. The council was critical of the tendency in some Cegeps to deconstruct rather than to construct knowledge.

There are those that hold that freely encouraged liberty of expression contributes less to the development of a critical sense, than to the adoption of a very superficial subjectivity. (p. 61)

The sequel to this institutional hardening of the arteries, astonishing in such a young organization, is the development of sentiments of isolation and sometimes of discouragement. (p. 63)

On the positive side of the balance sheet, more than half the projects in the Cegeps financed by the Minister of Education dealt with how students learn or with teaching techniques and methods. Course plans had been developed and served as a form of contract with students, inservice training for college professors had become an established program, and lecturing was being questioned as a method of teaching. University teaching services were now established at McGill, Laval, Montreal and the University of Quebec at Montreal. To deal with mass education and the resulting depersonalization, it was suggested that professors should reconsider their role as transmitters of knowledge and aim at teaching students to think for themselves, to provide them with the capacity to be their own teachers, rather than covering all the subject matter.

Through the 1980s, the annual reports of the Superior Council dealt with many varied issues, from evaluation (1982-1983), basic or core education and the quality of education (1983-1984), the learning process (1984-1985) and changing needs (1985-1986) to the development of ethical competence (1989-1990). In addition, the Superior Council published recommendations or advisory bulletins in conjunction with its Commission on Higher Education. These ranged from the effects of budgetary compressions and the future of the university (1981), the role of the professor (1982), information technology and instruction (1983), adults in postsecondary education (1985), professional training (1986) to teaching and research in the social sciences (1987). The Council of Universities also published a series of recommendations (avis), primarily on new programs, but also on topics in higher education, for example, on university financing (1984). Overall, the level of attention paid to postsecondary education had increased geometrically. To deal with increasing pressure on the postsecondary system, particularly for greater emphasis on science and technology education, in 1985 a Ministry of Higher Education and Science, responsible for postsecondary education, science and technology was created. The Superior Council then became a consultative body advising both the Minister of Education and the Minister of Higher Education and Science.

Twenty-five Years After the Parent Commission

In 1987-88, twenty-five years after the Royal Commission of Inquiry on Education and twenty years after the inception of the Cegeps, the Superior Council of Education dedicated its annual report to a review of how well the objectives of the Commission had been met. The number of students completing secondary school, and attending college and university had surpassed expectations. In 1961, the Commission had predicted that 45% of the college-age population would attend college; in 1986, 63% were doing so. More Cegeps had been opened than planned, and the numbers attending any one Cegep often exceeded the expected enrollment of 1500 students, rising to over 5000 in some of them.

More women than men were attending college, both in the general and the professional programs, although men outnumbered women in the science and technology programs. Higher percentages of anglophone and allophone students (those with neither English nor French as the first language learned) than francophone were enrolled in Cegeps. The location of the Cegeps reflected the distribution of the population, with high concentrations in the Montreal and Quebec City regions. Because Cegeps set their own admissions policy rather than being open-door institutions as are colleges elsewhere in Canada, accessibility had become a responsibility of the Cegep network, rather than of each establishment. Some Cegeps, because they could admit fewer than all applicants to their programs, had become fairly selective; others had to ensure general access to the system.

In spite of the enormous gains in attendance at Cegep, in its 1986-87 report, the Superior Council made increasing access to Cegeps a strategic target. This objective was based on the fact that the first year of Cegep was a twelfth year of education, and that elsewhere in North America, a greater percentage of students were completing grade 12. Students were also prolonging their time in Cegep, delaying career choices or changing programs, and the number of changes, withdrawals, and failures had escalated markedly. The 1986-87 annual report did not discuss the extent to which these problems were due to the great increase in the total numbers attending Cegep, but it did recognize that fewer and fewer individuals defined themselves as students.

Evaluation became a key issue for college planners in the eighties, both of student progress and college programs. One long-standing problem was the fact that diplomas were awarded by individual colleges without examination by the Minister of Education or the universities and often without stated institutional policies. The fact that the Cegeps had multi-faceted roles to play meant that they had to deal with conflicting demands. The Council suggested a return to their primary mission of providing a basic training for students. The colleges were called upon to provide better support and guidance services and to improve programming by instituting qualifying programs and bridges between programs. College professors were asked to foster open learning situations, to articulate learning objectives more precisely, to employ diagnostic formative evaluation and summative evaluation so that students "could assume responsibility for their learning" and teachers could "master a pedagogy centered on learning and success" (Superior Council of Education, 1990, p. 95). Comparison with the recommendations of previous reports suggests that these objectives were much less abstract and more modest.

One change in the Cegeps which was totally unpredicted in the Parent report was the increased emphasis on research activity. With a maturing professoriate, the number of research projects increased in the colleges, and provision was made in the collective agreements concerning research. By 1985, the Conseil des Collèges, which had a parallel function to that of the Conseil des Universités, suggested in its report on *Le Cégep de demain: pouvoirs et responsabilités,* that the renewed mandate of the colleges should consist of a teaching mission, a research mission, and a mission of service to the community. Pedagogical, disciplinary, and technological research were to become a part of college life, complementing university research and aiding in staff development.

In the universities enrollment had surpassed predictions, but the greatest leap was in part-time studies for adults over 25. In 1986, over 28,000 were enrolled full time, and over 94,000 were enrolled in university programs on a part-time basis. The number of students in the expected university age group (18–24) who were studying part-time or had interrupted their studies had also not been predicted. In a study reported in 1982, over three-quarters of part-time students were attending university for the first time; 80% were attending university after entering the labor market (Roberge, 1982). The number of university degrees awarded had increased from approximately 4500 in 1950 to over 43,000 in 1986. Quebec was producing the same proportion of science graduates as the United States but more teachers and fewer commerce graduates (Superior Council of Education, 1990, p. 35). Regional disparities within Quebec persisted, with outlying regions as in the northwest (Outaouais, Abitibi-Temiscaming) having lower rates of postsecondary attendance. But some Montreal districts, particularly the north and south shores, also had lower postsecondary school attendance rates.

In response to the recommendations of the Parent Commission, the universities had been asked to provide specialized education to students who had two years of general education in the Cegeps and to broaden their mission to include service to the community. The report of the Superior Council of Education (1990) noted that this specialization of education had indeed occurred but that it had resulted in a fragmentation and proliferation of courses. The report further noted that this movement had prevented students from establishing a clear idea of the discipline or field of study in which they were engaged, leading to confusion about educational goals. Quebec students, particularly those attending francophone universities, compared to Canadian students overall, spent more time obtaining their bachelor's degrees; proportionately fewer registered full time in undergraduate and graduate programs, and fewer of them obtained degrees.

Professors, meanwhile, had to deal with increased demands on them to teach, do research, and serve the community. In a major report based on interviews with some forty Quebec spokespersons on the evolution of Quebec society and its educational priorities, Lamarre (1987) called upon the university to redefine its goals. Not only were universities to enrich basic education and to evaluate their attempts to do so, they were also to assume leadership in research, particularly by collaborating with enterprise.

University administrators were called upon to ensure that teaching and scholarship in the university were increased.

In its review of the effects of the Parent Commission, the Superior Council noted that universities had failed to properly supervise graduate students, provide areas for research, and encourage students to become more involved with university activities. A bias toward the natural and applied sciences in the allocation of research funds, facilities and equipment had also contributed to disequilibrium and polarization in the universities. The only course open to academics seeking excellence in their fields was specialization and research (p. 112). The report noted that because an explosion in knowledge had occurred at the same time as the demand for specialization, integrating knowledge, offering an overview of a discipline, and establishing links between different fields of knowledge had become more difficult for universities. Even more perilous in terms of teaching outcomes, many universities, especially francophone ones, dealt with the pressure to do research and the increase in student numbers by depending upon sessional lecturers (chargés de cours) to take on the responsibility of teaching undergraduate courses. Originally hired because of their acknowledged competence in a field of study and for a limited time period, sessional lecturers, although a minority of the teaching staff, had become members of their own profession, unionized and carrying the equivalent of full-time teaching loads, often while pursuing graduate studies.

In response to this situation, the Superior Council recommended that universities emphasize greater coherence in undergraduate programs, both vertically (in relation to Cegep programs) and horizontally. Programs were to stress the development and epistemological underpinnings of various fields of knowledge, foster the development of basic intellectual skills, ensure the mastery of communications, mathematics, and computer skills, and make students more aware of the values inherent in intellectual work and professional practice. The objectives stated for the universities were more challenging and perhaps more difficult to operationalize than those stated for the Cegeps.

Toward the Year 2000

In 1990 the Council of Colleges published a report entitled *Vers l'an 2000: Les priorités de développement de l'enseignement collégial.* In it were documented the questions facing Quebec colleges, the socio-economic challenges resulting from a global economy, increased socio-economic inequality, the crisis of the family, interculturalism, and the increase of women in the work force. New socio-cultural trends noted were environmental quality, peace, and the search for personal services, which led the Council of Colleges to suggest that individualism would be one of the principal values of Quebec society in the year 2000. This represented a major shift in Quebec values from the constant focus on the *collectivité* in the seventies and eighties. To meet these challenges, the Cegeps were to continue to provide a solid basic education, broadly based professional training, and continuing education for lifelong learning. Teaching was to be aided by learning centers and tutorials, the provision of frameworks for learning within disciplines, orientation programs, formative evaluation, mastery learning, and integrated approaches to learning.

The number and size of Cegeps and the territories they served had expanded. In 1990, there were 46 public Cegeps throughout Quebec, seven of which had more than 5000 students. The Cegeps had become a major factor in the social, cultural and economic development of their regions. At the same time, a study of the Cegep system done by the Ministry of Education found that one-third of college level students changed their program, usually in the first year and usually from natural sciences to social sciences, often changing college at the same time (Falardeau, 1992). Better students were less likely to change, and failure was a principal reason for change but so was indecision in choosing a career. Program changes were accompanied by a prolonged period of study and an adjustment to a more appropriate career path.

As an advisory body to the Minister of Education, the Council of Colleges used the report *Vers l'an 2000* as a document of consultation and distributed 4000 copies throughout the province. Round tables in Cegeps and consultations during the next year led to the production of a book in 1992 entitled *L'enseignement collégial: des priorités pour un renouveau de la formation*. Its definition of college, of which there were 105 in 1990-91, included 46 Cegeps, 25 privately supported colleges, 23 colleges with permits and another 11 establishments. The report confirmed that knowledge was at the center of modern society, that it is necessary to aid young people to find a place in society through a career, and that school is the place where both young and not so young will find culture. The extensive dissertation identified four major needs for education in the future: competence, the ability to adapt, the ability to make choices based on a system of values and a critical approach, and openness to diversity. The college system was to be renewed through changes to the curriculum, greater responsibility, and more developmental research.

Meanwhile, the Council of Universities (1992) studied the institutional planning process. In this report, university autonomy was recognized to be of the utmost importance in order that universities be able to adapt to rapid change. The Council, however, called upon universities to use quantifiable and measurable objectives so that they could evaluate how well their priorities had been met and so that they could link priorities with budgets. The Council that year reorganized itself by adding a commission on university development and finance. The Quebec government dismantled the Council of Universities and the Council of Colleges as of 1993.

In its final report, entitled *Challenges and Choices Facing the Quebec University System: Redefining the Relationship Between Universities and Society* (1993), the Council of Universities emphasized, as had the report of the Council of Colleges, the need for renewal, but great attention was also paid to the number of graduates from and the research funds allocated to Quebec universities. Although there were a quarter of a million students enrolled in Quebec universities, just over 33,000 degrees and diplomas had been granted in 1991-92. The spotlight was no longer on access per se but on output into the labor force. Over 80% of Quebec university students were enrolled in professional programs or programs leading to the labor market, but only 50% of the students enrolled in university programs obtained a degree. The argument advanced was that graduation rates had to rise to enhance the self-esteem of students, faculty, and institutions. The analysis of university research was somewhat more positive. Quebec was considered to have good performance compared with Ontario and with a range of developed nations. To ensure international competitiveness in research, however, Quebec's universities were exhorted to cooperate and to develop more system-wide strategies. Funding constraints and new funding objectives were also highlighted in this final report. Flexibility, contractual funding, and public funding linked to the results of program evaluation, especially at the graduate level, were suggested responses.

In its retrospective report (1969-1993), the Council of Universities noted that in 24 years of existence it had produced more than 450 advisories and reports. It had evaluated 335 new programs and approved 249 of them. The report concluded with concern that the Ministry of Education would no longer have a mechanism for consultation on the development of teaching and research in the universities, an intermediary for the evaluation of new programs, or a commission on university research. These functions were allocated to the Superior Council and the Conference of Rectors and Principals of the Universities of Quebec (CREPUQ) (Bordeleau, 1994).

The Superior Council during the 1990s continued its interest in questions of university pedagogy, stating the need for a renewed pedagogy in which the university culture is valued and supporting teaching and teachers (Conseil Supérieur, 1990). It recommended that universities adopt a planning perspective based on the pedagogical activities in their programs. Teachers were called upon to encourage creativity in their classes and to cultivate the spirit of research; students were invited to participate as active partners, taking charge of their own learning and development. The question of the postsecondary student population remained a priority, especially the increasing diversity among students (Conseil Supérieur, 1992a). The Council again noted that few of those enrolled in postsecondary programs considered themselves to be students. Colleges and universities were asked to provide additional help to students coming from deprived backgrounds, for example, by setting up orientation programs, to create work-study programs, to aid students to understand professional life and the workplace and, finally, to establish real communities of scholars with authentic communication and true milieux of intellectual exchange.

This report was followed by an advisory report to both the Minister of Education and the Minister of Higher Education and Science (Conseil Supérieur, 1993) on integrating the new cultural (immigrant) communities into Quebec society. This policy initiative was founded on the recognition of rapid changes in the demographic make up of society and the idea of the school as a crucible of social integration, confirming the continued extended role of education in Quebec. Linked to the theme of integration were internationalization, the global economy, and the development of a planetary conscience (Conseil Supérieur, 1992b). Later that year the two ministries of education and higher education and science were reintegrated as one, and in September 1994 there was a change in government. Since that time, political upheaval has put educational concerns in the background.

What are the major trends that arise from this review of objectives and priorities in Quebec? One is an increasing emphasis on the quality of education. In the context of global competition, in which a greater level of general and specialized competence is required, education is viewed as a measure of success for a nation (Conseil Supérieur, 1992b; 1994). Education is also seen as contributing to a reduction in social fragmentation. Social justice and access are continuing themes and the theme of integration has developed from them. By the year 2000, the Council proposed an objective of 70% access to college for Quebecers less than 20 years old, with a 60% graduation rate within 25 years. This can be compared with an actual access rate of less than 64% in 1992-93 (*Indicateurs de l'éducation*, 1995). The objective for access to university undergraduate studies for Quebecers younger than 30 was 35%, with a 25% graduation rate. Masters and doctoral degree objectives were 10% and 5% and 1.2% and 1% respectively.

In spite of major cuts in government spending, the Council recommended that education should be considered a short-, medium- and long-term investment and should remain a priority in public spending. Actual investments through the federal established programs financing entitlements for postsecondary education in 1993-94 for Quebec were 25% of the total for Canada; Quebec expenditures represented 37% of the total amount spent by Canadian provinces, the highest in Canada (*Toward the 21st century*, 1995). The measurement precision introduced into educational financing is exemplified by the procedure for allocating funds to the universities: a 1993 Law of the Quebec Ministry of Education required that the rules and modalities for financing Quebec universities be set out (Règles budgétaires et calculs des subventions de fonctionnement aux universités du Québec (1994-95), (1994). In this document were the amounts for 1994-95 allocated to each university and the method, process, and parameters used, including student weights, special programs, indirect costs of research, centers of excellence, student services, number of students graduating, the amount allocated to the university for each graduate ($500 per B.A., $600 per M.A., $1000 per doctorate), and new program development.

Has the planning and consultative process been a success? Has the message of councils, conferences, and commissions been heeded? On a percentage basis, the recommendations of councils appear to have been discussed but responded to decreasingly over the years. The Parent Commission had a major impact, undoubtedly because its recommendations were critical to Quebec's development, specific, and funded. Since that time, policy recommendations have tended to be more abstract and hence more difficult to pursue. Time has worn down belief in broad-scale consultation, and institutions are guided in their tendency to respond to the recommendations by their understanding of the relative impact that statements of policy have had over the last 30 years. Economics has proved to be a stronger policy maker: if there are insufficient funds, it is difficult to expect new initiatives. Greater efficiency in policy making could be expected with one council rather than three examining the needs of postsecondary education, but the number of policy advisory reports in the early 1990s appeared to increase rather than decrease. One finding is certain, Quebec has taken great strides to provide a good education to its citizens, and has been careful to take into account its citizens' wishes, involving them in the planning process. This has enabled massive changes to take place in higher education in Quebec.

Over the last 50 years, the number of students who gain access to postsecondary programs in Quebec has gone from the lowest in Canada to the highest. Organized systems of postsecondary academic and vocational training have been put into place. Planning has become a consultative process of great sophistication. If young people are less willing to adopt a student's life exclusively, lifelong learning, or *education permanente* has been instituted. Geographically isolated regions have established postsecondary facilities which aid in regional development and stability. One important question for Quebec postsecondary educational institutions is the role they will play in the global economy and whether they will be able to meet competitive pressures. But this is a question for all postsecondary institutions to consider.

References

Audet, M. (1982). *Rélance à l'université*. Gouvernement du Québec: Ministère de l' Éducation.

Black, C. (1977). *Duplessis*. Toronto: McClelland & Stewart.

Bordeleau, J. (1994). *Rapport d'activités 1993-1994*. Conférence des recteurs et des principaux des universités du Québec (CREPUQ).

Clarkson, S., and McCall, C. (1990). *Trudeau and our times*. Toronto: McClelland & Stewart.

Commission d'étude sur les universités. (1978). *Document de consultation*. Gouvernement du Québec: Ministère de l'Éducation.

Conseil des Collèges. (1985). *Le Cégep de demain: Pouvoirs et responsabilités*. Québec: Gouvernement du Québec.

Conseil des Collèges. (1990). *Vers l'an 2000: Les priorités de développement de l'enseignement collégial*. Québec: Gouvernement du Québec.

Conseil des Collèges (1992). *L'enseignement collégial: Des priorités pour un renouveau de la formation*. Québec: Gouvernement du Québec.

Conseil des Universités. (1977). *Huitième Rapport Annuel, 1976/77*. Quebec: Editeur officiel.

Conseil des Universités. (1979). *Dixième Rapport Annuel, 1978/79*. Quebec: Editeur officiel.

Conseil des Universités. (Avril 1992). *Bulletin d'information, numéro 8*. Quebec: Gouvernement du Québec.

Conseil des Universités. (1993). *Challenges and choices facing the Quebec university system: Redefining the relationship between universities and society.* Quebec: Gouvernement du Québec.

Conseil Supérieur de l'Éducation. (1990). *La pédagogie, un défi majeur de l'enseignement supérieur: Avis au ministre de l'enseignement supérieur.* Québec: Author.

Conseil Supérieur de l'Éducation. (1992a). *Les nouvelles populations étudiantes des collèges et des universités: des enseignements à tirer: Avis à la ministre de l'Enseignement supérieur et de la Science.* Québec: Author.

Conseil Supérieur de l'Éducation. (1992b). *L'enseignement supérieur: Pour une entrée réussie dans le XXIe siécle: Avis à la ministre de l'Enseignement supérieur et de la Science et au ministre de l'Éducation.* Québec: Author.

Conseil Supérieur de l'Éducation. (1993). *Pour un accueil et une intégration réussis des élèves des communautés culturelles: Avis à la ministre de l'Éducation et ministre de l'Enseignement supérieur et de la Science.* Québec: Author.

Conseil Supérieur de l'Éducation. (1994). *L'enseignement supérieur et le développement économique: Avis au ministre de l'Éducation.* Québec: Author.

Dandurand, P., Fournier, M., and Hétu, C. (1979). *Condition de vie de la population étudiante universitaire québecoise.* Montréal: Département de sociologie, Université de Montréal.

Dominion Bureau of Statistics. (1960). *Student progress through the schools by grade.* Ottawa: Queen's Printer.

Edwards, R. (1990). Historical background of the English-language CEGEPS of Quebec. *McGill Journal of Education, 25*(2), 147-174.

Falardeau, I. (1992). *Les changements de programme au collégial: Changer de cap sans perdre le nord.* Ministère de l'Enseignement Supérieur et de la Science, Direction générale de l'enseignement collégial.

Harris, R.S. (1976). *A history of higher education in Canada: 1663-1960.* Toronto: University of Toronto Press.

Henchey, N. (1973). Revolution and education in Quebec. In D. Myers, *The failure of educational reform in Canada*, pp. 157-167. Toronto: McClelland & Stewart.

Henchey, N., and Burgess, D.A. (1987). *Between past and future: Quebec education in transition.* Calgary: Detselig.

Higher Education: Report of the Committee appointed by the Prime Minister under the Chairmanship of Lord Robbins, 1961-1963. (1963). London: Her Majesty's Stationery Office.

Human Resources Development Canada. *Profile of post secondary education in Canada: 1993 edition.* (1994). Ottawa: Education Support Branch, Author.

Lamarre, M. (1987). *Tendances de l'évolution de la société québecoise et priorités qui s'en dégagent pour l'éducation.* Quebec: Conseil Supérieur de l'Éducation.

Loi du Conseil des Universités. (1968). Statuts de 1968, Chapitre 64, Quebec: Editeur officiel.

Magnuson, R. (1980). *A brief history of Quebec education: From New France to Parti Québecois.* Montreal: Harvest House.

Ministère de l'Éducation. (1995). *Indicateurs de l'Éducation.* Québec: Author.

Paltiel, S. (July 1992). *Personal communication.* Montreal, Quebec.

Règles budgétaires et calculs des subventions de fonctionnement aux universités du Québec (1994-95). (1994). Gouvernement du Québec: Ministère de l'Éducation.

Roberge, P. (1982). *Les étudiants à temps partiel des universités québecoises.* Quebec: Conseil des Universités.

The Royal Commission of Inquiry on Education in the Province of Quebec (Parent Commission) (1963). Quebec: Queen's Printer.

Rumilly, R. (1966). *Histoire de l'École des Hautes études commerciales de Montréal.* Montreal: Beauchemin.

Snow, C.P. (1964). *The two cultures and the scientific revolution: And a second look.* London: Cambridge University Press.

Sorécom. (1982). *Les Québecois face aux universités et aux universitaires du Québec.* Montréal: Société de recherches en sciences du comportement.

Superior Council of Education. (1966). *Participation in educational planning: Annual report 1964/1965.* Quebec: Minister of Education.

Superior Council of Education. (1980). *The state and needs of education—1979/1980 report.* Quebec: Editeur officiel.

Superior Council of Education. (1983). *Educational activity: Present practices and ways of renewal—1981-82 report.* Quebec: Editeur officiel.

Superior Council of Education. (1990). *1987-1988 Annual report on the state and needs of education: The Parent Report, 25 years later.* Quebec: Editeur officiel.

Toward the 21st century: Federal and provincial support to postsecondary education in Canada: A report to Parliament, 1993-94. (1995) Ottawa: Education Support/ Student Assistance Branch, Minister of Human Resources Development.

New Brunswick

Sheila A. Brown[*]

The development of higher education in New Brunswick since 1945 is a study of the evolution of individual institutions and the historical, religious, social, and political forces which shaped them, including the role of government in bringing about planned change. The church was initially a prime influence in the establishment and development of the province's universities. Gradually, however, that influence waned and the government played a larger role, planning and shaping the university system through the implementation of the recommendations of the Royal Commission on Higher Education in 1962 and a follow-up Committee on Higher Education Financing in 1967. The government's role is also clear in the creation and development of the New Brunswick Community College, established by an act of the Legislature in 1974, and the history of a number of other colleges and schools. From 1974 onwards the cooperative regional efforts of the governments of the three maritime provinces of New Brunswick, Nova Scotia, and Prince Edward Island, under the auspices of the Council of Maritime Premiers and its Maritime Provinces Higher Education Commission, complement solely provincial initiatives. In 1991 another Commission, the Commission on Excellence in Education, took stock of the postsecondary education sector and made a number of far-reaching recommendations, several of which have already been implemented.

At least four readily identifiable forces have contributed to the establishment, location, and form of the province's postsecondary institutions. First, many of the early settlers of the province, English-speaking Loyalists and French-speaking Acadians, placed a high value on education. Second, the different cultural and linguistic backgrounds of the

[*] Appreciation is expressed to Tim Andrew, Craig Carter, Beth Corey (MPHEC), Leandre Desjardins, Jean Fisher, Ellen Herbeson, Jim O'Sullivan, Bernard Paulin, Bill Smith, W.B. Thompson, and W.A. Spray for help in gathering information; to Tom Condon and John Reid for permission to cite symposium papers; and to Bill Godfrey, Ellen Herbeson and her students, Gail Hilyer and Bill Smith for their comments on earlier drafts.

population required that higher education be available in both English and French. Third, the dispersion of the population across a province of 72,000 sq. km. resulted in geographically distributed institutions to serve the different regions. Finally, there was a recognition, from at least the mid-nineteenth century, of the importance of providing opportunities for women, as well as men, to participate in higher education.

In this chapter a brief overview of the creation and early development of postsecondary institutions in New Brunswick is provided with reference to the four factors outlined above; key events which affected higher education in the province are examined and recent developments described.

New Brunswick Higher Education in the 1990s

The Institutions

Today New Brunswick has a range of public institutions of higher education. These include four universities, two with multiple campuses, creating seven distinct entities, established from the eighteenth to the twentieth centuries: the University of New Brunswick at Fredericton (UNB) and at Saint John (UNBSJ); St. Thomas University in Fredericton; Mount Allison University in Sackville; and Université de Moncton (U de M) at Moncton, Edmundston, and at Shippagan. University-level education is also offered by the privately owned Atlantic Baptist College in Moncton. The New Brunswick Community College, established in 1974, has nine campuses located throughout the province to serve both anglophone and francophone populations. Locations include anglophone campuses in Miramichi (Chatham), Moncton, Saint John, St. Andrews, and Woodstock. Francophone campuses are located in Bathurst, Campbellton, Dieppe, and Edmundston. There are several other postsecondary institutions: the Maritime Forest Ranger School, established in 1946, which offers education and training in English at Fredericton and in French at Bathurst; the New Brunswick School of Fisheries in Caraquet, established in 1959; and the New Brunswick College of Craft and Design, created in the 1940s. As well, there are five Diploma Schools of Nursing—one in Bathurst, Edmundston, and Saint John and two in Moncton. A number of private institutions also offer education and training at the postsecondary level. The main focus in this chapter is on the public institutions.

The New Brunswick universities fulfil different missions and together offer a wide range of opportunities for students. Statements of their role were requested and published by the Maritime Provinces Higher Education Commission (MPHEC) in the early 1980s (MPHEC, 1981) and updated in the early 1990s (MPHEC, 1993). These statements, along with publications from the universities themselves, provide a summary of each university's view of its distinctive character and contribution.

Mount Allison and St. Thomas are primarily undergraduate liberal arts institutions with some professional programmes. Université de Moncton offers French language education at the undergraduate and graduate levels in basic and applied disciplines. The University of New Brunswick also offers a wide range of programmes, including undergraduate, masters, and doctoral studies. Within the province professional programmes are offered in most major fields except medicine, dentistry, veterinary medicine, and pharmacy, which are offered elsewhere within the Maritimes. The Atlantic Baptist College offers undergraduate education in a limited number of disciplines and describes itself as a Christian liberal arts and science institution.

Each campus of the New Brunswick Community College offers a programme of basic education and academic courses, different speciality programmes in selected occupational areas and educational services designed to meet the needs of the local community (Landry and Downey, 1993). One- and two-year programmes are supplemented by short training courses offered under contract. The Maritime Forest Ranger School provides a one-year training programme for forest technicians and a continuing education programme, the School of Fisheries provides fishing training and continuing education, and the College of Craft and Design offers a three-year diploma as well as some part-time and certificate options.

The Diploma Schools of Nursing have long offered preparation for registered nurses. As a result of changing professional requirements for nurses, a baccalaureate degree in nursing will be required of nurses by the year 2000, and this change will lead to the eventual disappearance of the diploma schools and the full incorporation of nursing education into the universities.

Enrollment

Enrollment at all the universities has grown steadily during the study period and today stands at over 18,000 undergraduate students (Table 1) as well as about 600 masters and over 100 doctoral students. Part-time enrollment has also grown and now exceeds 5,000 students (Table 2).

The Atlantic Baptist College has about 220 students, mostly full time, and there are plans for an increase in two phases—450 and 650—once a new campus is opened.

Table 1

Full-Time Undergraduate Enrollment in New Brunswick Universities*

University	Enrollment				
	Years				
	1961-62	1971-72	1981-82	1991-92	1994-95
Mount Allison	1,219	1,347	1,544	1,932	2,232
St. Thomas	199	1,095	889	1,683	1,968
Université de Moncton	985	3,192	3,034	5,070	5,185
University of New Brunswick	2,170	4,678	6,052	8,312	8,971
Maritime Forest Ranger School	n/a	60	91	88	58
Total	4,573	10,372	11,610	17,085	18,414

*Sources: Report of the Royal Commission on Higher Education, 1962; Report of the Committee on the Financing of Higher Education in New Brunswick, 1967; Statistics Canada; Association of Atlantic Universities, 1969; Maritime Provinces Higher Education Commission.

Full-time regular enrollment in Community College programmes totalled 6,466 in 1993-94, up from 6,010 two years earlier. The report of the Commission on Excellence in Education (Landry and Downey, 1993) comments on the disparity in enrollment growth between the universities and the colleges. According to MPHEC data, the participation rate at the

New Brunswick Community College has scarcely changed over the past 25 years, while Canada wide it has tripled to approximately 10.5% of the 18 to 24 age group. At the same time, the New Brunswick universities, like their counterparts elsewhere in Canada, have seen a doubling of the participation rate to over 20% of the same age group. Such data should be interpreted with caution since they likely do not reflect the considerable numbers of students who attend the Community College for short-term job-related training. Full-time total enrollments at the community college in 1993-94 were 15,673, when students taking contract training and apprenticeship training are included (New Brunswick Advanced Education and Labour, 1994).

Table 2
Part-Time Undergraduate Enrollment in New Brunswick Universities*

University	Enrollment			
	Years			
	1980-81	1986-87	1991-92	1994-95
Mount Allison	73	95	110	129
St. Thomas	167	226	215	240
Université de Moncton	1,578	1,859	2,622	1,882
University of New Brunswick	2,044	2,756	2,845	2,968
Total	3,862	4,936	5,792	5,219
FTE of PT	2,330	2,055	n/a	n/a

*Source: Maritime Provinces Higher Education Commission.

Funding

The Provincial Government supports the universities of New Brunswick and the Maritime Forest Ranger School through the MPHEC from funds generated from provincial tax revenues and fiscal transfers from the federal government under EPF (Established Programs Financing). In 1991-92 EPF covered approximately 71% of the cost of postsecondary education in New Brunswick, a decrease from 88% in 1986-87 (MPHEC Financial Plan, 1992-93). The MPHEC calculates that, over the decade 1982-92, government funding to the maritime universities increased by 13%, but enrollment increased by 46%. Consequently, government funding per student has decreased markedly, being partially offset by increases in student fees. As Table 3 shows, fee revenue now constitutes between 24% and 36% of operating income, compared to 18% to 29% in the mid-1980s.

Table 4 gives financial data for New Brunswick universities and the Maritime Forest Ranger School. Total unrestricted operating grants from government make up the bulk of the total revenues, divided approximately 53% to UNB, 30% to U de M, 10% to Mount Allison, 5% to St. Thomas, and 1.3% to the Maritime Forest Ranger School. Restricted operating assistance, usually about an additional 5% of the unrestricted funding, is also allocated for particular purposes, specifically alterations, renovations, equipment, and library resources.

The Atlantic Baptist College's operating funds come from private sources—donations from the churches of the Atlantic United Baptist Convention, individuals, businesses, and alumni—and from tuition and ancillary revenues.

Major capital grants are dealt with separately and vary from year to year. Some new capital construction for the universities has been approved in recent years. The Atlantic Baptist College is now permitted, under its recently revised by-laws, to accept government funding for capital purposes. The MPHEC and the provincial governments now also appear to be paying particular heed to concerns about physical plant deterioration and the deferred maintenance problems which characterize all of the campuses (MPHEC, 1991).

The financing arrangements of the Community College are quite different because, as a department of government, the government funds expenditures while tuition fee and training revenues accrue to the province (Landry and Downey, 1993). Today NBCC's gross expenditures are $60–70 million, with $30 million in revenues generated from tuition and the sale of training spaces in programmes. The School of Fisheries operates similarly under the provincial Department of Fisheries and the College of Craft and Design is administered by the Department of Advanced Education and Labour.

Table 3
Operating Grant and Fee Increases in New Brunswick Universities*

University	Operating Grant Increase (%)	Fee Increase (%)	Fee Revenue as Percentage of Fee and Government Grant**		
			Years		
	1993-94		1986-87	1990-91	1993-94
Mount Allison	1.03	5	23.9	25.8	34.8
St. Thomas	3.95	5	29.0	30.2	36.6
Université de Moncton	2.39	5	18.7	20.4	24.5
University of New Brunswick	1.65	5	21.0	21.8	27.3
Maritime Forest Ranger School	1.70	-	-	-	-

*Source: Maritime Provinces Higher Education Commission.
**Fee revenue calculated as product of enrollment and basic student; no allowance made for higher fees, or increase in university assistance to students.

Table 4

Unrestricted Operating Grants for New Brunswick Universities*

University	Operating Grants ($,000)		
	Years		
	1981-82	1986-87	1993-94
Mount Allison	7,180	10,225	13,981
St. Thomas	2,807	4,712	7,335
Université de Moncton	20,596	30,661	42,831
University of New Brunswick	38,598	55,398	74,922
Maritime Forest Ranger School	667	1,209	1,899
Total	69,848	102,205	140,968

*Source: Maritime Provinces Higher Education Commission.

Historical Foundations

Origins of the Institutions

This brief overview of the roles of the New Brunswick postsecondary institutions provides a snapshot of higher education in the province in the mid-1990s. To appreciate how the current situation has come about it is important to understand the origins and evolution of the institutions and to go back prior to 1945 to review the historical foundations on which they were established. For the universities these reflect, as noted earlier, the early importance of the church, combined with the other factors which have been outlined, and the role of planned change since the 1960s. For the Community College and the other schools, the role of government has been paramount although the pulp and paper and lumber industries and the fisheries community have supported the Forest Ranger and Fisheries schools respectively.

The Loyalists' concern for education resulted in the establishment of an Academy in Fredericton in 1787 (Royal Commission on Higher Education, 1962). In 1800 the province granted a charter to the Academy, which became the College of New Brunswick and subsequently King's College under Royal Charter. Although legislation in 1846 allowed that members of the governing council need not be Anglicans, the College continued to be seen as an Anglican College, which was a matter of concern to some (Cameron, 1991). Others felt that the College's classical emphasis was not best suited to the needs of the population—who wanted more comprehensive and practical education, according to the province's first Royal Commission on Higher Education, appointed in 1854. Consequently, the Commission recommended that King's College become a non-sectarian provincial university, and hence, in 1859, the University of New Brunswick came into formal existence (Cameron, 1991; Royal Commission on Higher Education, 1962).

Several other colleges and universities also grew up, each connected in some way with a particular religious denomination, connections which continued for some time. Mount Allison was established in Sackville in 1839 when Charles Frederick Allison, a Methodist business leader, approached the Wesleyan Methodists and offered to provide land, buildings, and an endowment to establish an institution of higher education (Reid, 1984). In 1843 a Boys' Academy was opened, followed by a Ladies' College in 1854. The first degrees were granted in 1863. Thus, from its origins, Mount Allison was associated with the Methodist (now United) Church of Canada although the University was always open to students of all denominations. From originally having a majority on the Board of Regents (Reid, 1984, p. 335), the United Church now names two of the twenty-four members.

St. Thomas University in Chatham started as part of the Roman Catholic school system serving the Miramichi region. The University's forerunner, St. Michael's College, was established in 1860. For a time, it was run by the Christian Brothers, who left in 1878, following a major fire. In 1910 the College, renamed St. Thomas College after St. Thomas Aquinas, reopened under the Basilian Fathers (Fraser, 1970). In 1912 there was an unsuccessful attempt to affiliate St. Thomas with the University of New Brunswick. In 1923 the diocesan clergy again took over the operations of the College, which offered a two-year programme in arts, with students wanting a degree transferring to another institution. The

College first granted degrees in 1936 (Royal Commission on Higher Education, 1962) and formally became St. Thomas University, by an act of the legislature, in 1960, primarily at that time serving English-speaking Catholics.

In addition to the three anglophone institutions, there were three francophone institutions, St. Joseph's and its affiliates, Sacre Coeur and, later, St. Louis-Maillet. St Joseph's, in the Memramcook Valley in the southeast was incorporated and given degree-granting powers in 1868, although its roots go back a further fourteen years. Serving Acadian and Irish Catholics, it was, until the early 1940s, a traditional classical college, but in 1942 the curriculum was broadened with the addition of first commerce and then science and education programs. Notre-Dame d'Acadie College, established by the Sisters of Charity in Memramcook in 1871, was a girl's school, which became affiliated with St. Joseph's. A later affiliate was Collège de l'Assomption for boys, founded in 1943 (Royal Commission on Higher Education, 1962).

Collège du Sacre Coeur, established in Caraquet by the Eudist Fathers in 1889, became a degree-granting institution in 1900. The College moved to Bathurst in 1915. Collège Jesus-Marie founded in Shippagan by the Sisters of Jesus-Marie and offering opportunities for girls, became affiliated with Sacre Coeur in 1960. In 1946, the Eudists opened another university for boys, St. Louis in Edmundston. Its affiliate, Collège Maillet for girls in nearby St. Basile, was established in 1949 although schooling had been offered there since the late nineteenth century by Les Religieuses Hospitalières de Saint Joseph (Royal Commission on Higher Education, 1962).

By the early 1960s then, there were three anglophone and three francophone universities or colleges in New Brunswick, each with degree-granting powers, dispersed throughout the province. The francophone institutions also had affiliates offering all or part of degree programmes which provided opportunities for women to participate in higher education. To varying extents the Anglican, Methodist, and Roman Catholic Churches had played a role in the establishment and development of these institutions. As well, the founding of the universities appears to owe much to the value placed on higher education by the settlers themselves, whose needs and aspirations also gradually helped to shape the curriculum. The bilingual and multicultural history of New Brunswick, settled by Loyalists and Acadians, and later emigrants from Scotland, Ireland, England, and other European countries created a need to serve both English- and French-language constituencies.

The Maritime Forest Ranger School was established in 1946, a joint venture of New Brunswick and neighbouring Nova Scotia, in conjunction with UNB and the forestry industry. Its mandate was to offer technical education in forestry. For some years the School was affiliated with UNB but funded through the provincial department of Natural Resources. Its governance was provided by an Executive Committee comprising representatives of the joint venture partners. The School of Fisheries was established in 1959 to offer technical education to the fishing industry through direct training and continuing education. The School fell under the jurisdiction of the Department of Fisheries. The College of Craft and Design was established in the 1940s. The privately owned United Baptist Bible Training School was established in Moncton in 1949 as a bible institute and high school.

New Brunswick also has a long history of vocational education, dating back to the nineteenth century. The Vocational Education Act of 1918 supported the development of technical and vocational education. Vocational Committees were set up in a number of communities and a number of vocational schools came into existence. In 1948 one of these, the Canadian Vocational Training Centre in Moncton, became the New Brunswick Technical Institute, and in 1963 the Saint John Technical Institute opened. These were the historical roots of the New Brunswick Community College.

Teacher training was also offered through a succession of institutions with their origins in the nineteenth century, until the universities assumed the responsibility for teacher education in 1973. The first teacher training school was established in Fredericton in 1848. A new Normal School was opened in that city in 1877, and it was quickly recognized that arrangements must be made to address the training of teachers for both the English- and French-speaking schools. With the passing of the Vocational Education Act in 1918, the Normal School also had to train vocational teachers. In 1947 the Normal School became the Teachers' college, and the first degree programme was introduced in the 1950s (Picot, 1974).

Role of Government

The provincial government clearly had played a role during this early period, with the provincial legislature conferring degree-granting powers on the institutions and passing legislation affecting the governance of King's College (later UNB). The recommendations of the government-appointed Royal Commission on Higher Education of the mid-nineteenth century led to the formal establishment of UNB as a non-sectarian provincial university.

The government also played a role through its funding of universities. Up until 1951 the provincial government provided operating grant support only to the University of New Brunswick, as it had done since its inception. The government did not support the other institutions. However, in 1951 the five other institutions persuaded the provincial government to broaden its support by granting small annual operating allowances to each of them while restricting capital grants to UNB (Royal Commission on Higher Education, 1962; Reid, 1989). At approximately the same time, 1952, the federal government initiated fiscal transfers to the provinces for education of 50 cents per capita (Cameron, 1991).

Evolution from Historical Roots

Several events can be identified which have had a major impact on how postsecondary education in New Brunswick evolved from these historical roots up to the present time. One, in 1962, was the Report of the Royal Commission on Higher Education (Deutsch Commission) established by the provincial government to make recommendations on the nature of higher education in the province and the follow-up Committee on the Financing of Higher Education. A second was the founding of the New Brunswick Community College in 1974, and a third was the creation, also in 1974, of the Maritime Provinces Higher Education Commission. The last major event was the Commission on Excellence in Education, established in 1991. Consequently, the following discussion is organized in three sections: 1962 to 1974, 1974 to 1990, and 1990 to 1995.

The Period 1962 to 1974

The Royal Commission on Higher Education

Chaired by John J. Deutsch, the Royal Commission on Higher Education was established in 1961 by order of the Lieutenant Governor to study "the Province's resources in the field of higher education and their future development and utilization" (Royal Commission on Higher Education, 1962, p. 116).

The Royal Commission studied the issues of university funding, student financial aid, and access—including demands for a university in

Saint John and for increased educational opportunities for francophones. A report on these issues was submitted in 1962.

A New Institutional Framework

The Commission proposed what it termed "a new institutional framework" for the province and what Cameron has termed "a massive dose of institutional centralization" (Cameron, 1991, p. 110). The plan called for the continuation of UNB in Fredericton with the establishment of a second campus in Saint John; the movement of St. Thomas from Chatham to the main campus of UNB in Fredericton and a federation between the two institutions; the continuation of Mount Allison as a liberal arts university in Sackville; and the creation of the new Université de Moncton in the City of Moncton. The northern New Brunswick colleges serving the francophone communities of Bathurst, Shippagan, and Edmundston and environs would be affiliated with the Université de Moncton. The implementation of these changes in the early to mid-1960s resulted in a provincial pattern of education which continues to the present day.

Financing

The Commission recommended substantial increases in both operating and capital funding to universities by the province based on a funding formula to be in effect for five years with a subsequent commission to review the matter and recommend on the next five years. The financial formula had two components—a flat grant to cover fixed costs and an enrollment-driven portion to cover variable costs associated with enrollment increases. The second component, based on New Brunswick students only, was to be $300 per student in 1962-63, increasing to $420 by 1966-67 (Cameron, 1991; Royal Commission on Higher Education, 1962).

In its funding recommendations the Commission explicitly recognized that, if the system were designed to avoid "duplication of effort or wastage of resources" (p. 102), then Provincial Government financial assistance should be available to all universities, so that New Brunswick students could attend the provincial university of their choice, each of which would enjoy support. The Commission also recommended that provincial support for capital projects be restricted to academic and administrative facilities and exclude ancillaries like residences and dining rooms. The Commission recognized the importance of financial and other arrangements with provinces offering programmes not available to New Brunswick students in their home province—such as English-language programmes in medicine, dentistry, social work, and pharmacy offered at Dalhousie University in Nova Scotia and similar programmes for French-speaking students offered elsewhere (Royal Commission on Higher Education, 1962).

Student Financial Aid

The Commission recommended an increase in student aid, noting that it was below the level elsewhere in Canada. They proposed Provincial Government university entrance scholarships to recognize students' achievements and also made provision for part of a student's loan to be treated as a non-repayable bursary, based also on academic achievement (Royal Commission on Higher Education, 1962).

Although the Deutsch Commission was concerned primarily with the universities, it did suggest that there would be economies in locating new teacher education facilities on the UNB and U de M campuses—a Teacher's College opened on the UNB campus in 1964 and École Normale (bilingual) opened on the U de M campus in 1968. These arrangements continued until 1973 when, following recommendations made in a study by St. Thomas University President Duffie, the government decided that teacher education would be integrated into the universities, and the two schools formally became part of the two universities (Picot, 1974).

The Committee on the Financing of Higher Education in New Brunswick

In February 1966, the provincial government established the Committee on the Financing of Higher Education in New Brunswick, with the same members as the Deutsch Commission, to make financial recommendations for the next five years. The Committee was also empowered "to consider and report upon any other related matter" (Committee on the Financing of Higher Education in New Brunswick, 1967, p. 11), which allowed it to take stock of the status of the institutional changes it had previously recommended. As Cameron (1991, p. 147) notes, "Few royal commissions are ever given the opportunity of returning to review their handiwork some years after their recommendations have been put in place." The Committee commented positively on the extent to which the new institutional framework was meeting the province's needs. However, it identified two areas warranting attention, the administrative organization of the Université de Moncton and the urgent need for facilities at UNBSJ (Committee on the Financing of Higher Education in New Brunswick, 1967).

The Committee believed that the Université de Moncton should become a public institution. Under the 1963 Charter, a seven-member council, largely composed of members of the Holy Cross Order, had executive authority. It was now recommended that the University have the typical bicameral governance structure of a Board of Governors, with executive powers, and a Senate responsible for the University's academic affairs (Cameron, 1991; Committee on the Financing of Higher Education in New Brunswick, 1967).

UNBSJ was, by 1967, offering the first two years of arts and science programmes as well as first year business administration, forestry, engineering and physical education but in scattered and temporary quarters. Enrollment was growing, and clearly permanent facilities were needed. The Committee urged that physical development proceed as quickly as possible, but that existing academic offerings be strengthened before new ones were added.

The Committee believed that formula financing should continue and recommended the level of government assistance for the New Brunswick universities for a two-year period—believing the environment was changing too rapidly to make a five-year recommendation. Subsequent recommendations would be the responsibility of a permanent Commission on Postsecondary Education which the Committee proposed be established to advise the government and to help plan and coordinate future developments. This recommendation was quickly adopted.

The New Brunswick Higher Education Commission

In 1968 the New Brunswick Higher Education Commission (NBHEC) was created. In 1969 the NBHEC proposed grant allocations for the next three years and a continuation of the policy of formula financing (New Brunswick Higher Education Commission, 1969). The Commission continued its work until 1974, making recommendations on operating and capital assistance for universities and technical schools, student aid, inter-university cooperation, and other issues of concern.

An Assessment of Higher Education in New Brunswick by the Late 1960s

By the late 1960s New Brunswick higher education had undergone major change in a short period of time, largely as a result of government policy initiatives. Reid comments that the Deutsch Commission is one of a few such commissions which has "produced demonstrably lasting results" and that "to a remarkable extent, the Deutsch Commission's recommendations were carried into effect, and have had a continuing influence" (Reid, 1989, p.2). The changes were significant and were undoubtedly thought radical by many at the time. Reid argues that change was inevitable as "the status quo in New Brunswick higher education had become untenable" (Reid, 1989, p. 24) and that three broader developments provided an environment which facilitated such significant changes. First, there was increased public investment in higher education, as during the 1950s, the federal government initiated and then increased fiscal transfers to the provinces for education with funds to be divided among institutions according to enrollment.

Second, public interest in higher education led to increasing pressure from the public in cities like Saint John and Moncton for more access to higher education.

Third, the provincial government of Louis Robichaud (1960-70) placed a priority on economic and social reform. Robichaud, the province's first Acadian Premier, believed that the path to economic prosperity was through a well-educated population and workforce (Stanley, 1984). As an Acadian he was particularly concerned that francophone higher education best serve the needs of the Acadian community. It was with these objectives in mind that the Robichaud government established the Deutsch Commission.

Overall, the implementation of the recommendations of the Deutsch Commission and the subsequent Committee on Financing Higher Education placed higher education in New Brunswick on a sounder financial footing and allowed for the resources allocated to be used to greater advantage than might otherwise have been the case. Nonetheless, the preservation of a large degree of geographic dispersion allowed for the needs of New Brunswickers throughout the province as well as some residents of the neighbouring provinces of Nova Scotia and Quebec to be met. The creation of the New Brunswick Council on Higher Education ensured a continuing role for government in monitoring and coordinating higher education in the province, in recommending levels of funding for the universities and in acting as a buffer between the provincial government and the institutions.

The Shift to a Regional Focus

In 1968, the Council of Maritime Premiers (CMP) announced a Maritime Union Study which was to consider the benefits of closer economic and political cooperation among New Brunswick, Nova Scotia, and Prince Edward Island. The CMP asked the Association of Atlantic Universities (AAU) to undertake a study of higher education in the region, a particularly timely issue given concerns about the relative underfunding of Maritime universities compared to universities elsewhere in Canada. The study undertaken recognized that there already existed considerable movement of students from province to province and considerable cooperation and coordination among universities in the Maritimes. The joining of three institutions to form the Université de Moncton and the federation of St. Thomas with UNB were cited as two examples of cooperation as was the existence of only one professional programme within the region in fields like medicine and dentistry to serve students from the entire Maritimes. The creation of APICS, the Atlantic Provinces Inter-University Committee on the Sciences, in 1962, also was given as an example of cooperation among universities as was the AAU (founded in 1964).

The AAU emphasized the importance of a regional approach to higher education planning with increased cooperation and coordination. This would be facilitated by the establishment of a single university grants committee for the region, even without political union (Association of Atlantic Universities, 1969).

The Period 1974 to 1990

The Maritime Provinces Higher Education Commission

In 1974 a regional commission, the Maritime Provinces Higher Education Commission (MPHEC), was established by legislation in each of the three provinces. Chaired by Dr. Catherine Wallace, the MPHEC existed for a few months in parallel with the provincial body it replaced, the New Brunswick Higher Education Commission, to allow for a smooth transition. The purpose of the Commission was: "To assist the Provinces and the institutions in attaining a more efficient and effective utilization and allocation of resources in the field of higher education in the region" (MPHEC, 1975a, p. 52).

The Commission, which has responsibility for the universities and the Maritime Forest Ranger School, acts as a buffer body between the institutions and the government. Proposals for new and modified programmes are considered by the Commission for approval as are recommendations to government for additional funding if required. The objective of this approval process is to maximize the use of resources and avoid duplication. The Commission makes recommendations on operating and capital expenditures, tuition fees, and any other matters it believes affect higher education in the region. Each provincial legislature then decides on the level of grants for the province.

Initiatives of the MPHEC

In the twenty years of its existence, the Commission has undertaken a number of studies of interest. One of the earliest, initiated in 1974, was a Study by the Committee on Higher Education in the French sector of New Brunswick. The New Brunswick Higher Education Commission had pointed to some problems experienced by the affiliated colleges of the Université de Moncton and called for a reassessment of "the future structure of higher education in the French sector of New Brunswick with special emphasis on the role to be played by the various institutions involved" (NBHEC, 1975, p. 20). In its report, the Study Committee referred to

> the tensions caused by the present structure of affiliation of the various colleges to the Université de Moncton and of the insufficient assurance provided by this structure for the security and cohesion of Francophone higher education in New Brunswick. (MPHEC, 1975b, p. 39)

While reiterating that there should be a single French-language university for all francophones of New Brunswick, the Committee recommended the creation of l'Université Acadienne. The Committee expressed the view that the affiliation arrangements for the colleges outside Moncton were inadequate. Competing with the Université de Moncton the northern colleges were experiencing enrollment declines and feeling, according to the Committee, isolated from U de M. As Reid (1989) notes, the "apparent imbalance in favour of southern New Brunswick . . . plagued the Université de Moncton in its institutional relationships with its northern affiliated colleges" (p. 23). The colleges felt they received insufficient support from U de M which had not been able to create "a feeling of solidarity between francophones of all regions" (MPHEC, 1975b, p. 41). To deal with this perceived problem and expressed fears that U de M was slipping into bilingualism rather than French-language education, the Committee proposed that as of July 1, 1976, the new L'Université Acadienne replace Université de Moncton, Saint Louis-Maillet, and Jesus-Marie Colleges.

The MPHEC considered the report of the Committee. While recognizing the problems identified in the report, the Commission did not recommend the creation of a new university as such. However, different arrangements were developed to integrate more clearly the institutions at Edmundston and Shippagan with Moncton, and in 1976 an Act to amend the University of Moncton Act was introduced. The University was declared to be a degree granting French-language institution with campuses in Shippagan, Edmundston, and Moncton. In 1988, when Université de Moncton celebrated its 25th anniversary with a major ceremony on the Moncton campus, video linkages to the other two centres symbolized the university's structure.

Other studies initiated by the Commission have included the study of the role and goals of all the maritime institutions discussed earlier (MPHEC, 1981), a Study on Learning Disabilities (Golick, 1988), a study on Student Aid (MPHEC, 1988), a major study of the deterioration of the physical plant of the universities, and a major recent study of the role and capacity of the institutions within the region (MPHEC, 1993). This last initiative is discussed in more detail below.

Institutional Role and Planned Capacity Statements

In 1988, concerned about the continuing appropriateness of the method of funding Maritime universities, the MPHEC commissioned a review by Alan Adlington. After consultation with representatives of the Maritime universities, Adlington submitted his report proposing changes in the funding formula. Enrollment would be de-emphasized in funding calculations and more focus would be placed on the roles and capacities of the universities (MPHEC, 1989). Each would express its role in the higher education system and its planned capacity for the Commission's consideration, suggesting a more pro-active approval role for the

Commission with respect to the overall system of universities and how each fit within it. An enrollment corridor would be created representing plus or minus 3% or 4% of the planned capacity. Universities could vary their enrollment within that corridor but would not necessarily get increased government funding for going above the corridor, although fee income would increase accordingly. As well as the basic operating grant there would be funds for particular policy initiatives such as infrastructure costs, new developments, or special functional needs. The implementation of this concept in New Brunswick is discussed in more detail later.

An Assessment of the MPHEC's Impact

In the past twenty years the MPHEC has had a major impact on higher education in New Brunswick as well as in the other maritime provinces. Like commissions elsewhere have found, there is value in placing a buffer body between the universities and the government. The Commission acts as a conduit through which the needs and funding requests of the universities are transmitted and interpreted to government. In turn, government policy and decisions are passed on to the universities through the MPHEC which can assist in their interpretation. The programme approval process, described earlier, helps to avoid unnecessary duplication of programmes as well as providing an opportunity for other universities to be informed about and comment on the initiatives of the proposing institution. The Commission has also undertaken a number of studies which have contributed to our knowledge of education needs and initiatives in the region, maintains a data base of historical and current information on Maritime and Canadian higher education and provides assistance to universities, individual researchers, government, and others requiring information on educational topics.

From time to time the MPHEC has been criticized by universities for not being as strong an advocate for the universities with government as the universities might wish. There has existed a perception in some quarters that the Commission has had a tendency to recommend funding at a level the government can afford rather than at the level the universities state that they need. It should be said that this is not a particularly unusual criticism of such commissions. Moreover, in its Financial Plan 1992-93 the Commission clearly recognized the difficulties facing universities and recommended a level of funding it believed "necessary to maintain services and programmes at their existing level" (MPHEC, 1992, p. 11). Whatever the accuracy of the perception, it is true that the MPHEC's funding recommendations were typically adopted by the Government of New Brunswick. In recent years the MPHEC has not made recommendations for funding levels. Rather, it has outlined the consequences for university budgets of different funding scenarios. Some have argued that the MPHEC should be more pro-active in evaluating existing, not simply new and modified programmes, and more rigorous in its examination of programme proposals. Nonetheless, Condon (1989) comments favourably on the Commission's willingness to conduct research and disseminate its results and on the openness and clarity of its funding recommendations.

Perhaps the major catalyst for debate on the role of the MPHEC has, in recent years, been the creation in 1989 of the Nova Scotia Council on Higher Education (NSCHE). In 1993 the Council of Maritime Premiers (CMP) established in 1993 an inter-provincial task force to study and make recommendations on the functioning of the MPHEC. The CMP accepted several of the task force's recommendations on enhancing the Commission's effectiveness and reaffirmed their commitment to the Commission.

Other Postsecondary Institutions

In 1974 the Maritime Forest Ranger School was shifted to the jurisdiction of the MPHEC for funding purposes. In 1978 the School was incorporated with the passage of the Maritime Forest Ranger School Act (MPHEC, 1981). A French-language programme was introduced in Bathurst in 1980. The School continues to offer technical education in forestry through a full-time, one-year programme as well as continuing education opportunities. The School of Fisheries remains under the Department of Fisheries, rather than the Department of Advanced Education and Labour, primarily because of its strong link to the fishing industry. However, the St. Andrews Community College assumed responsibility for fisheries training in the Bay of Fundy as of 1988 (Landry and Downey, 1993). The College of Craft and Design is administered by the Department of Advanced Education and Labour and offers a diploma as well as certificate programmes and individual courses.

In 1970, the United Baptist Bible Training School was renamed the Atlantic Baptist College, and two years of university-level arts courses were introduced alongside the biblical diploma program. The high school program had been phased out a few years earlier. In 1983, the College was granted a provincial charter to confer baccalaureate degrees.

The Community College

Neither of the Commissions in the 1960s addressed the vocational and technical aspects of postsecondary education, focusing solely on the universities and their affiliated colleges. By the early 1970s a number of people felt that the structure of technical education in the province also should be examined and that there would be value in bringing the various technical and vocational schools under one umbrella. Hearings conducted by the NBHEC in 1972 were told that postsecondary institutions were not responding adequately to community needs (Dennison and Gallagher, 1986). Accordingly, the Community College Act was passed in 1973 bringing the New Brunswick Community College (NBCC) into existence in 1974. A corporation, with a board of governors, was established to oversee the affairs of the College. This single entity incorporated the vocational and technical schools, encompassing nine campuses, and their staff became staff of the College. Its Board reported to the Minister of Education.

For six years the NBCC operated in this way, quite satisfactorily in the view of a number of people, as it seemed to be gaining respect and acceptance in the community. The province was divided into five regions, each with a regional advisory board which could make recommendations to the Board of the NBCC and which facilitated a responsiveness to local needs. Flexibility can be said to characterize the NBCC in its early years of operation, as it responded to local needs and job training requirements. A plan commissioned by the Board in 1978 confirmed the College's success in meeting its mandate while suggesting changes to respond to the province's bilingualism and growing needs for educational upgrading and job training (Dennison and Gallagher, 1986). This assessment notwithstanding, the government made the decision in 1980 to change the administrative structure of the College. It ceased to be a separate corporation and came under the direct supervision of a government department, then called the Department of Continuing Education and subsequently the Department of Community Colleges. The Regional Advisory Boards disappeared with this centralization in the College's administration.

The motivation for this change appears to have been a desire to make NBCC more clearly an instrument for carrying out government economic and social policy including labour market requirements and accessibility for both anglophones and francophones to postsecondary education. Muller (1990) conceptualizes these changes in human resource development terms. He describes how the centralized administration was facilitated by computerized infrastructure, access to standardized information, and centralized curriculum development and evaluation. He outlines how programmes are assessed and how decisions are made centrally about the resources allocated to the programmes.

The dropping of some programmes that can be offered by the private sector and the focus on others identified as being relevant to regional needs in different parts of the province underscore the role the government sees for the College in provincial economic development. In order to establish the extent to which programmes meet labour market objectives, they are continually reviewed based on an annual graduate follow-up survey, student retention and consultation with stakeholders in the educational and workplace sector and the general public (Dennison, 1995). The College is not a junior college but rather an institution managed by two senior civil servants in the Department of Advanced Education and Labour as co-CEOs with labour market objectives in mind.

Each campus of the College offers programmes in basic education which may also prepare students for more specialized courses. These specialized programmes provide more in-depth preparation and vary from campus to campus to avoid duplicating effort. Finally, the College offers educational services geared to local needs.

Dennison (1995), in his summary of the current status of the NBCC, notes the shift from corporate entity with advisory committees to government administration with little external input. He comments favourably on the College's commitment to serving New Brunswickers in both French and English and the efficient use of resources that administrative centralization allows, while reserving judgement on whether the structure that has been developed is the best one for the circumstances.

The Period 1990 to 1995

In the fall of 1991 the New Brunswick Government of Premier Frank McKenna announced the creation of a Commission on Excellence in Education, co-chaired by former Deputy Premier Aldea Landry and former President of UNB, James Downey. The Commission's first issues paper and report dealt with elementary through secondary education while the second addressed postsecondary education. The latter Report made thirty-nine recommendations which the Commission classified as relating to foundational issues, life-long learning, the Community College and other postsecondary institutions, and universities (Landry and Downey, 1993).

The Commission on Excellence in Education

Foundational Issues

The Commissioners outlined the principles which guided them and to which they felt many who presented to the Commission also subscribed. These included eliminating the dichotomy between education and training, commitment to lifelong learning, and the importance of a core set of skills for students to develop in computation, analysis and communication. They also reaffirmed the link between education, training, and research for the economic well-being of the province. The Commissioners saw that these goals were best likely to be achieved through an integrated but diverse higher education system in New Brunswick, which included distance education as well as on-site instruction. To this end they called for the establishment of the New Brunswick Distance Education and Training network to complement the existing research network in conjunction with the communication sector. The Commissioners also addressed the need for accessibility to educational opportunities for all New Brunswickers, including First Nations people, persons with disabilities, and women.

Lifelong Learning

The Commissioners stressed the importance of continual learning as social and economic demands change and the population must adjust to these changes. They believed that the province must have a range of learning opportunities available to its citizenry including foundation education, skills development, apprenticeship programmes, and portability of credits, including prior learning assessment. They made a number of recommendations which addressed these needs. For example, they called for a thorough review and modernization of the apprenticeship system and, from a policy perspective, recommended a federal-provincial partnership to foster labour-market objectives.

Community College

A significant number of the recommendations concerned the Community Colleges which the commissioners believed have been "quite successful in fulfilling their role as a comprehensive training system" (Landry and Downey, 1993, p. 40). Nonetheless, they identified weaknesses in the College's administrative structure and recommended the establishment of the Community College as a crown corporation with very different administrative and funding arrangements than in the period since 1980. They also recommended that the New Brunswick College of Craft and Design be included in this corporation. Their recommendations addressed administrative structure as well as accessibility, operating and capital funding, professional development of instructors and curriculum considerations, including the need to ensure some consistency in curriculum quality and content in the short courses offered.

The Universities

The Commissioners stressed the need for universities to pay appropriate attention to the importance of good teaching, providing opportunities for instructors to develop and maintain good teaching skills and for universities to recognize good teaching in tenure and promotion decisions. The Commission also called for a common applications centre and student information system which would enhance service to students and provide consistent, province-wide data on student participation and success rates. Other recommendations dealt with student mobility, financial aid, tuition fees and government funding of institutions. Notable among the funding recommendations was a call to continue the existing system of formula funding but with additional targeted funding to bring about change which is seen as desirable, presumably by the government. The Commission also called for the government to take appropriate steps to ensure the long-term effectiveness of the MPHEC as an agency which can foster and support regional initiatives in higher education. They also suggested that the MPHEC take the lead in developing appropriate performance indicators and encouraging the universities to employ these indicators in demonstrating accountability.

The Government's Response

On April 28, 1993, the Minister of Advanced Education and Labour, Vaughn Blaney, presented the Government's response to the Commission's report, following a number of public consultations. Predicated on the philosophy that education and training are the keys to economic development, the response outlined an approach based on the principles of "life-long learning, accessibility, flexibility, quality and partnerships" (Blaney, 1993). The "learner-centred strategy" he announced was to include the establishment of a New Brunswick Council on Education for discussion and action, initiatives in distance education, career skills and literacy development, initiatives to ensure gender equity, and ease of credit transfer. Provisions would be made for an additional 400 Community College places and admission to programmes was to require Grade 12 completion. The Community College was to become a Special Operating Agency of the Department of Advanced Education and Labour by 1996-97 and not a Crown Corporation as recommended (Dennison, 1995). The Department of Advanced Education and Labour, created in 1991, has responsibility for the universities, the NBCC, vocational training, and apprenticeship training—a clear demonstration of the relationship the Government of New Brunswick sees between education and training and labour market development. The government's role is one of leverage to achieve public policy objectives through incentives and disincentives for job creation and economic development and preparation for the job market. In his response to the Commission's report the Minister also challenged the universities to focus on ensuring, enhancing, and recognising teaching quality and to develop performance indicators to demonstrate publicly their accountability.

Role and Planned Capacity Statements

Another initiative in the 1990s will also shape the postsecondary sector. As noted earlier, the MPHEC asked the universities in New Brunswick and Prince Edward Island to submit statements of institutional role and planned capacity which they did in 1992-93. The MPHEC then prepared a composite report, as it had done earlier in Nova Scotia. In this report (MPHEC, 1993), each university's history and current and future roles in teaching, research and community service were outlined. Trends in enrollment, funding, and student outcomes were considered and a number of challenges which confront the universities suggested. Many of these challenges echo the comments of Landry and Downey, including quality of teaching, accessibility, gender equity, lifelong learning and education/workplace issues, against a backdrop of declining government funding and the need for postsecondary institutions to be as effective and efficient as possible under this constraint.

A number of general recommendations were made about such areas as quality assessment of academic programmes, credit transfer both among universities and between universities and the Community College, inter-university cooperation in programme delivery, including distance education, accessibility, accountability, and teaching quality and priority. The Universities offering the programmes singled out for attention were recommended to review those programmes and the resources allocated to them. As the report followed the report of the Commission on Excellence in Education, it also offered comments on one of the earlier Commission's recommendations on teacher education, contained in its first report on K-12 education. The MPHEC recommended a phase-out of four-year teacher education programmes which would be replaced with combined or sequential B.A. or B.Sc/B.Ed programmes. The MPHEC also called for a review of university acts to address the appropriateness of governance structures and suggested the need for post-tenure reviews to ensure continued satisfactory performance of faculty.

At the moment it is not clear what impact this report will have on the New Brunswick universities and this represents a currently evolving issue. Some recent initiatives do appear to have their origins, or at least their current impetus, in the MPHEC's comments. For example, a first-year university programme is currently being offered at the New Brunswick Community College campus in Chatham through cooperation of St. Thomas, Mount Allison, and UNB, primarily through on-site instruction. It seems probable that this initiative might be extended in the future to other communities since it has proved attractive to students who might not otherwise have enrolled in university. In March 1995, the four New Brunswick universities announced that they were studying the possibility of forming a consortium for delivery of distance education and are actively pursuing those discussions.

TeleEducation NB was established as a five-year project under the Canada-New Brunswick Cooperative Agreement on Entrepreneurship and Human Resource Development (TeleEducation NB, 1994). The network provides New Brunswickers with ready access to education and training in both English and French through telecommunications. Approximately 50 distance education sites exist throughout the province and a growing number of courses are becoming available. Funds have been earmarked for course development. TeleEducation reports through the Department of Advanced Education and Labour. Its establishment addresses issues raised by both the MPHEC and the Commission on Excellence in Education.

Other recent developments include the introduction of Bachelor of Nursing programmes, a corollary of the phasing out of the diploma schools of nursing. UNB is offering a programme in English in Fredericton, Saint John, Moncton, and Bathurst. U de M is offering a programme in French in Moncton, Edmundston, and Bathurst, with coordination among the three sites, including the use of distance education. The MPHEC noted in its Role and Planned Capacity Report the possibility of the diploma schools staying in place for a transitional period of two years after the introduction of the degree programmes (MPHEC, 1993).

The Atlantic Baptist College has plans for expansion. It will move to a new campus with opportunities for future development in 1996, add programmes, students, and faculty, and change its name to Atlantic Baptist University.

Conclusion

The number, location, and nature of postsecondary institutions in New Brunswick owe much to the historical influences on their establishment. Up to the mid-1850s in the case of UNB and much later for the other universities, the church had a major influence. Since the 1960s government influence has been very apparent in the lives of the universities and instrumental in the creation of the Community College. It can be argued that it is through the efforts of government and the adoption of the recommendations of the commissions and committees government has established, that a unique system of higher education has been shaped in New Brunswick. In turn, this forms part of a broader regional system. Within this system the different institutions play clearly distinctive roles one from another, cooperate in a number of ways, and, through the monitoring and approval process for programmes, unwarranted duplication of programmes can be avoided and an attempt is made to allocate limited resources in the most efficient way.

Notwithstanding the effort of government to shape and monitor a provincial and regional system of higher education, the different ways in which the universities have developed make clear the interests and strengths of the individual institutions. They retain their autonomy and represent distinctive entities each with its own programme mix, philosophy of education, and historical traditions. The Community College falls under direct government control and is not an autonomous institution, and the distinctiveness of one campus from another is a direct result of decisions on programme specialization and regional needs.

Undoubtedly the MPHEC's report on university roles and capacities and the government's excellence in education initiatives will lead to close scrutiny of university and college programmes in New Brunswick. Nonetheless, the implementation of the recommendations of the Deutsch Commission in the 1960s, the subsequent work of the New Brunswick Higher Education Commission and the Maritime Provinces Higher Education Commission, and the government initiatives that have led to the creation of both the New Brunswick Community College and the three specialty colleges, have resulted in a system of higher education which appears to meet the needs of New Brunswick students and shows a considerable degree of rationality in the different roles played by the postsecondary institutions.

It seems likely that a very pro-active public policy agenda will continue to influence the postsecondary education sector, particularly the Community College through the clear link between college programmes and workplace demands but also the universities through the Role and Planned Capacity exercise, incentives to develop distance education and multimedia initiatives, and funding which includes a targeted component to encourage particular developments in the public interest.

References

Association of Atlantic Universities (1969). *Higher education in the Atlantic Provinces for the 1970's.* A study prepared under the auspices of the Association of Atlantic Universities for the Maritime Union Study. Halifax, NS.

Blaney, V. (1993). *Response to the excellence in education recommendations.* Ministerial Statement to the New Brunswick Legislature April 28, 1993.

Cameron, D.M. (1991). *More than an academic question: Universities, government and public policy in Canada.* Halifax, NS: The Institute for Research on Public Policy.

Committee on the Financing of Higher Education in New Brunswick. (1967). *Report.* Fredericton, NB: Government of New Brunswick.

Condon, T.J. (October 1989). Higher education in New Brunswick: Challenges for tomorrow. *Shaping the system: Higher Education in New Brunswick*. Symposium at University of New Brunswick, Fredericton, NB.

Cormier, C. (1975). *L'Université de Moncton historique*. Moncton, NB: Centre d'études acadiennes, Université de Moncton.

Dennison, J.D. (1995). *Challenge and opportunity: Canada's community colleges at the crossroads*. Vancouver, BC: UBC Press.

Dennison, J.D., and Gallagher, P. (1986). *Canada's community colleges: A critical analysis*. Vancouver, BC: UBC Press.

Fraser, J.A. (1970). *By force of circumstance: A history of St. Thomas University*. Chatham, NB: Miramichi Press Ltd.

Golick, M. (1988). *Learning disabilities in postsecondary education. Report to the Maritime Provinces Higher Education Commission*. Fredericton, NB: Maritime Provinces Higher Education Commission.

Landry, A., and Downey, J. (1993). *To live and learn: The challenge of education and training. Report of the Commission on Excellence in Education*. Fredericton, NB: Government of New Brunswick.

Maritime Provinces Higher Education Commission (1975a). *Annual report 1974-1975* Fredericton, NB.

Maritime Provinces Higher Education Commission (1975b). *Report of the Committee on Higher Education in the French Sector of New Brunswick*. Fredericton, NB.

Maritime Provinces Higher Education Commission (1975c). *Financial plan. 1975-76 to 1992-93*. Fredericton, NB.

Maritime Provinces Higher Education Commission (1981). *Maritime provinces postsecondary institutions: As we see ourselves*. Fredericton, NB.

Maritime Provinces Higher Education Commission (1988). *Student aid for the 1990s. Student Aid Study Committee Report*. Fredericton, NB.

Maritime Provinces Higher Education Commission (1989). *Annual Report*. 1988-89. Fredericton, NB.

Maritime Provinces Higher Education Commission (1991). *Annual Report, 1990-91*. Fredericton, NB.

Maritime Provinces Higher Education Commission and Nova Scotia Council on Higher Education (1993). *Role and planned capacity report 2. New Brunswick and Prince Edward Island universities and general recommendations*. Fredericton, NB.

Maritime Provinces Higher Education Commission (1994). *Annual Report, 1993-94*. Fredericton, NB.

Muller, J. (Ed.). (1990). *Education for work, Education as work. Canada's changing community colleges*. Toronto, ON: Garamond Press.

New Brunswick Advanced Education and Labour (1994). *Annual report 1993-94*. Fredericton, NB.

New Brunswick Higher Education Commission. *Annual Reports. 1967 to 1974.* Fredericton, NB.

New Brunswick Higher Education Commission (1969). Investing in the future. *A programme for government assistance to universities, technical schools and their students.* Fredericton, NB.

Picot, J.E. (1974). *A brief history of teaching training in New Brunswick 1848-1973.* Fredericton, NB: Department of Education.

Reid, J.G. (1984). *Mount Allison University: A history, to 1963.* 2 volumes. Toronto, ON: University of Toronto Press.

Reid, J.G. (October 1989). Some historical reflections on the Report of the Royal Commission on Higher Education in New Brunswick. 1962. *Shaping the system: Higher education in New Brunswick.* Symposium at University of New Brunswick, Fredericton, NB.

Royal Commission on Higher Education in New Brunswick (1962). *Report.* Fredericton, NB: Government of New Brunswick.

Stanley, D.M.M. (1984). *Louis Robichaud: A decade of power.* Halifax, NS: Nimbus Publishing Ltd.

TeleEducation NB (1994). *Annual report.* Fredericton, NB.

Higher Education in Nova Scotia: Where Past Is More Than Prologue

Brian D. Christie

I. Our Feature Attraction, The Universities

Program Notes

The story of university education in Nova Scotia is an incomplete opus, a drama in two acts, with the Great Depression and World War II as intermission. Some will view this presentation as a tragi-comedy, while for others, including many who appear in the most recent scenes, it takes on at times epic proportions. It includes characters, heroes and villains, whose roles have great dramatic impact. Audiences seem fascinated by it, finding enjoyment in each retelling. New scenes are currently being authored, and the next twist in its plot-line has yet to be revealed. Whatever is to come will best be understood in the context of the scenario that we now rehearse.

The Overture

In 1945 Nova Scotia's higher education institutions were either small private college foundations or agencies of the provincial government offering professional and technical education. The private colleges received no government funding to support their operations except for that provided for some professional schools like Dalhousie University's Faculty of Medicine. Privately endowed to varying degrees, the colleges subsisted on endowment income, augmented by tuition fees, donations from individuals, and, for some, subventions from their sponsoring churches. Several of the colleges were dependent on clerical academics for a significant part of the teaching complement, augmenting the contributions of underpaid faculty. Government was not involved in the direction of the private colleges nor in higher education policy or planning.

The administration of the institutions was authoritarian, even autocratic, with control that extended into many aspects of the lives of students. Most students enrolled in arts, science, or pre-professional programs—professional education opportunities were limited to medicine, law, dentistry, engineering, and a very few others.

Admission standards were high and courses of study tightly defined. Extracurricular life was rich as students actively engaged in managing most of the programs and clubs. Faculty members knew their students by name, and a graduate could often point in later years to a professor who had had a profound effect on his or her career and life.

In the past fifty years Nova Scotia's universities have been transformed in many of the same ways as their counterparts in other provinces. Enrollments have grown by an order of magnitude, and the demographics of the student population have altered profoundly. Female students are now in the majority at most institutions; enrollments from minority populations occur in greater measure in undergraduate and professional programs, and mature students have increased substantially.

New facilities have been built to accommodate this growth. New institutions have also been created, although not to the extent of some other provinces. Many new programs, particularly in graduate and professional education, have been added, and the number of courses from which an undergraduate student may choose has proliferated tremendously. The increasingly occupational orientation of university studies has undercut the former dominance of liberal education.

Numbers of faculty have increased, most faculty complements are unionized, and faculty and students have greater formal voices in the administration of their institution's affairs. There is a much greater reliance at many institutions on part-time instructors. The aging professoriate is no longer a new phenomenon. A cadre of equity officers has arrived on campus.

Sponsorship of university education in Nova Scotia has shifted from largely religious to primarily governmental and now is shifting again to a greater reliance on market support from fees, contract income, and fundraising. Growth in research activities and the amount of time that faculty devote to the search for new knowledge have altered the nature of the academic enterprise and the cost of operating the institutions. The three camels of Canadian research, the granting councils, are firmly ensconced in the tents of academia.

And yet, for all this change, those who read the history of Nova Scotia's universities, over more than two centuries, will find that the central debate about university education in the province is unchanged. Despite numerous attempts to remake the institutional structure of Nova Scotia's university system, the arguments continue about how many universities the province should have and how government funding should be divided among them. Anyone who wishes to understand the current condition of university education in Nova Scotia must look to the history books and the long series of failed attempts to merge some or all of the institutions. This debate has engendered bitter rivalries among some of the universities and has produced some of the most peculiar decisions on the structure and funding of university education that this country has seen. The debate continues in full force. For, despite many attempts, the organizational structure established in the nineteenth century has endured and been fortified.

Dramatis Personae

Higher education in today's Nova Scotia is a scene of unique contrasts. There are more universities per capita than in any other province, and there is the least developed community college system in the country. The universities receive the lowest provincial operating grants per student and the second highest per capita of provincial population. According to a popular magazine rating scheme, Nova Scotia's universities are among the best and worst in Canada. Every one of the degree-granting institutions has a distinctive or specialized purpose or a particular catchment demographic for its students, yet provincial politicians call repeatedly for rationalization and elimination of duplication. At the same time, the current government, which has forced amalgamation on unwilling school boards, hospitals, and municipalities across the province, has refused to act in the same way with the universities, despite repeated appeals by some of the institutions.

The university system in 1995 contains six specialized institutions (soon to be five), six comprehensive and predominantly undergraduate universities of varying size and with particular audiences, and one research-intensive multiversity, small and truncated by the absence of the usual applied science and teacher preparation faculties. Indeed, all are small by national standards. These institutions are joined by a web of affiliation agreements, program linkages, cooperative academic and academic support endeavours, cost-reducing administrative arrangements, and computer and library networks. Seven of the thirteen are located in the capital city of Halifax and have a combined enrollment that approximates that of the University of Calgary, or Ottawa, or Western Ontario. Two of the thirteen offer community college technology programs in addition to university-level studies.

The current cast of characters includes the following, in order of appearance:

The University of King's College (1789). Canada's oldest university, located on a corner of the Dalhousie University campus in Halifax, is formally associated with Dalhousie in the offering of studies in the Humanities and Social Sciences. King's offers a first-year Foundation Year Program following which students can proceed to studies at Dalhousie or to a small jointly offered Contemporary Studies Program. King's also provides the only programs in Journalism in Nova Scotia. The university enrollment is about 800 students.

Dalhousie University (1818). Nova Scotia's largest university (about 11,000 students) is Canada's smallest multiversity. Programs are offered in Arts, Science, Management, Law, Graduate Studies, and a wide range of health professions. Dalhousie and the Technical University offer the only doctoral degrees in Nova Scotia. Dalhousie receives about 70% of granting council research funding to Nova Scotia universities and is the most heavily engaged in international development activities. Unlike most of its peers across Canada, its Engineering program is small, limited to the first two years, while its Education school is in process of closing as the result of a government edict. It has an international reputation for work in Ocean Studies. It also offers the majority of continuing education activities in the province.

Acadia University (1838). Located in the small town of Wolfville in the Annapolis Valley, Acadia is primarily an undergraduate university with a limited number of masters programs. It has an excellent reputation for liberal education and the exposure of its honours students to research activities, and it is active in distance education and houses one of the province's four remaining Education (teacher preparation) programs. Enrollment is about 4,400. A Baptist divinity school is associated with Acadia.

Saint Mary's University (1841). This Halifax university was operated by various Roman Catholic religious orders until 1970. Primarily an undergraduate institution, it is the second largest university in Nova Scotia following a doubling of enrollments in the 1980s. Saint Mary's has a major concentration in business and commerce (about 40% of its 8,000 students). With its emphasis on accessibility, more than one-third of Saint Mary's students study part-time, and the University uses a variety of off-campus sites.

St. Francis Xavier University (1853). A primarily undergraduate institution that emphasizes its socially engaged Roman Catholic tradition, St. Francis Xavier is the birthplace of the internationally known Antigonish Cooperative Movement. The majority of its 3,700 students are in Arts and Science. Programs in Education, Business Administration, and Nursing are also offered.

The Nova Scotia Teachers College (1854). Reputed to be the last remaining normal school in North America, this teacher training facility in Truro is in the process of being phased out by the provincial Department of Education which operates it. NSTC prepares students for teacher certification and has an arrangement with Mount Saint Vincent University for degree completion.

Mount Saint Vincent University (1873). Located in Halifax, Mount Saint Vincent, founded by the Catholic Sisters of Charity, is a primarily undergraduate university focusing particularly on the higher education of women who make up about 85% of its 3,600 students. Almost half of its students are part-time, and the majority have come to the university as mature students following various life experiences. Programs unique to the University include Human Ecology, Public Relations, and Tourism Administration.

Nova Scotia College of Art and Design (1887). NSCAD is the oldest degree granting professional college of its kind in Canada. The College prepares students for professional careers as artists, craftspersons, communication designers, environmental planners, and art educators. Its location in historic buildings on the Halifax harbourfront has contributed to the revitalization of that part of the city. Bachelors and masters programs are offered to about 600 students.

Université Sainte-Anne (1890). The only francophone university in the province, Sainte-Anne was founded to serve the educational, linguistic, and cultural needs of Nova Scotia's Acadians. Located in the small town of Pointe-de-l'Église on the southwest French Shore, Sainte-Anne offers undergraduate programs in Arts, Education, Administration, and Management and the first two years of Science to a total of about 500 students. Programs in French immersion are also provided.

Nova Scotia Agricultural College (1905). NSAC is a regional facility for the Maritime provinces, offering university and college level education related to the agri-food industry, as well as continuing education and professional development activities. It has the third largest research volume among the universities. Bachelor and masters degrees in Agriculture are offered in association with Dalhousie University, while Agricultural

Engineering is a cooperative effort with the Technical University. The College is operated by the Department of Agriculture and enrolls about 800 students at its Truro campus.

The Technical University of Nova Scotia (1907). TUNS, located in Halifax, offers programs in engineering, architecture and urban planning, food science and technology, and computer science. The initial two years of the engineering and computer science programs are offered by up to nine associated universities in the three Maritime provinces. Most of its 1,400 students are fulltime, and about one-quarter are in masters or doctoral programs. Research funding is the second largest in Nova Scotia at about 12% of granting council support.

Atlantic School of Theology (1971). AST was established to provide an ecumenical approach to the preparation of persons for ministry, lay and ordained, and to the study of theology. Created by the merger of the Divinity Faculty of the University of King's College (Anglican), Holy Heart Theological Institute (Roman Catholic), and Pine Hill Divinity Hall (United Church), its masters programs in Divinity, Theological Studies and Theology enroll about 80 full-time and 50 part-time students, primarily from the founding churches but also from other denominations. It relies on grants from both government and the sponsoring churches and is located in Halifax.

University College of Cape Breton (1974). UCCB in Sydney, Cape Breton Island, was the second institution created in the post-war period through a merger. Xavier College, a junior college campus of St. Francis Xavier University, was amalgamated with the Nova Scotia Eastern Institute of Technology, creating an institution that offers both university education in the liberal arts and sciences and community college training in trades and technology. Hybrid programs such as a Bachelor of Technology (Environmental Studies) and a Bachelor of Arts (Community Studies) have emerged from the resulting synergy. UCCB has a strong economic development element to its mission. It is the only degree-granting institution in Cape Breton and enrolls 2,700 university program students.

Act One

Our curtain rises with the founding of King's College, in Windsor in 1789, with funding from both colonial and imperial coffers. King's charter limited the granting of degrees to those who swore allegiance to the thirty-nine articles of faith of the Church of England, denying access to over three-quarters of Nova Scotia's population. This situation set the stage for

Lord Dalhousie, the newly arrived Lieutenant-Governor of the province, to establish a college based on ideas that were, it turned out, far ahead of the views of most of the populace he governed. Modeled on the University of Edinburgh, non-sectarian, and with a decidedly practical bent to its educational philosophy, Dalhousie College was to be, in the Governor's vision, the provincial university.

A fine building was built in the heart of Halifax, consuming all of the endowment (and more) that his Lordship had provided with funds collected from the Americans during the War of 1812. By the time the new facilities were ready for occupation, however, Lord Dalhousie had moved on and the Anglican-dominated Legislative Council refused to grant funds for his college to operate. In 1824 the Boards of King's and Dalhousie, recognizing that their rivalry promised continuing hardship and lack of success, agreed to merge, only to have the amalgamation vetoed in Britain by the Archbishop of Canterbury and the Colonial Secretary. A second attempt in 1832 also failed. And so, Lord Dalhousie's fine edifice was rented out to a pastry shop and for other uses, while King's College, with most of its grants cut off, was reduced to four students by 1834.

In 1838, the Reform government of Joseph Howe provided operating funds to Dalhousie College. A President was selected, and faculty were recruited. But when President McCullough's preference for the appointment of a well-qualified Baptist, E.A. Crawley, was overridden by the Presbyterian trustees in favour of two of their co-religionists, Crawley and his Baptist supporters founded Acadia College. This opened the door to the establishment of more church-sponsored institutions. 1842 and 1843 saw the provincial government's attempts to establish "One Good College" fail in sectarian battles in the legislature and in November 1843, with the college issue a major factor, Howe's government was defeated. By 1845, government funding was flowing to King's (Anglican), Saint Mary's (Roman Catholic), Pictou Academy (Presbyterian), and a Methodist college in Sackville, New Brunswick, which was to become Mount Allison University. Dalhousie, unfunded, closed.

In 1863, new legislation and funding allowed the re-opening of Dalhousie despite vigorous attempts to repeal the legislation by Baptist legislators. A new approach to rationalization was attempted in 1876 with legislation creating a University of Halifax. This institution, modeled on the University of London, was to act initially as a central examining agency. The government's long-term plan was for it to become the provincial university. Six colleges, including St. Francis Xavier in Antigonish, were provided funding as an incentive to cooperate, but most were opposed to the idea. When the legislation expired five years later so did the government grants to all the colleges as another burst of sectarian rivalry and opposition to the funding of the non-denominational Dalhousie College led to the defeat of all proposed compromises. This funding lapse lasted for a total of 82 years.

Many of the colleges found themselves in dire straits as a result of the cessation of government grants. Saint Mary's closed its doors from 1881 to 1903. Those which managed to continue did so because of the support of their church sponsors, alumni, and/or benefactors. Merger discussions between Dalhousie and King's and later between Saint Mary's and Dalhousie again led nowhere.

In the meantime, the growing costs of education in the sciences and engineering were increasing the burden on the small colleges. Government funding was assisting Dalhousie to provide professional education in Medicine and Dentistry, in addition to its schools of Law and Pharmacy. However, the other colleges did not want Dalhousie to acquire the increasingly popular engineering programs, as well. The solution consisted of the government establishing and operating the Nova Scotia Technical College (now the Technical University of Nova Scotia) to provide the costly upper years of engineering education, while a number of the colleges provided the less expensive introductory two years. In 1908 the Technical College joined the ranks of the Nova Scotia Agricultural College, founded in 1905, and the Nova Scotia Teachers College, 1854, as government-operated professional education institutions.

The closing scene of Act One took place in the early 1920s and featured the efforts of two would-be guest directors, sponsored by the New York-based Carnegie Foundation for the Advancement of Teaching. Dr. William Learned of the Foundation's staff and Dr. Kenneth Sills, the President of Bowdoin College in Maine, conducted a study of the state of higher education in all three Maritime provinces. While generous with its praise, their report (1922) found much to criticize in the dissipation of effort across too many institutions, the underfunding, understaffing, low salaries, poor libraries, inadequate scientific equipment, and generally poor preparation of entering students. Learned and Sills concluded that the elements of first-class value which they had discovered at Dalhousie, St. Francis Xavier, and Acadia, for example, could be turned into a very good structure and a model for North America through an infusion of money from the Foundation for buildings and endowment and a re-organization of the institutions into a federation along the lines adopted at the University of Toronto. The new University of the Maritime Provinces would bring all the region's colleges together at one site in Halifax, retaining many of their names and their endowments. The numerous Catholic colleges would be combined. Dalhousie College would turn over most of its buildings and endowments and its programs in the professions and sciences to the new university, becoming the non-denominational University College. As the Carnegie Report stated (p. 36):

> Dalhousie would undergo almost any sacrifice of prestige, control, and even of name, if thereby the educational facilities of the province could be placed upon a permanently satisfactory and well-ordered foundation.

The offer was tempting and the colleges throughout the region engaged in many rounds of negotiations. But in the end, they could not surmount their long-held rivalries, their attachments to their original locales and supporting communities, and their antipathy to the non-denominational Dalhousie. Acadia officials even agreed in private that the new university should bear and preserve the Dalhousie name and then used this issue to attack the proposal. Dalhousie's President offered to compromise on the name but the proposal was doomed. One by one, each college rejected the Foundation's offer or failed to respond until only King's and Dalhousie were left to share a million dollar endowment as the reward for their coming together. This small step was doubtless due to a fire in Windsor that had razed the King's building in 1920 and left the College with no alternative way to secure new facilities.

Intermission

As the curtain came down on this anticlimactic final scene of Act One, the players withdrew backstage to cope with the financial rigours of the Depression, the absences of faculty and students during the war, and the challenges of accommodating the wave of returning veterans in the period immediately after the great conflict.

This first century and a half presented many possibilities for the merging and strengthening of Nova Scotia's colleges and universities. Virtually all of these opportunities were missed and the total results were insignificant, particularly when compared to the potential gain from the Carnegie offer. The early history of sectarianism that other provinces either surmounted or avoided, Nova Scotia embraced wholeheartedly so that the patterns that were established early remain today. They are apparent both in the structure and the attitudes that have bedeviled university education in Nova Scotia throughout its history.

Why did this come about? In part, it appears, these problems were the result of the timing of the initiation of college education in British North America. The climate of sectarian rivalry in Nova Scotia became fixed before the full development of responsible government, the introduction of scientific education (and its expenses), and the possibility of learning from others' experiences could have a salutary effect. In part, it was the premature vision of Lord Dalhousie who established a non-denominational college before its time so that it became the natural target for all sectarian interests, uniting them only in a common enmity for the "atheistic" institution. Dalhousie's lack of foresight in failing to ensure an operating endowment for his college doubtless played a role. The inability to obtain public funding for colleges with no denominational support was, however, pervasive across North America during the early nineteenth century. In part, it was the economic impact of Confederation that impoverished the region and provided few resources for provincial funding of higher education until federal government transfer payments changed the situation in 1963. Political factors were also important. For successive provincial governments, the lesson of Joseph Howe's defeat on the college issue loomed large. The style of government in Nova Scotia, where personal and political considerations dominate over public and social concerns, has kept governments since Howe's time well away from involvement in controversial "university politics." In part, it was individual personalities: the Archbishop of Canterbury, Crawley, and the Presbyterian Seceder McCullough, the Kirk trustees of Dalhousie College, the King's alumni who long opposed merger, and the Bishop of Antigonish who vetoed St. Francis Xavier's acceptance of the Carnegie offer. Each had an impact at a critical time that shaped the future, or more correctly, left the future to be shaped by the past.

Act Two

As the curtain rose for the second act of this performance, a new impressive piece of stage scenery met the eye. Saint Mary's University had constructed in the early 1950s an imposing granite structure in the south end of Halifax, capable of housing more than 1000 students in its high school and college programs. The story of how this project was financed is an intriguing one, involving a last-minute rescue of the Catholic Episcopal Corporation of Halifax (the diocese) from financial embarrassment, and the major contractor from bankruptcy, through the provision of an emergency line of credit by wealthy financier Norman Stanbury. To finance the carrying charges on the bonds that eventually were floated to cover the massive overrun construction cost, every church property in the diocese, excepting cemeteries, was mortgaged. And, it was later discovered, Archbishop McNally had not obtained the necessary permission of the Vatican to borrow the funds, although he had publicly announced that he had done so after a hurried trip to Rome. This episode illustrates, among other things, the commitment, willingness to sacrifice, and attachment that many in the church communities had for the higher education institutions they sponsored.

The 1960s saw a restoration of general public funding of universities in Nova Scotia after a hiatus of more than eight decades. In receipt of a windfall increase in federal transfer payments, the province finally found it possible to respond to the urgent needs of the institutions. A University Grants Committee, the first such buffer agency in Canada, was established in 1963 and distributed close to a million dollars in operating support and a half-million dollars in capital grants in the first year. The Committee also advised that Acadia, St. Francis Xavier, and Saint Mary's should increase their enrollment levels to meet projections of future enrollment growth, that graduate and professional programs should continue to be concentrated at Dalhousie and the Technical College, and that out-of-province supplementary fees should be considered for the 40% of students at Nova Scotia universities whose homes were elsewhere in Canada. This latter recommendation at least was not acted upon. Nevertheless, despite a modest decline in the proportion of out-of-province students, the issue continues today to be a concern of the provincial government, particularly in the context of federal transfers for postsecondary education that are based on provincial populations rather than student enrollments.

During the 1960s provincial funding for the universities became a legislated responsibility of the provincial government. A formula approach to the allocation of the operating grants, largely historically driven but including a weighted enrollment element modeled on the Ontario allocation formula, was introduced. In the latter half of the 1960s and the early 1970s many of the church-based colleges were re-chartered as public institutions as the founding churches turned over control to lay boards. Saint Mary's University became co-educational and, following the refusal by Mount Saint Vincent of a merger proposal, absorbed the university-level instruction of young women at the Convent of the Sacred Heart in Halifax.

The University Grants Committee took up the challenge of further reducing the duplication of effort and unnecessary expenses by promoting a series of bilateral negotiations, each involving Dalhousie and another Halifax institution. A number of cooperation and affiliation agreements were concluded, and, in an excess of optimism, the Committee announced in 1969 that Mount Saint Vincent would become a college within Dalhousie University. This was not to be, although cooperative arrangements in honours programs did continue. The only lasting effect of this initiative was the merger into Dalhousie of the formerly independent Maritime School of Social Work.

Merger discussions were not limited at this time to the higher education arena. The political union of the three Maritime provinces was also under study, and in 1971 a modest step in that direction occurred with the creation of a Council of Maritime Premiers and a number of pan-provincial agencies reporting to it. One of these was the Maritime Provinces Higher Education Commission, which replaced the provincial grants committees in each of the three provinces in 1974.

The Commission, with members appointed by the Council and a staff establishment in Fredericton, New Brunswick, was given legislated responsibilities for advising the Maritime governments on university financing matters and for promoting the efficient and effective use of resources in higher education in the region. Review of new program proposals, promotion of cooperative planning activities, gathering and transmission of data and information about the institutions, and facilitation of the special financing arrangements for regional programs were identified as its main duties. The regional programs include Dalhousie's health professional programs, the Agriculture College, the Atlantic Veterinary College in Prince Edward Island, and the Maritime Forest Ranger School in New Brunswick. MPHEC's purview encompassed all degree-granting institutions in the region, including Nova Scotia's thirteen universities and colleges, and three specialized applied arts and technology postsecondary institutions in the region. This latter group includes the Nova Scotia College of Geographic Sciences in Lawrencetown, Annapolis County, which in a typical Nova Scotian peculiarity is a campus of the Nova Scotia Community College.

The same year, 1974, also saw the creation through merger of the College of Cape Breton in Sydney. As well, there was yet another failed attempt at merger in Halifax. The Technical College and Dalhousie University had reached an agreement to join together. Enabling legislation passed second reading in the Legislative Assembly. But the College's alumni and Acadia University mounted such strong opposition to the plan that the bill was referred before final reading to a select committee that never reported. In due course, the College was renamed the Technical University of Nova Scotia (1980). Some of the other remaining colleges were also renamed, for instance the University College of Cape Breton, and all were awarded degree-granting status.

Attention next shifted to concerns about funding. A number of the Nova Scotia universities had been complaining for some time about inequities in their levels of government support. After much discussion the Nova Scotia government agreed to fund a 10-year program intended to remedy this deficiency. Additional funds were to be provided to bring the universities to the regional average grant per weighted student through the annual allocation of equalization grants which became part of an institution's permanent base funding. The allocation of each year's grants was determined by the relative size of the gap between an institution's weighted funding per student and the regional average.

This program, which began in 1978/79, had two major unanticipated consequences. First, it gave the "underfunded" universities major incentives for enrollment growth. Increased fee revenues, allocations through the regular enrollment element of the operating grant, and the equalization grants all rewarded higher student numbers. During the 1980s Saint Mary's University doubled its enrollments, and Mount Saint Vincent University grew substantially. Others grew to a lesser extent. As a result, equalization was not achieved. Instead, the enrollment increases offset the effect of the equalization grants to such an extent that the equalization gap actually grew over the twelve years that the funding program was in effect. Saint Mary's still regularly petitions for redress of its inequitable underfunding.

The second effect resulted from a combination of factors, in particular the government's failure to provide base funding that met inflationary needs so that the equalization grants were not supplementary funds as had been promised but drew from what the universities believed should have been increases to the regular grants. Equalization began to demand an unexpectedly large portion of the annual increase in government assistance to the universities, almost 40% in 1986/87 compared to only 8% or less in the earlier years. Moreover, the Commission in its allocation mechanism gave first priority to the equalization funding and second priority to the enrollment-driven element of the regular allocation formula. The result was wide variations in the grant increases to the various universities. In 1986/87, for example, while inflation was running at over 4%, Dalhousie and St. Francis Xavier received grant increases of about 3% while grants to King's, Mount Saint Vincent, Saint Mary's, and UCCB increased from 9% to 11% each. In one year the Commission had to suspend the application of its formula to prevent an absolute decrease in funding to Dalhousie, which, having expanded its enrollments in the 1960s before equalization, was now concentrating on increasing its research intensity, for which there was no funding allowance.

Dalhousie and St. Francis Xavier mounted a spirited attack against the continuation of this funding framework, convincing the Nova Scotia government that a review was in order. The MPHEC engaged Alan Adlington, a retired deputy minister and university administrator from Ontario, who reported in December 1988. Adlington advised that formula approaches to university funding had run their course, that quality considerations should now be given precedence over accessibility concerns, and that the universities which were responsible for regional programs and were research intensive ought to be protected from further funding reductions. Adlington proposed a funding system based on a "planned capacity and role" approach, much as the Bovey Commission in Ontario had recommended, with pre-determined enrollment corridors and special policy envelopes. The government's response was to discontinue the use of the MPHEC formula in Nova Scotia; the equalization program was wound up with two final instalments and a new funding approach was introduced employing fixed shares for the base grant with a small amount of targeted funding for research overheads and policy issues. The universities were asked by MPHEC to provide Statements of Institutional Role and Planned Capacity which they did in late 1989.

In the meantime, Nova Scotia was in receipt of the report of a Royal Commission on Postsecondary Education (1985). This was, in fact, the second Royal Commission on the subject within a dozen years—the province never being averse to duplication on matters of university education. The previous Royal Commission had produced, in 1974, a voluminous report on education, public services, and provincial-municipal relations which had been largely ignored. Foreshadowing Adlington, it had called for an emphasis on quality and a de-emphasis of accessibility concerns as well as increased student assistance and full-cost tuition fees. The 1985 Report recommended that the universities in the province perform as a coordinated system and that a Council on Higher Education be created with "executive authority" and discretionary powers over funding. The objectives were rationalization, the achievement of increased efficiency and effectiveness through reduced duplication, and increased coordination of activities. If the Council approach proved inadequate, the Royal Commission recommended consolidation into a single University of Nova Scotia.

The Nova Scotia government had become unhappy with the MPHEC primarily because it had for a number of years been recommending increases in funding for the universities larger than the government was willing to provide. Embarrassingly, the other Maritime governments were funding the full amounts that the Commission recommended. Accordingly, pointing to the MPHEC's failure to accomplish its coordinating and rationalizing function, Nova Scotia established a new body in 1989, the Nova Scotia Council on Higher Education.

The NSCHE was created by order-in-council to advise the government of Nova Scotia on university funding, long-range planning, and cost-efficient program delivery, ostensibly the same functions as the MPHEC. Members of the Council were the Nova Scotia representatives on the Maritime Commission which continued in yet another duplication. The Council, with offices and staff, including a full-time chair, was established in Halifax as an agency of the Department of Education.

The creation of the Nova Scotia Council inaugurated a new era of intensive consideration of the rationalization of university affairs in the province. Unfortunately, the next event was an inauspicious beginning. Dalhousie, TUNS, and the provincial government had reached an agreement to conduct a feasibility study of the relocation of the Technical University to an area of the Dalhousie campus, this time without an organizational merger. But the premier unexpectedly failed to appear at the press conference announcing the study and the government remained mute during a vicious campaign against this proposal by the campus neighbourhood, led by a former president of Saint Mary's. The universities quickly abandoned the project.

In July 1990, the Minister of Advanced Education conveyed to the university presidents a report from the NSCHE resulting from a review of the Role and Planned Capacity Statements. It contained recommendations that a wide variety of subjects be reviewed: low-demand programs and small departments, quality assessment, graduate programming, transferability of credits, distance and continuing education, shared administrative services, the rationalization of specific program areas, and limits on enrollment growth and extra-regional students. It called for increased cooperation among the universities and invited them to respond to the concerns raised in the report.

The Council of Nova Scotia University Presidents (CONSUP) took on the responsibility for responding to the Minister. In May 1991, it reported on a variety of studies that were underway, recommended that the government establish a permanent structure to support a coordinated university system, and supported a number of propositions, including a Graduate Faculty of Nova Scotia, the creation of one business school in Halifax, and some reduction in teacher preparation sites (i.e., closing the Teachers College). But by June 1992 CONSUP was forced to concede to the Minister that it could not resolve the program rationalization issues that had been identified. It called for assistance from a strengthened NSCHE. In response, the Minister appointed a new full-time chair for the Council, Janet Halliwell, a former federal civil servant with the Science Council of Canada.

In December 1992, the Council issued a paper describing how it proposed to revitalize and renew (and rationalize) the university system through the following means: a long-range planning process; changes in areas such as transfer of credits, distance education, the structure of graduate studies, and a revised funding mechanism; system-wide program reviews; and the further development of shared systems and services. The first accomplishment was announced in May 1993 when the universities reached an agreement on the transfer of credits for first- and second-year courses.

Meanwhile, government funding to the universities had been falling steadily since 1980 on a weighted-student basis, adjusted for inflation, and the pace of the decline had accelerated since 1988/89. The total amount of operating assistance was held constant in the period 1991-1994 before absolute decreases were imposed. After more than a decade of budget cutbacks, Dalhousie began calling in July 1993 for fundamental change in the system structure to bring about economies. It proposed the consolidation of the seven Halifax universities, and perhaps the Agricultural College, into a single federated university.

The first of the Council's system-wide program evaluations was released in January 1994. The Education Review Committee, composed of out-of-province experts, recommended the requirement of a two-year post-degree Bachelor of Education for teacher certification in Nova Scotia, reduction in the number of annual graduates, and the closing of the Teachers College and the Education programs at Dalhousie, Saint Mary's, and St. Francis Xavier. The Council accepted the recommendations and the Minister concurred with one exception. He retained the program from which he had graduated at St. Francis Xavier. The universities accepted the outcome although Dalhousie was critical that the cost implications had not been identified. As implementation proceeded, the anticipated cost savings from the phased closure of the Teachers College did not emerge from the government's budget, those of the faculty at Dalhousie's "inadequate" School of Education who did not retire were re-settled at Mount Saint Vincent's expanding department, and the Council reneged on its undertakings to compensate Dalhousie for the full net financial impact of closing its programs.

The Engineering Review Committee reported in April 1994, recommending the maintenance of the current program structure, increased cooperation among the Halifax universities, and the imposition of standards that would threaten the closure of some of the small feeder programs at the Associated Universities. The Council deferred response to this report.

The next review report appeared in June 1994 and unleashed a storm of controversy. The Computing Science Review Committee, despite being highly critical of the commitment to the discipline at TUNS, recommended that only TUNS and Acadia should be permitted to offer computing science undergraduate degrees, that other universities be limited to service teaching classes, and that a new institution be created for research and graduate studies in Computing Science. Dalhousie was outraged, because it had the only Computing Science unit where all the faculty were NSERC-funded and because, as the pre-eminent science university in the province, it could not see itself giving up the discipline. The Committee was now proposing more, not fewer, institutions. More fundamentally, Dalhousie began to distinguish a pattern in the review reports that aimed at its dismemberment, solving its funding problems by reducing its size and scope to that of the other universities. Education had been something of a cash cow for Dalhousie; the next scheduled review was to be of Business schools which were even more important to Dalhousie's finances and stature. Factor in Saint Mary's 40% concentration in Business and Commerce and the Minister's view that only one Business School was required in Halifax, a view with which Saint Mary's agreed, and the possibilities were frightening. Dalhousie denounced the Computing Science report and called for the long-awaited, much delayed framework plan that the Council had promised. The Council, its credibility severely damaged, deferred response to the Computing Science review and suspended the review process.

A document entitled an Overview of the Green Paper (Critical Choices) was released by the Council in October 1994. It contained a proposed system mission, along with values, visions, goals, and strategies, and described without recommendations a number of options for system restructuring and governance/coordination. In February 1995 an interim report from a Council committee proposed a new grant allocation mechanism, using weighted enrollments, support for research costs based on granting council funding, approved enrollment corridors and policy envelopes. The Council later confirmed its plans to proceed with the development of this new formula approach.

As 1995 continued, Dalhousie stepped up its campaign for a Halifax merger and the Technical University also proposed a federation of all Halifax universities. In response, Saint Mary's, Mount Saint Vincent, the College of Art and Design, and Atlantic School of Theology announced a Partnership arrangement involving shared administrative services and coordination of academic programs while retaining separate identities and governance structures. Dalhousie released a consultants' report that confirmed its estimates of ten million dollars in potential administrative savings annually from a merger. The Partners responded that they could save three to four million dollars, but later developments revealed that this figure was unsubstantiated. Public opinion polls showed Dalhousie's proposal had large popular support, but the government, reportedly concerned about possible backlash from the Catholic community and other alumni of Saint Mary's and Mount Saint Vincent, was unmoved. In the end, the seven Halifax universities agreed to examine jointly the financial savings and other benefits achievable through a consortium that would maintain the independent identity and governance of each institution. A business plan was developed and submitted to the government, detailing how financial savings could be realized through faculty attrition, early retirement and non-replacement, and the creation of a jointly run service corporation to provide administrative and academic support services.

Initial reaction to the Business Plan on the part of the Minister was positive. As the curtain falls at the end of 1995, the universities await a formal response to their proposal. Still, an air of scepticism prevails about the notion of the universities working together; as yet, no one has detected a sense of urgency or priority for the implementation of the consortium plan.

II. Also Playing: The Community Colleges and the Other Attractions

Vocational and technical education has a long history in Nova Scotia, although not a particularly well-developed one. One of the first uses of the original Dalhousie College building was as a Mechanics' Institute that put on very well-attended lectures on a wide variety of topics. In 1872 the Halifax Marine School was founded to teach navigation skills. In 1890, the School of Nursing at the Victoria General Hospital began operations that carried on for 105 years. Both the Agricultural College and the Technical College, founded in the first decade of this century, had responsibilities for technician and technology training. From 1907 to 1947 the Principal of the Technical College, Dr. Frederick Sexton, was also Director of Technical Education for the province, responsible for local technical courses and "schools" for miners. As well, the universities have for many years offered vocational diploma programs: Some, such as secretarial science, have been discontinued; others continue. However, in areas such as building trades, commercial enterprise, and manufacturing skills, training was historically delivered either through apprenticeship programs at the worksite, on-the-job training, or private commercial colleges teaching business skills. Not until well after the war was the reluctance of the provincial government to invest in facilities and programs overcome.

The first major step took place in 1951 with the opening of the first of fourteen regional vocational high schools with federal government funding support. The late 1950s and the 1960s saw the creation of a series of technological institutes: The Nova Scotia Land Survey Institute (Lawrencetown, 1958), which later became the College of Geographical Sciences, the Nova Scotia Institute of Technology (Halifax, 1958), the Eastern Institute of Technology (Sydney, 1968), which later was to become part of the College of Cape Breton, and the Nova Scotia Nautical Institute (Halifax, 1973), founded by the merger of the navigation school and a Marine Engineering School that had been established in 1948. These institutions offered a variety of one-or two-year programs in business and technology as well as overseeing apprenticeship training in the industrial trades and providing short courses of technical training. A number of hospitals added health technology programs to their nursing education activities. (In 1995, the last nursing diploma schools were closed, and the two university degree programs expanded their enrollments.)

There was little further change until the 1980s when the Royal Commission on Postsecondary Education (1985) documented a long list of complaints about occupational education in the province under the general rubric of lack of responsiveness to industrial and job market needs: out-of-date equipment, curricula and instructors; insufficient contact with industry; poorly functioning advisory committees; underutilized facilities; insufficient numbers of graduates; dispersal of effort and lack of prestige.

Essentially, while the rest of the country had been developing community college systems, Nova Scotia had been neglecting the whole area.

In response the government announced in 1986 its intent to create a community college system for the province. A White Paper was produced in 1988 and a multicampus Nova Scotia Community College was created from the collection of existing technical institutes and several federally operated schools. In 1991 the government moved to incorporate into the Community College the vocational schools that were previously under the jurisdiction of local school boards. This step had the unfortunate effect of stripping the province of secondary-level vocational education opportunities and denying such training to those who had not completed grade 12. And it burdened the Community College with facilities, instructors, and traditions that better suited the instruction of adolescents than adults. Enrollments at some of the former vocational schools dropped dramatically.

The Nova Scotia Community College currently operates in 14 communities on 19 campuses, offering 140 programs to about 7,000 full-time and 10,000 part-time students. An associated francophone Collège de l'Acadie has six campuses. Originally operated directly by the Department of Education, the Colleges will soon acquire independent Boards.

The Community College is now going through a major shake-down with program terminations, staff layoffs, and the closure of five campuses. Approximately 800 student places are being eliminated. While only one-third of the qualified applicants to college programs are currently accepted, the College faces a situation where its programs are seen to be out of alignment with market needs. According to one estimate, some 60% of its students were being trained for jobs that made up only 10% of the labour market. Programs with poor job placement results for graduates are now being deleted. Much of the change, however, is being driven by budgetary rather than quality concerns.

One recent positive development is the increase in contact training for individual companies for employees such as call centre operators, casino dealers, and manufacturing technicians. Last year the NSCC, which has a budget around $70 million, obtained $10 million in revenue from such contracts.

Community college education in Nova Scotia is still very underdeveloped. The ratio of college students to university students in the province is the lowest in Canada and is falling as a result of the current program deletions. Only tiny Prince Edward Island has fewer college teachers.

III. The Reviews

After the performance, one turns to the newspapers for the critic's comments. According to *The Globe and Mail* (1992), "In business, when you offer a product or service for which there are more than enough buyers, they call you a success. Nova Scotia's university system, by that measure, is a remarkable success story." Nova Scotia has been successful in creating institutions which have made university-level education accessible to much of its population, so that its participation rate in university education is the highest in the country. Indeed, it is often remarked that Nova Scotia's leading export is "brains" as the universities are a major industry and important employer in the province. Through regional agreements, students in the Maritime provinces can attend the expensive professional programs that are concentrated in only one of the region's universities. Much of this interprovincial enrollment flow comes into Nova Scotia. The additional inflow of many students from other parts of Canada and the rest of the world gives Nova Scotia by far the highest ratio of full-time university students to population, 50% higher than the national average. This accessibility success results from the widespread geographic dispersion of the universities, their reputation for offering quality education with personal attention, and a sense of community, the long tradition of university attendance for major parts of the provincial society, generous admission requirements at some of the institutions, and a financial regime that in the early and mid-1980s gave tremendous incentive for enrollment growth and, more recently, has made the institutions highly dependent on tuition revenue.

The emphasis on accessibility and enrollment growth has had its price. The underdevelopment of the community college system may be attributable in part to the draw on provincial government financial resources that the universities represent: in recent years, Nova Scotia has devoted the highest percentage of government expenditures to the combination of university operating grants and student aid of any province in the land. And, with government fiscal capacity increasingly constrained from the combination of declining federal transfers and the burden of high provincial debt and escalating social program costs, a number of the major Nova Scotia universities are describing a future of staff reductions, program deletions, continuing tuition inflation, and the curtailment of other services.

In addition, the current configuration of the Nova Scotia university system is less than optimal in a number of regards. The fragmentation of the system and the lack of scale of its individual components present particular problems. Difficulty in competing in national competitions such as the recent Networks of Centres of Excellence is one, especially when the province itself provides little base support for research activity. Many of the institutions find it prohibitively expensive or financially taxing to meet the costs of information technology innovation and price increases for library materials, let alone to provide essential or desirable services in such fields as employment equity, employee assistance and counselling, student placement, or occupational health and safety.

There are concerns often expressed about the quality of programming in several of the specialized institutions that prepare highly skilled professionals essential to the economic and social development of the province; their existence outside of the critical review environment of a university raises doubts. Indeed, the education of engineers, teachers, and agriculturalists in institutions lacking the liberal arts exposure of a comprehensive university is a subject of concern that has begun to be addressed, at least in regard to teacher preparation. If nothing else, the segregation of applied scientists at the engineering and agricultural institutions from the basic scientists at the leading research university limits the synergy that could enhance the various enterprises and generate greater technological and economic benefits for the provincial economy.

Finally, uncoordinated activity, lack of joint planning, competition, and duplication among the institutions lead to a waste of resources, lost opportunities, and a misdirection of leadership activities on the various campuses. For example, voluntary cooperation among mistrustful entities requires much greater effort and more resources to initiate and sustain than is commonly considered. The competition for scarce provincial resources and political support demands considerable effort. It often results in government responding with politically determined actions or, not responding at all. Indeed, this has been the history of higher education politics in Nova Scotia for almost two centuries and the way in which the system has arrived at its current structure and relationships.

References

Aird Associates Ltd. (1995). *Nova Scotia Community College new campus programming, Volume one, Report*. Halifax, NS: Aird Associates.

Cameron, D.M. (1991). *More than an academic question: Universities, government, and public policy in Canada*. Halifax, NS: The Institute for Research on Public Policy.

Cameron, D.M. (1995, April). *It's not as easy as it looks: Reflections on Nova Scotia's experience*. Paper presented to a conference entitled Restructuring Postsecondary Education: Accountability, Rationalization, Finance, sponsored by the Ontario Council for Leadership in Educational Administration, Toronto.

Campbell, G. (1971). *Community colleges in Canada*. Toronto, ON: McGraw-Hill.

Dennison, J.D., and Gallagher, P. (1986). *Canada's community colleges: A critical analysis*. Vancouver, BC: UBC Press.

Fraser, D. (1992, April 18). The dynamic of university change. *The Mail-Star*, Halifax, p. B2.

Hanington, J.B. (1984). *Every popish person: The story of Roman Catholicism in Nova Scotia and the Church of Halifax 1604-1984*. Halifax, NS: Archdiocese of Halifax.

Learned, W.S., and Sills, K.C.M. (1922). *Education in the Maritime Provinces of Canada*. New York, NY: Carnegie Foundation for the Advancement of Teaching.

Nova Scotia Community College, *Calendar 1995-96*.

Nova Scotia Council on Higher Education (1995). *The institutions—Their individual roles and characteristics*. Halifax, NS: Nova Scotia Council on Higher Education.

Royal Commission on Post Secondary Education (1985). *Report of the Nova Scotia Royal Commission on Postsecondary Education*. Halifax, NS: Commission.

Students, money and universities. (1992, December 26). *The Globe and Mail*, p. D6.

Terry, J. (1980). Atlantic Canada's community colleges. *College Canada*, 5(2).

Tripartite Committee on Interprovincial Comparisons (1992). *Interprovincial comparisons of university financing; Eleventh report of the Tripartite Committee on Interprovincial Comparisons*. Toronto, ON: Tripartite Committee.

Waite, P.B. (1994). *The lives of Dalhousie University, volume one, 1818-1925, Lord Dalhousie's College*. Toronto, ON: McGill-Queen's University Press.

Prince Edward Island

Ronald J. Baker

A colleague of mine, Frances Frazer, began an article on the literature of Prince Edward Island, "No one, to my knowledge, talks of the literature of Burnaby or Mississauga, and if population alone were considered, 'the literature of Prince Edward Island' would be an equally improbable topic. But in the Island's case, history and geography also have a bearing. By Canadian standards P.E.I. has a lot of eventful history. And its natural isolation has given its people a strong feeling of communal identity . . ." (Frazer, 1978, pp. 78-87). Prince Edward Island, she might have added, is the smallest province by far—224 km long, and from 4 to 60 km wide. It is 0.1% of Canada's total land area and has 0.5% of its population.

One might just as well ask why this book has a whole chapter on postsecondary education on Prince Edward Island and not one on, for instance, St. Catharines, Ontario. The total population of P.E.I.(about 130,000) is only a little above that of St. Catharines (125,000), and St. Catharines has a much larger catchment area. But St. Catharines, its university (Brock), and its community college (Niagara College) will not get a chapter in this book.

Even accepting that P.E.I.'s status as a province more or less demands a chapter, one could ask why it is necessary to spend time on the history of postsecondary education on P.E.I. rather than simply to describe the two institutions that started in 1969, the University of Prince Edward Island (UPEI) and Holland College. It is necessary because nearly everything on P.E.I. begins with its history and is explained by its history. The UPEI, for example, says in its 1994-1996 calendar that one of its defining characteristics is tradition, and it gives as part of that tradition not only the two universities immediately preceding it, Prince of Wales College and St. Dunstan's University but also their predecessors, the Central Academy and St. Andrew's College, high schools founded over 150 years ago.

UPEI, unlike other new universities founded in the sixties, Brock, for example, or Simon Fraser, inherited faculty, students, Board members, non-academic staff, property, and many attitudes and beliefs from its immediate predecessors. Some of the inherited faculty were relatively recent appointees, not deeply committed to the previous institutions, but even they had been attracted to the institutions as they were.

Holland College, on the other hand, except for inheriting some property, was absolutely new. History, however, is needed to understand why Holland College was the first real attempt in P.E.I. and one of the first in the Maritimes to provide a postsecondary education that could be an alternative to university.

The historic strands of postsecondary education in P.E.I. were all intertwined till the 1960s and some continue to be. Whatever their origins, Islanders are extremely conscious of being Islanders. Whether Irish, Highland Scots, Lowland Scots, English, Acadian, or from the very small minority of other origins; whether Protestant or Roman Catholic, rural or urban, rich or poor, Liberal or Conservative—and all those sub-divisions can be important—and whether or not they supported Prince of Wales College or St. Dunstan's University, they nearly all had opinions about postsecondary education on the Island, as they have had since the founding of St. Andrew's College in 1831 and the Central Academy in 1834. They have favoured university education but tended to ignore other forms of postsecondary education. In a province long based on agriculture and fishing, with little industry, other education and skills could be learned by example rather than in institutions.

St. Andrew's College (1831-1844) was founded by the Roman Catholic Bishop MacEachern. It was intended, as was St. Dunstan's for much of its history, to educate boys for the priesthood, recognising, however, that some pupils would not have vocations and should go into the professions. The enrollment was never large, being only 10 in 1844, but in its brief history, two bishops and 22 priests received at least part of their education there. Internal dissent and lack of funds led to its demise, but as G. Edward MacDonald says:

> In the long run, St. Andrew's greatest contribution was the legacy it bequeathed its success, St. Dunstan's College. As the first school of its kind anywhere in the Maritime region, St. Andrew's was, as one admirer claimed for it, "a very essential element of the life of Catholicity in the Maritime Provinces." (p. 38)

As early as 1769, there was a proposal for a public institution of higher education in P.E.I., and in 1794, Governor Edmund Fanning donated land "for the purpose of laying the foundation of a College for the education of youth in the learned languages, the arts and sciences, and all branches of useful and polite literature." For two decades, schools operated on the site, and in 1834, the Central Academy was founded by Royal Charter. In 1860 it was renamed Prince of Wales College in honour of the visit of the then Prince of Wales, later Edward VII.

For a long time, St. Dunstan's and Prince of Wales competed in a mild way, but they were sufficiently different in connections and goals—St. Dunstan's with a four-year program geared to Laval and very much to the Roman Catholic Church; Prince of Wales with a two-year program geared to Protestant or secular universities—that the competition was not serious. But in the 1960s when both institutions shared in the general expansion of higher education and when Prince of Wales got degree-granting powers (1964), the competition for students and funds concerned government, many members of the public, and some members of the two institutions.

The story of the events of the sixties that led the government to establish UPEI is told in Lorne Robert Moase (1972), *The Development of the University of Prince Edward Island: 1964-1972*. Essentially the two existing institutions were unable to agree on any significant degree of cooperation or rationalization. In 1968 therefore, Premier A. Campbell, with the backing of a Federal Provincial Development Plan, issued a Policy Statement on Postsecondary Education. It included a proposal to develop a College of Applied Arts and Technology (the future Holland College) and a program to develop a single, public, non-denominational university.

He said," But, let one thing be very clear; the Government will support financially, with all the funds at its disposal, only a single public university in Prince Edward Island." In spite of major opposition from Prince of Wales College, the Government persisted in its plans. Eventually, legislation for what were to become UPEI and Holland College passed unanimously, supported by the opposition as well as by the government.

That the time was ripe is borne out by the first president of UPEI Ronald J. Baker. In 1973, four years after its founding, he said, "I had expected that it would take about ten years to put together the former institutions, but after three years, I estimated that only six faculty out of about 140 want to return to pre-1969. Actually, I know only three, but I'm allowing for a 100% error."

So, in 1969, the two new institutions began. Holland College, a community college, brand new in everything and the University of Prince Edward Island, technically new but carrying both debts and benefits from the two previous institutions, Prince of Wales College (PWC) and St. Dunstan's University (SDU).

It is common to speak of UPEI as a merger of PWC and SDU, but it is not strictly true. St. Dunstan's University, with funds resulting from the sale of the campus to UPEI (via the P.E.I. government), continues to exist, dispensing money for scholarships, lectures, and other university activities. Prince of Wales College has never been formally dissolved. With no funds and no property, and its faculty and students gone, its Board has gradually faded away, leaving, however, an active and loyal Alumni Association (loyal to UPEI as well as to PWC).

The appearance of a merger or amalgamation, especially to Islanders, comes from the fact that the programs, and the rights of students and faculty at PWC and SDU, were guaranteed for a period in U.P.E.I., but many people overlooked the substantial number of faculty appointed to PWC and SDU in their last few years with no significant connections with their traditions and the faculty appointed to UPEI in its early years. An Islander like Sister Olga McKenna (1982) in "Higher Education in Transition, 1945-1980" completely ignores their role in the development of UPEI. Like this writer, however, to discuss post-WW II higher education on P.E.I., she devotes a considerable part of her space to the history of higher education on P.E.I.

An examination of department, faculty, and Senate minutes for the first few years indicates that the faculty with few significant connections with PWC or SDU played a major part in decisions. Baker has said that he thinks that the more traditional PWC and SDU faculty were often brought together by their reservations about the proposals of the new faculty. None of the radical ideas of new faculty were considered seriously at all.

Ronald J. Baker, president from 1969 to 1978, was a compromise candidate. The University Planning Committee, chaired by Dr. E. Sheffield, was made up mainly of equal numbers of faculty, students, and administrators from PWC and SDU. Each side had favorite candidates thought to be sympathetic to its goals, candidates naturally opposed by the other side. Eventually, Baker, then head of English and formerly the original Academic Planner at Simon Fraser University, was appointed. He later said that he thought that the committee had kept moving west until it got to someone who didn't know a Catholic from a Protestant. He also said later that he thought that the lack of very strong support from or connection with either side was an advantage in the early days of the University. Baker had some experience with new institutions. Before planning Simon Fraser, he had written the section of the Macdonald Report in British Columbia that led to the B. C. community colleges and to Simon Fraser and—in part—to the University of Victoria. He had been involved in the planning of the B.C. Institute of Technology and several community colleges in B.C.

As the author of this chapter, I am reluctant to say much about the first presidency. Immodesty, however, plus some respect for the historical record, allows me to quote from a framed presentation given to me by the then Lieutenant Governor of P.E.I., Gordon L. Bennett, Q.C., formerly the Minister of Education who had introduced the legislation establishing UPEI:

> Whereas the anticipated turmoil, disorder, and disruption of the university program, through the merger did not materialize largely as a result of the skill, diplomacy, understanding and fair-mindedness which President Baker brought to this task. . . . the citizens of Prince Edward Island will be forever grateful to Professor Ronald J. Baker for the skilful and successful leadership he provided . . . as the first President of the University of Prince Edward Island. (Bennett, 1978)

The Visiting Committee sent by the Association of Universities and Colleges of Canada to consider UPEI's application for membership made similar remarks.

The University of P.E.I. started in July 1969. It had to accept its first students in September. Between July and September, it had to integrate the curricula of PWC and SDU and establish the academic and administrative mechanisms of a new university. That would have been difficult in two months under any circumstances. It was especially difficult given the suspicions still existing among the inherited faculty and students, given the general rebellious mood of universities in the late 1960s, and given the new University Act which gave significant powers to a Senate consisting almost entirely of elected faculty and students.

In July and August of 1969, it was impossible to establish legitimately even the procedures for elections, let alone elect members of Senate. Students were not even registered. Many faculty were off-campus. Even if all faculty had been on-campus and all of the future UPEI students had been available, those from PWC knew little of those from SDU and vice versa, certainly not enough for normal elections.

Consequently, the president asked each group of faculty likely to become a department to agree unanimously on an interim chair. All but one of what were to become the new departments were able to agree. That one finally agreed without dissent. ("Interim" and "without dissent" were key words in the first year.) Those interim chairs then advised on interim deans and such administrators as the Librarian, the Registrar, and the Comptroller. It was not possible to follow the same procedure with the students, but the Committee of Interim Chairs invited members of the joint committee of student officers from PWC and SDU to join in their deliberations, and student opinion was often significant.

The election of students and faculty to the Board of Governors posed similar problems. The government had appointed nine lay members in June 1969, but the Act also called for two members elected by faculty, two student members elected by students, and two members elected by and from the Senate. The Board had to begin to make decisions immediately. It overcame the difficulties of faculty and student membership by inviting two participating observers appointed by the new Faculty Association of the university, two from the joint committee of the Student Councils of PWC and SDU, and two from the committee of interim chairs.

A detailed outline of the work of the interim chairs, the Board of Governors, and the Senate when it was able to meet for the first time in October 1969, can be found in the president's first Annual Report, UPEI, 1970. The Board adopted an interim Faculty Handbook and decided upon such matters as fees, fringe benefits, terms of appointment. As the annual report says:

> The Senate had an extremely difficult task in its first year. As one member said, there were at least twenty items of business which were of such importance that each must be dealt with first. In addition to being responsible for all academic policies and regulations of the University, the Senate, under our legislation, has responsibility for the procedures for appointments of faculty and administrative staff. Complicating such formidable and extensive responsibilities was the fact that the University inherited differing policies from Prince of Wales College and St. Dunstan's University in many areas, and—as always in a new university—there was a considerable desire to develop completely new policies in many areas. (p.10)

What the Report does not say but the president said later was that the situation was not made any easier by the fact that not one of the faculty had ever served on a university senate other than in PWC and SDU where senates were not set up until not long before the merger. In fact, only a very few faculty had held full-time teaching appointments anywhere else. Many of the new and recent faculty were products of the sixties and were sure that they knew how to run universities, even ones like UPEI that began with at least two of everything—two heads of every department, two sets of administrators, two student unions, two sets of accounts, two sets of estimates, two sets of academic regulations, two campuses . . . and so on. And five pension plans, plus some people without pensions.

The Senate met 26 times in its first eight months. Committee meetings were extra, of course. Sometimes issues were hotly debated and meetings did not finish until one or two in the morning, but in spite of all those difficulties, UPEI was essentially organized—if a little weary of debates and committees—by its second year. It also settled on the former St. Dunstan's campus, gradually turning over the former PWC campus to Holland College.

Since then, the goal of UPEI, with perhaps the exception of the addition of the Atlantic Veterinary College, admitting its first students in 1986, appears to have been to become a typical small Maritime university. Like the others, it has added buildings—a residence, an excellent library, a large sports centre, a dining hall, a Veterinary College. It has also carried out a number of major renovations to old buildings. The former Library became an administration and academic building. The former chapel and convent became a recital hall and a Music Building. Two residences were completely remodelled as academic buildings. The oldest building on the campus, Main, was remodelled, renovated, and *restored* to what it would have been had SDU been able to afford it. The various remodelling and renovations enabled the university to preserve the traditional and attractive main quadrangle.

The holdings of the Library have increased dramatically, from 95,000 items generously counted and with many duplications in 1969 to 611,913 items in 1995. These include 285,000 volumes, 86,388 microfilm volume equivalents, 72,525 bound periodical volumes, and 168,000 government documents. On-line searches have been available since 1980. The catalogue is computerized and available on-line, and some CD-ROM bibliographies are open to all users. The public is welcome to use the Library, the research library for the whole province. The BOBCAT system of completely integrated library services instituted in 1991 makes it one of the most up-to-date libraries in the region.

Given the small size of the university and the small population of the province, the library is more than well used; In 1994, the entrance gate counters registered nearly half a million.

Computing has developed from none in either PWC or SDU in 1969 to extensive facilities in 1991. A full account of the facilities, developing all the time, does not belong here. An indication, however, is that the Computing Centre has a full-time staff of 14, all students have accounts, and that in addition to the Centre's main computers, there are approximately 1,000 microcomputers on campus as well as 154 public access terminals for students.

The development of library and computing services is perhaps the best example of the benefit brought by moving from two small and competing universities to one.

The enrollment has grown from a total of 1,555 full-time, 504 part-time students in PWC and SDU in 1968 to 2,300 full-time, 800 part-time in 1994-95. Of those, 200 are in the Veterinary program, and 35 in an M.Sc. program, primarily in the Veterinary College.

The qualifications of faculty have also increased. Whereas relatively few of the faculty at PWC and SDU, until the mid-sixties, had doctorates, most of the faculty now do. The faculty has also become more cosmopolitan, with members from most Canadian universities and from many U.S. and other foreign universities. Research has expanded substantially, especially in the Veterinary College.

The offerings, again, with the exception of the Veterinary College, are typical and fairly traditional and conservative. Arts has departments of Canadian Studies, Classics, Economics, English, Fine Arts, History, Modern Languages, Music, Philosophy, Political Studies, Psychology, Religious Studies, and Sociology and Anthropology; Science has Biology, Chemistry, Engineering (a three-year diploma leading to later years at The Technical University of Nova Scotia, the University of New Brunswick, and other Canadian Universities), Home Economics, Mathematics and Computer Science, and Physics. There is a Faculty of Education, a School of Business Administration and a School of Nursing. With the exception of Nursing, Computing, and the Veterinary College, no department has been added that was not in embryo in PWC or SDU. A proposal to add geography, totally non-existent in the Maritimes at the time, was turned down by the Faculty of Arts in spite of the fact that land utilization has been and continues to be a major issue on P.E.I. Geography was seen as a new subject and one that would compete for funds and students with traditional subjects.

Until recently UPEI was restricted by its Act to first degrees, but it is now able to offer graduate work almost entirely in, or connected with, the Veterinary College. It is the Atlantic Veterinary College that makes UPEI different from the other small Maritime universities. It is the fourth Canadian veterinary college, the third anglophone college. Taking approximately 50 students a year, it is designed by federal-provincial agreements to serve primarily the Atlantic region. Its operating budget for 1994-95, $14,596,095 for a total of about 200 students, is about two thirds that of the budget of the rest of the university, $21,997,546 for over 2,500 FTE students. Its building cost over $40,000,000, more than the rest of the buildings on the campus put together, though their replacement cost would perhaps be more.

Just as the history of UPEI exemplifies the Island tradition of postsecondary education, the history of the Atlantic Veterinary College illustrates the kind of provincial rivalries in the Maritime region, the kind of rivalries that left Nova Scotia in the 1970s with more degree-granting institutions than the whole of western Canada.

Just as some Islanders urged PWC to give more agricultural education and just as the Carnegie Foundation (Learned and Sills, 1921) had suggested in 1921 that SDU might concentrate on agriculture, it was suggested that UPEI should begin a faculty of agriculture. Experience of the major changes in faculties of agriculture and their relative decline persuaded UPEI not to begin agriculture, but it did begin to investigate the possibility of a veterinary faculty. PEI had the advantages of a varied animal population and the fact that it was unlikely to become urbanized as Guelph was becoming. There was no veterinary faculty teaching in English east of Ontario, and it was extremely difficult to get into veterinary schools, more difficult than into medical schools.

While UPEI was investigating the possibility of a veterinary school, the then Federal Minister of Agriculture, the Hon. Eugene Whalen, announced at the Nova Scotia College of Agriculture in Truro that it would be the site of the fourth veterinary college in Canada. There had been no consultation with either the Maritime governments or universities. Truro was a non-degree-granting, essentially vocational school of agriculture; it did offer the first two years of a degree program so that students could transfer to such universities as Guelph in agriculture or veterinary science. Its faculty and facilities were far from adequate for a veterinary college.

After UPEI made representations to the Premier of P.E.I., the Honorable A. Campbell, he took the matter to the Council of Maritime Premiers. They, in turn, asked the Maritime Provinces Higher Education Commission to consider it. The MPHEC asked the then Dean of the Veterinary College at Guelph, the very highly respected Dr. D. Howell, to recommend a location. After an extensive study, he recommended, in order, UPEI, New Brunswick, and Acadia. He thought the Nova Scotia College of Agriculture quite unsuitable.

Political squabbling over the location, (typical of the region and the universities, particularly of Nova Scotia), and too convoluted to detail here, followed, delaying the start of the College for ten years and increasing the cost significantly. Eventually the Honorable Eugene Whalen intervened again, this time ensuring the location at UPEI.

If the squabble over the location was typical of the region, the bitter internal arguments at UPEI about accepting the College were also typical. The Senate was frequently almost deadlocked as those who saw UPEI as a traditional liberal arts college fought against what they considered to be its increasing move towards professional faculties. Eventually the Atlantic Veterinary College was opened at UPEI in 1986. It brought graduate work, greatly increased research, and enormously expanded computing, audio-visual, and teaching facilities.

Holland College

The significance of the presidents of postsecondary institutions, even the first presidents, is often exaggerated, and not only by themselves, but the significance of the first president of Holland College cannot be overestimated. Dr. Donald Glendenning, the first president of Holland College (1969-87), had been a vocational school teacher. He had gone on to take a doctorate at the University of Indiana, and he came to Holland College from the Federal Department of Manpower and Immigration, having been involved in various training and retraining programs. He was a passionate and persuasive believer in making education accessible to the whole province, in the importance of vocational and technological training, and of methods that concentrated on demonstrable skills. Moreover he believed in the decision that the College Planning Committee had made pragmatically—that the College would not offer university transfer or general education programs. He thought that they distracted the attention of community colleges from their primary purposes.

For the first ten years of its life, Holland College was Glendenning's creation; indeed it still is. He was responsible for its teaching methods, its staffing, and its development as one of the most innovative—and entrepreneurial—postsecondary institutions in the country. As John Dennison said in *Canada's Community Colleges*:

From the outset, at a time when preparatory or remedial education was still in its pioneering stage in other parts of Canada, it welcomed adults who had not completed secondary school. As a result, it quickly established a broad base of citizen support. Its emphasis in the curriculum on education for employment provided it with additional popular support. It encouraged community advice on college policy and programme development and became a "community" college from the start. (p. 46)

He goes on:

But Holland College's reputation in the rest of Canada, as well as at home, rested primarily on its instructional methods. From the beginning, its programmes were organised for individualized, self-paced learning which subdivided course materials into modules or building blocks so that all students could progress through the programmes at their own paces, with instructors serving as tutors of individuals rather than as teachers of classes. (p. 47)

Its method of instruction, STEP (Self-Training and Evaluation Process) has attracted so much attention, both in Canada and internationally.

For each program a DACUM (Developing A CurriculUM) chart is prepared, a breakdown into small units of the skills to be learned. Students can demonstrate their mastery of particular units at their own pace.

Recognizing current jargon, the College now describes its system as CBE, Competency-Based Evaluation. Within that general description, STEP is the specific system used in most programs. Most community colleges in Canada are aware of the Holland College system and have adopted it or parts of it for some of their programs. Holland College, however, remains the only college based entirely on it.

Many universities, however, tend to remain intentionally ignorant of the increasing demand for Competency-Based Education. Those interested might read a recent essay by Charles W. Joyner, "The DACUM Technique and Competency-Based Education" (Joyner, 1995).

He says that "[t]he most frequently cited example of the successful implementation of a CBE system is Holland College in PEI" (p. 251). He goes on to give a number of reasons for its success.

These reasons are no doubt valid and useful to anyone attempting to introduce CBE, but I believe that the main reason for the success at Holland College was Dr. Glendenning's leadership plus the fact that Holland College, unlike UPEI, inherited no faculty or traditions. Indeed there were no traditions of non-university postsecondary education in the Atlantic provinces because there was no alternative to university.

Dr. Glendenning introduced the instructional technique, based on the DACUM system and was responsible for training the instructors in it. The original instructors remain, after 23 years, dedicated to the system. In recent years, the College has been offering employers guarantees of the students' competence. If the College record shows that a student can perform a particular operation or has mastered a particular skill and the employer finds that is not so, the College will retrain the student free.

The system is based on performance, and during Dr. Glendenning's presidency, students did not receive diplomas or certificates. They took with them a chart showing the particular skills they had mastered. They did not need to finish a complete program, but only to master those skills that they wanted or a particular job required. Frequently, they return to complete further modules.

Recently, the College has bowed to student demand for diplomas and now issues them, partly because employers outside Prince Edward Island do not always understand the system.

The College began in 1969 with Electronics, Secretarial Arts, Commercial Art, Resources Planning, and PreTech (Occupational Foundations). There were 97 students, plus another 70 in night classes. Since then, the College has offered a very wide range of technological and vocational courses plus a number of courses of general interest. In 1994-95, full-time enrollment was 1,519 and part-time, 4,211. Details of the growth of the College can best be seen briefly in the Diary of Holland College, 1968-1979, Holland College, Charlottetown, 1979, and its unpublished successor, Diary Update. Annual Reports give detailed information.

Two programs deserve special attention, the Culinary Institute and the Atlantic Police Academy. The Culinary Institute began in 1984. It is designed to train the highest level of chefs, an over-ambitious goal some thought in a region not known for *haute cuisine*. It has been very successful, winning prizes in international competitions and attracting foreign students (at full cost!). It regularly has more applicants than it can accept. It is now incorporated into a larger unit, The Atlantic Tourism and Hospitality Institute. The Atlantic Police Academy is the only Police

Academy in Canada that is not under the control of a particular police department or a Police Commission. All four Atlantic provinces use it, an example of the kind of cooperation badly needed. A recent development is an Institute of Educational Technology.

No institution is without problems, of course, and although Holland College's system of performance-based instruction remains the basic one for the College, it has had, according to some, one major difficulty. In 1975, the College took over the running of the vocational programs in the public schools. Students, often those having difficulty in academic programs, were able to take some academic courses and some vocational courses in such subjects as bricklaying and cosmetology. The College inherited over a hundred vocational teachers from the school system. Partly because the students were not as motivated and directed as the postsecondary students in Holland College's full-time postsecondary programs, partly because many of the teachers were set in their ways, and partly because the College did not provide enough in-service training, the system never really worked for the school students. For a variety of reasons, not all of them related to the instructional system, the vocational programs will leave the College in 1995.

A mixed success is the College's provision of services throughout the province. Responding to Glendenning's belief in accessibility, the College offers programs in a number of centres. Secretarial programs are offered in five places, for example. Although undoubtedly popular with the public, some people think that the costs are high given the small size of the province. The College disputes that judgment, although agreeing that main campuses in Charlottetown and Summerside are underutilized.

The STEP system has been of major interest to educators. Many from elsewhere in Canada, from the U.S.A., and from overseas visit the College to see it. The College has helped train teachers for other colleges, and it has helped some colleges and universities design DACUM charts for particular programs. Since his retirement from the College presidency in 1986, Dr. Glendenning has been in constant demand as a consultant on vocational and technological education in the Third World, and some of the staff he trained are also in demand. Glendenning was made a Member of the Order of Canada in 1985, one of the very few community college presidents to be so honoured.

In their own terms, both Holland College and UPEI are successfully established. Their support from the public and the government is strong and growing. Their main problems are those they share with almost all postsecondary institutions in Canada—funding and what many see as an increasing tendency towards *interference* from governments or outside agencies such as the Maritime Provinces Higher Education Commission.

References

Bennett, G.L. (June 30, 1978). *Topics.* UPEI

Dennison, J., and Gallagher, P. (1986). *Canada's community colleges: A critical analysis.* Vancouver: UBC Press.

Diary of Holland College, 1968-1979, Holland College, Charlottetown, 1979.

Frazer, F.M. (Summer 1978). Island writers. *Canadian Literature.*

Joyner, C.W. (1995). The DACUM technique and competency-based education. In J.D. Dennison (Ed.), *Challenge and opportunity: Canada's community colleges at the crossroads* (pp. 243-255). Vancouver: UBC Press.

Learned, W.S., and Sills, C.M. (1921). *Education in the Maritime Provinces.* Carnegie Foundation.

MacDonald, G.E. (1989). *The history of St. Dunstan's University, 1855-1956.* Charlottetown, PEI: Board of Governors of St. Dunstan's University and Prince Edward Island Museum and Heritage Foundation.

McKenna, M.O. (1982). *The garden transformed, Prince Edward Island, 1945-1980.* Charlottetown, PEI: Ragweed Press.

Moase, L.R. (1972). The development of the University of Prince Edward Island: 1964-1972. Unpublished master's thesis, University of New Brunswick, Fredericton, New Brunswick, Canada.

Newfoundland: More Canadian Than British, But Longer Getting There

Kathryn Bindon and Paul Wilson

The Historical Context

The European history of contemporary Newfoundland and Labrador stretches back to the Norse sagas of Vinland and the North Atlantic cod fisheries of the fifteenth and sixteenth centuries. During the pre-Conquest colonial period the area was an outpost of both the British and the French empires. Although the effects of settlement policies and patterns of both imperial periods are evident still, it is the legacy of the United Kingdom that is most tangible in the area of public policy and institutional organization.

For Newfoundland and Labrador, the resolution of authority in favour of the British government in the eighteenth century *did not* foster a pattern of political, economic, or social development that parallelled that of the rest of British North America. The Island was exploited for centuries according to mercantilist principles that prized the economic potential of the transient fisheries above that of colonists; permanent settlement was prohibited as inimical to the interests of commerce. The Newfoundland fishery was also considered a training ground for the British navy. The custom of sending out new men each season and then insisting upon their return to England was reiterated in legislation throughout the seventeenth century, fully formalized in the Act of 1699, and remained unchanged until the 1800s.

Legislation, however, did not affect the decisions of many of the "green men" (MacNutt, 1965, p. 5), who chose the unknown possibilities of the New World over the known consequences of return to Europe. Nor could regulations inhibit the smuggling of "passengers" to the New World; "the shore population of Newfoundland not only maintained itself but became an important by-product of the fishery" (MacNutt, 1965, p. 5). The ongoing pattern of development was of small outports and one major entrepôt located on the east coast of the Island. The distant outports were

ruled in patriarchal and isolated fashion, while the eastern urban centre
(eventually the city of St. John's) was not only the outpost of British
authority and economic control but also the home of the colonial elite. Thus
a pattern of "Townies versus Baymen," or St. John's versus the outports,
which persists to this time, was established.

This development, trenchant and persistent as it was, emerged in a
vacuum of governance, under a "fiction that Newfoundland was not a
colony" (MacNutt, 1965, p. 176). By 1803 there were almost 20,000
people on the Island, and it was clear that "'the nursery of seamen' now
sheltered landsmen who only occasionally took to deep water" (MacNutt,
1965, p. 143); but, it was not until 1813 that the legal entitlement to small
grants of land was established, and the terms of the Act of 1699 prohibiting
cultivation of the soil were altered (MacNutt, 1965). In 1824, the Act for
the Better Administration of Justice in Newfoundland and for Other
Purposes began a very slow progress towards the traditional entitlements
of British colonial government. In these developments as well, the
predominance of the east coast over the rest of the colony was evident and
continuously reinforced—partly through a chosen isolationism, partly as
a result of colonial snobbery, and undoubtedly because of geography.

The geography of the colony was daunting, and the patterns of
settlement reflected not only the role of the fisheries industry but also the
impenetrability of the interior. Until the completion of a trans-island rail
line in 1898, the sea was the usual means of communication and
transportation for most Newfoundlanders. Even then, St. John's remained
a more difficult and expensive place to get to than the mainland for many
west coast Newfoundlanders whose access to the Inter-Colonial (later
Canadian National) Railway network consolidated their connections with
the Maritimes and Upper and Lower Canada.

Geography also served to reinforce relationships with mainland
institutions that were based on other considerations. The Catholic
communities of the West Coast, for example, preferred to send their
children to St. Francis Xavier University in Nova Scotia for reasons of both
religion and economy:

> On the Newfoundland railway, serpentine proof of the island's
> modernization, there were eight hundred kilometres of distance
> and expense between St. John's and Corner Brook. Looked at
> from Corner Brook's viewpoint, Antigonish in Nova Scotia, and
> therefore Saint Francis Xavier University, were just as close. Not
> only that, but a good proportion of pre-paper-mill settlers in

western Newfoundland belonged to families whose forbears had migrated into the area from Nova Scotia during the 1840-60 period. When the church developed St. Francis Xavier as a centre for Catholic and Celtic learning, for many families on the west coast it was not only the closest but also their own university. (MacLeod, 1990, p. 39)

A complex blend of historical factors also influenced the development of education in the colony and the province. The stages of political maturation that marked the experience of other provinces did not occur in similar fashion or order in Newfoundland. The colonial legacy was both more bitter and more trenchant, and the processes of achieving representative and responsible government came late to this area despite its much longer history of European contact and presence.

Responsible Government was achieved in 1855 (as compared to 1848 in the Canadas), but the decision not to participate in Confederation in the 1860s left Newfoundland fixed firmly in the British colonial sphere and resulted in a very different and unique century of development. The replacement of Responsible Government by a Commission of Government in the years 1934-39 reflected the colony's political vulnerability and bankruptcy but also further delimited the experience and development of self-governance prior to the decision to join Confederation in 1949.

Sparse population, limited accessibility, community-based cultural differences, and internal regional and religious hierarchies, coupled with the persistent traditions of the fishery contributed to the particular characteristics and qualities of education in Newfoundland and Labrador. These factors continue to contribute to the development of institutions within the tertiary level to the present day.

The east coast, with its direct link to Europe and its role as purveyor of goods and governance, developed an infrastructure that was more traditional. Although the linkages to Britain and the Imperial elite were directive, St. John's had a sufficient mass of population enjoying the benefits of colonial metropolitanism to support the foundation of fortunes and the development of educational aspirations and institutions.

West coast communities lagged behind in terms of basic recognition of the need for institutional and social development until well into the twentieth century, when industrialization created new communities demanding and requiring service and support. These historical differences of origin, settlement and orientation—the east coast toward London and the west coast toward Canada—were reflected in the formation of social institutions and patterns of usage; education was no exception.

In this sector, Newfoundland's early experience was marked by the negative constraints characteristic of its colonial development, including a delayed start and a high degree of sectarian and geographic regional contentiousness. The first tangible evidence of institutional development for higher learning, the Newfoundland School Society, was founded in 1823 to train teachers for the outport communities. Its merchant champions in St. John's were "inspired by the missionary zeal of Lord Liverpool" (MacNutt, 1965, p. 168) in their thinking, and the Colonial Office acquiesced to their demand that the religious denominations play a significant role in managing the Society despite the opposition of the Governor. The advent of Responsible Government in 1855 heightened political, and therefore sectarian feelings in every sector, and both Catholic and non-Anglican Protestants demanded more recognition (MacNutt, 1965).

Denominational organization was thus confirmed as an essential part of the foundation of educational development in the primary and secondary levels and in the training of teachers. It was not to be an attribute of institutions at the tertiary level, which emerged much later, in response to a different set of social, economic, and political circumstances and with a mandate intriguingly devoid of denominational influence or interest.

The development of postsecondary education within the Province of Newfoundland and Labrador is entirely a twentieth-century phenomenon and largely occurred after 1945. Moreover, the history of university education within the Province is the history of a single institution which emerged in 1925 as a College, became a University with Confederation (1949) and will celebrate its 50th anniversary as a degree–granting institution as the century ends.

The Memorial University College, 1925-1949

Newfoundland established the senior partner in its current postsecondary profile in 1925. The Memorial University College, a War Memorial, was created within an educational environment of sectarian tension but had a clearly non-denominational identity and a mandate to provide higher education. The reasons for its appearance at that particular time were many, but an historian of its early years, Malcolm MacLeod, summarized the moment as follows:

Why was there nothing like a university in Newfoundland prior to 1925? The answer lies apparently in the country's relatively sparse, relatively poor, very scattered population and small middle class. Until the 1920s the system of basic elementary education was still being established. High levels of illiteracy suggest a limited appreciation for education in general, let alone higher learning. Some combination of economic diversification, industrialization, growth of the middle class, the spread of schooling and literacy, modern communications, greater awareness of mainland examples—and perhaps a desire to emulate conditions in the Maritimes—together provided the context in which plans for increased higher education in Newfoundland were implemented with such deliberation. The lengthening tradition of fair balance among the religions created an atmosphere in which former animosities were permitted to subside. National grief and pride after the slaughter in Europe were translated into public spending on a new facility. Canadian curriculum, American funding, and an English headmaster, properly packaged, could form a Newfoundland institution. (MacLeod, 1990, p. 32-33)

Memorial University College (MUC) offered two-year programming in the arts and sciences that allowed its students to proceed to British or mainland universities for completion of degrees. But although examinations were returned to the University of London for grading, the College was, from the beginning, tied into the Canadian system by a decision to replicate the course arrays and requirements of Maritime universities. "This paradox," notes MacLeod, "represented a near-final stage in the transition of Newfoundland from the British to the Canadian cultural empire" (MacLeod, 1990, p. 60).

Expansion of the College was related to the assumption of responsibility for all teacher training and the absorption of the Normal School, and the development of pre-Engineering and Household Science programming in the 1930s. The latter was made possible by the building of new facilities in 1931-32. Thus, within its first decade, Memorial University College had evolved programmes reflecting "an amalgam, perhaps not entirely satisfying to anyone, of core studies in science and the humanities and in narrowly specialized preparation for engineering, teaching, and household science" (MacLeod, 1990, p. 82). This pattern of mixed orientations and a debate between education versus training would characterize Memorial's development for some decades to follow, although little further development would occur until after Confederation.

Faculty also supported the early identification of the College with the mainland. Despite the British postures of early years, the practice of recruiting Newfoundlanders who had completed their studies at mainland universities was the norm after 1933. By 1939, of 18 full-time instructors, 11 were Newfoundlanders, and 8 were former Memorial students (MacLeod, 1990). It was also the stated policy of the College to afford "special consideration and interest" (MacLeod, 1990, p. 86) to faculty who were both Newfoundlanders and graduates of Memorial. Thus the faculty represented the particular experiences of Newfoundlanders, plus exposure to the Canadian pattern of undergraduate and professional education.

The College continued to serve mainly the citizens of the east coast area. Elitism and inequity characterized student life for many of the early graduates, although these differences tended to be commented upon mainly by those who were not from St. John's. Moreover, the uneven distribution of secondary programming and the extremely low literacy rate in the colony combined to exaggerate, rather than minimize, the inner regionalisms of Newfoundland.

Memorial University College survived its early years only with the support of the Carnegie Corporation of New York. Between 1924 and 1938, these external resources accounted for the establishment, the development, and the survival of the College. While public funding preceded its transition to University, the College experienced a significant amount of external bureaucratic meddling and manipulation through control of resources from the Commission of Government and the Dominion Government prior to 1949, when it became Memorial University of Newfoundland (MUN) (MacLeod, 1990; Williams, 1966).

Memorial University of Newfoundland, 1949-68

At the time of Confederation in 1949:

> . . . only the middle class residents of St. John's (at six denominational colleges) and people in the larger resource towns such as Grand Falls and Corner Brook (in company-supported schools), could hope to finish high school. Other than Memorial College—which offered the first two years of a university degree programme—and a rudimentary vocational institution, the new

province had no postsecondary system of education. (Royal Commission on Employment and Unemployment, 1986, p. 1)

For Memorial, the transition from college to university involved both a legal and a philosophical restatement, but the necessity of its evolution revolved around a public debate that had been ongoing for at least a decade. Experience with the Commission of Government, and the near demise of MUC during the depression had raised the issue of status for both the institution and its graduates. In the matter of degree-granting status, the President's Report of 1937-38 noted that, in the interest of not remaining "more backward in higher education than Tasmania" (President's Report as cited in MacLeod, 1990, p. 209), degree-granting status should ensue. Apart from concerns for the quality of the programmes, the same report noted the importance of finding "some compensation . . . for the wider experience now enjoyed by those of our graduates who proceed abroad" (President's Report as cited in MacLeod, 1990, p. 209).

The debate about completion, exposure, and the benefits and detractions of insularity was ongoing. But nationalism, constitutional reform, and the natural urge of the university to grow and develop led to the creation of a degree-granting institution. From the perspective of government, a variety of public pressures combined in the Confederation era to urge them to action in the area of education. A population boom during the 1940s and 1950s, coupled with "the revolution of rising expectations of our Newfoundland people" created "a belief that education is essential for future progress" and "a demand that life here be as good as that elsewhere in Canada" (Warren, 1975, p. 333).

People were not satisfied with comparisons with the past; they wanted to compare their lot with that of people across the nation. And when they found their way of life wanting, they looked to education as the means of improving the situation. Ordinary families developed expectations that their children would progress through school and get a better job than their parents; they demanded education as a right. (Warren, 1975, p. 333)

The University Act (1949) encompassed governance and mission and built upon the mixed responsibilities that had characterized the College. Guidelines are provided in the description of disciplinary duties that relate particularly to the province's sense of the University's role and the College's history as a public institution in a province with only very rudimentary vocational training:

> 8.—(1) The University shall, so far as, and to the full extent which its resources from time to time permit, provide (a) such instruction in all branches of liberal education as may enable students to become proficient in and qualify for degrees, diplomas, and certificates in science, commerce, arts, literature, law, medicine, and all other branches of knowledge; (b) such instruction, whether theoretical, technical, artistic, or otherwise, as may be of especial service to persons engaged or about to be engaged in the fisheries, manufacturers or the mining, engineering, agricultural, and industrial pursuits of the province; (c) facilities for the prosecution of original research in science, literature, arts, medicine, law and especially the application of science to the study of fisheries and forestry . . . (Newfoundland, 1973, p. 3523-3524).

In addition to the traditional requirements of any university, the identification of fishing and forestry, among other applied and professional pursuits, figured prominently in the legal identity of the institution. Thus, the University was viewed as a key participant in the economic development of the new province from its very inception.

The historical debate and the specificity of the University's charter provides at least part of the explanation for some of the philosophical musing that characterized the next 20 years within the University. The 1950s, in fact, was a decade of ruthless rigour in the matter of faculty credentials and institutional symbols, as MUN worked to establish itself as a full and credible university (MacLeod, 1990, p. 94). In 1951, the Board of Regents appointed Robert Newton, former President of the University of Alberta, to undertake a survey of the tasks awaiting the new university. His findings were published in 1952 and presented an intriguing portrait of past and present in the assessment of Memorial he provided and his recommendations for its future.

Newton (1952) stressed the historical predominance of the Arts and Sciences and drew clear distinctions between what is appropriate to vocational schools and to universities. His concern about the pre-eminence of the government's economic priorities in the mission of the university was clear. For example, he considered the number of government appointees to the University's Board of Regents "disproportionately large, considering the supreme importance of maintaining public confidence in the University as an independent institution, completely free from any suggestion of political control" (Newton, 1952, p. 8). He also suggested quite clearly that the basic industries of forestry and fishery required only a few educated specialists for leadership in research and scientific instruction in the University (Newton, 1952). Indeed, as he elaborated at one point:

> Newfoundland is unique in having such a large proportion of its population thinly scattered along its six thousand miles of shore line. These fisher folk do not for the most part require a university education, even if that were financially practicable for them. Neither is their main need for vocational education—they are born to the trade—though doubtless they could profit by winter short courses featuring the latest technical developments. (Newton, 1952, p. 64)

Similar themes of autonomy and tradition were sounded in 1967 in a Report entitled *The Government and Administration of Memorial University of Newfoundland* produced by a Committee chaired by Les Harris, who later became President of the University. Having identified the main tasks of the university as the acquisition, expansion, and dissemination of knowledge, and the "training of adults to apply the acquired knowledge and the developed critical temper in their lives and activities" (Harris, 1967, p. 1-2), the Committee pointedly noted:

> It may well be that governments will regard the last of these three as by far the most important and that they will thus measure the success of a university . . . by the social service it renders . . . when the motivating force becomes not intellectual endeavour but the desire to produce more and more technicians, the university is no longer true to itself; it is no longer a university. (Harris, 1967, p. 1-2)

This need to state and restate the limits of government and the necessary autonomy of the university in interpreting its mission and mandate undoubtedly reflected the physical proximity of the sole University to the seat of government and the historical experience with fiscal links to internal controls and fears for the independence of the University as an institution.

Memorial had always maintained an active continuing education and upgrading programme, although teachers had traditionally been the major client group. Until 1936 the College had offered extension and evening classes on a regular basis. This disappeared partly as a result of understaffing and underfunding but also because the Newfoundland Adult Education Association became the focus of continuing education in the province. Started in 1929 with funding from the Carnegie Foundation, the Association offered traditional subjects in addition to home economics, navigation, and community welfare courses throughout the province. In 1936, the Province provided public funding in the amount of $12,000, and the mandate rested with the Association for the next few decades.

The University responded to demands for increased access in 1959 when the Extension Service of Memorial University reached out to the province through the technologies of radio and television. This was not an entirely new initiative, but the commitment in 1959 was to technology and distance education on a new scale, and it was an approach to delivery that the University would remain involved in and continue to develop. Evening and summer courses were mounted, and access to the service was supported by regional representatives of the University.

Memorial's return to a provincial extension mandate in 1959 reflected the availability of technology as well as the university leadership's desire to ensure that the development of university programming would remain centred in the existing institution. To a significant extent as well, the expansion through distance technology reflected the work of Dr. Max House of the Medical School in identifying innovative ways of extending medical services and education to distant parts of the province. Distance education, through technology and correspondence delivery, provided an important additional source of access and later complemented the first-year programming available in some of the community colleges. The principle of transfering to St. John's for the completion of programmes remained characteristic of all University programming.

The Royal Commission on Education and Youth

Philip J. Warren, a member of the Faculty of Education at Memorial University, and later Minister of Education, chaired the Royal Commission on Education and Youth that reported to the Province in 1968. The report of the *Warren Commission* provides a good audit of postsecondary opportunities as well as attitudes and philosophies at this point almost two decades after Confederation. Although the major focus remained on primary and secondary education, in keeping with enrollment patterns in the province, there was significant attention paid to the tertiary system and the manner in which it ought to develop. One of the emerging themes in the discussion was the need to diversify and to move beyond the existing programmes of university or vocational learning in responding to a growing postsecondary population in Newfoundland:

> Many people throughout the Province . . . consider any type of education other than university or vocational education as a frill. Just as elementary education had to overcome great obstacles in the nineteenth century, further education in the broad sense has yet to establish itself in the minds of many as an essential in today's society. Where it is recognized, it is often thought of as something to be indulged in by intellectuals who would rather study history than watch television, or as something for the under-privileged who for some reason or other have missed regular schooling. This attitude must change. Further education, both postsecondary and other, must be regarded as the new hope of an educated democracy. (Royal Commission, 1968, p. 96)

The expansion of Memorial University and the growth of the vocational system introduced a process of clarifying institutional roles that remains unfinished to this day. In all of this, a commitment to increasing accessibility to education generally, but with a political *leitmotif* of fostering "economic development by upgrading the workforce through higher education and technical training" (Smallwood, 1984, p. 665) that had a certain applied edge to it running throughout, continued to inform the argument.

The Warren Commission, quoting other reports, projected that enrollment in the University could climb to between 11,000 and 14,000 students by 1975-76, with as many as 7,000 to 9,000 first- and second-year students. The challenge in terms of the balanced development of the University was clear; in terms of the province, both demand and need appeared undeniable.

In attempting to recommend a development policy for postsecondary education in Newfoundland at this point, the Warren Commission turned their attention to high school, putting aside the matters of qualifications and the high number of failures and dropouts in the first and second year of the university. The conclusion that Newfoundland students required another year of study, for both academic and social preparation for university, suggested either the expansion of the secondary curriculum to include Grade XII or a transitional college programme that would support successful transfer to the university.

The Commission surveyed developments in other provinces, including British Columbia, Alberta, Ontario, and Quebec. The model that appeared most attractive was the junior college or college system that provided for a post-high school levelling of learning to a point of university preparation in combination with the completion of courses that would equate to some university-level credit. The example of the Lethbridge Junior College, which comprehended university, technical-vocational, and adult eduction sections, was cited. Another model cited was that recommended by the Quebec Royal Commission on Education, through which an additional postsecondary institutional level that would combine pre-university, general, and vocational programmes was introduced to the Quebec system.

In this light, the recommendation to establish regional colleges in which first- and second-year university courses could be pursued was not surprising. An additional year of high school was rejected on the grounds that it would pose financial difficulty for many school boards. Moreover, there was a "belief that education beyond Grade XI would be handled more efficiently by a more centralized authority" (Royal Commission, 1968, p. 97).

In 1968, Newfoundland was in an intriguing position to learn from other provincial experiences, to adapt models of postsecondary systems that reflected a longer and larger experience with the constraints of public education, and to respond to the general demands for accessibility and the growing recognition that economic and social development depended upon increasing opportunities for citizens and their children.

Toward a Provincial Community College System

The vocational system in Newfoundland had evolved from its rudimentary form in 1949 in a traditional manner in terms of curriculum and inspiration, but it too displayed the constraints of island geography and attitudes toward education. Moreover, while vocational capacity was expanded significantly in the post-Confederation decades, there was no overriding framework or long-term developmental plan established:

> At its inception, the vocational school system formed an integral part of the Smallwood industrial strategy of the 1960s and 1970s, whereby the schools were to supply the modern industrial

expansion of the province with skilled tradesmen. Although specific goals for the system were not legislated, the vocational schools set about providing pre-employment courses in a variety of trades, particularly those under the apprenticeship system. Some attempts were made to suit local training requirements . . . (Royal Commission on Employment and Unemployment, 1986, p. 82).

A federal/provincial cost-sharing programme signed in 1950 supported the expansion of vocational or *trade* schools. The Vocational Schools Assistance Agreement was renegotiated in 1960 so that the federal government assumed 75%, rather than 50%, of the costs of these programmes. By 1978, a total of 16 vocational schools, a Craft Training Centre, the Bay St. George Community College, the College of Trades and Technology, and the College of Fisheries were operating through the Province (Newfoundland and Labrador Department of Education, 1980).

The degrees of development and variety of course offerings, as well as the administrative structures in place, did not reflect a unified provincial attitude toward vocational training. The courses of study were, to a great extent, determined by the needs of each sub-region or urban setting; varied courses were accompanied by varied standards of admission. The system was administered by the Department of Education, and training in traditional apprenticeship trades areas such as welding, plumbing, and motor vehicle repairs, together with academic upgrading predominated (Newfoundland Department of Career Development and Advanced Studies, 1985).

The community college concept only gained currency during the 1970s. The Bay St. George area, centred in Stephenville at the site of the former American Harmon Air Force Base, spearheaded this move. In 1974, a reorganization within the Vocational Education Division of the Department of Education was inaugurated in the hopes of establishing "a comprehensive adult education plan for the province" (Gough et al., 1987, pp. 7-8). A regional Director for Adult and Continuing Education was appointed, with "specific responsibility for the development of a pilot community college in the Bay St. George area, with general policies for guidelines in other regions of the province" (Gough et al., 1987, pp. 7-8). The task of pulling together programmes and facilities of the District Vocational School and the Adult Education Centre created the Bay St. George Community College, established in 1977 (Gough et al., 1987; Newfoundland and Labrador Department of Education, 1980).

For many years this institution was unique on the west coast. Very much the product of local activism, the College mounted programmes that spanned a wide variety of trades and technological areas of endeavour; its consolidation and effectiveness were a source of community pride for the Stephenville area for the decade of its existence.

A government White Paper on *The Reorganization of the Vocational School System* appeared in 1985, largely in response to unemployment statistics describing the graduates of 1982. Graduates who possessed a trade school education indicated an unemployment level of 37%; those from colleges and the University were at 10%. At the same time, federal funding for training was disappearing. The White Paper posited that while vocational schools were equipped to provide pre-employment training in the traditional trades, there had been little innovation in programmes for years: "the 1984-86 Prospectus for the Vocational school system clearly shows the continuing influence of early 1960s policy" (Royal Commission on Employment and Unemployment, 1986, p. 88).

The need to make training programmes more responsive to provincial needs led to a proposal to consolidate existing vocational schools under Boards and to identify generic skill group areas—such as engineering technologies, fisheries and marine-related employment, computer and computer applications, management skills, and public sector service areas including tourism and hospitality—as a focus for future educational planning (Gough et al., 1987; Royal Commission on Employment and Unemployment, 1986; Newfoundland Department of Career Development and Advanced Studies, 1985). The suggested provincial college system of "six institutions with twenty campuses" (Newfoundland Department of Career Development and Advanced Studies, 1985, p. I) was to be operational within three years, or by the end of 1988.

In St. John's, the College of Fisheries, Navigation, Marine Engineering and Electronics, commonly known as the Fisheries College, had a somewhat different mission and fate from its sister institutions. It first admitted students in the 1963-64 session. Its function was "to train men for the marine industries (shipbuilding, marine electronics, and so on), for the fisheries industries (the hunt and the catch), for the seafood industries (handling and processing), and ancillary industries" (Royal Commission, 1968, p. 91). Programmes were directly linked to the maritime resource industry as it existed in Newfoundland; and the Departments of Basic Training, Naval Architecture, Nautical Science, Mechanical Engineering Technology, Electrical Engineering Technology, Food Technology, and

Extension Services supported a span of programmes ranging from the most basic courses to research-oriented programs.

The introduction of the community college model of organization, resulted in 1992 in a system of five Regional Colleges of Applied Arts, Technology and Continuing Education with twenty-three campuses. This reflected the desire to move into more technological and applied areas of education, while the establishment of Boards of Governors indicated awareness of the need for some distance between government and the institutions. The development of an administrative system, however, was not built upon inter-institutional consensus, established standards, or common philosophies. There was little articulation among the community colleges and transfer from one college to another, even within the same program, was made difficult by the idiosyncrasies of programming, the lack of formal transfer credit agreements, and the differing philosophical and practical understandings of mission and mandate that existed between the new partners.

Nursing Education

The training of registered nurses has traditionally been a three-year hospital-based program. The nursing assistants programs were also hospital based, but these programs are now offered in the regional colleges. Interestingly enough, the Registered Nursing program in St. John's had a quasi-denominational structure. The program at St. Clare's trained Roman Catholic nurses by and large. The General Hospital and Grace Hospital accommodated nursing students from the other denominations. The remaining School of Nursing was based at Western Memorial Regional Hospital in Corner Brook. Since 1966, Memorial has offered a five-year Bachelor of Nursing Degree. Transfer credit arrangements were such that a Registered Nursing Diploma graduate could complete the B.N. with approximately three years of study at MUN.

Recent restructuring has seen the amalgamation of the St. John's schools under the aegis of the General Hospital and the near demise of the Corner Brook school. Current plans call for the elimination of the Registered Nursing as the entry-level qualification and its replacement with the Bachelor of Nursing. This is being done with the cooperation of the Nurses' Professional Association and is viewed as one way of improving the professional status of nurses within the health care system. Plans call for the Bachelor of Nursing to be the entry-level qualification by the year 2000.

University Developments in the 1970s and 1980s

Coincident with the publication of the Warren Commission, which recommended that the University not create branches around the province but cooperate in the development of multi-purpose colleges, Memorial's Senate tabled a report on the creation of junior colleges: *The Report of the Senate Committee on the feasibility and desirability of Junior Colleges* (Sullivan, 1966).

The term "regional college" became more commonly used than "junior college," but neither should be confused with "community college." Two colleges outside of St. John's were envisaged, and they were to be creatures of the University. The Report clearly established the parameters of the University's responsibility within the tertiary sector:

> There is no doubt that technical and vocational and continuing education are of considerable importance for the Province of Newfoundland. But the provision of technical and vocational education programmes is the responsibility of the provincial Department of Education. Considerable and commendable efforts have been made in this area through the co-operation of the Provincial and Federal Governments. Recommendations for further developments in this area will undoubtedly be made by the Royal Commission on Education and Youth. Adult Education programmes are, as well, primarily the responsibility of the provincial Department of Education, although the Extension Department of the University will play an increasingly important role in this area. (Sullivan, 1966, p. 11)

The rationales presented in support of a Junior College system—one on the St. John's Campus of MUN and two in regional centres (Central and Western Newfoundland)—included the age of first-year students, the "inadequacies in the Newfoundland system of high school education" (Sullivan, 1966, p. 12), and the special instruction and counselling needs of first- and second-year university students. In addition, the Committee felt that the free tuition policy of the provincial government (a short-lived experiment of the sixties) would increase enrollments: "It should, therefore, not be necessary to attract students into the University by way of transfer programmes from vocational and technical education" (Sullivan, 1966, pp. 12-13).

This Committee also surveyed international and national experiences of junior, regional, and community colleges. They were insistent not only that Newfoundland's position of having a single university offered an opportunity to be truly innovative and unique but also that vocational training should be kept separate from any endeavour within the University. Their recommendation of a two-year Junior Division programme to be followed by a three-year Senior Division curriculum was premised upon the notion that the entire programme would be within the University's control.

Concerns about university control, autonomy, and the potential of the Warren Commission's recommendations prompted the University to implement a Junior Division in 1968 after arrangements for appropriate support and programming to ensure student success had been made. It was both a pragmatic and idealistic initiative, governed, predictably, by resource considerations and changes in the political and social climate. However, one of the results was an open-door policy that became difficult to resource and impossible to manage. It should be noted that the Junior Division mandate extended only to first-year programming, and the Senior Division, with a traditional faculty or professional school structure, covered the second-year and beyond.

From the days of relocation to a new campus in St. John's in 1961, the University had grown quickly. Yet throughout the 1970s and 1980s, there was lingering concern about Newfoundland's participation rate:

> The participation rate (i.e., the total full-time enrollment related to the 18–24 year age group) shows Newfoundland in a similarly unfavourable light—for the 1983-84 year, 10.3% compared with 19.4% for Nova Scotia and 15.9% for New Brunswick. . . . Although Newfoundland's participation rate has more than doubled (from 4.2%) since expansion to the new campus in 1961, 10.3% in 1983-84 was still the lowest in any Canadian province. (Memorial University of Newfoundland, 1985, p. 7)

This argument, coupled with the fact that Memorial has taken the position that it is obligated to accept all qualified students who present themselves for admission because it was the only university in the province, created the context for Junior Division and an eventual first-year system, General Studies, that was intended to ensure academic competence and social readiness for university-level studies.

In its origins in 1968, the Junior Division identified teaching as a priority, and in many instances hired high school teachers as designated faculty. There was a marked de-emphasis of the traditional complement of research expected of University faculty. The commitment to teaching was reiterated in the University's self-study of 1976, which recommended:

1. That the University reaffirm that its first priority is education and, in the first instance, teaching.
2. That among teaching programmes, the undergraduate teaching of the Junior Division, the Faculties of Arts and Science, and the Faculty of Education should be the first priorities. (Memorial University of Newfoundland, 1976, p. 148)

One Regional College of Memorial University of Newfoundland was created in 1975. The Corner Brook Regional College was to provide a transitional opportunity for students from the west coast and Labrador who otherwise would have had to go to St. John's or outside the province to pursue University programmes as well as to provide access to diploma programmes. These opportunities were to be in addition to the vocational college programmes available in the catchment area, since none of these institutions offered first-year university programming.

Establishment of the Regional College reflected the University's internal planning, although the decision to implement was political. Certainly, capital resources were provided by government for the purpose of establishing the College in Corner Brook and were not designated from within the University envelope.

The College operated as contemplated in the 1966 Sullivan Report—that is, as a two-year feeder institution for the University. However, the Warren Commission's recommendations regarding combined diploma and university-level programming were not implemented. While the rudiments of a college diploma were outlined in programming in the early years, all facilities were quickly adapted to more traditional purposes, and the diploma program was withdrawn entirely within four or five years.

During the late 1970s, faculty were increasingly engaged according to university-wide standards and as full university colleagues, with credentials and research playing as important a role as a commitment to undergraduate teaching. The shift in emphasis in the hiring of faculty and the demise of the diploma program reflected the vision of the second principal. Cyril Poole, who succeeded Arthur Sullivan in 1977, had previously served as the Vice-President (Academic) of Mount Allison University in New

Brunswick. Increasingly an atmosphere of university standards and orientation evolved that, while on a different scale from that of St. John's, nevertheless identified with the life of the University rather than the role of the Regional College.

In 1979 the Regional College was given a name, The Sir Wilfred Grenfell College of Memorial University. While the connection with the late nineteenth-century medical pioneer was tenuous at best, the act of naming the institution provided a symbolic consolidation of the physical presence of the University on the west coast and an identity with which students, faculty, and the community would increasingly connect.

In 1983, Grade XII or Level III was added to the reorganized secondary curriculum with an immediate, short-term relief of first-year intake into the University. This step met the Warren Commission's 1968 objective of adding a 16th year to the educational system in Newfoundland, which was in keeping with patterns in other provinces, and it provided students with more time to prepare themselves for university. It also complicated the coherent development of the Commission's plan to structure a postsecondary system that joined two years in regional colleges with a required three years at the University. The reorganized high school system was conceived as a broadening of the junior matriculation and did not incorporate a senior level of matriculation. Consequently, it did not respond to the call for a higher level of academic or intellectual preparation, even though it provided for a more mature first-year class.

Concern about the varied levels of preparation of high school graduates and the argument for accessibility continued to inform university planning. Definitions of qualified for purposes of admission were decided by Senate, but the door was open to anyone with a 60 average in the required courses. The first year, intended as a leveller, became a winnower, at significant cost to the institution and to many students whose lack of preparation predisposed them to early failure even though they could not be required to withdraw until the end of the first year. In this, the University met its obligation to accessibility by moving the decision point to the end of first year, when limited and limiting choices were available to students.

The School of General and Continuing Studies was established in 1988. In many ways a reconfiguration of Junior Division, this administrative reorganization brought together extension, educational television services, and non-traditional student entry with first-year programming. It further formally recognized the abandonment of the

University's plan to create a two-year Junior Division in several regional locations and a three-year Senior Division located in St. John's.

The University undertook two major initiatives at Sir Wilfred Grenfell College in the later 1980s. Consistently growing enrollments coupled with the pressures of a core of academic faculty led to discussions of further development of programmes at the Corner Brook campus. A committee of representatives from St. John's and Corner Brook prepared a report recommending the completion of four-year degree programming in the Arts and Sciences at Grenfell. Such programmes were to be distinct from those available in St. John's, and the orientation of the College was to be to a small, personalized undergraduate experience. In a time of increasing resource concerns, it was clear to the Senate of the University that the College could develop only with the infusion of additional funding.

Concurrent with this movement toward completion of undergraduate programmes in Arts and Sciences was the inauguration of Fine Arts programming at the Corner Brook campus. While a School of Music existed in St. John's, the decision to establish a School of Fine Arts for the study of visual and theatre arts at Corner Brook was taken in 1983 and was confirmed in the provincial government's decision to fund a building for that purpose.

A further significant development in the delivery of university education was the offering of first-year university programs at various sites around the province. Since the late 1980s, first-year courses were implemented at a number of community colleges throughout the province. The University played a role in approving instructors, course content, and examinations in these programmes that were originally offered on designated college campuses in Labrador City, Burin, Grand Falls, and Lewisporte. Structurally, the programmes were marginalized rather than integrated into the University's system. Memorial exercised an indirect control over hiring through retaining the right to approve applicants for teaching positions in the programmes only if they were acceptable university-level teachers. On the other hand, faculty hired were in the direct employ of the respective College and enjoyed none of the benefits of University colleagueship or employment. The courses offered were limited to those that could be replicated exactly in terms of curriculum and content, and library resources were extremely limited. The text-based course was clearly easier to mount in these circumstances, and any natural development of curriculum was limited by distance, institutional culture, and the separation of faculty from their academic milieu.

The "System" in 1995

The White Paper on Education presented in 1990, *Equality, Excellence and Efficiency: A Postsecondary Educational Agenda for the Future* (Newfoundland Department of Education, 1990), posited an ambitious schedule for capital and programme development within the tertiary system. In this, the expansion of first-year programming throughout the province and the development of Grenfell as a full, four-year campus were projected, the latter to be fully implemented by 1994-95. But the pace of change in the sector has been far quicker, the range of developments more comprehensive, and the pressure of external circumstances more profound and immediate than was contemplated five years ago.

The five Regional Colleges of Applied Arts, Technology and Continuing Education joined with the Department of Education and Memorial University to form the Newfoundland and Labrador Council on Higher Education in 1992. The new structure facilitated progress in the area of standardization and transfer of credit, and by 1995 the first semester of two-year technical programmes and the first year of three-year technical programmes were common. Further, the Council undertook, as a part of its basic mandate, to prepare *1995-1996 Transferguide: A guide to transfer of credit in Newfoundland and Labrador Public Postsecondary Institutions* (Newfoundland and Labrador Council on Higher Education, 1995) and to establish a Provincial Articulation Committee, with sub-groups working to formalize high school to college, college to college, and college to university transition.

Budget cuts in the spring of 1995 led the regional colleges to discontinue their involvement in adult basic education programming. Amid much public protest, a new phase of college structuring was mooted by the Department of Education. The thrust of the concept is a further consolidation of administrative and governing board structures into a single unit, as well as the designation from within the system of a technical college that would provide programming leading to applied, technical degrees. While the final vision of the structure is not public, the goal appears to be further administrative consolidation to support standardization, respond to fiscal restraint, and provide more sophisticated technical training and education.

As the maritime industrial capacity of the province developed, so did the sophistication of some of the programmes and teachers at the Fisheries College, which was renamed the Marine Institute. Informal links with university scholars and programmes and the need to evolve some of the disciplines beyond the traditional limitations of the vocational college emerged naturally. The distinction between the vocational training and education/research elements of the institution were not clearly drawn. Also, the pressures of both economic and educational development in the province prompted its merger with the University as the Fisheries and Marine Institute of Memorial University of Newfoundland in 1991. Legislation to codify the merger was accompanied by a transitional process in which the Board of Governors of the Marine Institute became an advisory committee to the Board of Regents of the University, and the Senate of the Institute was authorized to act in the stead of the Senate of the University. While programme and faculty related developments continue to evolve, by the spring of 1995 the Institute was operating as a faculty of the University with representatives elected to the Senate of the University, an industry-based advisory board appointed by the Board of Regents, and one full undergraduate programme, a Bachelor of Maritime Studies with options in Marine Engineering Technology and Nautical Science Technology approved for implementation in the fall of 1995.

Within the University, fundamental changes have occurred in admissions and student advising. The open-door admissions policy was replaced with a required 70% high school leaving average, effective fall 1995; the practice of not applying re-admission standards at the end of the first semester was discontinued; and the School of General Studies was closed in 1993 and replaced by an academic advising centre. The general degrees require four years and the professional degrees five, with the first year's performance being decisive in admission to professional faculties and many programmes in the Arts and Sciences.

Sir Wilfred Grenfell College now offers B.A. and B.Sc. programming as well as the B.F.A. (Bachelor of Fine Arts), coming close to meeting the deadline for development contemplated by the White Paper of 1990. The institution is developing a singular identity within the Memorial system, with four-year programmes that are based upon a core curriculum, general education, and cognate/specialization requirements. Selected professional programmes appropriate to the region and the mandate of the institution are currently under development for implementation over the next few years.

Both campuses are involved in various outreach activities, in which relationships with other partners in the educational sector are being developed and acted upon in matters of information technology, distance delivery, and programme planning. The Open Learning and Information Network (OLIN) was funded in 1994 by the Human Resources

Development Agreement, and Memorial is a key player in the development and activities of this network.

Finally, economic reversals and impending changes in federal-provincial fiscal relationships have had significant, unanticipated impact upon the development of the tertiary sector during the past few years. The moratorium in the cod fisheries and the resulting training requirements of the Northern Cod Adjustment and Recovery Program (NCARP) and the Atlantic Ground Fish Strategy (TAGS) Training programme have channelled approximately 17,000 individuals into adult basic education and a broad spectrum of postsecondary programming but not typically university study.

A significant number of seats in the regional colleges of applied arts, technology, and continuing education were taken to support TAGS retraining, and this had an impact upon the traditional population of young people who were used to accessing spaces on a first-come, first-served basis. The real sectoral growth has been among private institutions. From a handful of established private institutions, the Department of Education now identifies almost fifty private institutions. While the educational demographics of the displaced fisherpeople was complex, the result of federal programming has had a visible impact on one facet of the tertiary sector. While the social and economic results of millions of dollars of investment in these training/education programmes are as yet largely untested, the fund has supported the opening of a plethora of new private institutions that have little accountability in terms of outcomes or standards. Moreover, there has been little attempt to integrate these institutions into any plan, philosophical or practical, for the longer-term development of either education or training in the province.

To accompany these fundamental issues of social and economic restructuring, the continuing elaboration of definitions relating to education and training, and the role of various partners in the tertiary sector, the Province of Newfoundland and Labrador finds itself contemplating the unknown impact of the federal budget of 1995. The disappearance of Established Program Financing and the implementation of the Canada Social Transfer will require the provincial government to establish a new approach to funding institutions and setting priorities in the areas of health, education, and social support.

From the vantage point of the spring of 1996, government has announced its intention to proceed immediately with an amalgamation of the community college system. Although the details of implementing the plan are as yet not clear, the goal is to establish a single administrative headquarters and board of governors for the five community colleges that were previously autonomous; Cabot, Eastern, Central, Westviking, and Labrador community colleges will thus all become part of an as yet unnamed provincial institution. As part of this process, a number of satellite campuses have been closed altogether.

Another unanticipated announcement in the Spring of 1996 was that all first-year university course offerings at community colleges on the Island of Newfoundland (not in Labrador) would be discontinued effective September 1996. While one campus (Grand Falls) has proposed retention of the programme for one year on the basis of advanced student enrollments, it is not apparent this will have any impact on the government's plan.

This leaves the province and postsecondary educators pondering very interesting times and new relationships as we head towards the next century.

References

Gough, W.H.C., Evans, R., and Germani, A. (1987). *We alone: The story of the Bay St. George community college*. Stephenville, NF: Bay St. George Community College.

Harris, L. (1967). *The government and administration of Memorial University of Newfoundland: A report*. St. John's, NF: Memorial University of Newfoundland.

MacLeod, M. (1990). *A bridge built halfway: A history of Memorial University College, 1925-1950*. Montreal: McGill-Queen's University Press.

MacNutt, W.S. (1965).*The Atlantic Provinces: The emergence of colonial society*. Toronto: McClelland and Stewart Limited.

Memorial University of Newfoundland (1976). *Summary of the report of the task force on university priorities*. St. John's, NF: Division of University Relations.

Memorial University of Newfoundland. (1985). *Memorial's story*. St. John's, NF: Division of University Relations.

Newfoundland. (1973). *The revised statutes of Newfoundland 1970: A revision and consolidation of the public general statutes of Newfoundland as contained in the revised statutes of Newfoundland, 1952 and as passed in the years 1953 to 1970 both inclusive*. St. John's, NF: E.R. Davis, Queen's Printer.

Newfoundland and Labrador Council on Higher Education (1995). *1995-1996 transferguide: A guide to transfer of credit in Newfoundland and Labrador public postsecondary institutions*. St. John's, NF: Author.

Newfoundland and Labrador Department of Education (1980). *Annual report 1978-1979*. St. John's, NF: Author.

Newfoundland Department of Career Development and Advanced Studies (1985). *The reorganization of the vocational school system*. St. John's, NF: Author.

Newfoundland Department of Education (1990). *Equality, excellence, and efficiency: A postsecondary educational agenda for the future*. St. John's, NF: Government of Newfoundland and Labrador.

Newton, R. (1952). *Memorial University of Newfoundland: A survey*. St. John's, NF: Memorial University of Newfoundland.

Royal Commission (1968). *Report of the Royal Commission on education and youth* (Vol. 2). St. John's, NF: Newfoundland Book Publishers.

Royal Commission on Employment and Unemployment (1986). *Education for self-reliance: A report on education and training in Newfoundland*. St. John's, NF: Author.

Smallwood, J.R. (Ed.). (1984). *Encyclopaedia of Newfoundland and Labrador* (Vol. 2). St. John's, NF: Newfoundland Book Publishers.

Sullivan, A.M. (1966), *Report of the Senate Committee on the feasibility and desirability of Junior Colleges*. St. John's, NF: Memorial University of Newfoundland.

Warren, P.J. (1975). Dramatic change in education. In J.R. Smallwood (Ed.), *The book of Newfoundland* (pp. 333-350). St. John's, NF: Newfoundland Book Publishers.

Williams, A.F. (Ed.). (1966). *Memorial University of Newfoundland and its environs: A guide to life and work at the university in St. John's*. St. John's, NF: Memorial University of Newfoundland.

Postsecondary Education in the Yukon: The Last Thirty Years [1]

Aron Senkpiel

"In the North," so goes an oft-repeated truism, "geography is *the* major challenge." Yet, as intimidating as the region's geography may be, a second challenge also figures prominently in the development of social, educational, and judicial services in the North: addressing the disparate and sometimes conflicting needs of a small, culturally heterogeneous population. This is especially obvious in the history of postsecondary education in the Yukon. It is the brief yet intense story of adopting and adapting institutional values, practices, and structures from elsewhere in the country to meet the challenges of the territory's geography and the diverse educational needs and aspirations of its residents.

If this history is to make theoretical and practical sense to the reader who, following traditional definitions of higher or postsecondary education, expects a discussion of university education or who, based on experience outside the region, expects dollars spent or students served to cross certain thresholds of significance, some qualifications are necessary. First, the Yukon—which is geographically much larger than Prince Edward Island, New Brunswick, and Nova Scotia together—is demographically a very small community. In 1941, just 4,914 people lived in the territory (*Yukon Census Figures*, 1941). In 1992, just 31,000 people lived here; of these, 22,000 lived in a single community—Whitehorse (*Yukon Statistical Review*, Second Quarter, 1992).[2] To put this in perspective, the entire population of the territory is smaller than the enrollment of some of Canada's universities.

Not surprisingly, then, the Yukon's economic, social, political, and educational apparatus is conspicuously less developed than those of other regions of the country. Because of its small population, simple economy, and federal dependence, the Yukon, along with the Northwest Territories, has often been regarded as a developing region or even as a northern "colony" (Coates, 1987). As such, it is arguable that the Yukon is more interesting, in terms of the development of its institutions, for what it might yet do rather than what it has already done (Stenbaek and Senkpiel, 1989).

Second, the entire formal history of postsecondary education in the Yukon spans not several centuries or even several lifetimes. Even if one uses 1963, the year in which the Whitehorse Vocational Training School was opened, as the start of formal higher education in the territory, it spans just thirty years. Moreover, it is really the history of two institutions: the Yukon Vocational and Technical Training Centre and its successor, Yukon College.

These observations suggest that a study of postsecondary education in the Yukon must necessarily be on a much smaller scale than   such a study would be if it were conducted in another region of the country. They also suggest that such a study must necessarily be more qualitative than quantitative. There is, for example, almost no scholarly literature to cite. As well, when dealing with such small numbers, even the simplest of statistics can mislead. Clearly, the scholarly distance easily attained by scholars writing in other jurisdictions is more difficult, if not impossible, to attain here.[3]

Third, if by the term "postsecondary education" is meant, as it often has, university education, then even today some conceptual liberty must still be taken to use it to describe events in the Yukon. To state the obvious, the Yukon, like the Northwest Territories, does not have a university. Indeed, if one accepts the 60th parallel as the southern edge of Canada's Far North (Maslove and Hawkes, 1990, p. 13), then Canada does not have a truly northern university. This fact is of national and international consequence. It not only makes the north unique among the regions of Canada, it makes Canada unique among circumpolar nations.

In an odd fashion, these very facts, which make the inclusion of the territories so difficult in the study of postsecondary education in Canada, also make it essential. To discuss what has not happened in the north or is just now starting to happen in the north is to identify not just a major gap but a major opportunity within postsecondary education in the country, in terms of both education and research.[4]

Given these observations, it is interesting to note that in the Yukon, as in the Northwest Territories, the emergence of a representative territorial government and the establishment of the Yukon's first postsecondary institution are contemporaneous events. Indeed, Yukon College, like Arctic College, can be seen as a very tangible expression of the Yukon's resolve to be a self-determining region. Consequently, the development of postsecondary education in the Yukon—which is, as noted above, very recent—can be usefully divided into two periods. The 1960s and 1970s were a time of articulation and aspiration; the 1980s and early 1990s have been a time of realization.

The 1960s and 1970s—Simple Beginnings, Growing Aspirations

The history of formal postsecondary education in the Yukon begins with the official opening of the Whitehorse Vocational Training Centre on June 11, 1963. About one hundred students registered for the various vocational programs that the Centre's twelve faculty, four administrators, and seven support staff offered. As principal Jack Bredin stated several years after the Centre opened, students could "learn a skill which would enable [them] to gain employment in a chosen field" (Yukon College official opening commemorative edition, 1988, p. 2). From the outset, then, the primacy of "training for employment" was firmly established. Although the Centre grew considerably over the next fifteen years—it was renamed the Yukon Vocational and Technical Training Centre in 1965—the vocational focus was not to shift significantly.

That the Centre was devoted to vocational training is obvious from the fact that neither it nor its staff figured significantly in the considerable public discussion about new higher education opportunities in the Territory that emerged in the 1970s. This can be accounted for by the fact that the Centre simply did not figure in the educational planning of affluent Yukoners who equated postsecondary education with going "Outside." To them the Centre was seen as largely irrelevant. Put baldly, many viewed it as a place for those members of the community who, while they might be trained, could not be educated. By the mid-1970s, the Centre seems to have been firmly entrenched in the public's mind as an example of what the Territory had been, not of what it might become.

These discussions of postsecondary education grew out of the general spirit of optimism which pervaded the Territory at the time. In the early 1970s, rising energy costs, federal cutbacks, and frequent disruptions in production at the Cyprus Anvil Mine in Faro had caused a recession. However, by 1976, things were changing. The Federal Government was once again publicly expressing interest in the development of its northern territories. The Alaska Highway Natural Gas Pipeline was being promoted. A settlement of the north's land claims, which had been given considerable impetus by the recommendations of the Berger and Lysyk inquiries, seemed imminent. And, perhaps most importantly, representational government and party politics were being pursued by the Territory (Smyth, 1991). When the 1979 session of the Yukon Legislative Assembly was opened, Commissioner Ione Christensen captured some of this optimism in the *Speech from the Throne*. She spoke positively of the introduction of party politics as "necessary to continue our evolution towards full responsible government" and then went on to outline the newly elected Progressive Conservative Government's agenda:

> We seek an early and just settlement of Yukon Indian land claims; a full state of preparedness for the construction of the Alaska Highway Natural Gas Pipeline and the development of a firm and aggressive development policy for the Yukon. (*Speech from the Throne*, 1979)

The significance of this growing spirit of self-determination cannot be overstated. As historians Kenneth Coates and Judith Powell note in *The Modern North* (1989), "since the mid-1970s, the North has been set on a radically different course" (p. xv). Clearly, at the start of what Coates and Powell rightly call a "period of transition" (p. xv), many people anticipated a new prosperity, one built on an economy expanded by resource exploitation and the settlement of land claims. This optimism fuelled, in turn, various and at times contradictory efforts to establish a truly northern, postsecondary academic institution.

In fact, if the economic projections of the 1970s seem optimistic today, some of the educational plans of the times seem downright futuristic. Spurred on by all the federal talk of the country's future lying in its north, Richard Rohmer and a diverse group of northern Canadians secured letters patent for the University of Canada North (UCN) in March 1971.[5] However, as Amanda Graham has noted, UCN was unable to do the things which would have established it in the public's mind as a *bona fide* institution: namely have recognized faculty teach students in classrooms. Consequently, public support for the initiative waned, and by 1979 UCN was seen as something of a joke. The January 25, 1979, editorial in *The Northern Times* observed:

> The so-called University of Canada North, which currently exists as little more than a file folder . . . and an office in the T.C. Richards Building . . . is probably worse than useless in the attempt to get a real institution of higher education in the North. (p. 4)

At the same time that UCN was trying to secure support for its endeavours, another quite separate, national effort to establish a northern university was underway. Given the renewed federal interest in the North—no doubt because of the oil rush in the Beaufort—there was an increase in grant money available for northern scientific research and, consequently, an increase in scientific interest in the north. It was specifically with a view to improving northern research that the Science Council of Canada, in 1977, urged the establishment of a northern university (*Northward Looking*, 1977). From the Council's perspective, the "most immediate value of a University of the North would be to provide a focus for the development of northern research activities specifically designed to solve northern problems" (p. 57). It was in the context of securing grant monies that the Council should have "all the prestige that attaches to the word 'university'" (p. 58). The actual educational role of the university was seen as of secondary importance (pp. 58-59).

Then, in December 1978, William Gauvin, Director of Research for the Noranda Research Centre and head of the Science Council's special committee on northern development, released a paper entitled *A Northern Resource Centre: A First Step Towards a University of Canada North* in which he, too, supported the establishment of a northern university. Again, a facility of primary use to southern scientists was envisaged:

> The resource centre could provide adult education, be a focal point linking northern education institutions with those in the south, a meeting ground and a forum for discussion of northern problems and a training ground for young northerners. . . . While the focus here is on science and technology and the development eventually of an indigenous northern scientific community, it should be understood that the University of the North must be seen in a wider educational context. (Orton, 1979, p. 3)

Also, several statements in the report suggest that the intended readership of the report was not northerners but southern decision makers interested in promoting Canadian sovereignty: "The northern resource centre would provide an institutional 'flag' to remind Canadian scientists that indeed Canada is a northward looking nation" (p. 3). Clearly, the Science Council was looking northward but from about as far south as one could get in Canada.

Other groups were also pursuing the notion of a northern institution. Anticipating the imminent and lucrative settlement of land claims and displeased by the inattentiveness of the Yukon Government, which was seen as a vehicle of the non-Native population, Native groups like the Yukon Native Brotherhood and the Yukon Association of Non-Status Indians were making their own plans. For example, the *Whitehorse Star* of November 27,

1978, notes that Jennifer Mauro of the Yukon Native Brotherhood had approached the Saskatchewan Indian Federated College about the possibility of delivering its programs in the Yukon. Then in December 1978 delegates to the general assembly of the Council for Yukon Indians passed a "resolution to establish a Yukon Indian education centre" as a "focal point from which native people can be served" ("CYI Plans Native Education Centre," 1979, p. 6).

A fourth line of inquiry, the one which was finally to succeed, was being pursued by the Yukon Government. The Government, no doubt influenced by aspirations of the indigenous non-Native community that went back at least to 1960 when James Smith and F.H. Collins (both of whom had served as Commissioners of the Yukon) had identified a site for a university, was eager to do something substantial to address the growing interest in and support for university-level education. It, like the electorate it represented, was clearly not satisfied by the current programming offered by the Yukon Vocational and Technical Training Centre or by the extension courses that were occasionally offered by the University of Alberta in Whitehorse. Consequently, it undertook work on several fronts. Given that these were to merge in the creation of Yukon College in 1983, they merit discussion.

In July 1977, the Government of the Yukon signed an agreement with the University of British Columbia for the establishment of a program to train long-time Yukoners to teach in Yukon elementary schools. That fall the Yukon Teacher Education Programme (YTEP)—the territory's first full-time university-level program—started classes in a small group of portable structures in Whitehorse. The program continued until 1982. At that time, the need for locally-trained teachers was considered met. However, a growing number of local residents had found that if they claimed that they wanted to become teachers, they could acquire up to two years of university-level coursework. Consequently, the Yukon Government, now quite consciously working towards the establishment of a college and feeling pressure from the University of British Columbia, agreed to convert the teacher education program to a two-year liberal arts program. Thus, in the summer of 1982, UBC Programs was created.

Whether or not the Yukon Teacher Education Programme was successful depends a great deal upon with whom one talks (Senkpiel, 1986). For those who believed the program was to train "Native" Yukoners—meaning students of First Nations ancestry—the program failed. For example, of seven Native students admitted into the programme in 1981 from a special year of preparatory studies, none graduated. However, for those who believed the program was to train "Native" Yukoners—meaning students born in the territory, as the Yukon Government was careful to indicate in the first YTEP contract—it was reasonably successful. In its five years, it trained seventy-three teachers, many of whom still teach in Yukon schools. But from the perspective of this study, the importance of the program was that it resulted in the first university-level liberal arts program in the Canadian North, what was ultimately to become the Academic Studies Division of Yukon College.

The other major step taken by the Government during the late 1970s was its decision to ask a group of educational researchers from the University of Alberta's Centre for the Study of Postsecondary Education and the Department of Educational Administration to undertake a major study of continuing education opportunities in the Yukon. More specifically, the research team—led by Professors Ingram, Konrad, and Small—was asked to "ascertain the educational aspirations of adults in the Yukon, examine promising alternative program, delivery, governance and financing arrangements, and recommend alternatives for continuing education which might be most desirable and feasible in the Yukon" (Ingram et al., 1979, p. iii). The primary recommendation of the 173-page report published at the end of the study, *Toward a Yukon College* (1979), was the creation of a comprehensive community college. Significantly, it took the idea of a Yukon postsecondary institution out of the conjectural realm and articulated a philosophy of continuing education and an institutional structure that still figure prominently in current decision-making in Yukon higher education.

Working with a committee of interested community representatives, the research team conducted personal interviews with 128 "knowledgeable persons" (Ingram et al., 1979, p. 39) from across the Territory. As well, in an effort to identify "levels of involvement, barriers, interests, and preferences in continuing education" (p. 47), the team sent out a continuing education needs assessment which was completed by over 1000 Yukon residents. Based on the data from the interviews and the survey, the team was able to confidently describe current educational opportunities in the territory and, as well, Yukoners' educational aspirations.

Of particular significance to this study are the major themes or inferences that the team identified from its interviews and its recommendations. Because these continue to be major issues in postsecondary education—as evidenced, for example, by the ongoing deliberations of the Yukon College Board of Governors—these are worth noting. In all, the team identified eight inferences. First, the team noted a "cultural polarization" (p. 40) between Natives and non-Natives. They also noted that many Yukoners, especially those in the communities, felt "too much power was . . . centralized in Whitehorse" (p. 41). The team also found that "there were important differences in the continuing education needs of small communities" (p. 41) and a strong desire to use "local resources" (p. 42). Among non-Natives, the team concluded, "high value was placed on the opportunity to study . . . outside" (pp. 42-43). But it is the team's final inferences that are, perhaps, most interesting. It found that "there was an expression of general dissatisfaction with the present operation of the Vocational Centre" (p. 42) and "little support for the creation of a Yukon University and little or no interest in [the] University of Canada North" (p. 42). However, "strong interest . . . was expressed in a community college type of institution which would offer a broad range of courses, both credit and non-credit, to high school leavers and older adults" (p. 42).

Based on their findings, the researchers made a total of 29 recommendations in five major areas: governance, finance, programming, delivery, and implementation. As noted above, their primary recommendation was:

> That a college, centered in Whitehorse, be established to serve all
> of the postsecondary and continuing education needs of the Yukon
> and to assume various investigative and social critic functions. (p.
> ix)

This and the twenty-eight other recommendations delineate an institution familiar across North America: an independently governed, comprehensive community college offering a range of credit and non-credit training and educational programs using a variety of instructional techniques and media.

But, in the final clause of the first recommendation an important, additional role is given to the proposed college. That is, Ingram et al. subsumed to the college a role more often associated with the university: that of investigator and social critic. Also, having identified this as an important role, they suggested that it was for this reason that while "the present Vocational Centre . . . could, at least initially, be the major component of the new college" (p. 127), what was "needed [was] a new institution, one or two steps removed from the Government" (p. 127). In short, they suggested a college with a difference, that difference being investigation or research.

When one looks back from the vantage point afforded by the 1990s, it becomes clear that *Toward a Yukon College*—published at the end of the 1970s—has functioned as a blueprint, guiding the establishment of Yukon College. (Indeed, the recommendations could still serve as a useful checklist, indicating not only what has been accomplished but what remains to be accomplished.)

The 1980s and 1990s—Creating the Yukon's College

That the Yukon Government quite methodically pursued the goals set out in *Toward a Yukon College* is evident from several steps it took during the early 1980s. It selected a site for a new college complex and began ground preparation. Then, on March 23, 1983, Minister of Education Bea Firth announced "the Yukon Vocational and Technical Training Center and [UBC Programs] had been merged to form a new Yukon College" (Smyth, 1991, p. 130).

Initially, the proclamation of the new College was little more than the renaming of the Yukon Vocational and Technical Centre. Admittedly, the Centre's programming base had expanded considerably over the previous few years with the addition of a network of community centres and a new two-year Business Administration program brokered from Red Deer College. Additionally, the Government decided to move the UBC arts and science extension program which had continued after the dissolution of the Yukon Teacher Education Programme from its own small facility on Nisutlin Drive to the old vocational centre campus on Lewes Boulevard, the latter being the new College's home. But two points need to be stressed here. First, the College continued to be, administratively, a unit of the Advanced Education Branch of the Government's Department of Education. Interestingly, the College did not have a principal or a president; rather its senior officer was a director who reported directly to the Assistant Deputy Minister of Advanced Education. That is, the Department of Education had complete control over the College—a fact it demonstrated more than once but perhaps most dramatically in March 1985 when the then Deputy Minister of Education walked the short distance from the government buildings to the College and terminated the College's Director. Second, the university-level programming offered in the College remained administratively and academically separate from it. It continued to be administered by the University of British Columbia. In short, while the establishment of Yukon College had been proclaimed, it was a college largely in name only.

Following the proclamation of the College, the Government took several additional steps to realize the recommendations of the Ingram report. A detailed development plan was submitted to the Government in March 1984. Later that year, a design competition for a new college complex to be constructed at a site in Takhini was announced. Then, on March 28, 1985, cabinet approved the conceptual design submitted by Carlberg Jackson Partners.

On May 13, 1985, the Progressive Conservatives, who had been in power since the advent of party politics in 1978, lost the territorial election. The new government was formed by the New Democrats led by Tony Penikett. It was a nervous time for the new College. Its officials were uncertain whether the new government would support its continued development. For example, while the ground for the new Takhini complex had been prepared, construction had not yet begun. There were rumours that "they" were not pleased with the plans approved by the previous government. Several months passed before the Government, somewhat reluctantly, gave its go-ahead for construction of the new campus.

However, by 1986, the NDP Government was solidly behind the continued development of Yukon College. This support seems to have crystallized just prior to and then during a massive community consultation initiative called Yukon 2000 which allowed hundreds, if not thousands, of Yukoners to state their views about the "future of their economy and society" (*The Things That Matter,* 1987). In March, a consultant from Manitoba who had served in the NDP Government there, Lionel Orlikow, submitted his report *The Option to Stay: An Education/Strategy for the Yukon* (1986). In it, he observed that Yukoners often did not have the "option to stay" (p. 3) in the Territory, that employment and education often forced people, who would have preferred to stay in the territory, to leave. "Education," wrote Orlikow, "now encourages migration out" (p. 3). Given this, he strongly advocated the continued development of the College. In fact, five of his twelve recommendations dealt with the College. All dealt with increasing the College's autonomy and strengthening its community-based responsibilities and activities.

The impact of Orlikow's report is obvious when one looks at the documents that came out of the Yukon 2000 process. For example, in *The Things That Matter* (1987), the NDP Government identified four broad goals. One of these was "the option to stay." The other three were "control of the future," "an acceptable quality of life," and "equality." Clearly, the further the Government proceeded with the Yukon 2000 process the more central a strong, autonomous Yukon College became to the accomplishment of its objectives. This is particularly obvious in the Yukon 2000 document entitled *Training for the Future: The Yukon Training Strategy* (1987). In Part II, in which the Government talks about "expanded local opportunities" (pp. 5-9), the continued development of the College's community learning centres figures prominently. Specifically, the centres were not to be tightly controlled by Whitehorse but were to be directed by a need for "local decisions" and "local development" (p. 7).

If more community control is the conclusion of Part II, more college autonomy is the conclusion of Part III. The report states "the time has come to consider establishing an independent Board of Governors to operate the College—a board whose agenda is fully dedicated to the College" (p. 12). Significantly, such a board should represent "all sectors of Yukon society" (p. 12). Clearly, the idea of an independent college with a strong, flexible network of locally directed community campuses was seen to fit, fundamentally, with the economic, cultural, and educational agendas set by a government which had been elected in the territory's small communities. In short, although the idea of a Yukon college housed in a large new complex had been developed by the previous government, by 1986 the NDP government was fully committed to its further development.

A little more than a year later, with the construction of the new facility nearing completion, the Minister of Education, Piers McDonald, released his government's *White Paper on College Governance and Phased Implementation* (1987). Early in the paper *The Yukon Training Strategy* is quoted, thus establishing an explicit link to the Yukon 2000 process. Interestingly, the quote is one which adds another dimension to the government's thinking about the College:

> The Government believes Yukoners must participate fully in decisions that affect them. In keeping with this principle, the Government will be transferring responsibilities to Yukon College so that it can take its place as a mature member among community colleges in Canada. (*White Paper on College Governance*, p. 10)

The suggestion that Yukon College should take its place in the future of the territory was a familiar one. What was new here was the recognition that Yukon College would not just belong to the Yukon community but also to a second community: a community of colleges. It seems that by August 1987 the Government, energized by the Yukon 2000 process, saw its actions as not just regionally significant but nationally as well.

Part 3 of the report describes the Government's "preferred college governance model" (pp. 13-16). The model entrenches strong community and First Nations representation on the board: "The permanent Yukon College Board will consist of a minimum of ten public members, of which at least three shall be Indian representatives, three shall be regional

Community Campus representatives . . ." (p. 13). That is, while the main college facilities were to be in Whitehorse—the new $50 million Ayamdigut campus was nearing completion—power on the board was to be held by the predominantly Native rural communities. As well, the paper urged the development of a program advisory council that would be appointed by the board and advise it on programming matters. This council was to have as members all the chairs of what were now being called the community campuses, thus further securing community control.

The duties of the new board were to be considerable; it would have all the powers of a corporation, but, the "primary authority for identifying and analyzing overall territorial postsecondary educational and training needs [were to be] retained by the Minister" (p. 15).

Regarding actual implementation, the paper delineates the establishment of an "interim" board (p. 13) that would sit during a three-year transition period during which time it would, with the assistance of a conversion team made up of government officials, effect the necessary transfers and put in place the necessary policy and administrative structures.

Given the release of the *White Paper* (1986), there were no major surprises in the new *College Act* which was assented to on May 18, 1988.[6] The number of governors to be appointed by "the Commissioner in Executive Council" (p. 10) was increased slightly to twelve, including a student representative. As well, it entrenched the role of and community representation on the Program Advisory Council and the existence of community campus committees. It also allowed for the creation of an interim board of governors which would sit until the transfer was effected which would occur "on a date to be specified." Later, it was decided that independence would occur on January 1, 1990.

The new campus was nearing completion, the College Act had been passed, board governance was guaranteed, and the conversion team was working. It was an impressive range of accomplishments. One would have thought it would have been considered enough. But during this time, the Department of Advanced Education and college officials were also busy working on the third side of the triangle: programming. They felt that when the College moved to the new campus in 1988, with governance assured in the immediate future, some new programs should be in place. A territorial election was also in the offing.

This impending happy confluence had been recognized early in 1988 by some of the College's faculty. Following a three-year transition plan, academic responsibility for the university transfer program had been transferred from UBC to the College. The transfer had, in fact, been completed in two years and the College's new Arts and Science Division—now the north's first autonomous university-level academic program—was anticipating a major influx of students because of its new, somewhat more flexible admissions criteria and the completion of the new college campus. Given what had happened and what was about to happen, the faculty prepared a major proposal for the Government. Entitled *The Diploma of Northern Studies: A Proposal for Integrated Programs in Native Studies, Northern Science, and Northern Outdoor and Environmental Studies* (March 1988), the proposal urged the establishment of the first comprehensive university-level northern studies program in Canada. Such a program would, if implemented, allow northerners to do what people from other regions of the country could do: learn about their region while living in it. Senior college and government officials both supported the proposal, and, following some modifications, funding was granted.

On October 1, 1988, the new College was officially opened. The official guests represented both traditions of learning which, it was hoped, were to flourish at the College: elders from many of the territory's communities sat beside senior university officials. Two other things stood out that day. Government Leader Tony Penikett bestowed a $1 million gift to the College so that it could establish a permanent Northern Studies Research Fund. And a Tagish Elder, Mrs. Angela Sidney, bestowed on the campus a new name. *Ayamdigut* is Tagish for "the house that moved." A year later, on December 31, 1989, the moving process that had begun ten years earlier when *Toward a Yukon College* was completed. The following day, on January 1, 1990, the independent college envisaged by Ingram et al. was finally a reality.

It should be clear from the preceding discussion that the Yukon's decision to create its own postsecondary institution—a step taken by the government with almost unqualified community support—was made in faith, in the belief that such an institution would help the territory take control of and shape its own future. As such, it was a decision probably not dissimilar to that taken by other ambitious communities early in their development. As such, it was done with a view of what a community can or should become than what it currently is. The institutional model that was finally chosen—the comprehensive community college—was a sound one. Unlike the University of Canada North concept, the somewhat more modest college model better fit the actual educational needs and economic resources of the community. Rather than focusing only on the more advanced educational needs of the community, the comprehensive college could meet very broad educational and cultural needs, from basic literacy training in the communities to first-

and second-year university education in the capital. Indeed, Yukon College provides a useful example of an institution which has been able to marry, somewhat successfully, the community development values more often associated with adult education and the academic or scholarly values more prevalent in discussions of higher education. Given the breadth of expectation and responsibility, it is not surprising that Yukon College has sometimes stumbled. What, perhaps, is surprising are the many times that it has not.

Notes

1. The following paper was first prepared, in a somewhat different form, for a special study of higher education in Canada sponsored by the Canadian Society for the Study of Higher Education.

2. Statistics Canada gives the population of the Yukon in 1986 as 23,360 (Maslove and Hawkes, 1990). The difference between the 1992 Yukon Government and 1986 federal figures should not be interpreted as growth but rather the result of different methods of data collection. Traditionally, the Yukon Government's Bureau of Statistics gives higher figures. There has been only limited population growth during the last two decades.

3. This question of objectivity is not theoretical. The author came to the territory in 1980 to lecture for the University of British Columbia in its Yukon Teacher Education Programme. Since then he has personally been involved in many of the events described in this paper, and his own notes have served as an important source of dates and names.

4. The long-standing absence of postsecondary opportunities in the territories, which are both under federal jurisdiction, can be seen as just one result of the British North America Act's assignment of responsibility for education to the provinces. Another consequence, of course, is the enormous variety of postsecondary systems in Canada.

5. Amanda Graham has just completed the first comprehensive study of this important initiative. Some of the data given in the following discussion of the University of Canada North are from her MA thesis, The University That Wasn't (1994).

6. The act did include one provision which might be considered "surprising": it includes a "cop out" clause. Section 16(1) reads: "If the board of governors fail to direct the programs and activities of the College in accordance with this Act, the Executive Council Member may appoint an administrator to replace the board and manage the programs and activities of the College until a newly constituted board is appointed."

References

Another spin on the same merry-go-round (January 25, 1979). *Northern Times*, p. 4.

Coates, K. (1987). *Canada's colonies*. Toronto: James Lorimer.

Coates, K., and Powell, J. (1989). *The modern north: People, politics, and the rejection of colonialism*. Toronto: James Lorimer.

College act (1988). *In Statutes of the Yukon, 1988* (pp. 9-13). Whitehorse, Yukon: Government of the Yukon.

CYI plans Native education centre (January 31, 1979). *Yukon Teacher*, p. 6.

Diploma of northern studies: A proposal for integrated programs in Native studies, northern science, and northern outdoor and environmental studies (March 1988). Whitehorse: Yukon College.

Graham, A. (1994). The university that wasn't: The University of Canada North, 1970-85. Unpublished MA thesis, Lakehead University.

Ingram, E., Konrad, A., and Small, J. (1979). *Toward a Yukon college: Continuing education opportunities in the Yukon*. Edmonton: University of Alberta, Centre for the Study of Postsecondary Education.

Lotz, J. (1971). *Northern realities: Canada-U.S. exploitation of the Canadian north*. Chicago: Follett.

Maslove A., and Hawkes, D. (1990). *Census 1986: Focus on Canada: Canada's north: a profile*. Ottawa: Supply and Services Canada.

Northward looking: A strategy and science policy for northern development (August 1977). Report No. 26. Ottawa: Science Council of Canada.

Orlikow, L. (1986). *The option to stay: An education/strategy for the Yukon*. Whitehorse, Yukon: Government of the Yukon.

Orton, M. (1979, January 25). North needs its own university. *The Northern Times*, p. 3.

Senkpiel, A. (1986). An unlikely alliance: The Yukon Teacher Education Programme, 1977-1982. Unpublished manuscript.

Senkpiel, A. (1989). A new northern reality: Northern research and education at Yukon College. In *The role of circumpolar universities in northern development* (pp. 190-94). Occasional Paper #4. Thunder Bay: Lakehead University Centre for Northern Studies.

Smyth, S. (1991). The Yukon chronology. Vol. 1 of *The Yukon's constitutional foundations*. Whitehorse: Northern Directories.

Speech from the Throne, opening the 1979 first session of the Yukon Legislative Assembly (March 6, 1979). Whitehorse: Government of the Yukon.

Stenbaek, M., and Senkpiel, A. (1989). Making connections: The Association of Canadian Universities for Northern Studies and Canada's two northern colleges. In *The role of circumpolar universities in northern development* (pp. 158-63). Occasional Paper #4. Thunder Bay: Lakehead Centre for Northern Studies.

The things that matter: A report of Yukoners' views on the future of their economy and their society (1987). Whitehorse: Government of the Yukon.

Training for the future: The Yukon training strategy (1987). Whitehorse, Yukon: Department of Education, Government of the Yukon.

Whitehorse Star (November 27, 1979), p.9.

White paper on college governance and phased implementation (1987). Whitehorse, Yukon: Department of Education, Government of the Yukon.

Yukon Census Figures (1941) Ottawa: Statistics Canada.

Yukon College official opening commemorative edition (1988, October 1). Whitehorse: Government of the Yukon.

Yukon Statistical Review, Second Quarter, 1992. (1992). Whitehorse, Yukon: Bureau of Statistics, Government of the Yukon.

Higher Education in the Northwest Territories

Gail M. Hilyer

Introduction

Until the late 1980s higher education opportunities in the Northwest Territories were certainly not "all of a piece" (Aird, no date, p. 36). An overview requires reference to a series of educational delivery sources which essentially have no common superstructure and which, in some ways, do not even touch each other substantively.

Picture a single college, which was referred to as a college or a college system, sometimes simultaneously. Add to the picture, a federal delivery system which both funds and, to some extent, directs the nature of the education/training content and has recently restructured to reflect the expressed need for ownership by the majority Aboriginal population. Then overlay a plethora of external university and college involvements, including distance delivery activities, articulation arrangements, and extensive national and international research. This will provide a glimpse of the complexities of postsecondary education in the Territories.

There are many challenges to understanding this situation. One of the major factors is the current political, cultural, and social revolution, which has given immediate cause for review of all other structures within the Territories. The magnitude of this revolution must be considered within the context of the higher education system in the Northwest Territories. An accurate description of the pace of change occurring within the Territories cannot be fully documented. Perhaps a visual mini-series might better portray what is happening. Some of what has been written has gone from present to past tense within the space of a few months.

A Territory and Its People in Transition

A cursory environmental scan of the Northwest Territories demonstrates the challenges to any educational structure which functions within its parameters. The Northwest Territories consists of an area of 3,376,698 square kilometres, which is approximately one-third of the total land mass of Canada. With a population of 57,650, the population density is approximately 1 person to every 67 square kilometres (*Canadian Almanac & Directory*, 1992, p. 85). Of the sixty-six communities in the Northwest Territories, the largest is the capital, Yellowknife, with a population of 15,000 (p. 83). There are four centres with populations of approximately 3,000 and others have populations under 1,500. Transportation is primarily by air. There is a partially-paved highway system in the southwest and the Dempster Highway from the Yukon to the Alberta Border serves Inuvik and some of the Mackenzie Delta communities. A water-based transportation system enables barges and ships to resupply coastal and Mackenzie River communities during the short summer season with fuel, equipment, and other bulk supplies, including those required for household use. Transportation is expensive, given the distances involved, and the vagaries of the weather.

In the Territories, which is about the size of the subcontinent of India, with three time zones, flights from larger centres to farthest distant communities may cost as much as $2500 round trip and a single hotel room may cost $150 per person per night. Most communities have access to television and radio communications. Telephone service is also available in most centres, although a single telephone in the Band Office or radio phone may be the only communication link available. It would be interesting to consider the impact of these demographics on one specific service, such as registration, which is taken for granted in a traditional southern college. The registration process at the College is complicated not only by distance but by the extent of services which are provided, including housing for students and their families and transportation arrangements. The challenges of distance and communications are difficult and costly to address.

Unique administrative questions must be addressed by higher education in the Northwest Territories, for example, whether to have convocation before the closing of the ice roads that provide families with an economically viable way to celebrate with the graduates. This question precipitates discussions related to holding the ceremony before course work and practica are complete or maintaining the academically traditional model and, thereby, excluding many people from what may be the first graduation ceremony to be shared with their family. This one dilemma exemplifies the complexities, sensitivities, and interrelationships of the cultural, economic, transportation, and political environments. It provides another dimension to add to the picture of higher education in the Northwest Territories.

The economy of the Territories is a major factor in considering the complexity of providing higher education services to residents. The largest private sector employer is the mining industry. The estimated value of mineral production in 1985 was six hundred million dollars, which is 17% of the Canadian production produced in a Territory with less than 1% of the population.

Government services is also a very large employer in the Territories. According to Malone, ". . . in smaller communities, it is often the only business" (Aird, no date, p. 138). Not only is the Government of the Northwest Territories the primary employer, it is also the purveyor of the policies of both the federal and Territorial governments as these relate to services and economic opportunities for the residents of the Northwest Territories. Government employment makes up about 46% of all wage employment in the Northwest Territories, while in the rest of Canada it is approximately 21%. The Northwest Territories is the only jurisdiction in Canada where Aboriginal people comprise the majority of the population. It is estimated that 63% work in the wage economy at some point during a year, sometimes coinciding with opportunities provided by the service industry involved with tourism and, more particularly, construction. Both of these occupations are seasonal and some pay low wages. The Government of the Northwest Territories (GNWT) presently employs 2,080 Aboriginal people or about 34% of the total of 6,123 employees. The percentage of managers who are of Aboriginal origin is 14% (p. 142). Malone states that ". . . the GNWT delivers services to Aboriginal people that the Federal government often supplies in southern Canada and that Northerners do not enjoy many of the subsidies which are part of the revenue from Federal services, including equalization payments" (p. 139). Of specific concern to those providing higher education opportunities to the residents of the Northwest Territories is the estimate, provided by Malone, that "it costs three times more to provide services in the North." (p. 139). For those concerned with Full-Time Equivalencies (FTE's) as a basis for the funding of institutions of higher education, this statement provides another example of the challenges faced by educational administrators in the Territories.

For some Native peoples, the traditional sources of revenue and supplies are still from hunting, trapping, and fishing. Another increasing source of revenue is from the sale of northern art, including carvings and prints. In a newsletter published in March 1993, there is an outline of the 1991-96 Canada-NWT Economic Development Agreement (EDA). It reports that the annual sale of art production, including soapstone sculpture, fine prints, paintings, tapestries, beadwork, jewellery, and moosehair tufting—to name a few—is approximately $28 million dollars. Interestingly, half of this income is reported as going directly to the artists, who then supplement their income with other work.

There are many factors to be considered in attempting to understand the opportunities and challenges facing the people of the Territories. A recent statement from the Canadian Advisory Council on the Status of Women indicates that more than one out of every ten women in the Territories, ages fifteen to nineteen, has a baby each year. This means that, given any school year, and considering Grades 9-12, there will be forty-three babies born for every one hundred young women of high school age. Despite this fact, it is known that Aboriginal women are more likely to graduate from high school than are Aboriginal men. The birth rate among Aboriginal peoples is three times the national average and 45% of the population is under twenty.

A recent Labour Market survey, conducted by the government of the Northwest Territories, indicates that based on the 1986 census, 33% of the adult population had less than a Grade 9 education, and 56% had not completed high school. The same census reported that 17% of adult Canadians had less than a Grade 9 education, and 44% had not completed high school (p. 17).

Recent figures available from Advanced Education in the Territories indicate that one hundred and thirty Aboriginal people have university degrees, with more than three thousand positions requiring degrees for entry. Other figures provided by Advanced Education indicate an increase in the Dene student postsecondary population of 535% between 1984 and 1992 and in the Inuit student population there has been an increase of 879% in the same time frame. The enrollment in Arctic College increased 272% in that time period.

There are other unique issues which have to be considered. If the fundamental skills of reading, writing, and mathematics add value to the life of each individual, then the need for access to education is clear. In considering this, however, within the culture of the Territories, fundamental skills often have a very different meaning related partly to the on-the-land skills which have maintained life and continue to support life for some. The whole issue of clarifying *value*, including the opportunities for enhancement of the economic position of individuals and their communities, is not as simple to define as it may be in other jurisdictions. Individuals must have the skills and opportunities to make decisions based on understanding their culture and the information age with which they must interact.

Malone refers to a territorial unemployment average, including the discouraged worker, of 26% with rates as high as 50% in smaller communities. The cycle begins early. Many Aboriginal children drop out of the educational system before Grade 10. In a report prepared for the Canada Employment and Immigration Commission, Northwest Territories Directorate, and the Department of Education, Government of the Northwest Territories, in March 1992, the contents alone reflect the necessity to revisit the complexity of the factors which must be a part of any study of higher education services in the Northwest Territories. Topics include the socio-economic context, community attitudes about the expectations of education, attitudes in the home about education, students' household responsibilities and their employment, teaching styles and methods, self-esteem, and suicide, to name a few (Lutra Associates Ltd., 1992, p. 2). Of specific interest to the providers of higher education in the Northwest Territories is the finding in the study that

> school more often plays an influencing and/or guiding role in the future plans of Aboriginal students and most Grade 12 students plan to continue their education in the next year through Postsecondary education or by continuing in high school . . . (p. 48).

This report indicates approximately 58% of the population of the Northwest Territories is Aboriginal. This indigenous population, speaking seven distinct languages, makes up 72% of the school enrollment. Only 5% of the Aboriginal students who start school, however, graduate from Grade 12 (Lutra Associates Ltd., 1992, p. 10). The report indicates that 72% of the Aboriginal working-age population in the Northwest Territories is functionally illiterate and that among those unemployed, 67% have less than a Grade 9 education. Another startling fact, which speaks to the challenge of change in the Territories, is the fact that the Territories has the highest rate of suicide in Canada (p. 2). The challenge of providing services must also be seen in the context of related data which indicate that only 2%

of Aboriginal persons in the Northwest Territories annually attend university.

The current system of government in the Northwest Territories is in itself unique in Canada, affecting the process of planning and development of its institutions. There are twenty-four elected representatives, one for approximately 2,375 residents. The style of government is consensus, although motions are decided by majority vote.

In looking at the Northwest Territories in transition, of all of the factors which are currently driving change and affecting the life of every resident of the Territories, the proposed separation of the Northwest Territories into two distinct political, economic, and cultural entities is paramount. The eastern territory is called Nunavut, while the western territory is yet to be named. Both territories will have territorial governments, services, and independent status in relationship with the federal government and other provincial governments. The population of Nunavut will be approximately 19,000 and that of the western territories 38,000.

Of interest, is the work of the Commission for Constitutional Development. This Commission is charged with the creation of a constitution for the new western territory. The work of the Commission involves the responsibility to create a new relationship between the Dene, Metis, and non-Aboriginal Northerners. This new relationship involves defining jurisdictions and designing institutions which will be responsive to varying approaches to educational, social, legal, and health responsibilities. It requires statements of respect for the unique and shared values of the cultural groups. Embedded in the imperatives of authority and responsibility are the matters of Aboriginal self-government; a new Constitution; and the devolution of the Government of the Northwest Territories, with its resources and services, from large communities to all communities.

It is also critical to be sensitive to the very real issues of reclaiming cultures, identities, languages, and control, which is inherent in this climate. The elected Representatives, who currently hold seats in the Legislative Assembly, represent the Aboriginal peoples who live within the Territories, as well as the non-Natives, including a total of seven different cultural groups, speaking as many languages and more dialects. The Legislative Assembly of the Northwest Territories works in more languages than does the United Nations. One signal of the interesting transitions occurring is the change of community names from the obviously non-Aboriginal to the original or alternate Aboriginal name. For example, the community of

Snowdrift, with a population of 286, has changed its name to Lutsel K'e, sending a clear message to the institutions of the Territories to acknowledge the ownership and investment of its peoples in their land, their language, and their lifestyles.

An Overview of Higher Education in the Northwest Territories

It was not until 1982 that postsecondary education was described as being the responsibility of the yet unborn Arctic College and was defined as education beyond Grade 10. Long before the establishment of its own College, the Northwest Territories had a number of educational relationships with southern universities—Canadian universities south of the 60th Parallel. These relationships provided research opportunities for southern-based students and research information for northerners, although the latter function had occasionally been a source of some frustration for the hosts of such research. It is now a requirement to share the outcomes of research through licensing arrangements with the Science Institute of the Northwest Territories (SINT), which was created by the Northwest Territories Legislative Assembly in 1984. Interestingly, the Canadian Circumpolar Institute (CCI) is located at the University of Alberta.

Another postsecondary opportunity for northern people continues to be attendance at southern institutions. Based on information provided by Advanced Education, there were approximately 400 students from the Northwest Territories attending southern postsecondary institutions in 1991-1992, of this number, one hundred were either Inuk, Dene, or Metis.

From the perspective of an outsider looking into the Territories, it may be thought that a likely source of delivery of higher education would be distance education. While there is a long history of discrete projects, until very recently the majority of the registrants in courses delivered through distance education were registered with southern universities. While there is no accumulated data available covering all sources, one piece of information suggests a possible profile of utilization. In the period from fall 1990 to spring 1992, there were 298 registrants in Yellowknife enrolled in university-transfer credit courses with Athabasca University. In the same time period, there were 32 registrants in Fort Smith. This suggests that most of the registrants are residents of the larger centres. This is likely to be related to the availability of the technology and also of the economic, educational, cultural, and language profile of students who register in university courses through access to distance delivery.

In 1992, Television Northern Canada (TVNC) was established, and for the first time courses were offered through this network, potentially to all of the communities of the north. This delivery system is too new to provide specific data. Several other systems were considered, including Distance Education by Radio (DEBRA), a radio-based delivery structure, intended to be piloted by Arctic College in the winter of 1993. While distance delivery seems to be one way to serve the needs of distant and relatively small populations, the challenges for the technology and instructional methodologies are tremendous.

Other sources of educational information are to be found in a network of twenty-three community libraries serving the north. The north also has an extensive number of newspapers and newsletters, approximately 170 in 1986.

Research

An adequate overview of the type and kind of research currently being done by universities in and about the Northwest Territories is beyond the scope of this chapter. In an Association of Canadian Universities for Northern Studies (ACUNS) Occasional Publication/Publications occasionnelle, No. 8, 1983, thirty-four Canadian Universities were identified as being involved in northern research projects. In fact, in the ACUNS brochure, the mission of the Association is defined, in part, as being "to establish mechanisms through which resources can be allocated to member universities and colleges so as to increase knowledge of the North and ensure an appropriate supply of trained northern researchers, managers, and educators" (Witty, 1983, p. 2) and "to enhance opportunities for northern people, particularly indigenous northeners, to become leaders and promoters of excellence in education and research matters important to the North" (p. 3). Arctic College was one of the two colleges that are members of this organization; and the college headquarters in Yellowknife was identified as one of the regional offices of ACUNS. The second member college is Yukon College.

In *Education, Research, Information Systems, and the North* (1986), there is a partial listing of the staff specialists and graduate students engaged in northern studies at the University of Alberta. Of the one hundred and twenty names and accompanying projects listed, most projects that indicate the geographical location of the research are related to the Northwest Territories. Two examples of the level of academic and public interest in the Territories are to be found in the current research related to the Franklin expedition and the Wood Buffalo National Park, a portion of which lies within the boundary of the Territories.

Arctic College was also affiliated with The Natural Sciences and Engineering Research Council of Canada (NSERC), the Science Institute of the Northwest Territories (SINT), Northern Information Network (NIN), Northern Scientific Training Program (NSTP), and the South Slave Research Institute (SSRT). There are also a number of American and International Postsecondary institutions with which Arctic College has had research/adjunct relationships—the Hertzen Institute, St. Petersburg, Russia; the Michigan Community Colleges Consortium; and the University of Ohio.

The Arctic College Story

Arctic College was the single higher education institution based in the Northwest Territories. It was founded in response to the economic skill training needs of the population. It had a colourful and well-documented history which, to some extent, paralleled the development of the Institutes of Technology which evolved into Colleges of Applied Arts and Technology in Ontario in the 1960s.

Arctic College, which was the institution of higher education, was neither a sole source nor a sole focus for postsecondary education in the Northwest Territories. It strived diligently to work in partnership with a multi-sector client group and had many formal and informal channels which did not always functionally provide for clear governance of, structure for, or access to higher education. Unlike most provincial systems, where colleges, both private and public, have some formal and publicly accepted relationship with each other, with prospective students, and with their funding agencies, the college system in the Territories was not so clearly defined nor were the opportunities it provided for education and training always known.

In a letter written by Jack Witty, Director, Thebacha College, in November 1983, the origin of the College is described. Some quotations from this letter will help to bring the beginnings of this institution into focus:

> . . . made a deal to buy the whole camp . . . cook trailer, power house trailer and . . . five sleeping trailers. The trailers were then pulled out of the bush and brought over to Fort Smith. . . . During the early part of the winter of 1967 a company in Ottawa, Snow

Removal and Ice Control, approached Indian Affairs with the idea of putting on a heavy equipment training program in the north for northerners . . . permission was given in August of '69 . . . land was cleared by students using bulldozers. There were no water or sewer connections so cess pits were dug, . . . scrounged two warehouse . . . using heavy equipment again moved them onto the present site, set them up 50 feet apart and then with a couple of carpenter instructors began to put a floor between them and a roof over them and couple of more walls. By January we had closed the building in and had accommodations for the nursing assistance program, and upgrading program . . . (p. 3).

Keep in mind that the average temperature in Fort Smith in January is -35 degrees Celsius! Oral histories describe barbed wire around the original trades training centre in Fort Smith, positioned to discourage the visitation of local residents, whose presence distracted from the serious purpose which the trainees were expected to espouse.

One predecessor institution of Arctic College was the Adult Vocational Training Centre (AVTC) which evolved from the project described by Jack Witty and opened in 1969. Initially, it was the base for the Heavy Equipment Operators' Program. Between 1969 and 1971, a number of programs were delivered by AVTC, including Pre-employment Welding, Carpentry, Clerk Typist, and Certified Nursing Assistant. In 1971, the Centre received Canada Manpower (now Employment and Immigration Canada) sponsorship for its programs.

In 1977, the Head of AVTC became the Superintendent of Vocational Education, and the Centre became responsible for all vocational training in the Northwest Territories. At this time, Fort Smith was the Administrative Centre of the Territories. Given the geographical location, specifically the expanse of the jurisdiction, the Centre faced enormous communication challenges.

AVTC and, later, Arctic College had all of the responsibilities of providing residence, recreation, counselling, and often other services beyond the traditional role of higher education. The term, *in loco parentis*, practised in the small university environment of the 1950s, continued, in many ways, to be part of the business of Arctic College.

A Special Committee on Education was formed in the Northwest Territories in 1980. It was composed of five Members of the Legislative Assembly, and its task was to:

inquire into current problems and public concerns about education including reviewing existing legislation, consulting in all parts of the NWT, initiating action research projects to demonstrate new approaches to solving education problems, and charged to present a final report and recommendations to the Legislative Assembly in 1982. (Legislative Assembly of the Northwest Territories, 1982, p. 7)

One of the many recommendations made by the Committee was the establishment of Thebacha College. The first members of the Board of Governors were appointed in early 1982. The Board commissioned a strategic plan to guide the establishment of the new College and in 1984, the Executive Council of the Legislative Assembly approved a mandate for the College to deliver adult education and training programs throughout the Northwest Territories. Specific areas of program responsibility included technical and vocational programs, compensatory or upgrading programs, adult and continuing education, general education, and the initial years of university programs. To deliver education and training in a decentralized structure was a key element of the College's mandate. Two other interesting recommendations were that students should be admitted solely on the basis that they demonstrate responsibility to profit from programs and that Arctic College be developed as a community college concept. In 1986, the name was officially changed from Thebacha College to Arctic College, a designation which reinforced the geographical mandate of the College to serve the population across all of the Northwest Territories.

In October 1984, a vice-president was appointed to direct the development of the Frobisher Bay Campus. In the mid-1980s, the name of the community of Frobisher Bay was changed to Iqaluit and, in keeping with the College's sensitivity to the culture and language of its students, the campus was then called *Nunatta*, an Inuktitut word meaning "of this land." The organizational structure of Nunatta is essentially parallel to that of Thebacha College. *Thebacha* is a Chipewyan word meaning "by the rapids" and reflects the location of the College near the banks of the Slave River.

In 1986, the Arctic College Act was approved by the Legislative Assembly, and the Board of Governors became responsible for the operation of the Corporation. The headquarters of Arctic College moved from Fort Smith to Yellowknife. In 1987, the Aurora campus in Inuvik was established, and in 1988, two other campuses—Keewatin, in Rankin Inlet and Kitikmeot, in Cambridge Bay—were opened. In 1989, the Yellowknife campus was opened by the Board of the College, intended essentially for continuing education students. In 1990, responsibility for the Western Arctic Adult Education Centres was assigned to Arctic College. Previously, the centres were managed by the Divisional Boards of Education. The Eastern Arctic Centres joined the College in 1987.

One of the major tasks taken on by the Board of Governors was to develop a strategic plan, with a mission statement and goals. The mission statement, designed to lead the College through the period 1990 to 1995, read:

Arctic College is a multi-campus institution designed to provide a wide variety of educational services to adult learners of the Northwest Territories. The programs are directed specifically to the Northern environment and the needs of individual northeners, the work force and the northern communities. The college recognizes the need to make appropriate educational opportunities available to any adult who wishes to learn. To accomplish this, courses and services are delivered at campuses and in communities across the N.W.T. In this manner, Arctic College strives to encourage life long learning in a rapidly changing world. (Board of Governors, 1990, p. 2)

Arctic College combined a centralized and decentralized delivery structure which was built on a foundation of twenty years of program experience and tradition. It engaged in establishing language and policies which defined its role as an institution of higher education. The institution continued to be faced with the ramifications of an unclear operational definition of whether it was a college or college system. This type of shift in focus has been seen to be a reflection of the relative youth of Arctic College.

The fundamental structure of Arctic College was changed in late 1992. The Legislative Assembly, which currently governs the Northwest Territories, directed the College to become two colleges, one with headquarters in Iqaluit, and the other with headquarters in Fort Smith. This transition was to be completed by spring 1994.

Also, the concept of system, as in Arctic College system, is often referred to in descriptions and discussions about the College whereas the language of the recommendations of the Special Committee of Education, which established the College, specifically refers to *an* Arctic college. This contradictory use of terms to describe the structure of relationship within the College presented an interesting management challenge.

Mark Cleveland, President of Arctic College, in *Arctic College: The Development of a Territorial College System* (1986), identified a number of issues the College would have to either define or resolve within the next developmental stage, including legislative establishment of base funding, definition of the College's mandate, and authority and approval for increased program offerings. One issue identified was the rate at which additional College campuses would be approved and funded. Another issue involved the duplication of certificate and diploma programs and the resultant competition for funding. Also, from the initial recommendations which resulted in the formation of the College, there has been discussion concerning extensions and distance delivery, which would enhance the ability of the College to meet its mandate. These initiatives would require designated financial resources to support the acquisition of expertise as well as the technical and physical resources implicit in the delivery of such activities.

The major concern identified by Cleveland was the need for Arctic College to "establish its credibility, in part through a conscious effort to establish its focus on its unique 'community,' and its inclusion of the strengths of the socio-cultural milieu in which it has been established"(Cleveland, 1986, p. 98). Arctic College is still struggling with these identity issues, a struggle which often consumes corporate energy which could be profitably used to fulfill its mandate to deliver education and training.

One indicator of the challenge of credibility faced by Arctic College is found in the paper, *Managerial Training in Nunasi* (Tunraluk, 1987). The author is the business management officer with the Nunasi Corporation, the business arm of the Inuit Tapirisat Tungavik Federation of Nunavut, the group responsible for the 1992 plebiscite related to the definition of the boundary for the Nunavut Territory. He described a program to train managers for the Corporation. While he applauded the initiatives of the Government of the Northwest Territories and Arctic College to provide advanced education for the Inuit people, he indicated that the Corporation did not feel that it "was an acceptable position to vest all of the training requirements of the Inuit into established institutions of higher education" (Association of Canadian Universities for Northern Studies, 1992, June, p. 102). The task of defining economic partnerships and becoming an effective, responsive educator and trainer in this incredibly fast-changing environment is not simple.

In a letter to the campus vice presidents in March 1992, on the occasion of the fifth anniversary of Arctic College, Cleveland acknowledged the organization's experience "of change and rapid growth" (Cleveland, 1992, March, p. 1). One specific structural move identified as critical to the future direction of the College was the consolidation of the campuses and community adult education programs. The intention of this reassignment was to link the College more closely to the communities and to centralize program delivery under a single organization which would coordinate delivery of "the academic and career preparation programs required to meet the needs of Northerners" (p. 1). To provide benchmarks for measuring the success of the College structure after five years of operation, Cleveland identified (1) maintenance of permanent College staff in over 30 communities, with at least some services on an annual basis to more than 85% of all of the communities; (2) delivery of training worth more than $6,000,000 in partnership with private and public sector organizations in 1991/1992; (3) enrollment increases of 30% between 1989/1990 and 1990/1991. This rate of increase continued into the 1991/1992 year. Part-time enrollments have also increased by similar percentages over the same time period.

In 1991-1992, Arctic College had 1,517 full-time students and 6,561 part-time registrants. This is an increase of 19% over 1990-1991. Over the period 1988/89 through 1991/92, full-time enrollment increased by 63%, with an increase of 28% in part-time registrations in the same period. Enrollment in certificate and diploma programs has increased approximately 100% in this time period (Arctic College, 1993, p. 1). Of the students enrolled in 1992, 58% were women and 42% men. Approximately 14% of the students bring their children to the campus where they are studying if they are enrolled in full-time programs. Approximately 75% of the students are of Aboriginal origin, and they live in almost all of the 66 communities in the Territories. In snapshot data, compiled at Thebacha Campus, for example, during the period September 1992 to March 1993, students had come to the Campus from 58 communities in the Territories. This figure does not include a small number of students who came to Arctic College from outside of the Territories, mainly from the Yukon, Quebec, Labrador, and Alberta. English is the first language of 65% of the students, with Inuktitut being the language of 8.5% and North Slavey and Dogrib of 2%.

Arctic College, although it had always responded to training needs identified by residents of the Territories, did not establish a Native Studies Program until 1990. This Program was offered in partnership with the

Yellowknife Dene Band, Canada Employment and Immigration, and the Territories Department of Social Services. It was most successful, contributing to the sense of community and individual pride as well as being the winner of the Association of Canadian Community College's 1992 Partnership Award. This identifies a critical issue which faced Arctic College and its successor Colleges. The Colleges need to be identified with the culture of their many communities while establishing a clear identity as Canadian postsecondary institutions, maintaining appropriate academic standards and administrative portfolios similar to other Canadian Colleges, to ensure that graduates are prepared, if it be their choice, to move into mainstream southern education, to complete or obtain professional credentials, or to be further prepared to deal with the complexities of corporate management—all of this without any devaluation of traditional northern values and cultures.

Two Colleges—A New Beginning

In 1992, at the direction of the Cabinet of the Legislative Assembly, Government of the Northwest Territories, the process of developing a two-college system, which would also provide for the inclusion of the Science Institute Northwest Territories (SINT), was begun. At the Fall 1994 session of the Legislative Assembly, An Act to Amend The Arctic College Act, Bill 7, the Public Colleges Act, was passed to incorporate two Colleges, one to serve the proposed eastern territory and one, the western territory.

On December 31, 1994, the Corporation of Arctic College was dissolved, and on January 1, 1995, two Colleges were established. Each College has its own Board of Governors, President, supporting headquarters staff, including finance and policy, as well as staff for the Campus and Community Learning Centres. Although the process of naming the College was delayed until later in the spring, Aurora College began providing service to the people of the western Arctic, with headquarters in Fort Smith, enhanced by 14 community learning centres. The eastern Arctic is being served by Nunavut Arctic College, with headquarters in Iqaluit, campuses in Cambridge Bay, Rankin, and Iqaluit and Community Learning Centres located in 20 other communities in the eastern Arctic.

Each college developed a corporate plan, with goals both similar and discrete including increased community-based programming, strengthening basic education, establishing a northern research agenda, including the documentation and incorporation of northern knowledge. Nunavut Arctic

College's Plan includes support for strong communities, cultural appropriateness, with significant use of Inuktitut as the language of instruction and a focus on life-long learning. Aurora College also includes the goal of becoming a degree-granting institution in its Plan.

As these two colleges begin to mature in their individual cultures and relationships, they must still work within one Territory, and under a government and funding department, Education, Culture and Employment, which serves the whole of the Northwest Territories. All of the pre-established challenges remain, complicated by the new dual structures, which must quickly and effectively establish credible educational identities. The administrative and transitional complexities facing these institutions are enormous. With all of the political, social, and financial changes buffeting the foundations of government and all sectors of education, these new colleges are responsible for providing extensive and expanding opportunities in the face of fiscal restraint and increasing demand for services which are to be delivered within the communities of the north.

Conclusion

Education is a dynamic process, involving individuals, groups, and the society in which they live. It is a process which is shaped by the past and, at the same time, one which must be refined continuously to support a vision of the future. "The educational process in the Northwest Territories should reflect the unique nature of this people's past . . . their traditions, history and values . . ." (Northwest Territories. Legislative Assembly, 1991, p. ii). *Dynamic* is the operative word to define the energy required by higher education services in the Northwest Territories to respond to the multitude of unique and changing factors affecting the daily lives and lifetime learning opportunities of the residents of the Territories. To understand the present and potential role of higher education in the Territories, it is imperative to comprehend the large picture of the geography, the climate, the politics, the cultures, and the economics of this environment. To manage higher education, in whatever new configurations will emerge, will require "serious creativity" (DeBono, 1992, p. 4), defined by DeBono as using skills to change concepts and perceptions. The traditional Canadian college model which is built on an optimum enrollment of X numbers of full-time students and Y numbers of part-time students, with a few international students added, all living within a defined and comparatively small geographic space, with a relatively homogeneous expectation of the function of a higher education, is far removed from the configuration in the Territories. The sense of college as the "second-best" (Porter, 1991, p. 78) does not seem to be an issue in this environment. What is at stake, and must remain of primary concern to those who are responsible for the funding and delivery of higher education, is the ability to respond to the priority need for literacy training for the residents of the Territories, which will lead not only to completion documents but to a continuing process of educational opportunity for trades, professions, or professional training. In turn, this process will provide educated and skilled indigenous practitioners as leaders for the new Northern Territories. In *Canadian Community Colleges*, Dennison and Gallagher spoke to the need for innovative delivery of higher education which differs from that expected of other Canadian colleges. This requirement for innovative solutions is being tested even more in the environment of the 1990s than it was in the 1980s. No one solution, such as the increased availability of distance education opportunities, will provide all of the answers or even the best ones. One source of positive action is to be found in the talents of the people currently involved with higher education in the Territories. Change of the nature and pace currently being experienced by those responsible for higher education in the Northwest Territories is both draining and exhilarating. It requires a commitment to renewal for its managers. In the document, "Reshaping Northern Government," February 1992 (Northwest Territories. Legislative Assembly), a number of recommendations for consolidating government departments were made which led to the Departments of Employment, Education, and Culture consolidating in 1993-1994. The mission of this new, consolidated department is "to invest in and provide for the development of the people of the Northwest Territories, enabling them to reach their full potential, to lead fulfilled lives and to contribute to a strong and prosperous society" (Northwest Territories. Department of Education, Culture, and Employment, no date, p. 3). Major legislated changes such as these must be accompanied by well-developed human resource plans if both the intent of the changes and the services to be provided are to remain vital.

One topic not referred to within the scope of this document is the need to consider the impact of the global economy on the Territories and, therefore, on its higher education structure. Another challenge to be processed into a vision before much more time has passed is the role which the Territories see themselves playing in the global marketplace, a role which will partly determine the educational and training needs of its people. Porter, in his recent report, urges Canadian firms to "take a more pro-active approach if they want educational institutions to produce employees with both the general and specialized skills required for competitiveness" (Porter, 1991, October, p. 78). The Territories will have to determine and prepare for its place in the external market if it wishes to benefit from the opportunities available.

New perspectives face everyone in the Territories who has a stake in higher education professionally, politically, or economically as well as those who are and will be the consumers of the services. New directions, both externally and internally prescribed, must be responded to with a firm, perceptive, and creative wisdom which will bring into balance the struggle to blend the values of the disrupted past and the vision of what should lie ahead for the people of the Territories.

As Canadians face changing perspectives in a multitude of situations and as the Northwest Territories come to a crossroads in terms of governance, economy, languages of work, and educational structures, it would seem most appropriate to give the last word—a word of guidance—to a Chipewyan elder from Lutsel K'e: "We all can't walk on one path, but we can all work together as a people for our children and the future" (Commission for Constitutional Development, 1992, February).

References

Adams, W.P. (Ed.). (1986). *Education, research, information systems and the North.* Yellowknife: Proceedings of the ACUNS meetings, Yellowknife, 17-19 April 1986. Ottawa, ON: Association of Canadian Universities for Northern Studies.

Aird, R. (Ed.) (no date). *Running the North: The getting and spending of public finances by Canada's territorial governments.* Ottawa, ON: Canadian Arctic Resources Committee.

An Act to Establish the Arctic College (1986). *Northwest Territories Gazette.* VII, (2), C. 1.

Arctic College (1991-1992). *Annual report.* Yellowknife, NT.

Arctic College (1993). *Statistical overview—Student activities.* Yellowknife, NT.

Arctic College (1994), *People and communities: A partnership for learning, draft strategic plan of College West, 1995-2000.* The Author.

Arctic College, *Establishment of two colleges, A summary of directions* (March 1994).

Arctic College Act, Revised Statutes of the Northwest Territories, C. A-7-1-34 (1988).

Arctic College East, *Corporate plan* (October 1994).

Arctic College (West), *Corporate plan (draft)* (September 1994).

Association of Canadian Universities for Northern Studies/Association universitaire canadienne d'études nordiques. (1982). *Ethical principles for the conduct of research in the north.* Occasional Publication/Publication occasionnelle, 7.

Association of Canadian Universities for Northern Studies (1991-1993). *Brochure,* 1-2.

Association of Canadian Universities for Northern Studies. (1992, June). *Northline,* 12, 2.

Blishen, B.R., Carroll, W.K., and Moore, C. (1987). The 1981 socioeconomic index for occupations in Canada. *Canadian Review of Sociology and Anthropology,* 24, 465-488.

Blishen, R. (1950, November). The construction and use of an cccupational class scale, *Canadian Journal of Economics and Political Science,* 24, 4. Used in John Porter. (1956). *The vertical mosaic.* Toronto, ON: University of Toronto Press, 1965.

Board of Governors (1983). *Strategic plan.* Thebacha College. Fort Smith, NT.

Board of Governors (1984). *Thebacha College strategic plan discussion paper.* Thebacha College. Fort Smith, NT: Government of the Northwest Territories.

Board of Governors (1990). *Strategic plan.* Yellowknife, NT: Northwest Territories, Arctic College.

Canada's colleges forced to adapt to budget squeeze. (1992, February 5). *The Chronicle of Higher Education,* pp. A41.

Canadian almanac & directory (1992). Toronto, ON: Canadian Almanac & Directory Publishing Company Limited.

Cleveland, M. (1986). *Arctic College: The development of a territorial college system.* Yellowknife, NT. Association of Canadian Universities for Northern Studies Conference.

Cleveland, M. (1992, March). *President's report to Arctic College Board of Governors.* Inuvik, NT: Arctic College.

Cleveland, M. (1992, March 28). *Arctic College marks fifth anniversary.* (President's letter to Vice Presidents). Yellowknife, NT: Arctic College.

The Cohos Evamy Partners (1992). *Facility program: Final draft: Applied arts & library building, Thebacha Campus, Arctic College, Fort Smith, N.W.T.* Edmonton, AB: The Cohos Evamy Partners.

Commission for Constitutional Development (1992, February). *Interim report.* Tabled document No. 21-12-(2) tabled on Mar 90 1992 at the Legislative Assembly, Yellowknife, NT.

Commission for Constitutional Development (1992, April). *Working toward a common future.* Tabled document No. 66-12-(2) tabled on June 29 1992 at the Legislative Assembly, Yellowknife, NT.

Cunningham, J. (1991, March). *Political evolution of the N.W.T.* Thebacha Campus, Arctic College, Fort Smith, NT.

Dacks, G. (no date). *The view from Meech Lake: The constitutional future of the governments of the Yukon and Northwest Territories*. Unpublished report.

DeBono, E. (1992). *Serious creativity using the power of lateral thinking to create new ideas*. New York, NY: HarperCollins Publishers, Inc.

Dennison, J.D. (1991). Higher education in federal systems: A sharing of experiences. *The Canadian Journal of Higher Education* 21(2), 102-107.

Dennison, J.D. (1992). The university-college idea: A critical analysis. *The Canadian Journal of Higher Education* 22(1), 109-124.

Dennison, J.D., and Behnke, W.W. (1992) *Innovation in Canadian community colleges: A study of the relationship between innovativeness and organizational variables*. Vancouver, BC: University of British Columbia and Vancouver Community College.

Dennison, J.D., and Gallagher, P. (1986). *Canada's community colleges*. Vancouver, BC: UBC Press.

Devine, M. (1992, March/April). *The Dene Nation: Coming full circle*. Arctic Circle, pp. 12-19.

Dickerson, M.O. (1992, May). *Whose North? North political change, political development, and self-government in the Northwest Territories*. Alberta: The Arctic Institute of North America and UBC Press.

Diubaldo, R.J. (1981). The absurd little mouse: When Eskimos became Indians. *Journal of Canadian Studies*. 16 (2), pp. 34-40.

Donal, J.G. (1978). The psychodynamics of evaluation. *Journal of the Association of Canadian Community Colleges* 2 (1), pp. 34-27.

Education, Culture and Employment (September 1994). *People: Our focus for the future, A strategy to 2010*. Author.

Fumoleau, R. (1975). *As long as this land shall last: A history of Treaties 8 and 11, 1870-1939*. Toronto, ON: McClelland and Stewart Ltd.

Gallagher, P. (1985, May 31). *Prospectus*. Canada's Community Colleges (letter to R. Holtorf).

Government of the Northwest Territories (1991, November). *Strength at two levels: Report of the project to review the operations and structure of northern government*. Yellowknife, NT.

Government of the Northwest Territories (1992, December). *Statistics Quarterly*. Yellowknife, NT.

Government of the Northwest Territories (1993, January). *Education: Department mission statement*. Yellowknife, NT.

Guy, B. (1992). *Update on sources of labour market information and analysis*. Yellowknife, NT: Government of the Northwest Territories, Advanced Education.

Holtorf, R. (1984, Spring). *Skills growth fund submission, Thebacha College*. Fort Smith, NT: Government of the Northwest Territories.

Hughes, B. (1987). *Adult education and northern development: A major essay submitted in partial fulfilment of the requirements for the degree of Master of Education.* Vancouver, BC: University of British Columbia.

Indian Affairs (no date). *Administrative outline.* Outlining the historical development of the administration of Indian Affairs. Public Archives of Canada: Public Records Division.

Indian and Northern Affairs Canada (1957). *Treaty No. 11 June 27, 1921 and adhesions (July 17, 1922) with reports, etc.* Ottawa, ON: Queen's Printer and Controller of Stationery. (Reprinted from the edition of 1926).

Indian and Northern Affairs Canada (1966). *Treaty No. 8 Made June 21, 1899 and Adhesions, Reports, etc.* (IAND Publication No. QS-0576-000-EE-A-16). Ottawa, ON: Queen's Printer and Controller of Stationery. (Reprinted from the 1899 edition).

Krakana, M. (1978). Participatory evaluation and the decision making process. *Journal of the Association of Canadian Community Colleges* 2 (3), pp. 105-10.

Legislative Assembly of the Northwest Territories, Special Committee on Education (1982). *Learning: Tradition and change.* Yellowknife, NT: Outcrop Ltd.

Leslie, J., and Maguire, R. (Ed.). (1978). *The historical development of the Indian Act* (2nd ed.). Ottawa, ON: Indian and Northern Affairs Canada: Treaties and Historical Research Centre, Research Branch Corporate Policy.

Lovely, K. (1986). *College development plan.* Yellowknife, NT: Government of the Northwest Territories, Department of Education.

Lutra Associates Ltd. (1990, May). *A needs assessment of women in trades: "You can do it too."* Yellowknife, NT.

Lutra Associates Ltd. (1992, March). *Lessons for all: Factors contributing to early school learning in the Northwest Territories.* Volumes 1 and 2. Yellowknife, NT. Department of Education, Government of the Northwest Territories.

MacLachlan, L. (1992). *Comprehensive Aboriginal claims in the N.W.T.* Information North, Arctic Institute of North America. 18 (1).

Macpherson, N.J. (1982, Spring). *AVTC—Thebacha College, 1976-1982.* Fort Smith, NT.

Macpherson, N.J. (1991). *Dreams & visions: Education in the Northwest Territories from early days to 1984.* Yellowknife, NT: Government of the Northwest Territories, Department of Education.

Miller, K., and Lerchs, G. (1978). *The historical development of the Indian Act* (1st ed.). Ottawa, ON: Indian and Northern Affairs Canada: Policy, Planning and Research Branch.

Moffat, J.D. (1976). *Program forecasts for a proposed community college of the North.* Yellowknife, NT: Government of the Northwest Territories, Continuing Education Division of the Department of Education.

Northwest Territories Archives (1991, November). *Preliminary guide to holdings of the Northwest Territories Archives.* Yellowknife, NT. Prince of Wales Northern Heritage Centre. 4th edition.

Northwest Territories. Department of Education, Culture, and Employment (no date). *Department of Education, Culture, and Employment: Organizational profile and priorities.* Unpublished report.

Northwest Territories. Legislative Assembly (1980). *Hansard: Official report index.* 9th Assembly, 2nd Session Jan. 31, 180-Mar. 13, 1980. pp. 8, 40. 49, 57-8, 743, 949-50, 1015, 1022, 1034, 1067, 1094, 1096, 1098.

Northwest Territories. Legislative Assembly (1986). *Hansard: Official report index.* 10th Assembly, 7th Session Feb. 12, 1986-Jun. 26, 1986. pp. 216, 260-61, 729, 1026, 1194.

Northwest Territories. Legislative Assembly (1988). *Hansard: Official report index.* 11th Assembly, 2nd Session Feb. 10, 1988-Apr. 18, 1988. pp. 3-4, 295, 481-82, 626-27, 635-37, 646-48, 808, 1293-294, 1305-306, 1312-313, 1555.

Northwest Territories. Legislative Assembly (1991). *Hansard: Official report index.* 11th Assembly, 8th Session Feb. 13, 1991-Jul. 7, 1991. pp. 253-54, 627, 654, 662, 1035, 1040.

Northwest Territories. Legislative Assembly (1991). *Northwest Territories Education Annual Report.* Yellowknife, NT.

Northwest Territories. Legislative Assembly (1992). *Reshaping northern government.* Tabled document No. 10-12-(2), tabled on Feb 19, 1992, Legislative Assembly, Yellowknife, NT.

Northwest Territories. Legislative Assembly (1992, March). *Interim report on Arctic College made by the Standing Committee on Agencies, Boards and Commissions.* Yellowknife, NT.

Northwest Territories. Legislative Assembly (1992, March). Response to written question [W26-12(2)], asked by Richard Nerysoo. *Aboriginal employment statistics with the Government of the Northwest Territories.* Reply by Honourable Stephen Kakfwi, Minister of Personnel.

Northwest Territories. Legislative Assembly (1992, September). *On the multilateral meetings on the constitution and first ministers—Aboriginal leaders conferences on the Constitution of Canada*: Report of the Special Committee on Constitutional Reforms. Honourable Stephen Kakfwi, Chairperson. Yellowknife, NT.

Pineo, P.C., and Goyder, J. (1988). The growth of the Canadian education system: An analysis of transition probabilities. *Canadian Journal of Higher Education* 17 (2), 37-54.

Porter, M.E. (1991, October). *Canada at the crossroads: The reality of a new competitive environment.* A Study Prepared for the Business Council on National Issues and the Government of Canada. Ottawa, ON: Business Council on National Issues and Minister of Supply and Services.

Purich, D. (1992). *The Inuit and their land: The story of Nunavut.* Toronto, ON: James Lorimar & Company, Publishers.

Resources Management Consultants (N.W.T.) Ltd. (1983). *Thebacha College strategic plan, 1983.* Yellowknife, NT: Gerry Gallant, Senior Principal.

Ross, D. (1991). *Education as an investment for Indians on reserves: The causes of their poor education levels and the economic benefits of improving them.* Ottawa, ON: Canadian Council on Social Development.

Saywell, T. (1992, May 25). *$600,00 awarded to study Native self-government.* Yellowknife, NT: Northern News Services.

Small, J., Konrad, A., Hassen, M., and Pickard, B. (1976). *Renewal in post-secondary institutions: An analysis of strategies.* Edmonton, AB: Department of Educational Administration, University of Alberta, p. 23.

Tunraluk, A. (1987). Managerial training in Nunasi Corporation. In W.P. Adams (Ed.), *Education, research, information systems and the North* (pp. 101-102). Ottawa: Association of Canadian Universities for Northern Studies.

Ugoff, D., and Peggy, P. (1990, December 5). *The undergraduate learning environment: Challenges and opportunities.* Submission of the Canadian Association of College and University Student Services (CACUSS) to the Commission of Inquiry on Canadian University Education. Ottawa, ON.

Venne, S.H. (1981). An Indian future for our children: Helping to understand past oppression to build a strong Indian future. *Indian Acts and Amendments 1863-1975: An indexed collection.* Saskatoon, SK: University of Saskatchewan Native Law Centre.

West, E.G. (1988). *Higher education in Canada: An analysis.* Vancouver, BC: The Fraser Institute.

Western Constitutional Forum (1985). *Partners for the future.* A selection of papers related to constitutional development in the Western Northwest Territory.

Witty, J., Director (1983, November 3). *Letter to N.J. Macpherson, Senior Executive Officer, Executive Committee Government of the N.W.T.* Thebacha College.

Zuker, M.A. (1988). *The legal context of education.* Monograph Series/19. Toronto, ON: OISE Press-Guidance Centre.

Putting It All Together: Viewing Canadian Higher Education from a Collection of Jurisdiction-Based Perspectives

Michael L. Skolnik

Introduction

The purpose of this chapter is to provide some sort of synthesis based upon the thirteen jurisdiction-based essays which precede it. The emphasis here is on identifying major themes and issues across jurisdictions as well as noteworthy similarities and differences among them in regard to developments, trends, and patterns in higher education in the different parts of Canada.

Before turning to the substantive content of the preceding chapters, it is useful to take a minute to place them in context in relation to recent literature on Canadian higher education, say, of the past two decades. There have been relatively few publications on Canadian higher education, that is, ones which have attempted to provide a national picture, and most of these have been written by a single author or pair of authors, and have concentrated upon a single sector or a particular set of themes or issues. Examples of such works are *Canadian Universities 1980 and Beyond: Enrolment, Structural Change and Finance* by Peter M. Leslie (1980), *Canada's Community Colleges: A Critical Analysis* by John D. Dennison and Paul Gallagher (1986), and *More Than an Academic Question: Universities, Government, and Public Policy in Canada* by David M. Cameron (1991). Parts of all three books are devoted to systematic examination of their subject on a province-by-province (and territory as well in the case of Dennison and Gallagher) basis, but their thrust is to provide a national perspective with respect to the particular subject matter indicated in the title of the books. I cite these books specifically because province-by-province treatment of their subjects comprises a significant portion of their analyses, especially in Leslie's book. In most works which attempt to provide a national picture of higher education in Canada, the organization is entirely by thematic category rather than jurisdiction, with examples or instances taken from various jurisdictions to illustrate particular points.

The present book is somewhat unique in that it is organized totally by jurisdiction, with a different author for each jurisdiction, and it is intended to cover the whole of Canadian higher education rather than being restricted to particular components or issues. Of course, a single essay cannot span the whole of a province's or a territory's higher education activities, and each of the authors has had to be selective in deciding what to include. Inevitably such selection depends in part upon an author's own values and predilections but also upon the nature of developments in the jurisdiction about which he or she is writing and the tenor of and emphases in discussion of higher education activities and issues in that jurisdiction. Thus, one of the unobtrusive features of interest in a publication like this lies in observing what topics are emphasized or ignored in various jurisdictions and overall. For example, almost all the contributors to this book devote attention to financial aspects of or arrangements for higher education, no doubt symptomatic of the times in which we live. I will return briefly to this question of what topics the contributors chose to emphasize or not emphasize in the concluding section of this essay. For now, I should like to turn to the actual developments, trends, and patterns examined in the preceding chapters.

Historical Conditions and Influences

A nation's postsecondary education system can be viewed as consisting of the various policy and planning structures, institutions, programs, and related activities of each of its constituent political jurisdictions and the formal and informal interrelationships among those educational jurisdictions. In a nation with a highly centralized, unitary political structure, there may be only a single constituent jurisdiction with responsibility for all postsecondary education. In nations with federal systems, usually both the national and regional levels of government have roles in regard to postsecondary education, though the balance of influence and activity between these two levels varies considerably from one country to another. In some, such as China and India, both the national and subnational governments establish and operate many universities, and in

Australia, a single national university has been a prominent feature of a system otherwise made up of universities established by the states. In Canada and the United States, universities are under provincial or state jurisdiction, except for military academies, but the national governments support and influence postsecondary education in a variety of ways.

In Canada, postsecondary education, as a branch of education, is constitutionally under provincial jurisdiction. However, the federal government has long been involved in postsecondary education. The extent and nature of its involvement has varied over time depending, as David Cameron's chapter shows, upon prevailing constitutional interpretations, political trends and fashions, and economic circumstances. The role and influence of the federal government upon postsecondary education in Canada has been very significant. However, the story of postsecondary education in Canada is mostly a story of developments in each of the provinces, and more recently, in the territories as well. That fact is reflected in the organization of this book: twelve chapters on the provinces and territories and one on the role of the federal government. Of course, in being faithful to the division of political jurisdiction over postsecondary education, this organization is anomalous in other ways, as several of the authors have noted. For example, Ronald Baker observes that from a sheer population point of view it would be as reasonable to have a chapter on postsecondary education in St. Catharines, Ontario, as on Prince Edward Island, and Aron Senkpiel points out that the Yukon has fewer people than attend some Canadian universities.

The difference in size among the jurisdictions accounts for one of the major thematic differences among the chapters of this book. Several chapters consist primarily of detailed case studies of a single institution, while others focus mainly on system-level development and issues. In some cases, of course, the difference between these two perspectives is not very great. Gail Hilyer's description of the evolution of Arctic College in the Northwest Territories is at the same time a story of the development of a bi-institutional, multicampus system for providing postsecondary and adult education to a culturally and linguistically diverse population spread sparsely over an area the size of the Indian subcontinent. On the other hand, Baker's description of the development of the University of Prince Edward Island is quintessentially the tale of an institution. It reveals how long it can take and how difficult it may be to overcome religious division and to make an institutional merger gel, but ultimately both are possible.

The comparative recency of the heat generated in PEI by the merger of two institutions of different religious orientations is a reminder of what a major force religion once was in Canadian higher education. As the corresponding chapters of this book show, religious rivalries were a particularly persistent factor in the development of higher education in Nova Scotia, Ontario, and Manitoba, albeit to a lesser extent in New Brunswick with the reconstitution of the University of New Brunswick in 1859 as a non-sectarian institution. In both Toronto and Winnipeg, an early accommodation was reached whereby the University would be an examining and degree-granting body, and instruction would be provided by federated colleges, most of which were denominationally controlled. This arrangement, as Alexander Gregor observes, was modelled upon that of the University of London, and as Brian Christie notes, was recommended but failed to be adopted in Nova Scotia. As events unfolded in both Manitoba and Ontario, the role and influence of the University relative to its affiliated denominational institutions continued to increase, except that in Manitoba, the Collège Universitaire de Saint-Boniface emerged as an administratively autonomous institution. If the autonomy of Saint Boniface was justified on linguistic grounds, the same could not be said of St. Mary's University in Nova Scotia. Brian Christie argues that unlike the case in other provinces, which ultimately overcame the barriers of religious factionalism, the Nova Scotia university system continues to be held hostage to it to this day. In contrast to the Nova Scotia experience, for example, Glen Jones describes how denominationalism gradually ceased to be a significant force in the Ontario university system.

While denominational institutions in Canada were originally private in nature, now in nearly all cases those institutions have come into the public systems and have become recipients of public funding either as autonomous institutions or within the framework of affiliation with larger secular universities. There are only a handful of independent, denominational institutions in Canada which grant degrees—one in British Columbia, one in Ontario, and to a limited degree some of the private colleges in Alberta. While church-affiliated postsecondary education has become rather marginalized in Canada, William Muir notes the important role played by private bible colleges in Saskatchewan. He reports that Saskatchewan has the largest number of bible colleges on a per-capita basis of any province and that the training which they provide goes beyond theology. Muir notes, for example, that one college provides airplane pilot training, no doubt useful for missionaries in some situations, and that another offers training in cooking for evangelical camps. Muir suggests that bible colleges offer some of the same attractions to a lower-income rural population that liberal arts colleges offer a more affluent, urban population.

Besides differences in religion and, to a lesser but important degree, in language and culture, the other factors which have served to shape higher education in Canada were geography, demography, and economics. All of the chapters describe the challenge of devising an efficient and practical way of organizing provincial or territorial resources to serve a population that was unevenly, and usually sparsely, distributed over vast areas. Concentrating resources in a single provincial centre was the strategy favoured initially in the four western provinces and, until recently, in Newfoundland. The chapters on the western provinces trace the gradual spread of degree-granting institutions to other communities, and the chapter on Newfoundland describes the ongoing dilemma of how to provide wider access, particularly for the west coast, while concentrating resources as much as possible in St. John's. As several chapters indicate, a favourite Canadian approach to university development was for new free-standing institutions to emerge from under the wing of more established ones. John Dennison notes that—in a cross-national movement that seems remarkable by today's standards—the University of British Columbia started under the aegis of McGill University, and the former institution, in turn, helped bring the University of Victoria into existence. Senkpiel describes also the instrumental role of "UBC Programs" in the process which led to the establishment of Yukon College. This type of dynamic has continued to the present in British Columbia with five university colleges which started under the wing of provincial universities recently obtaining degree-granting status.

Expansion of Postsecondary Education

The chapters of this book differ in the rapidity with which their historical treatments proceed to the last half of the twentieth century. It is clear from all of them, however, that the immediate aftermath of World War II was an important watershed in the evolution of Canadian higher education. The precise dates varied, but commencing anywhere from the 50s to the early 60s, and lasting as late as the early 70s was a period of identification and elaboration of provincial needs, innovation and expansion, and the establishment of what might be described as provincial systems of postsecondary education. Government-appointed commissions played a major role in articulating the visions for these systems, and an affluent economy and burgeoning provincial treasuries provided the funds for their implementation. As Janet Donald notes in the case of Quebec, which was mirrored in most other provinces, in those years recommendations of commissions were acted upon by governments with a regularity and promptness not encountered since. Indeed, Jones observes how not responding to commissions and like bodies became the norm in Ontario in the 1980s.

Of the commissions during the formative period, the one which had the broadest national impact was the Massey Commission, which reported to the Government of Canada in 1951. The recommendations of this commission resulted in a major alteration of the role of the federal government in education. As Cameron notes, until the mid-twentieth century, the federal role was confined to technical/vocational education at the secondary level or outside the formal education system. Massey thrust the Government of Canada squarely into the funding of universities and other postsecondary education, and along with funding, came federal influence on priorities and directions of development for postsecondary education in the provinces. Cameron traces the evolution of this relationship from the direct grants to universities introduced after the Massey Commission through the "data wars" over the attribution of funding under the Established Programs Financing Arrangements to the recent attempt by the Honourable Lloyd Axworthy to replace these grants to the provinces with income-contingent loans to students and their folding into the Canada Health and Social Transfer.

Of provincial commissions during the expansion phase of postsecondary education, the most pervasive and impactful, and for those reasons the most venerated, was undoubtedly the Parent Commission in Quebec (1963), the recommendations and legacy of which are documented by Donald. Emphasizing democratization and access, and taking a total system view, this commission was responsible for a major reorganization not only of the postsecondary sector but also of the interface between the secondary and postsecondary systems. The key element in that interface, of course, was the CEGEP, a unique type of educational institution in North America. Besides providing a one-time plan for an integrated educational system, the Parent Commission emphasized the need for ongoing mechanisms for consultation and coordination. In this regard, a legacy of the Parent Commission whose accomplishments Donald reports in considerable detail is the Superior Council of Education, the keystone of a vast network of consultation.

Other formative provincial commissions and related initiatives described by the contributors to this book were the Deutsch Commission in New Brunswick (1962), the Macdonald Report in British Columbia (1963), the Warren Commission in Newfoundland (1968), the Oliver Commission in Manitoba (1973), and the Worth Commission in Alberta (1974). Of these, the ones in New Brunswick and British Columbia were particularly fruitful for postsecondary education in those two provinces. One of the major accomplishments of the Royal Commission on Higher Education in New Brunswick chaired by John Deutsch was to provide a plan for the institutional organization of university level education in the province, not unlike the state level master plans in the United States. As Sheila Brown reports, this plan involved the establishment of a second campus of UNB in St. John, the movement of St. Thomas University from Chatham to Fredericton and a federation between it and UNB, and the creation of the new Université de Moncton. Brown supports the views of others that the Deutsch Commission "produced demonstrably lasting effects." So too, according to Dennison, did the Report of UBC President, John Macdonald, which recommended that British Columbia should have two other universities besides UBC and a number of two-year colleges which would offer university transfer courses and occupational programs.

What I have described as the expansionary period was also the time during which systems of community colleges and other non-university postsecondary institutions were created in all provinces except Newfoundland, where the movement occurred a little later, and Nova Scotia, where it was much later. From the first community or junior college in Lethbridge in 1957, the story of the establishment of these colleges in the 1960s and 1970s has been related in detail by John Dennison and Paul Gallagher (1986). The present collection provides additional insights into the founding of the colleges, particularly for Newfoundland and Manitoba and, of course, the Yukon and Northwest Territories, but its main contributions in regard to the college sectors pertain to more recent developments, particularly involving articulation with university sectors.

Dennison describes the establishment of the university colleges in British Columbia and the full movement of some of them toward degree-granting status, along with the experience of the BC Council on Admissions and Transfer, and the introduction of Associate Degrees in the non-university sector. Michael Andrews, Edward Holdaway, and Gordon Mowat trace the considerable progress made in Alberta regarding degree-completion opportunities for students who begin their postsecondary studies in the non-university sector. They also summarize the impressive list of "firsts" for Alberta in regard to this sector: the first junior college, the first provincial transfer council, the first inter-provincial college (Lakeland

College, serving Northeast Alberta and Northwest Saskatchewan), the first private colleges accrediting board, and the first applied degrees for community colleges. Two other related firsts they note were Canada's first open university (Athabasca) and its first community adult learning councils. William Muir relates the reorganization of Saskatchewan's famed local community colleges without walls into nine regional colleges and the amalgamation of four technical institutes and some other non-university sector institutions into Saskatchewan Institute of Applied Science and Technology (SIAST). In contrast with these three provinces, Gregor's chapter reports the comparatively little change in Manitoba's community college sector, with the exception of a recent move to establish institutional governing boards for the colleges, the effect of which he says it is too early to tell. A recurrent theme in Gregor's chapter is the lack of provincial or institutional response to the Oliver Commission (1973), including its call for articulation between the two sectors.

Turning to the non-university sectors in the eastern part of the country, Kathryn Bindon and Paul Wilson relate the arduous process through which Newfoundland arrived in 1992 at a system of five regional Colleges of Applied Arts, Technology, and Continuing Education with 23 campuses. In perhaps the most pedagogically detailed part of any chapter, Baker describes the CBE and STEP instructional paradigms at Holland College which have given the Prince Edward Island institution national and international prominence. Brown reports that New Brunswick Community College continues as Canada's most centralized system and the most dedicated to carrying out provincial economic policy. Christie notes that while Nova Scotia finally brought a community college system into existence in 1991, it is still "very underdeveloped," and the ratio of community college to university enrollment in Nova Scotia is the lowest in Canada and falling, as "a result of current program decisions."

It is interesting that in both Ontario and Quebec, commissions with similar names, Vision 2000 in Ontario and Vers l'an 2000, reported in 1990. The principal thrust of the Ontario report was to reaffirm the original vision for the colleges in changed social, cultural, and technological circumstances. The recommendations which attracted the most attention were those to improve articulation between the CAATs and provincial universities and to ensure uniformly high standards and comparability of certificate and diploma programs from college to college. Vision 2000 did not recommend any significant moves toward program rationalization or system restructuring in spite of widespread expectations that it would do so. The Quebec document also reaffirmed the mandate of the CEGEPs to, as Donald notes, "provide a solid basic education, broadly based professional training, and continuing education for lifelong learning." Vers l'an 2000 also emphasized teaching strategies such as learning centres, mastery learning, formative evaluation, and integrated approaches to learning.

Structural Similarities and Differences Among the Provinces and Territories

It is sometimes said that although there are considerable differences in provincial structures of postsecondary education, one safe generalization is that all provinces have a binary system. While this assertion may have some validity at the most general level of observation in that there are both degree-granting and non-degree-granting institutions in each province, the extent of differentiation of institutional types in British Columbia and Alberta render the term, binary, an inappropriate descriptor. In British Columbia, the picture which Dennison paints is of an extraordinarily diverse array of types of postsecondary institutions. So many different types of institutions are now awarding degrees that degree granting can no longer be the basis for distinction between sectors. Moreover, the thrust of recent government policy has been to reinforce the interdependence and interrelationships among the various types of institutions. A good example of this policy thrust is the Open University, the mandate of which is to be "a flexible, distance learning, degree-granting alternative to the conventional universities." The Open University allows students to "bank" credits earned in other postsecondary institutions, and it also has agreements with a number of colleges and institutes for joint programs in areas such as music, fine arts, and health sciences.

A similar conclusion about the inappropriateness of the binary distinction would fit the Alberta postsecondary scene as laid out so conveniently in a chart by Andrews, Holdaway, and Mowat. Not only do the five categories after the universities include an incredible variety of different institutional types, but Athabasca University would appear to have more in common with some of these institutions than it does with the University of Alberta or Lethbridge. Nor is there much of a binary look to Nova Scotia's postsecondary system, with the great diversity of institutional type and size in the degree-granting sector and the underdevelopment of the community college sector.

Of course the binary description still fits some provincial systems pretty well. The gulf between Manitoba's four universities and three community colleges provides a quintessential illustration of a binary divide. Perhaps the most noteworthy structural feature of this system is that three of four universities are located in the same metropolitan area. In New Brunswick, the juxtaposition of five universities and a regionalized, nine-campus community college gives a definite binary look to postsecondary education, though qualified a little by the existence of separate specialized institutions: the Maritime Forest Ranger School, the New Brunswick School of Fisheries, the New Brunswick School of Craft and Design. The coexistence of the University of Prince Edward Island and Holland College is perhaps the easiest binary system to appreciate, although a third element, the Atlantic Veterinary College, is a particularly noteworthy feature. AVC is more than a part of the University. As Baker notes, it accounts for two-thirds of the university's budget and almost all of its graduate work. An interesting historical fact about AVC related by Baker was the considerable role played by the federal government in the decision to have this professional school at UPEI, suggesting how difficult it is to pigeonhole the federal role in postsecondary education in categories corresponding to its statutory powers and obligations.

In recent years, organizational changes in Newfoundland and Saskatchewan have taken them further in the binary direction. With the merger of the former Fisheries College with Memorial University and the reorganization of nursing education, almost all public postsecondary education in Newfoundland—with the possible exception of adult basic education—will soon be done by either the university, including Sir Wilfred Grenfell College, or the Colleges of Applied Arts, Technology, and Continuing Education. In Saskatchewan, the amalgamation of specialized technical and vocational institutions, along with the four urban community colleges into SIAST, and the reorganization of the local colleges into a regional college system, have reduced the diversity of the provincial system. These moves could be seen as creating a more simplified binary system or, alternatively, as resulting in a system that has three distinct and delineated parts.

And of course, the binary structure appears to be alive and well in the two largest provinces. While there are a few other small postsecondary institutions outside these sectors, postsecondary education in Ontario is formally organized in a binary structure. Moreover, Jones describes how higher education policy in Ontario has been developed exclusively within sectors rather than for the totality of provincial higher education, although recently there has been concern about the relationship between the two sectors, particularly in regard to enhancing opportunities for CAAT graduates to subsequently complete degrees in the universities. The Quebec system is also normally described as a binary structure, though its binary structure is mitigated somewhat by the partitioning of its universities into a multicampus system, the Université du Quebec, and the others, as well as between French- and English-language universities and CEGEPs.

System Planning and Accountability

When they turn their attention to the present and future, the contributors identify some major issues which, while taking on different forms in various provinces, involve the same set of challenges. These include pressures for postsecondary education systems to increase accessibility and quality of education in the face of shrinking resources and, therefore, to increase efficiency; to be more responsive to student and societal needs, including those pertaining to movement of students between institutions and sectors; and to demonstrate their effectiveness to governments and to the public, i.e., to become more demonstrably accountable. There has been considerable variation among the provinces in their responses to these challenges. In some, provincial-level visioning and planning has been a major vehicle for reshaping higher education, while others have relied mainly upon the initiatives of the individual institutions. In addressing the inevitable tension between provincial accountability and institutional autonomy, some have tilted the balance toward accountability, while others have retained emphasis on autonomy.

Before commenting upon what contributors have to say about provincial developments regarding planning and accountability, it is important to appreciate the national context of these developments. Although calculating the exact amount of its contributions for postsecondary education has been a flash point of controversy, the Cameron paper makes quite clear that the federal government has been contributing a substantial amount of funds to the provinces which have helped the provinces to support their postsecondary education systems, and the amount of these funds has been declining and has appeared more and more in jeopardy in recent years. With the apparent withering away of the major source of federal funds for postsecondary education, so, too, has the prospect for significant federal government influence over postsecondary education policy in Canada. The unsuccessful attempt by Minister Axworthy to substitute an income-contingent repayment loan plan for the Established Programs Financing arrangements might have been the last chance for the federal government to use financial leverage to steer postsecondary education in a significant way, though the national granting councils and the Canada Student Loan Program still provide for some leverage. In any event, the folding in of EPF grants along with Health and Welfare transfers in the Canada Health and Social Transfer—and the announced plans to reduce the total value of this transfer—has thrust upon the provinces greater pressure for efficiency, accountability, and self-reliance in postsecondary education.

One possible response to this new environment is increased effort at provincial planning for postsecondary education. I noted earlier that in the expansionary, formative period of the 1960s and early 1970s, all provinces articulated if not plans at least explicit visions for their postsecondary systems. However, these were largely "one-shot" initiatives. Unlike the United States, where all states have agencies responsible for management and/or coordination of postsecondary education, and system master planning is one of their major responsibilities, in Canada there are no agencies with this type of responsibility for planning. There are, of course, intermediary bodies in Manitoba, Ontario, and Quebec, as well as the Maritime Provinces Higher Education Council, and recently established councils in Nova Scotia and Newfoundland. However, these bodies have tended mainly to advise on new programs, funding levels, and other operating issues rather than produce plans for the postsecondary sectors.

Nevertheless, within just the past few years there have been attempts in several provinces to take stock of their postsecondary systems, and in a few cases to take some steps toward creating a comprehensive plan or vision of the whole system or at least for major parts of it. The most ambitious of these initiatives is the New Directions for Adult Learning document in Alberta which, as Andrews, Mowat, and Holdaway report, provides a framework for effectively interrelating all adult education activities in the province, from graduate studies to community adult learning, in both the public and private sectors. Andrews, Holdaway, and Mowat attribute the fact that Alberta has the highest adult education participation rate in Canada to the unique types of provision for adult education made within this framework. British Columbia also has made substantial advances toward the development of a highly interrelated system for postsecondary and adult education, building upon the Human Resource Development Project and the work of the BC Council on Admissions and Transfer. As in Alberta, the major impetus and leadership for these initiatives have come from the relevant government ministry. Nowhere else have visions of postsecondary systems of such breadth and grandiosity appeared, although there have been some valuable studies done in other provinces. Most of the studies in other provinces have been more concerned with evaluating present structures and performance, or with establishing better processes for accountability than with articulating new educational visions. Recommendations have often tended to focus more upon process than product or to appear as simply statements of wishes without specific means for making them come true, e.g., better coordination between university and community college sectors.

As an example of evaluative studies, all aspects of postsecondary education in Saskatchewan have recently been subjected to thorough review by the University Program Review Panel and similar bodies for other sectors. Muir notes that the sectors least controlled by government were judged most healthy in these reviews. The university review was generally positive about the efficiency and performance of the universities, and it is noteworthy that private vocational schools were given a favourable rating by an NDP-appointed commission. On the other hand, the reviews criticized SIAST for being overly centralized and top heavy administratively and the regional colleges for being less attuned to community needs than their predecessor institutions.

In contrast to the University Program Review Panel's favourable assessment of the performance of Saskatchewan's universities, next door the Roblin Commission concluded that Manitoba's universities could do much more with less and that the community colleges should get the first claim on any new funding that became available. In a similar vein as a subsequent discussion paper put out by the Ontario Council on University Affairs, the Roblin Commission expressed concern that much publicly supported university research was "only tenuously linked to Manitoba's social, cultural, and economic interests." The Commission left Manitoba with a challenge so eloquently and incisively described by Gregor and facing not just Manitoba, but all provinces: ". . . the development of clear and public provincial policy on the broad area of research, development, and training, such that the shape and development of the postsecondary system itself can be planned and measured against an articulated vision of the province's economic, social, industrial, scientific, social, and cultural future." To move in that direction, it recommended the replacement of the Universities Grants Commission by a Council on Postsecondary Education which would take "a 'proactive' role in mediating government policy into system-wide planning and budgeting, and for ensuring 'transparent' accountability."

In Quebec, as Donald notes, the Superior Council of Education has recently undertaken a number of critical studies of postsecondary education and raised concerns about the quality of teaching, graduation rates, and undergraduate curricula as well as the consistency of CEGEP diplomas. Similar concerns about quality and standards have been raised in Ontario, and one response to these concerns was the establishment of a provincial agency to establish and review province-wide program standards. However, as Jones notes, the major preoccupation in Ontario has been a continual search for adjustments in structure and process which could enable the system to accommodate reductions in funding without adverse affects on accessibility or quality. He reports how the province has moved from many years of making only modest changes to making more substantial changes to its postsecondary system in recent years but is still without any overall vision or plan for its postsecondary education system or a mechanism or process for creating and implementing one.

Further east, Brown reports the experience of the Maritime Provinces Higher Education Commission in trying to promote greater institutional cooperation and rationalization in New Brunswick and Prince Edward Island. She notes, however, that it is too soon to tell what will be the outcome of this process which began with the universities being asked to submit statements of their role and planned capacity. Further, she notes that institutions in New Brunswick already have distinct roles and cooperate in a number of ways and that duplication of programs "is minimized," but even more so than in other provinces, there is much to be done with respect to improving linkages between community colleges and universities.

As New Brunswick's university system is so much more rationalized than Nova Scotia's, it seems ironic that the latter province felt that it had to establish its own council in order to make progress in rationalization rather than doing so under the auspices of the MPHEC. Christie suggests, however, that it was probably embarrassment over the Nova Scotia Government's continual failure to comply with MPHEC funding recommendations that led the province to establish its own council. In any event, Christie reports that progress toward rationalization under the new council has been unspectacular, and Nova Scotia higher education is still plagued by the same old problems of fragmentation which have dogged it for more than a century: ". . . uncoordinated activity, lack of joint planning, competition and duplication among the institutions lead to a waste of resources, lost opportunities, and misdirection of leadership activities on the various campuses."

Conclusions

Among the areas of attention which the essays reviewed here generally have in common are historical discussions which are both descriptive and interpretive and elucidate how things came to be the way they are; descriptions of the structure of higher education in the various jurisdictions; identification and explication of major issues presently facing higher education; and some suggestion of immediate challenges and/or directions of change. The considerable variation in the way in which these topics are addressed and in the emphases given different facets gives, I believe, a freshness and engaging quality to the writing which might have been stifled had everyone had to write according to a common formula.

In the introduction I indicated that it might be of interest to note also topics which did not receive much attention. Three categories which stand out to me in this respect are privatization, pedagogy, and personnel.

The term, privatization, is widely heard in discussions of higher education in the 1990s, though less so in Canada than in the United States or United Kingdom. The term is generally not defined precisely, being used to refer to, among other things: increasing the share of the cost of higher education borne by students and their families; placing greater reliance on the interplay of market forces relative to provincial decision-making in determining the allocation of resources among institutions and institutional role and development; and encouraging or allowing greater scope for the provision of higher education by private institutions and organizations, including proprietary ones. The discussion of privatization in these essays was confined mostly to the second of these three concepts and that mainly in the Alberta and Ontario papers. The Alberta paper described the move to more of a market framework for postsecondary education, and the Ontario paper showed that on balance the movement there seems to be in the opposite direction, at least in the first half of the 1990s.

There was little discussion of privatization in the other two senses of the term in these essays. The Alberta paper was the only one to touch upon tuition fee policy, and it did so only briefly. As for private sectors in postsecondary education, the Alberta paper mentioned only briefly the role of private colleges and their receipt of the authority to grant baccalaureate degrees in certain areas. The British Columbia paper makes brief reference to the rapid expansion in the number of independent proprietary schools, reaching over 800 by 1995, and constituting "an issue which the public sector will be forced to accommodate in a systematic manner." In a somewhat related vein, the Newfoundland paper reveals that in response to the government support for retraining those adversely affected by the moratorium in the cod fisheries, "the real sectoral growth . . . has been among private institutions." Authors Bindon and Wilson express concern that this training fund has supported a growing number of private institutions that have little accountability in terms of outcomes or standards and that little attempt has been made to integrate private institutions into a plan for the development of education or training in the province. The latter observation, of course, would be true of privately provided higher education across Canada, with the exception of Alberta's private colleges. This book confirms that neither policy-makers nor researchers in Canada have yet even recognized the reality or potentiality of private postsecondary education.

With the exception of Donald's essay on Quebec and Baker's on Prince Edward Island, there is almost no mention of matters of pedagogy, not even of the word. Donald, of course, is sensitive to issues of forms of teaching and learning and of evaluation, and Baker describes the competency-based learning philosophy and strategy of Holland College. Those exceptions apart, in this respect the essays follow the common tendency in writing about higher education to distinguish between those phenomena which occur outside and those inside the "classroom," and confine discussions of the "big picture" and of higher education policy to the former. The fruitfulness of maintaining this distinction is increasingly problematic as learning becomes *the* main policy issue, and the Donald paper shows some of the benefits of trying to integrate the two perspectives in this regard.

Perhaps a little more surprising is the omission of personnel-related issues, for example, faculty role, morale, autonomy, working conditions, compensation, and unionization. The Ontario paper by Jones is the only one which deals with these issues to any extent, as he discusses the issue of centralization of collective bargaining in the CAATs, and the government's control of university and college salaries through the Social Contract. If there is to be only one mention of labour relations herein, it is fitting that it should be about the Ontario CAATs, as they have probably the most tumultuous and dysfunctional labour relations situation in Canadian higher education. Beyond that, it is not apparent what inference should be drawn from the fact that contributors do not see personnel issues as among the most noteworthy ones in Canadian higher education.

Overall, perhaps the most striking conclusion to be drawn from viewing these essays in total is the great diversity of situations surrounding higher education across the country. Beneath the surface of apparent binary structures or as provinces move away from straightforward binary structures, the essays reveal substantial differences with respect to composition, vision, and direction for their higher education systems. However, it would be dangerous to try to draw evaluative conclusions from these differences. For example, looking from one coast to the other, we see British Columbia experimenting with several new forms of postsecondary institutions perhaps fitting for the twenty-first century while Nova Scotia, according to Christie, is dealing with organizational issues of the nineteenth century. Yet, Dennison cautions that from a statistical standpoint, British Columbia's standing in postsecondary education is not overly impressive, at least as regards participation rates and accessibility. Rather, it is Nova Scotia that leads the country in these respects, at least in the university sector. Indeed, given the Nova Scotia system's very high university participation rate and the extent to which it attracts students from across Canada, I can't help but wonder if Christie is a bit harsh in his evaluation of the present structure. Could a structure have survived so many attempts to change it solely on the basis of irrational prejudices, or does its diversity and individuality confer some very tangible strengths? Be that as it may, this is an example of the kinds of provocative questions which arise through the comparisons of the experience of one province or territory with another which the chapters of this book provide. In summary, the jurisdiction-based essays in this book offer a unique perspective on Canadian higher education and a valuable complement to other works which are organized on thematic lines.

References

Cameron, D.M. (1991). *More than an academic question: Universities, government, and public policy in Canada.* Halifax, NS: The Institute for Research on Public Policy.

Dennison, J.D., and Gallagher, P. (1986). *Canada's community colleges: A critical analysis.* Vancouver, BC: UBC Press.

Leslie, P.M. (1980). *Canadian universities 1980 and beyond: Enrolment, structural change and finance.* Ottawa, ON: Association of Universities and Colleges of Canada.

Contributors

Michael B. Andrews (Ph.D., Alberta) is Associate Professor of Higher Education at the University of Alberta. Previously he was President of the Alberta Vocational College-Edmonton from 1981-1994. Dr. Andrews was Chairman of the Board of the Pembina Educational Consortium from 1984-1990 and Chairman of the Canadian Medical Association Conjoint Committee on Program Accreditation for Respiratory Therapists from 1985-1992.

Ronald J. Baker served with the RCAF in Germany after training as a navigator (RAF). He emigrated to Canada in 1947. He took a first class honours degree in English (1951) and an M.A. at the University of British Columbia followed by study in linguistics at the School of Oriental and African Studies, University of London. At U.B.C. he wrote part of the *Macdonald Report*, the basis of the creation of the B.C. community colleges, Simon Fraser University and the University of Victoria. In 1963, he was the first faculty appointment to Simon Fraser, as Director of Academic Planning and Head of the English Department. He was the founding president of the University of Prince Edward Island (1969-1978). He retired in 1991 as the David Macdonald Stewart Professor of Canadian Studies. Baker is an Officer of the Order of Canada and has honorary degrees from the University of New Brunswick, Mt. Allison, the University of Prince Edward Island, and Simon Fraser University. He has been a member of the Canada Council, the CRTC, and the Board of the Association of Universities and Colleges of Canada.

Kathryn Bindon is Principal and Professor of History, Sir Wilfred Grenfell College, Memorial University of Newfoundland. She obtained a B.A. from Sir George Williams University (Montreal), and a M.A. and Ph.D. in History from Queen's University. She held various positions at Concordia University, including Principal of the School of Community and Public Affairs (1981-84) and Executive Assistant to the Rector (1985-87). Dr. Bindon was Vice-President (Academic) at Mount Saint Vincent University from 1987-91 and was a member of the Maritime Provinces Higher Education Commission and the Nova Scotia Council on Higher Education during this time. She served on the board of World University

Service of Canada, as member and chair of the Minister's Advisory Board on Gender Integration in the Canadian Forces, the Minister's Advisory Group on Defence Infrastructure, and the Committee for Social Change in the Canadian Forces. Her publications include *Queen's Men, Canada's Men: The Military History of Queen's University*, and *More Than Patriotism: Canada at War, 1914-1918*.

Sheila A. Brown is President and Professor of Business Administration at Mount Saint Vincent University. Before moving to Nova Scotia she was Vice-President (Academic) at Mount Allison University in New Brunswick. She has a B.A. (Honours) from the University of Cambridge and a M.A. and Ph.D. from the University of Alberta. She has worked at the University of Alberta, the University of Manitoba, and Mount Allison University. She was Interim President of Mount Allison in 1990-91. Her teaching and research interests are in Marketing, with a particular interest in consumer behaviour and marketing and management in not-for-profit organizations. Her interests in higher education include performance indicators, distance education, and faculty development. She currently chairs the Association of Atlantic Universities Faculty Development Committee. In 1993 she served on a Committee appointed by the Council of Maritime Premiers to review the Maritime Provinces Higher Education Commission (MPHEC) and was a member of the MPHEC Academic Advisory Committee from 1991-1994.

David M. Cameron is Professor of Political Science at Dalhousie University. From 1971 to 1975 he served as Senior Policy Advisor to the federal Ministry of State for Urban Affairs. In 1975 he was appointed the first Director of the new School of Public Administration at Dalhousie, a position he held until 1980. He then joined the President's Office, first as Executive Director of Policy and Planning and subsequently as Vice-President, Planning and Resources. He returned to full-time teaching and research in 1985. He has published extensively on Canadian federalism, intergovernmental relations, and education. He has also written for numerous commissions and task forces, including the provincial ministers responsible for manpower policy, the Task Force on National Unity, and the National Forum on Postsecondary Education. He recently published *More Than an Academic Question: Universities, Government, and Public Policy in Canada*.

Brian D. Christie is Executive Director of the Office of Institutional Affairs and Assistant to the President for Planning at Dalhousie University. A graduate of the University of Toronto, with degrees in mathematics and economics, he has been a faculty member at universities in Saskatchewan, Manitoba, and Nova Scotia. He taught one of the first courses on the economics of education in Canada. From 1975 to 1983 he was senior policy advisor and coordinator of research at the Saskatchewan Universities Commission in Saskatoon. With research interests in the areas of university management and government-university relations, he is the author of many planning studies and policy reports and has conducted workshops on planning for universities and governments in Canada, the U.S., and Europe.

John D. Dennison is Professor Emeritus of Higher Education at the University of British Columbia. His primary research interest is in the development of the non-university postsecondary education in Canada. He has authored or co-authored four books, the most recent being *Challenge and Opportunity: Canada's Community Colleges at the Crossroads* and has published over 100 journal articles dealing with policy, history, organization, evaluation, and related aspects of community colleges in all provinces and territories. He has served on numerous commissions of inquiry dealing with various topics in postsecondary education. He has also been a consultant on related issues in Australia, the United Kingdom, and with a number of provincial governments and organizations.

Janet G. Donald is Full Professor in the Department of Educational and Counselling Psychology and the Centre for University Teaching and Learning at McGill University. Her current research, funded by SSHRC and the Quebec FCAR, is on the quality of learning in postsecondary education and postsecondary students' conceptualizations of learning. Recent publications include articles on professors' and students' conceptualizations of the learning task in science courses and on the use of broad indicators to evaluate undergraduate education. She was President of the Canadian Society for the Study of Higher Education in 1990-91 and won the Distinguished Researcher Award in 1994.

Alexander D. Gregor is Professor of Higher Education and Director of the Centre for Higher Education Research and Development (CHERD) at the University of Manitoba. He is a Distinguished Member and Past President of the Canadian Society for the Study of Higher Education, and a former editor of the *Canadian Journal of Higher Education*. His research interests lie in the history and public policy of higher education. Recent publications include "The Universities of Canada," which he has prepared for the *Yearbook of the Association of Commonwealth Universities* since 1990, and *Higher Education in Canada*, which he co-edited with Gilles Jasmin.

Gail M. Hilyer has a B.A. (McMaster) in Social Sciences, a M.Ed. (University of Toronto) in Adult Education, an Ontario Teacher's Certificate and is in a long process of completing a doctorate in Education at the University of Toronto. Her previous major career commitment was to Niagara College of Applied Arts and Technology (1968-1990) in Welland, Ontario. Gail also has twenty years experience as a consultant/evaluator of curriculum materials and textbooks for the Ontario Ministry of Education and as a bias editor/consultant for a number of publishers. In March 1991, she joined the staff of Arctic College as Dean of Instruction, Thebacha Campus, with responsibility for Certificate and Diploma programs, including university transfer programs, delivered in Fort Smith and throughout the western Arctic.

Edward A. Holdaway (Ph.D. Alberta) is Professor of Educational Administration at the University of Alberta where he has been on staff since 1968. From 1978 to 1987 he was also Director of Institutional Research and Planning. Professor Holdaway has had editorial or editorial board responsibilities with *The Canadian Administrator*, *Educational Administration Quarterly*, and *The International Journal of Educational Management*.

Glen A. Jones (Ph.D. Toronto) is an Associate Professor in the Higher Education Group, Ontario Institute for Studies in Education. Before joining the Higher Education Group in 1995, he was a member of the Department of Graduate and Undergraduate Studies, Faculty of Education, Brock University. His current research activities focus on the politics of higher education in Canada under a grant from the Social Sciences and Humanities Research Council, including a recent national study of Canadian university governing boards. He is currently President (1996-97) of the Canadian Society for the Study of Higher Education and Associate Editor of the *Canadian Journal of Higher Education*.

Gordon L. Mowat (Ed.D. Stanford) is Professor Emeritus of Educational Administration, University of Alberta. A former Chairman of the

Department of Educational Administration and Acting Vice-President (Facilities) at the University of Alberta, Dr. Mowat has had many important government positions in education in Alberta. These include senior high school inspector, member of the Cameron Commission on Education, Chairman of the Board of Postsecondary Education, and Chairman of the Private Colleges Accreditation Board.

William R. Muir is a professor in the Department of Psychology at the University of Regina. He obtained a B.A. from McGill, a M.A. from the University of Manitoba, and a Ph.D. from the University of Alberta. He was hired at Regina shortly after Regina College became the Regina Campus of the University of Saskatchewan. He was Director of the Regina Campus Faculty Association during the 1967 "Potashville Crisis" and played a leadership role in the Association during the University of Regina's transition to independence and the Association's decision to unionize. He has been a long-time member of the University of Regina Distance Education Advisory Committee. His research interests include the historical development of faculty culture and faculty value systems.

Aron Senkpiel came to the Yukon in 1980 to teach in the Yukon Teacher Education Programme, an extension program of the University of British Columbia. Since then he has helped establish the first liberal arts and science program in the Canadian North and the first comprehensive Northern Studies program in Canada. He is also a founding senior editor of *The Northern Review*, a multidisciplinary journal of the arts and social sciences of the north. He has written extensively about the development of postsecondary education and scholarship in northern, remote regions and the literature of northern Canada. Currently, he is Dean of Arts and Science at Yukon College.

Michael L. Skolnik is a Professor in the Higher Education Group, Ontario Institute for Studies in Education where he teaches and supervises graduate students and conducts research in higher education. He has authored and co-authored numerous books and articles on higher education, some examples of which are: *"Please Sir, I Want Some More": Canadian Universities and Financial Restraint* (with N. Rowen, OISE Press, 1984); "The Shell Game Called System Rationalization: The Politics and Economics of Retrenchment in the Ontario University System" (*Higher Education*, 1987); and "The Evolution of Relations Between Community

Colleges and Universities in Ontario" (*The Community College Journal of Research and Practice*, 1995).

Paul Wilson is Counsellor, Sir Wilfred Grenfell College, Memorial University of Newfoundland. He obtained B.A., B.Ed., and M.Ed. degrees from Memorial University and an Ed.D. from the University of Toronto. He was Assistant to the Dean of Junior Studies at Memorial from 1973-74 and Proctor in Residence from 1975-76. Dr. Wilson teaches courses in education and he has been actively involved in a number of community organizations. He is Vice-President of the Memorial University Alumni Association. His research has included work on such subjects as access to higher education, admission standards, and student performance.

Index